IMPERIAL PALACE AT JEDDO.

JAPAN

AND HER PEOPLE.

BY

ANDREW STEINMETZ, Esq.

OF THE MIDDLE TEMPLE, BARRISTER-AT-LAW.

𝔚𝔦𝔱𝔥 𝔑𝔲𝔪𝔢𝔯𝔬𝔲𝔰 𝔍𝔩𝔩𝔲𝔰𝔱𝔯𝔞𝔱𝔦𝔬𝔫𝔰.

LONDON:
ROUTLEDGE, WARNES, AND ROUTLEDGE,

FARRINGDON STREET.

NEW YORK: 18, BEEKMAN STREET.

1859.

ADVERTISEMENT.

HAVING been for some time past meditating the Manners and Customs of all nations—in fact, *Man all the World over*—it was but natural that I should embrace the opportunity offered, in the present conjuncture, to enlarge on the intensely interesting topic of Japan and her People.

In fulfilling the engagement, it has been my object to select such facts and incidents as will enable the reader to form comfortably "some idea of the subject," striving to make every page (as indeed indicated by its "heading") a subject of interest to all, independently of its present aspect.

The materials involved are very extensive ; for, new as the topic is now to the Public, it is a very old one on the shelves. Perhaps we have the means of becoming better acquainted with Japan and her People than with any other Eastern nation. During nearly a century, from the year 1548, Japan was open, was familiar to the nations of the West. Not only Portugal, not only Holland, but England also had a footing there and mingled with the natives. The Jesuits—and what region of the globe has not been filled with their labours ?—were the pioneers of European adventure. To the Jesuits we owe our earliest accounts of this singular people.

Since the destruction of Christianity in Japan, in 1639, the Dutch have enjoyed the monopoly of the European trade with the country down to the present day, and from the Dutch, or the writers attached to their Factory at Nagasaki, we have ample details which, together with the accounts of the Jesuits, make a considerable book collection on Japan and her People. I believe I have read or consulted all that has been written on the subject.

In order to save time, Mr. MacFarlane's "Japan, Geographical and Historical," now out of print, the copyright of which belongs to my publishers, has been placed at my disposal, to use as much of the matter as could be made available in my design and arrangement. In doing so, however, I found it necessary sometimes to alter, constantly to re-arrange, and frequently to insert new matter throughout, besides collating the text with his sources, which were before me. This expedient has saved time, but increased the trouble of the performance ; for which, however, I am entirely responsible, and have therefore nowhere quoted Mr. MacFarlane, excepting for his individual facts or opinions.

In *The Chinese Repository* from May, 1832 to 1845, there appeared a series of interesting papers on Japan, compiled from the modern accounts supplied by members of the Dutch Factory. A volume of these articles was subsequently published, entitled, "Manners and Customs of the Japanese ;" and Jancigny, in his "Japon," still more copiously transferred them to his pages. The *Quarterly*

Review also worked interestingly the same inexhaustible mine, so that nothing remained for me but to choose from which of these warehouses I should take my materials. I have made free with them all.

From the recent American Expedition to Japan I have also culled a few curious facts and incidents; but it is remarkable that the Japan of the present day is essentially the Japan of the sixteenth century in her institutions. Old Kämpfer is still the standard and ponderous book on Japan; all subsequent writers have but illustrated, scarcely added, to his honest revelations. The salient moral of the tale is, that Japan presents the striking phenomenon of Oriental conservatism in her institutions, whilst she evinces a spirit of progress not surpassed by any Western nation! And if righteousness exalts a nation, it is certain that the honesty of Japan's merchants is now as trustworthy as it was represented to our childhood by Robinson Crusoe.*

Annexed is a list of the chief works read or consulted for my compilation; it pretends to be no more, excepting such elucidations as I have, on all appropriate occasions, ventured to advance on subjects so deeply significant and suggestive.

ANDREW STEINMETZ.

---

* See *Robinson Crusoe*,—towards the end.

CHIEF WORKS QUOTED OR CONSULTED.

Epistolæ Japanicæ, 1570.

MAFFEIUS, *Historiarum Indicarum*, libri xvi. 1590.

SOLIER, LE PÈRE FRANCOIS, *Histoire Ecclésiastique, du Japon*, 1627.

PINTO, FERD. MENDEZ, *Voyages Adventureux*, 1628.

PURCHAS, *His Pilgrimage*, 1617.

TRIGAUTIUS, NIC., *De Christianis apud Japonios triumphis*, 1623.

CARDIM, LE PÈRE. *Rélation de la Province du Japon*, &c., 1645.

VARENIUS, B., *Descriptio Regni Japoniæ*, 1649.

CHARLEVOIX, LE PÈRE DE, *Histoire du Japon*, 1715, 1736, 1754.

KÄMPFER, ENGELB. *History of Japan*, 1727.

MONTANUS, *Atlas Japonensis* (see p. 275, note).

THUNBERG, *Travels*, vol. iii., 1796.

GOLOWNIN, *Narrative of my Captivity in Japan*, 1818.

MEIJLAN (MEYLAN, G. F.), *Japan, voorgesteld in Schetsen*, 1830

FISSCHER, J. F., *Bijdrage tot de Kennis van het Japansche Rijk*, 1833.

DOEFF, *Herinneringen uit Japan*, 1833.

TITSINGH, ISAAC, *Cérémonies usitées au Japon*, 1819.

———————, *Annales des Empereurs du Japon*, 1834.

KLAPROTH, *Aperçu de l'Histoire mythologique du Japon*, etc., 1834.

SIEBOLD, PH. FR. VON, *Nippon, Archiv zur Beschreibung von Japan*, 1832, *et seq. ann.*

Moniteur des Indes Orientales, etc., 1846 and 1847.
Chinese Repository, from May, 1832 to 1845.
Asiatic Journal, 1838, *et seq. ann.*
RUNDALL'S *Memorials of the Empire of Japan.*
Histoire Générale des Voyages, vol. x.
Quarterly Review, vol. lii. and lvi.
Manners and Customs of the Japanese.
JANCIGNY, *Japon, Indo-Chine,* &c.
MACFARLANE'S *Japan, Geographical and Historical.*
HILDRETH, *Japan as it Was and Is.*
United States Japan Expedition.

This list includes more than enough to exhaust the
whole subject of Japan up to the present time.   It might
be swelled to a catalogue by quoting obsolete voyages of
the earliest date, and by making a book of every *Annual
Letter* of the Jesuits respecting " the Province of Japan ;"
but these Jesuit-letters, excepting the first, throw no
light whatever upon the subject, and might just as well
have been written respecting Timbuctoo.   Siebold's valuable but confused and motley publications have not been
translated into English; there are two volumes of a
French translation—the *first* and the *fifth* (!)—entitled
Voyage au Japon.   The Dutch books quoted above have
not been translated; but both these and Siebold's have
been completely ransacked in the *Chinese Repository* and
the *Quarterly Review,* as indicated.   I have endeavoured
to cull the most interesting facts from all of them ; and
those who are interested in Missions will find ample
details in Solier, Charlevoix, Trigaut, or the *History of
the Church of Japan,* by l'Abbé de T., 1705.   See *note,*
p. 368.

CONTENTS.

LIST OF ILLUSTRATIONS.

JUGGLERS AND TUMBLERS.

INTRODUCTION.

AT the present epoch events do not creep—do not even walk or run : they devour space, like light ; or, like the electric flash, they astound us by their suddenness. Japan, the pink of the Pacific, has opened once more to the ravished and lusty eyes of the Western World.

B

Four and twenty years ago in the same month, a politician exclaimed,—" We think it much more likely that the sole remaining link between Europe and Japan—the Dutch connection — should be severed by violence or obliterated by disuse, than that either force or persuasion should devise a new one between this country, or any of its dependencies, and that empire ; that New Holland, Borneo, or Central Africa have a fairer chance of being diplomatized or dragooned into hospitality or submission towards us, *within any period to which the speculation of mortal man can reasonably extend.*" *

After more than two centuries of aversion, suspicion, and contempt—secure in her proud, and perhaps justifiable self-sufficiency—she has at last—like Portia in the play —risked " the lottery of her destiny "—and, indeed, " without voluntary choosing." For, if she has consented to entertain the pretensions of her imperial, royal, and republican suitors, her past history—the character and characteristics of her people and their time-honoured institutions, seem to warrant us in concluding that her enlightened rulers and statesmen have yielded with a sigh or a groan—meditating, perhaps, the proverb which inculcates that " hanging and wiving goes by destiny."

The " moral force" by which this " political revolution" has been effected is frankly declared and honestly admitted :—" After the complicated and harassing work in which the allies have been engaged in China for the last year, it is matter of congratulation to them that a political revolution as startling to the Japanese themselves as it was unexpected by the world at large, should have been wrought by the application of moral force alone in this singular and hitherto jealously exclusive empire. Various causes have conspired to produce this result. The contact into which they were constantly brought with both English and Russians during the late war, the expedition of Commodore Perry, and the establishment at Simoda

* *Quarterly Review,* November, 1834.

of an American Consul, together with the indefatigable exertions of Mr. Harris, the gentleman who filled this post, doubtless operated largely in preparing the Japanese mind for the change which their own sound common sense and quickness of observation showed them was inevitable. It was not, however, until the intelligence reached Jeddo of the treaty of Tien-sin, accompanied by an exaggerated report of the naval force with which the allies intended visiting Japan, and the uncompromising attitude they would assume when they arrived there, that the plenipotentiaries appointed to treat with Mr. Harris put their signature to the treaty, which had already been for some months before them. The arrival almost immediately afterwards of both the Russians and ourselves confirmed to some extent the rumours they had heard, and plenipotentiaries were without delay appointed to treat upon the same base as that which had already been adopted in the American treaty. It is not to be supposed, however, that the Japanese Government succumbed feebly to the pressure from without, as though resigning itself in despair to an inevitable destiny. So far from such being the case, Lord Elgin, upon his arrival at Jeddo, found the late Liberal Government, with whom the Americans had treated, had been turned out of office only two or three days previously. The Conservative, or aristocratic party, had replaced the enlightened Prime Minister with whom we expected to treat, by men of anti-progressive tendencies, and it was evident that, so far from yielding to further pressure, there was a strong disposition manifested on the part of the hereditary nobility to break rather than bend further. This was the public opinion which the six plenipotentiaries appointed to treat with Lord Elgin, though of sufficiently enlightened views themselves, were compelled constantly to consider in their discussion of those points in which any advance was desired upon the treaties already signed. So determined, indeed, was the resistance made to any further innovation, and so keen their investigation of our demands, that the work of negotiation, though it proceeded rapidly, was not unattended

with difficulty, and afforded no prospect of a more liberal
tendency than that already manifested."*

Their country, we are told, leaves them nothing to
desire in the necessaries, comforts, and luxuries of life;
their industry makes the most of the gifts of nature—
according to their way of thinking. Abject indigence
is unknown; beggars—in our deplorable sense of the
word—are scarcely, if ever, seen; they have no human
caravans, human menageries, or unions. The testimony
of all who have frequented their islands attest their happy
lot—from the earliest times of European visitation; all
agree that there are few nations who can more easily do
without others than the people of Japan; and, what is
better still, they perfectly know and value this magnificent independence.

Has a nation any right thus to isolate herself under
any circumstances whatever? Political ambition says
No. Commercial interest iterates the negative. The
insatiable curiosity of our Western races—over-endowed
with the spirit of intellectual conquest, ratifies the decision.

We are infinitely behind, or in advance of, the age—
this epoch of commercial activity, which sees in the accumulation of material wealth the accomplishment of all
that is good and great—even "the Law and the Prophets"
—if we cannot see that both the sympathies and antipa-
thies of nature and of social institutions must bend to the
fiat of expediency, like the major force which sometimes
determines alliances of interest—marriages of convenience.
To Utopian dreams we refer such philosophical hesitation,
and we frankly admit that a common interest—conceived
and pronounced to be such—must override all national
prejudices, all diplomatic routine—even the everlasting
antagonism of races. We have read a rude lesson to the
Chinese. We have proved and are proving to the Hindoos that the star of our destiny is still in the ascendant.
What wonder, then, that Japanese exclusiveness should

* The *Times*, November 2nd, 1858.

wisely yield to the spirit of Anglo-Saxon energy and expansion—both indeed stubborn and implacable national " phenomena"—but nevertheless, by the very nature of things, capable of stretching, when absolutely necessary, to the force of circumstances—or, for a " consideration." In the present instance the fact is accomplished. The mountain has commenced her labour. She may be pregnant with Behemoth or Leviathan—most assuredly not with a mouse.

On the other hand, we are informed that Japan is a country of redundant population. It seems to have been so in the earliest times of European contact. In the sixteenth and seventeenth century her merchants, her colonies, her pirates, were scattered on the coasts of Tonquin, Cambodia, Siam, Formosa, the Philippines, the Islands of Sunda and the Moluccas. Multitudes of the inhabitants served as volunteers in the armies of these countries, and proved their bravery. They fought for the English and the Dutch in their Indian wars. When the Russians discovered Kamtschatka in 1696, they found that the children of ancient Niphon had long before made a settlement in that inhospitable region. In the beginning of the seventeenth century Japanese emigration embraced sixteen foreign countries; when, in 1639, the inexorable decree was issued which inflicted the penalty of death on all who should leave and return to their native country, whilst it as stringently shut out the foreigner. The vessels which the natives had built on the European model were burnt ; the old build was peremptorily restored by law, to insure the chance of shipwreck, if any attempt were made to sail beyond the coasts of that stormy ocean. Since then peace within and without, general prosperity, the action of a salubrious climate, and other natural causes, have conspired to increase the already teeming population of Japan. With a population of forty millions of wealthy and civilized inhabitants, it is averred that Japan is sinking under a human plethora. Her villages touch each other, and form streets many leagues in extent. Her towns are crowded :—Jeddo is more than one half larger than Paris, larger than Peking, and is only less populous than London by about three or four hundred thousand souls. Infanticide, that horrible resource of the Chinese and other nations, is utterly repugnant to Japanese humanity.

At least so affirms a recent writer on Japan.* According to the old Jesuits, however, the Japanese not unfrequently committed child-murder, and also had recourse to drugs to procure abortion.† Perhaps, however, these cruel crimes were not more salient characteristics in the Japanese than in European nations, amongst whom the severest penal enactments fail to repress these felonies. Indeed the expression used by the Jesuit might be applied by a Japanese traveller to all the western nations respecting these foul practices,—especially the second.

Now, if we consider this population of forty millions spread over Japan's twelve thousand five hundred and seventy square leagues of territorial extent, we find the colossal figure of three thousand one hundred and eighty-two inhabitants to the square league! Some idea may be formed of this fact when we remember that France—which is not a desert—has only twelve hundred and thirty-nine inhabitants to the square league, and the United Kingdom but a few more. There are in Germany only 127 ; in Italy 172 ; in Holland 224 ; in Spain 63 ; in Poland 52 ; in Turkey 36 ; in Sweden only 14 inhabitants to the square mile,—in France 154, in the United Kingdom, 152,—whilst in Japan there are 354 !

With so many mouths to feed we find no difficulty in believing that the Japanese are a highly industrious people, who turn everything to account, and do not waste the gifts of the gods. We are told that in 1775 Dr. Thunberg, physician to the Dutch factory, went botanizing in the environs of Desima, but could not find a single plant for his herbal,—agriculture had displaced

* Fraissinet, *Le Japon Contemporain.*
† Maff. *Rer. Indic.* l. xii. Prægnantes fæminæ partum haud rarò medicamentis abigunt, &c.

every plant that is useless for food or raiment, and husbanded every inch of soil for the support of life.

Assuredly these facts prove the necessity for removing all restrictions from emigration in Japan. Her intelligent, hard-working population would find an outlet in Australia and New Zealand. California and the other States of the American Union would welcome a race with which they need not be ashamed to mix and renovate their blood. And such of those eminently distinguished islanders who are well provided with the circulating medium, would be received throughout Europe with open arms, to grace with their elegance the courts of kings, to lionize in the saloons of aristocratic society, to vie with our fops without disparagement in the trifles which are the end of their existence upon earth—that is, in our theatres and other places of fashionable resort.*

For, in the essential characteristics of the superior human races, the Japanese are at least the equals of our interminably mixed European and Trans-Atlantic populations ; and by the general testimony of all who visited their shores, they claim the highest consideration. "Their motions and gestures," wrote Bayard Taylor only three years ago, "were characterized by an unstudied grace, and it was the unanimous opinion of all our officers that they were as perfect gentlemen as could be found in any part of the world."† St. Francis Xavier, the Alexander of the Christian missions, said of them more than two hundred years ago, ' I know not when to have done when I speak of the Japanese. They are truly the delight of my heart." Our old mariner, William Adams, lived long amongst them, and enjoyed their kindness and munificence. Father Froes, after a residence of some years, said,—"They are as gifted a nation as any in Europe." A Spanish grandee, in 1608, did not hesitate to exclaim, that "if he could have prevailed upon himself to renounce

* Fraissinet, *Le Jap. Contemp.*

† "In universum acuta, sagax, ac benè à naturâ informata gens est," says Maffeius, *ubi suprà*, "a sharp, intelligent, and naturally well-endowed people."

his God and his king, he should have preferred that country to his own." Lastly, the *Times* of November 2nd says :—

"Suffice it to be recorded as our general impression that, in its climate, its fertility, and its picturesque beauty, Japan is not equalled by any country on the face of the globe ; while, as if to harmonize with its surpassing natural endowments, it is peopled by a race whose qualities are of the most amiable and winning description, and whose material prosperity has been so equalized as to insure happiness and contentment to all classes. We never saw two Japanese quarrel, and beggars have yet to be introduced with other luxuries of Western civilization. It is not to be wondered at that a people rendered independent by the resources of their country and the frugality and absence of luxury, which so strikingly characterize them, should not have experienced any great desire to establish an intercourse with other nations, which, in all probability, would carry in its train greater evils than could be compensated for by its incidental advantages. Their exclusiveness has arisen, not, as in China, from an assumption of superiority over the rest of the world, but from a conviction that the well-being and happiness of the community would not be increased by the introduction of foreign tastes and luxuries ; and that very propensity to imitate and adopt the appliances of civilization, so foreign to the Chinaman, is so strongly developed in Japan that their rulers foresee that the changes now being effected will, in all probability, some day or other revolutionize the country,—an apprehension which need cause the Emperor but little alarm ; no one can doubt who has visited the two countries that the Chinaman will still be navigating the canals of his country in the crazy old junks of his ancestors, when the Japanese is skimming along his rivers in high-pressure steamers, or flying across the country behind a locomotive."

They have, consequently, not degenerated. Shall we ascribe their continued virtues to their rigid exclusion of

European "civilization?" Alas! how *much* is comprised in this word.

But let us contemplate the hand of Providence in this entrance of the Western wedge into the granitic block of Oriental stagnation. All the circumstances seem to remind us of those national necessities which, in all times, have repeatedly changed and renewed the face of the earth. The thirst for gold and the banner of Religion; diplomatic jugglery and scientific curiosity; the selfish ambition of kings, and the seductive, nay, rather the imperative hunger for food, are causes whose effects we can but dimly foresee, even with the everlasting light of experience which shines on the immense track *behind us*;—advancing as we are in our restless career, with " On! still onwards!" the motto of our dominant race— God only knows whither!

> "'Tis destiny unshunnable—like death."

or,—

> "There's a Divinity that shapes our ends,
> Rough hew them how we will."

PART OF JEDDO.

PART I.

CHAPTER I.

GEOGRAPHY ; CLIMATE ; VEGETABLE, ANIMAL, AND MINERAL PRO-
DUCTIONS ; THE SCENERY OF JAPAN.

JAPAN is a cluster of islands left by the ocean, or upheaved
from the deep by volcanic action, opposite the north-eastern
coast of Asia.

Three thousand eight hundred and fifty islands, islets,
or rocks, compose the empire : they lie like beavers
basking in the sun—as Venice in her Adriatic—as the

British Isles over against the continent of Europe. Here the comparison ends, but it may suggest ulterior meditation in the mind of the reflective reader. London has been shown to be the very pole geographical round about which the *inhabited* world rotates—significantly enough of her destiny amongst the nations : Japan has remained the very paradise of fixed and unchangeable ideas—stagnant in her material wealth—stagnant in her institutions—content to hold her own—content with internal peace and prosperity.

The difference is a matter of *race*. The race or races which have encompassed the earth from these islands so insignificant on the map of Europe, would have achieved the same destiny had their lot been cast in Japan, or perhaps even in Kamtschatka.

The writer in the *Quarterly*, before quoted, asks :—" Where, however, in the well-ordered empire of Japan Proper can we find the counterpart of *Ireland* ? Where is the Japanese Connaught ? Which of her sixty-eight peaceful provinces represents Tipperary ? When has a Buddhist been insulted by a follower of Sintoo ? What voice has been raised to repeal the union between Nankaydoo and Saykadoo, or to pronounce that Tookaydoo shall no longer contain the centre of government of both ?"

The most important islands of Japan are Niphon, Kiousiou, and Sikok or Sitkokf. It would but uselessly fatigue the eye of the reader to enlarge on the geographical catalogue of island-names, which will be found barbarously represented in the map, abounding in sonorous vowels, but nevertheless recalcitrant to *our* vocal organs. Suffice it to state that the empire of " the Sons of the Sun" extends over a vast expanse of land and sea, of various climates and exhaustless fertility. Together with its dependencies, it covers twenty-five degrees of latitude, and twenty-seven of longitude, or about 390,625 square leagues of the earth's surface, including land and water. Malte-Brun makes the territorial superficies of the empire of Japan to be 16,000 square leagues, but calculations founded on the maps of Robert, Broughton, Arrowsmith, and Krüsenstern, reduce it to 12,570. During the last fifty years the natives themselves have attained sufficient familiarity with science to perfect their charts and calculations. They have produced a graphic representation of all the islands, rocks, and visible shoals of their archipelago ; have sketched the relative extent of the various islands, and have even succeeded in tracing the effects of the great geological revolutions of which that immense labyrinth has been the theatre.

The Japanese themselves call their country *Niphon*, or *Nipon*, a name compounded of *Nitsi*, "Sun," and *Phon*, "origin" or "rising," equivalent to "eastern country ;" and the term *Japan* is but a corruption of the Chinese *Zipangu*, of the same meaning.

In the island of Niphon is situated the capital of the empire—Jeddo or Yeddo—which occupies more ground than London, with a population numbering between 2,000,000 and 3,000,000. Jeddo is said to be, without exception, one of the finest cities in the world : streets broad and good, and the Castle, which includes nearly the whole centre of the town, built on a slight eminence, capable of containing 40,000 men. There are three walls or enclosures round this quarter. Within the inner wall the Emperor and his heir-apparent reside. The houses of the princes and nobles are palaces, and we may imagine the size when some contain 10,000 followers. They are built in regular order, forming wide streets some forty yards broad, kept in perfect order ; an immense courtyard, with trees and gardens, forms the centre of each enclosure, in the midst of which is the house of the owner ; the houses containing the followers, servants, stables, &c., form this large enclosure. They are built of one uniform shape. The gateways leading to the courtyard are exceedingly handsome, of massive woodwork, ornamented with lacquer and other devices. From the road that leads by the moat to the second wall is one of the finest views ever seen—on one side the Gulf of Jeddo, with the high hills rising beyond, while on the other is a portion of the great city of Jeddo, with its trees and gardens, picturesque temples, and densely crowded streets, extending as far as the eye can reach towards the interior ; then there is a view of the trees and green fields in the distance, far away beyond a thickly built suburb ; but the most striking view of all is that close by, the well kept green banks of the second defence rising some seventy feet from the broad moat below, with grand old cedars, over a hundred years of age, growing from its sides. The fine timber, the lay of the ground, the water lilies in the moat, the grandeur, good order, and completeness of everything, equal, and in some ways far surpass, anything ever seen in Europe, or any part of the world.*

Every cottage, temple, and tea-house is surrounded by gardens laid out with exquisite taste, and the most elaborate neatness is skilfully blended with grandeur of design. The natural features of the country are admirably taken advantage of, and a long ride is certain to be rewarded by a romantic scene, where a tea-house is picturesquely perched over a water-fall, or a temple rears its carved gables amid groves of ancient cedars. The tea-house is a national characteristic of Japan. The traveller, wearied with the noonday heat, need never be at a loss to find rest and refreshment ; stretched upon the softest and cleanest of matting, imbibing the most delicately-flavoured tea, inhaling through a short pipe the fragrant tobacco of Japan, he resigns himself to the ministrations of a bevy of fair damsels, who glide rapidly and noiselessly about, the most zealous and skilful of attendants.†

The island of Kiousiou, or Kewsew, is extremely well cultivated and generally fertile, with the exception of its eastern coast, bordering on the Bungo Channel, where it is mountainous, barren, and comparatively thinly inhabited. The chief town is Nagasaki.

Nagasaki, sometimes pronounced Nangasaki,‡ the only

---

* The *Times,* November 3rd, 1858.

† The *Times,* November 2nd, 1858.

‡ The proper name is certainly Nagasaki. We find it written and printed in a perplexing variety of ways. The old Spanish and Portuguese writers frequently turn it into Langasaki, or Lampsaki.

place open to foreigners, lies on a peninsula formed by the deep Bay of Omura, in 32° 45′ N. lat. and 129° 15′ E. long. Its harbour is spacious and deep, extending in length about four miles, with an average width of more than a mile. At its entrance is the small island of Papenberg, where the water is twenty-two fathoms deep, but it grows shallower as it proceeds inward, so that, opposite to the town, it has only a depth of four fathoms; so far it runs north-east, it then turns north, and has less depth. The town is built on its eastern shores, in a narrow valley which runs eastward. It is three-quarters of a mile long, and almost as broad, and inclosed by steep, though not lofty, hills. There are some good buildings in the town; as the palaces of the two governors, and those of some princes and noblemen of the empire, but especially the temples, which were sixty-two in number, within and without the town, in the time of Kämpfer (1692). The population may amount to 40,000 or 50,000 souls. It is one of the five imperial towns of the empire.*

Nagasaki is remarkable for the apostasy of the Jesuit Ferreyra, an old missionary, the Provincial of the Order, and Administrator of the Bishopric during the terrible persecution of the Christians of Japan, at the beginning of the seventeenth century.

Dreadful times were those! They suspended the poor Jesuit over a pit, where, after four hours' torture, his Christian fortitude failed him, and he gave the fatal sign of apostasy. They suffered him to live, but compelled him to assume the Japanese costume and a Japanese name, and to marry a Japanese woman, the widow of a Chinese goldsmith, who had been executed for some offence; and, finally, they made him a Japanese Inquisitor, making him preside over one of the tribunals which tried and consigned the Christians to martyrdom! Here was a specimen of Japanese policy in its striking refinement, calculation, and design. Your western state-craft could never think of such a plan for damaging the cause of a

* *Penny Cyclopædia,* "Japan."

proscribed religion. To show the convert his own apostle,
sacrificing to idols, and dipping his hand in the blood of
those whom he had himself made guilty of the state-
crime !

We are assured on the best authority, that Ferreyra
performed his function as Japanese Inquisitor.   Five
Jesuits were brought before him. " Who are you ?" he
asked. " Priests of the Company of Jesus." " Abjure
your faith," said the renegade, " and you shall be rich and
raised to honour."   The Jesuits preferred martyrdom, and
died accordingly.*

The Jesuits believed that Ferreyra's marriage was
merely a sham on his part—never consummated—and
they were probably right.   They also assert that Ferreyra
subsequently repented, confessed himself a Christian, and
won the crown of martyrdom in the very fosse where he
yielded in human frailty.

Mr. Hildreth† calls this last fact " a fine story," for
which " there seems to have been no foundation, except
the wishes and hopes of those who circulated it."   Certainly, it may be an invention of the Jesuits ; but if it
be not a fact, it deserves to be believed under the circumstances—the poor man's second state having probably
turned out infinitely worse than the death which most of
us would shrink from and decline.

A small artificial island in the harbour of Nagasaki,
called Desima, is remarkable as the crib to which the
Dutch have been rigorously confined for two hundred
years in their trade with Japan.   It was built in 1635
for the seclusion of the Portuguese sailors and merchants,
who were there confined as a security against the introduction of missionaries.

Desima is built in the form of a fan, surrounded by a
wall of basalt, surmounted by iron spikes, and communi-
cates with the city of Nagasaki by a bridge, which is
always strictly guarded by the ever-watchful Japanese

---

* Cretineau-Joly, *Hist. de la Comp. de Jésus,* iii. 203.
† *Japan,* p. 191.

officials. Its greatest length is about 600 feet, and its
extreme breadth about 240. Two gates on the north
side are opened to admit the Dutch ships into the harbour,
which are always shut, excepting at the ingress or egress
of these vessels. The Dutch are not permitted to build
a house of stone on the island, and their miserable habitations are of fir-wood and bamboo. Japanese spies, acting
as interpreters, clerks, and servants, are supported by the
Dutch, who, cooped up in Desima, are constantly exposed to the intrusion of the police of Nagasaki. In
short, a more annoying and thorough system of espionage
and imprisonment can scarcely be conceived. Under no
pretence whatever can the Dutch enter the city unless
summoned by express order from Government : no
Japanese is allowed to speak to them, unless accompanied
by a police-agent.

The Dutch are forced to pay a rent for Desima. It is
not avarice which prompted this exaction, but simply to
accord with a fixed principle that strangers, alive or
dead, should never occupy an inch of Japan. Indeed,
formerly the Dutch had only the sea for a burial-place.

Kämpfer dolefully describes the miseries to which the
Dutch submitted for the sake of the "almighty dollar,"
or gilder.

"Our ships, which put into this harbour once a year,
after they have been thoroughly visited by the Japanese,
and proper lists taken of all the goods on board, have
leave to put their men on shore on this island to refresh
them, and to keep them there so long as they lie in the
harbour, commonly two or three months. After they
have left, the director of our trade remains in the island,
with a small number of people, about seven or more, if he
thinks proper.

"Thus we live all the year round, little better than
prisoners, confined within the compass of a small island,
under the perpetual and narrow inspection of our
keepers. 'Tis true, indeed, we are now and then allowed
a small escape, an indulgence which, without flattering
ourselves, we can by no means suppose to be an effect of

their love and friendship,—forasmuch as it is never granted to us, unless it be to pay our respects to some great men, or for some other business, necessary on our side and advantageous for the natives. Nor doth the coming out, even upon these occasions, give us any greater liberty than we enjoy on our island, as will appear,—first, by the great expenses of our journeys and visits, great or small,—and by the number of guards and inspectors, who constantly attend us, as if we were traitors and professed enemies of the empire.   *   *   *

" These are the days allowed us for our recreation, if it may be called a recreation to be led about like prisoners, under the narrow inspection of so many attentive eyes,—for as to the several officers concerned in the management of our island and trade, and permitted on that account to converse with us, no sincere friendship, good understanding, or familiarity, can be by any means expected of them ; for, before they are admitted into our service, they must oblige themselves, by a solemn oath, to deny us all manner of communication, credit, or friendship, any ways tending to support or promote our interest.

" The person who takes this oath prays the vengeance of the supreme gods of the heavens and the chief magistrates of the country upon him, his family, his domestics, his friends, and near relatives, in case he doth not sincerely fulfil and satisfy to all and every article, as they are read and specified after the form of the oath, which, together with these articles, must be signed by him, and sealed with his seal, dipped in black ink, pouring, for a still stronger confirmation, some drops of his own blood upon it, which he fetches by pricking one of his fingers behind the nail.   *   *   *   *

" No Japanese, who seems to have any regard or friendship for the Dutch, is looked upon as an honest man and true lover of his country. The maxim is grounded upon the principle that it is absolutely contrary to the interests of the country, against the pleasure of their sovereign,—nay, by virtue of the oath they have taken, even against the supreme will of the gods, and the dictates of their conscience,—to show any favour to foreigners."

Every Japanese official associated with the Dutch at the factory, is bound twice or thrice a year to take a solemn oath of renunciation and hatred of the Christian religion, and is made to trample under his feet crosses and crucifixes—the symbols of Christianity.

It has been stated that the Dutch also were required to perform this act, so awful in its significance ; but this has been denied, and it is difficult to believe it : still it seems that they wisely took every precaution to keep their religion in the background. A story is told of one who, in the time of the great persecution at Nagasaki, being asked by the Japanese police if he were a Christian, replied, " No ; I am a Dutchman." Kämpfer denies this also ; but in supporting his denial he clearly proves the fact in all its essentials. By his account, a certain Hollander, Sandwoort by name, was cast away on the coast, and with a companion took refuge in Nagasaki, where during the persecution, being asked if he were a Christian, exclaimed, in order to save his life, " What Christians ? Christians ! We are Dutchmen." Kämpfer affirms that he was assured by an old Japanese interpreter, " that the Dutch always said they professed Christianity, but that they were not of the sect of the Portuguese priests."* It seems, as the world wags, that a lie by equivocation is not a lie ; and it has been said that " we are not obliged to speak the truth to those who have no right to demand it ;" a convenient doctrine, if we could only answer for its safety.

Osacca, one of the five imperial towns, and the most commercial place in the empire, is situate in the northern angle of the Gulf of Osacca, on the banks of the river Yedogawa, which, near the town, divides into three branches, and, before it falls into the sea, into several more. The middle, or principal branch of the river,

---

* *Hist. Gen. des Voy.* x. 611. More on this topic in the sequel.

though narrow, is deep and navigable. From its mouth, as far up as the town, and higher, there are seldom less than a thousand barges going up and down. Several navigable canals, which derive their water from the river, traverse the principal streets of the town, and serve as means for conveyance of goods. The banks of the river and of the canals are of freestone, coarsely hewn, and formed into ten or more steps, so as to resemble one continued staircase. Numerous bridges, built of cedar-wood, are laid over the river and canals, some of them are of large dimensions, from 300 feet to 360 in length, and beautifully ornamented. The streets are narrow, but regular, and cut each other at right angles ; though not paved, they are very clean. A narrow pavement of flat stones runs along the houses for the convenience of foot-passengers. The houses are not above two stories high, and built of wood, lime, and clay. At the north-east extremity of the city is a large castle, occupying a superficies of one square mile. The population is more than 500,000 inhabitants. According to the exaggerated account of the Japanese, an army of 80,000 men may be raised from among its inhabitants. Many of the residents are very wealthy men, especially the merchants, artists, and manufacturers. The Japanese themselves call Osacca the universal theatre of pleasure and diversion ; and plays are daily exhibited in public and private houses. South of Osacca, on the shores of the same gulf, is Sakai, another imperial town.

Meaco, or Kio, the residence of the ecclesiastical emperor, or Daïri, is about twenty miles from Osacca, and contained in the time of Kämpfer, according to a census, more than 500,000 inhabitants, besides the numerous court of the Daïri, and 52,000 priests. From the latest Dutch accounts it appears that the population has greatly diminished, while that of Jeddo has greatly increased. All the authorities on the subject agree in representing this holy city as the most immoral, profligate place in the Japanese empire. It is nearly four miles long and three wide. The Mikado resides on the northern side of the city, in a particular ward, consisting of twelve or thirteen streets, and separated from the city by walls and ditches. On the western part of the town is a strong castle, built of freestone, where the Kobo, or secular emperor, resides when he comes to visit the Daïri. The streets are narrow, but regular, and always greatly crowded. Meaco is the principal manufacturing town of the empire, where every kind of manufacture is carried to the greatest perfection. Nearly every house has a shop, and the quantity of goods which they contain is astonishing ; at the same time it is the centre of science and literature, and the principal place where books are printed. The town is united by a wide canal to the river Yedogawa, which flows not far from its walls.

All the islands of Japan are very imperfectly known ; nearly all the coasts are very difficult of access, being surrounded by numerous rocks and islets, and by a very shallow sea. This shallowness is most remarkable in the numerous inlets and bays with which the southern coast is indented.

It has hitherto been supposed that the harbour of Jeddo was so shallow that even small boats could not approach the beach, the larger Japanese vessels being obliged to keep far out to sea. This seems to have been a cunning report purposely spread by the Japanese authorities, for the recent expedition of Lord Elgin proved the contrary. Without the least difficulty the steamer ran right up, and anchored within a mile of the forts of Jeddo ; still, it appears that this was in " seven feet water."

The sea in all directions, besides containing numerous rocks, has some very dangerous whirlpools, two of which especially have been noticed by navigators : one near the Island of Amakoosa, at the entrance of the Bay of Simabara, and the other near the southern extremity of Niphon, between the Bays of Osacca and of Mia.* To this must

* Striking descriptions of these phenomena will be found in Kämpfer's valuable old book. The Japanese give the most fabulous account of them. They appear to be constantly mentioned by their poets and other writers.

be added, that no part of the ocean is subject to heavier
gales than the sea which surrounds Japan.

There are very strong currents which set along the
eastern coast of Japan, and are dangerous to the navigator
who is not aware of their extraordinary rapidity.   Captain
Cook thus draws attention to the subject :—" On the 1st,
at which time we were about eighteen leagues to the eastward of White Point, the current set north-east and by
north, at the rate of three miles an hour ; on the 2nd, as
we approached the shore, we found it continuing in the
same direction, but increased its rapidity to five miles an
hour ; as we left the shore it again became more moderate,
and inclined to the eastward ; on the 3rd, at the distance
of sixty leagues, it set to the east north-east, three miles
an hour; on the 4th and 5th it turned to the southward,
and at one hundred and twenty leagues from the land its
direction was south-east, and its rate not more than a
mile and a half an hour ; on the 6th and 7th it again
shifted round to the north-east, its force gradually
diminishing till the 8th, when we could no longer perceive any at all."*

Some of our travellers (Thunberg, for instance) assert
that the whole surface of these islands is only a succession
of mountains, hills, and valleys ; but Kämpfer expressly
says that he passed through several plains of considerable
extent, as that which runs from the town of Osacca to
Meaco, a distance of about seventy miles, and a similar
plain west of Jeddo, and extending to that town.   A large
plain occurs also along the northern shores of the Bay of
Mia, and numerous smaller plains are noticed by Kämpfer ;
but generally the hills run down close to the sea, or leave
only a narrow strip of level ground between them and the
seashore.   Japan is called the " land of mountains," but
most of its hills and mountains are cultivated to the very
top, and those few which are not cultivated are left in
their natural state on account of the sterility of the soil.

The Dutch have observed only one single peak of great

* *Voyages*, vii. 367.

elevation—the Fudsi Jamma, not far from the Bay of
Tomina, west of the Bay of Jeddo. They compare it in
shape with the Peak of Teneriffe, and observe that the
snow seldom melts on its top. Recent Dutch writers
estimate the height of this remarkable peak at from
11,000 to 12,000 French feet. According to the accounts

THE FUDSI JAMMA.

of navigators, however, it would seem that the northern
part of Niphon is traversed by a continuous chain of
mountains with several peaks. Volcanoes, either in an
active state or extinct, are numerous. To the latter class
the Fudsi Jamma certainly belongs.

According to the annals of Japan, Fudsi Jamma is just
2143 years old : they say it rose out of the bowels of the
earth in the year B.C. 285. It arose in a single night,
and there was at the same time an enormous depression
of the land in the vicinity of Meaco, forming the lake

Mitsou-no-oumi, that is, " the lake of the guitar," from its resemblance in shape to that instrument.

Fudsi, or Fousi, seems to mean " star," and *jamma*, or *yamma*, is " mountain." In the year 864 it became one mass of fire during the space of ten days, and then it burst open at the base with a dreadful explosion. This volcano

THE CRATER OF THE FUDSI JAMMA.

is situated in a direct line between Jeddo and Meaco. The last eruption was in 1707, when it covered Jeddo with ashes one inch deep.

The Japanese annalists also mention the volcanic birth of an island which rose suddenly out of the sea in the form of a great mountain ; a rain which brought down from the heavens a prodigious quantity of *hair;* a comet such as had never been seen before ; sundry earthquakes, and terrible conflagrations.

No region of the globe is so violently desolated by volcanic fire as this part of the Pacific—little worthy of this name—and the Japanese archipelago is the very centre of the subterranean and submarine conflagration. Surely this region must be nearer than others to that mass of liquid incandescent Heaven-only-knows-what beneath the "crust" of the earth, which is said to be capable of melting, a thousand times over, the hardest known substances untouched by our superficial "devouring element." We are told that the first man who ventured on the ocean in a fragile bark must have presented the curious physiological anomaly of a heart encased in oak and threefold brass ; but what a set of careless, thoughtless, and courageous knight-errants we must be to float, and rock, and roll incessantly right over such a bubbling sea of inconceivably fierce fire, not further below our feet than the distance from London to Oxford !

Formerly it was Fudsi Jamma that thus gave the Japanese a taste of the "lower regions." Fudsi was lord paramount of these tremendous eruptions, compared with which your Etna and Vesuvius are mere squibs and pop-guns. Now-a-days it is Wountsendake, "the Peak of the Hot Springs."

This dragon of a mountain is about four thousand feet high, and is always covered with snow—as it were to keep up a sort of incognito—to "make believe," or to keep himself cool whilst making "hot work" for the natives. He lifts up his truncated pyramidal head on a promontory of Kewsew, an everlasting terror to the populations. His rugged and menacing aspect, his huge crater, which has crumbled down, constantly vomiting a thick black smoke, spreading off into vapoury clouds, plainly show that his immense furnace must have formerly had a great deal to do with geological distributions, sinkings, and displacements ; and that he may any day take it into his head, or his bowels, to repeat his exploits. For, near the shore round about him, there are sunken mountains, which have risen out of the sea, and new craters have formed in those spots where the earth was not dense enough to resist the volcanic fluid boiling in his entrails. Numerous streams of boiling-water bathe his sides ;

frequent or rather continual earthquakes, accompanied with the explosion of ancient and new craters, keep up the alarm, and bid men prepare for the time when Wountsendake, the Peak of the Hot Springs, shall rise in his might once more, and scorch up or crush down his thousands and tens of thousands. A thousand years ago the natives built and dedicated to him—*To the Spirit of the Mountain*—a chapel close to his feet; they worship him with offerings like those nations who worship the devil to prevent him from doing them evil, believing that God is too good to do them harm.

The peninsula of Wountsendake, and the greater part of Kewsew, bristle with volcanic mountains, some extinct, others still acting as safety-valves to the incomprehensible excitements of mother Earth ; but of all the manifestations of her internal throes and torment, and their consequent desolation inflicted on the habitations of her children, that of 1792 was the most terrible for ages before.

"On the eighteenth day of the first month of that year," say the *Annals of Japan*, "the summit of the mountain was seen to crumble suddenly, and a thick smoke rose in the air. On the sixth of the following month there was an eruption in a spur on the eastern slope of the mountain. On the second of the third month an earthquake shook the whole island. At Simabara, the nearest town to the mountain, all the houses were thrown down, amidst a general terror and consternation, the shocks following each other with frightful rapidity. Wountsendake incessantly sent forth a hail-storm of stones, showers of ashes, and streams of lava, which devastated the country for many leagues round. At length, on the first day of the fourth month, there was a new commotion, which increased in intensity from moment to moment.

"Simabara was now a vast heap of ruins. Enormous blocks of rock, tumbling from the top of the mountain, crushed and ground to atoms all beneath them. Thunder rolled overhead, and dreadful sounds rumbled beneath the feet at one and the same time. All of a sudden, after an interval of calm, when men thought the scourge had passed over, the northern spur of Wountsendake, the Mioken-yamma, burst forth with a tremendous detonation. A vast portion of that mountain was blown into the air. Colossal masses fell into the sea. A stream of boiling water rushed forth foaming from the cracks of this new volcano, and sped to the ocean, which at the same time advanced and flooded the land."

Then was seen a sight never seen before, intensifying the terror of the innumerable witnesses of that terrible day, which might well seem a Day of Judgment come. From the conflict of the boiling waters of the volcano with the cold waters of the tempestuous ocean, suddenly mingled, there arose waterspouts which ravaged the land in their devouring gyrations.

The disasters caused by this accumulation of cata-strophes, earthquakes, volcanic eruptions, waterspouts, inundations, united together, exceed all belief. Not a single house of Simabara and its environs was spared : only the citadel remained, whose Cyclopean walls were formed of gigantic blocks of stone. The convulsions of nature on that day so changed the coast-line, that the most experienced mariners could not recognise its once familiar shape and bendings.

Fifty-three thousand persons perished on that fatal day.

It is observed that the eruptions generally commence with the flow of the tide, and that inundations caused by an unusually high tide follow the eruptions as well as the earthquakes. The Japanese meteorologists and weather-wise astrologers have been able to predict with certainty the atmospheric changes which will follow the shocks of earthquakes. If they happen at noon or at midnight, they produce epidemic diseases ; at two or six o'clock in the morning they are the forerunners of a tempest ; in the morning or in the evening they announce fine weather. The credulous husbandman accepts these predictions with unhesitating faith, attributing all these subterranean convulsions to some monstrous whale, which strikes the coast with its tail. Educated Japanese believe, with the

Chinese, that they are caused by a conflict between the ethereal and terrestrial elements, but latterly it seems that our views respecting these phenomena have been pretty generally adopted. Nevertheless it is maintained that six of their volcanoes and four of their mountains, which have hot springs, are the ten hells of Japan.*

From the peculiar form of the islands of Japan it may be presumed that they have no large rivers; and the rapidity with which the streams run down shows that the country in the interior rises to a considerable height. Many of them are so rapid that no bridges can be built over them, and they are not passed without danger. Several others are less rapid, and though they cannot be navigated, timber and wood are floated down them. A considerable number, however, seem to be navigable for small river-boats to a distance of some miles from the sea. The most considerable and important of those which are known is the river Yedogawa, in Niphon, which rises in the Lake of Oity, or Mitsou-no-oumi, before mentioned, a sheet of water sixty miles in length, but of inconsiderable width. After leaving this lake, it traverses the fine plain which extends from its shores to the harbour of Osacca, and in all this course it is navigated by river-barges. Boating is a favourite pastime with the Japanese ladies and gentlemen. It appears from the accounts of several travellers, that they have rendered some of their rivers navigable for considerable distances by artificial means, and that they have some canals connecting their rivers and lakes.

We are, of course, very imperfectly acquainted with the climate of Japan, the meteorological observation made by Thunberg at Nagasaki only extending over one year. The southern part seems to resemble, in many points, the climate of England. In winter it does not freeze and snow every year, though in most years it does. The frost and snow, when there is any, lasts only a few days. In January, 1776, the thermometer descended at Nagasaki

---

* Jancigny, *Japon;* Klaproth, *Asiat. Journ.*, 1831.

to 35° Fahr., but it was considered a very mild winter ; in August it rose to 98°, and that was considered as the average heat of the season. The heat would, consequently, be very great but for the refreshing breeze which blows during the day from the south, and, during the night, from the east. The weather is extremely changeable, and rains are abundant all the year round ; but they are more heavy and frequent during the *satkasi*, or rainy season, which occurs in June and July. Storms and hurricanes seem to occur very frequently, and the descriptions of them in Kämpfer and Langsdorf are truly terrific. Thunder-storms are also common, and earthquakes have successively destroyed a great part of the most populous towns. Only a few spots appear to be exempt from these terrible phenomena. It is observed by Kämpfer that waterspouts are nowhere of such frequent occurrence as in the seas inclosing Japan.

As there is considerable variety of opinion as to the climate of Japan, we will quote a passage from the Russian writer, who resided a considerable time on one of the islands :—

" On a comparison of the geographical situation of the Japanese possessions with that of the countries of the Western hemisphere under the same degrees of latitude, it might be imagined that the climate, the changes of the seasons, and the atmosphere, were alike in both, but such a conclusion would be very erroneous.[*] The difference of these two parts of the world in this respect is so striking, that it deserves particular notice. I will take, as an example, Matsmai, where I lived two years. This town lies in the forty-second degree of latitude, that is, on a parallel with Leghorn in Italy, Bilboa in Spain, and Toulouse in France.

" In these places the inhabitants hardly know what frost is, and never see any snow, except on the tops of

* Charlevoix states that the Japanese are much prejudiced in favour of their own climate, and acknowledges that it must be very healthy, since the people are long-lived, the women very prolific, and diseases very uncommon.

high mountains. In Matsmai, on the contrary, the ponds and lakes freeze, the snow lies in the valleys and the plains from November till April, and gales besides in as great abundance as with us in St. Petersburgh. Severe frosts are indeed uncommon, yet the cold is often fifteen degrees of Reaumur. In summer the parts of Europe under the same latitude as Matsmai enjoy serene and warm weather ; in Matsmai, on the contrary, the rain pours down in torrents at least twice a week, the horizon is involved in dark clouds, violent winds blow, and the fog is scarcely ever dispersed. In the former, oranges, lemons, figs, and other productions of the warm climates, thrive in the open air ; in the latter, apples, pears, peaches, and grapes, hardly attain their proper ripeness.

" I have not, it is true, been in Niphon, the principal island of the Japanese possessions ; but I have heard from the Japanese that, in Jeddo, the capital city of the empire, in the thirty-sixth degree of latitude, snow often falls in the winter nights to the depth of an inch or more. It is true it melts immediately the next day ; but if we consider that Jeddo is under the same latitude as Malaga, in Spain, we shall be convinced that the climate of the Eastern hemisphere is much ruder than that of the Western. The Japanese assured me that on the southern part of Sagaleen, in the forty-seventh degree of latitude, the ground is often thawed during the summer only to a depth of a foot and a half. If we compare with this the climate of a place in Europe, the latitude of which corresponds, for example—Lyons, in France—how different are the results ! That the accounts given by the Japanese are true I cannot doubt, for we ourselves met with great fields of ice, so late as the month of May, off the Kurile Island, in latitude 47° 45'. At this season no ice is to be seen with us in the Gulf of Finland, in 60° north latitude, though the water there, from being so confined, has not power to break the ice, which vanishes more in consequence of the rays of the sun. Off Japan, on the contrary, the waves of the ocean must break it up much sooner, if the sun acted with the same power.

"This great difference of the climate proceeds from local causes. The Japanese possessions lie in the Eastern Ocean, which may be truly called the *Empire of Fogs*.

JAPANESE GARDEN.

In the summer months the fog often lasts three or four days without interruption, and there seldom passes a day in which it is not for some hours gloomy, rainy, or foggy. Perfectly clear days are as rare in summer there as fogs

in the Western Ocean. Though the fine weather is more
constant in winter, yet a week seldom passes without
two or three gloomy days. These fogs, and this gloomy
weather, make the air cold and damp, and hinder the
beams of the sun from producing so much effect as in
other countries which enjoy a clear sky. Besides this,
the northern parts of the Islands of Niphon and Matsmai
and Sagaleen are covered with extremely high mountains,
the summits of which are mostly above the clouds, whence
the winds that blow over these mountains bring an extraordinary degree of cold with them. It is also to be
noted that the Japanese possessions are separated from
the continent of Asia by a strait, the greatest breadth of
which is 800 wersts, and that the country of the Mant-
chous and Tartary, which form the east frontier of Asia,
towards Japan, are nothing but immense deserts covered
with mountains and innumerable lakes, from which the
winds that blow over them bring, even in summer, an
extraordinary degree of cold. These may be the three
causes of the striking difference of climate in the countries
situated on the eastern side of the old world, and those
of the western hemisphere under the same degree of
latitude."*

It appears, however, that, taking its whole extent from
south to north, and counting all its islands, Japan will
afford the cultivator all the productions both of tropical
and temperate climates, and that it is a most healthy
country to live in. "The air of all these islands," says an
old Spanish writer, "is very salubrious. The soil is very
fertile ; the fruits are most delicious."†

The abundance of running water affords everywhere

* Captain Golownin, *Recollections of Japan*. This Russian officer
is entitled to full credit whenever he speaks of the things which
came under his own observation. It must, however, be borne in
mind that he was a prisoner all the time he was in Japan. The
atmosphere of a prison does not improve one's notions of the climate
of any place.

† Don Pedro Hurtado de Mendoza, *Espejo Geographico*. Madrid.
1690. Count Benyowsky speaks of the excessive heat of the climate
in the month of July.

the means of irrigation, and in this art the Japanese seem even to surpass the Chinese. The longevity of the people appears to be a well-established fact.*

Kämpfer mentions a village in which all the inhabitants were sons, grandsons, and great-grandsons, all the descendants of one man *still living !* The asserted great longevity of the Japanese, and the fecundity of their women, seem to permit no doubt as to the salubrity of the climate. They are said to be subject to few diseases, being a very cleanly and temperate nation, perfectly innocent of alcohol as a general stimulant for the people.

With a population known to be dense from the earliest times, and now giving, it is said, three hundred and fifty-four mouths to the square mile against the one hundred and fifty-two of the United Kingdom, Japan must rank amongst the healthiest countries of earth.

Though, to some extent, rocky or mountainous, the islands may be described as well-wooded and shaded. Firs and cypresses are the most common trees in their woods and forests. Of both there are several different sorts. In the plains, the natives who, like the Chinese, make the most of every inch of ground, take care to plant them in barren and sandy soils, which are fit for nothing else. For the sake of ornament and shade, they are, however, planted in rows along the roads, and over the ridges of hills. This gives great beauty to the country, and renders travelling in warm weather very pleasant.

A noble Spaniard, who was shipwrecked on the coast, and made the journey to the Emperor's court in the year 1608, says :—" On whichever side the traveller turns his eye he perceives a pleasant concourse of people, passing to and fro, as in the most populous cities of Europe ; the

* *Ambassades Mémorables,* &c. By Jacob Van Meurs ; Kämpfer's *History of Japan ;* Charlevoix, *Histoire et Description Générale du Japon ;* Thunberg's *Travels in Europe, Africa, and Asia ;* Benyowsky, *Memoirs and Travels ; Adventures and Recollections of Captain Golownin ;* Siebold's *Japan ; Extracts from Fischer and Meylan ; Journal of Education,* vol. vi. p. 370 ; and vol. x. p. 184.

D

roads are lined on both sides with superb pine-trees, which keep off the sun ; the distances are marked by little eminences planted with two trees.*

No firs nor cypress-trees are allowed to be cut down without permission of the local magistrate, and for every full-grown tree that is felled, a young one must be planted. From remote time the Japanese appear to have bestowed an exceedingly great care on the growth and preservation of their timber-trees, thus shaming some nations of Europe, who pretend to more wisdom and civilization.

Cedars of great size and beauty, and compared with those that once flourished so luxuriantly on Mount Lebanon, are very frequently met with. A Portuguese missionary, who was in the country in 1565, vividly describes the approach to one of the temples, which was through an avenue of pines and cedars intermixed, the trees uniting over head, so as entirely to exclude the heat and glare of the hot summer sun. Some of the cedars he measured were more than eighteen feet in girth. The roof of the temple was supported by ninety columns of cedar, of prodigious height, regular in the stem, and perfectly round.† The Jesuit Charlevoix was much struck with one particular camphor-tree. One hundred and thirty-five years after his time Von Siebold visited the same tree, and found it still healthy and rich in foliage. It had attained to the circumference of fifty feet. Captain Sir Edward Belcher, being in want of some small spars, was supplied with a quantity at Nagasaki. They were all cedar, and measured about ninety-six feet in length.

The views of Japanese scenery, published in the works of M. Fischer and Von Siebold, convey the idea of a superb sylva, and of a luxuriantly wooded country. It appears that all the temples, of any size or consideration, are approached through an avenue of evergreen trees. The

---

* "Journal of Don Rodrigo de Vivero y Velasco." — *Asiatic Journal,* July, 1830. The whole of this paper is in the highest degree interesting.

† P. Almeyda, as quoted by Mr. Rundall, *Memorials.*

cedar timber would, no doubt, prove a valuable article of export.

The oak flourishes in two varieties, both of which are very different from any that grow in Europe. The acorns of the larger oak are boiled and eaten by the common people, and are said to be nutritious and not unpalatable.

The mulberry-tree grows in most parts of Japan, but in greatest plenty in the provinces to the north, where many towns and villages subsist almost entirely upon the silk manufactures. But the silk of Japan is coarse, and very inferior to that of China, a circumstance which arises from the natives allowing their mulberry-trees to grow to age and size, instead of keeping up a constant supply of young dwarf trees. The coarseness of the leaves of the old tree imparts its quality to the silk. Wherever fine silk is produced, the worms are fed on the leaves of saplings. The Japanese mulberry-tree grows with surprising quickness, and spreads its branches to a great extent. It is found in its wild state in the country, but, on account of its great usefulness, the people transplant it and cultivate it. From its bark they make much of their curious paper, as also ropes, matches, coarse stuffs for dresses, and several other things.

The *urusi* or varnish-tree, of which they make so extensive a use, is a noble tree when grown to its full size. On incision it yields a rich, milky, glutinous juice, out of which the Japanese make the celebrated varnish, known in Europe by the name of *Japan*. With this varnish they cover and coat all their household furniture, all their dishes and plates, and all their drinking vessels, whether made of wood or of paper. The use of plate, or porcelain or glass, appears to be very limited, and is probably interdicted by some rule of nationality or religion : from the emperor down to the meanest peasant, all make use of the light varnished or japanned cups and dishes, the inner substance of which is wood or paper, or what we term papier-maché.

Another tree, called *forasi*, renders a varnish of an inferior quality.

The camphor-tree exists in many parts, and bears black and purple berries, which are pleasant to the sight. The country people make the camphor by a simple decoction of the stem and roots cut into small pieces. The tea-plant, which was long believed to be peculiar to China, thrives luxuriantly, and the Japanese are great tea-drinkers. The pepper-tree, or a tree which supplies the place of pepper, is common. They have three different

OLD CAMPHOR-TREE.

sorts of fig-trees, one of which, introduced by the Portu-guese, produces a fruit larger and of better flavour than any in Europe. The chesnut-tree is still more plentiful, and the fruit of it excellent. The walnut-tree flourishes, but chiefly in the northern provinces. In the same pro-vinces is a tree called by the natives *kaja*, which produces an oblong nut, inclosed in a pulp, and not unlike, in size and shape, to the areca nut. The oil compressed out of these nuts is very sweet and agreeable, resembling the taste of the oil of sweet almonds. It is much commended for its medicinal virtues. They make much use of it in dressing their food. The condensed smoke and soot produced by the burning of the shells of these nuts is the chief ingredient of the best and blackest Japanese ink, much of which is sold in Europe under the name of Indian ink. Another sort of nut grows very plentifully almost everywhere, on a fine tall tree, with large, beautiful leaves. The nuts yield plenty of oil, which is also much commended for several valuable properties. The orange-tree and the lemon-tree grow very plentifully, and are of several sorts. The juice of a very small but delicious lemon is commonly used in cookery. The plum-tree, the cherry-tree, and the apricot are cultivated. But the cherry-tree and the plum are valued chiefly, not for their fruit but for their flowers. The people improve them so much by a peculiar culture, that the flowers become as large as roses,* and, in the season when they are in full blossom, these trees afford a delightful sight, about their temples, in their gardens, and public walks. The vine is not much grown.

They take great delight, and have extraordinary skill as well in enlarging as in dwarfing all manner of plants. The branches of some of their trees, springing at the height of seven or eight feet from the ground, are occasionally led out across ponds, and supported on props, so as to afford a shade and covering of 300 feet in circumference.

There are various other trees, not easy to describe, which appear to be peculiar to Japan and the neighbouring islands.

"Assuredly," says an old Neapolitan monk and missionary, "this is a right pleasant land, and abundantly supplied with fair, tall trees." Nobody that has ever been in the East can forget the soft, fascinating, poetical

---

* Kämpfer saw cherry-blossoms, on the common cherry-tree, as large as roses. Meylan observed plum-blossoms four times the size of our cabbage roses.

odour emanating from groves of cypress and clumps of cedar. It is a natural, living, growing incense, offered up to heaven at all seasons of the year, at all times of both night and day, and the man has no poetry nor devotion in him, if he fail to be soothed and enchanted by it.

The noble Spaniard whom we have repeatedly quoted, felt the charms of these woods and groves as a man of taste and sentiment ought ; and he was so pleased with the whole aspect of Japan, that he declared, " if he could have prevailed upon himself to renounce his God and his king, he should have preferred that country to his own."*

The bamboo, which is applied to many purposes, and so extensively used throughout India and all the eastern countries, is very common in Japan. It supplies materials for almost everything, from the partition-walls of their houses and the fences of their gardens to the sails of their ooats and junks. The fine sort of bamboo, which the Dutch exported by the name of rattan, and sold for walking-canes, was a Japanese production and preparation. Both firs and bamboos are highly prized among the natives, for their constant verdure, and from a superstitious belief that they have an influence over the happy occurrences of human life. The approaches to their temples and other holy places are fringed with them ; and they make frequent allusions to them in their poetical writings, particularly in congratulatory poems, for they believe that the fir and the bamboo, if respected by the elements and not disturbed by man, will live and flourish for an almost indefinite period of time. Thus, " May you live as long as the bamboo," is considered no bad compliment.

The *jusnoki* is a species of iron-wood which also is very much used in building.

The country abounds in flowers and flowering shrubs. The *subacki* is a pretty large shrub, growing in woods and hedges, and bearing flowers not unlike roses. There is a vast variety, the Japanese in their copious language,

* Don Rodrigo de Vivero y Velasco.

giving 900 names to the different sorts of *subacki*. The *satsuki* is another shrub bearing flowers like the lily, and offering many varieties. The two sorts which grow wild, one with purple, the other with scarlet flowers, are a great ornament to the hills and fields in the proper season, "affording," says the old German traveller, "a sight pleasing beyond expression." The *momidsi* is a kind of maple, having leaves of a beautiful purple colour. Our bulb-lily, narcissus, and gillyflower, are both cultivated and found growing in the wild state. There are other flowers, peculiar to the country, too numerous to be named, and all said to be superior to ours in brilliancy of colour, but inferior in odour. "Indeed," says Kämpfer, "I think that Japan may vie with most if not all known countries, for a great variety of beautiful plants and flowers wherewith kind nature hath most liberally and curiously adorned its fields, hills, woods, and forests. Some of these they transplant into gardens, and improve by assiduity and culture to the utmost, and indeed to a surprising degree of perfection."

This love of flowers is one of the most pleasing features in the character of this most singular people. Nearly every house has its little garden in its rear, and a few flowering shrubs in its front. The garden is commonly square, and very neatly walled in. "It cannot be denied," adds Kämpfer, "that the great number of beautiful incarnate, and double flowers, which they bear in the proper season, are a surprisingly curious ornament to the back part of the house. In some small houses and inns of less note, where there is not room enough either for a garden or for a large flowering tree, they place in the back window one or two flower-pots, or some dwarf trees, or some little plants which will grow easily upon pumice, or other porous stone, without any earth at all, provided their roots be supplied with water; and they generally add to these a small vessel full of water, with a few gold or silver fish in it." The gardens attached to the better sort of houses are kept with uncommon care and neatness, and, though somewhat artificial in their arrangement, are described as being very delightful. They are laid out by professional gardeners, who do no other work, and who proceed upon certain established and ancient rules. In such a garden there must be a small rivulet falling over rocks, or tinkling among stones.

As florists and gardeners they are indeed conspicuous, and the beauty of a production of the soil in this department is seen in the Camelia Japonica, now found in every English greenhouse. Like the Chinese, they possess the singular art of producing miniature samples of the larger products of vegetation, an art scarcely known in Europe, and only to be admired as a curiosity. A box was offered for sale to the Dutch governor of Nagasaki, in which were flourishing a fir-tree, a bamboo, and a plum-tree, the latter in blossom, and the box was only three inches long and one inch wide. The account is given by an eye-witness, who adds that the price demanded for so great a curiosity was 1,200 florins.* Another very small box is mentioned as having contained miniature specimens of every tree that grows on the islands.

The great industry, and even the skill of the Japanese, as agriculturists, have been praised by all the travellers who have visited and written about their country. Kämpfer says they are perhaps as good husbandmen as any in the world. This he attributes not only to the extreme populousness of the country, but chiefly to the circumstance that the natives, being denied commerce and communication with foreigners, must, of necessity, support themselves by what they can produce by their own labour and industry on their own soil. Hence the laws on this head are very particular and severe, the State making it its business to see not only that the lands are cultivated,

---

* "Account of Japan," by Door G. F. Meijlan. Amsterdam, 1830, as quoted in the *Quarterly Review*, vol. lii.

The Chinese method of producing these miniature plants is given in G. Bennett's *Wanderings in New South Wales*, &c. More information will be found in a recent French work, Le Baron Leon de Saint Denys' *Recherches sur l'Agriculture et l'Horticulture des Chinois*. Paris. 1850.

but also that they are cultivated in the best manner, or at least according to the best rules of such agricultural science as the country possesses. Not only the fields and flat country, which are seldom or never turned into meadows, or kept for pasture, but likewise the hills and mountains, are made to produce corn, rice, pease, pulse, and numerous edible plants. Every inch of ground is improved to the best advantage ; and it was not without astonishment that Kämpfer and his travelling companions, on their journeys to and from the Imperial Court, beheld mountains, inaccessible to cattle, cultivated up to their very tops. This is managed by a succession of walls and terraces, rising above each other, and by the people ploughing or hoeing without the help of oxen. The same system obtains in many parts of China, and in not a few parts of Europe. The Japanese are skilful in manuring their grounds, and use a variety of substances for manures. Their rice—their main food—grown in the low country— is said to be the best of all Asia. It is perfectly white, and so nourishing and substantial, that foreigners, not used to it, can eat but little of it at a time. The rice-fields are cut through and through by little canals, and irrigated in the most careful manner. The rice grown in the upper grounds, where irrigation is difficult, is of an inferior quality. From rice they brew a sort of strong thick beer called *sackee.* Among their many laws relating to agri- culture, there is one by virtue of which whosoever leaves his ground uncultivated for the term of one year forfeits his title and possession. All lands must be surveyed every year by certain officers, who are called *Kemme,* and who are held in such repute that they have the privilege of wearing two swords, which is otherwise allowed to none but to the nobility and soldiers.

Maize, or Indian corn, millet, and in general all sorts of grain, are said to grow well in most of the islands. Turnips are exceedingly plentiful and of very large size. They have pease, horse-radishes, carrots, fennel, lettuces, cucumbers, gourds, and good melons. The natives also derive sustenance from a variety of wild plants and fruits, as well as from the leaves of certain trees, and from the flowers and berries of certain shrubs. They possess the art of depriving poisonous plants of their noxious qualities, and rendering them edible. The mushroom, under several varieties, is found everywhere. Both hemp and flax thrive well under Japanese management, and the people, being great smokers, grow vast quantities of tobacco. In fact, through the goodness of the soil, and the skill and care of the natives, all the most valuable of the productions of the earth are brought to great perfection.

If we assume the perfection of the arts of tillage and manufacture as a test of civilization, Japan may at least compete with any Oriental nation. M. Meijlan places it higher than any. The same recent Dutch observer bestows an amount of praise on their field cultivation which could not be justly applied to many European nations.*

Though abundantly stocked with pictures and carvings, with dragons and all other sorts of monsters, borrowed from the Chinese, the Japanese empire is but sparingly provided with four-footed beasts, wild or tame. The country is too much cultivated and peopled to afford cover to the wild quadrupeds, and the tame are bred only for carriage and agriculture. The use of animal food is interdicted by the national religion, and they have not left pasture enough to support many sheep and oxen. The horses are generally small, but there is a breed said to be not inferior to that imported into India from the Persian Gulf; but horses of this kind now appear to be rare. In the time of old Captain Saris they were common enough. "Their horses are not tall, but of the size of our middling nags, short and well trussed, small headed, and full of mettle, in my opinion far excelling the Spanish jennet in pride and stomach."† The Japanese relate most marvellous stories of the performances of some of their steeds. There is also a breed of ponies, which, though small, has been much admired. Oxen and cows are kept only for

* *Quarterly Review*, vol. lii.
† Saris's *Narrative in Purchas.*

ploughing and for carriage. Of milk and butter the Japanese know nothing. They have a large humped buffalo, sometimes of a monstrous size, which they train to draw carts or to carry heavy goods on their backs.

A JAPANESE FISHING FAMILY.

The elephant, the camel, and the ass are unknown animals. Sheep and goats were kept formerly at the Dutch settlements, in the neighbourhood of which some few may yet be found. They might be bred in the country to great advantage, if the natives were permitted to eat the flesh, or knew how to manage and manufacture the wool. They have a few swine, which were brought over from China, and which some of the country people near the coast still keep, not, indeed, for their own use, but to sell to certain Chinese junks which are allowed to come over to trade, most of the Chinese mariners being addicted to pork. Captain Sir Edward Belcher was supplied with some hogs that were overwhelmed with their own fat, and weighed about 150℔s.

Dogs or common curs they have, and in superfluous numbers. These dogs are as much the pest of the towns of Japan as they are of Constantinople and the other foul cities and towns of the Ottoman Empire. This vast increase of the canine species, and the encouragement and immunity accorded to it, arose (according to the popular account) out of a curious superstition and an extravagant imperial decree. An Emperor who reigned at the close of the eighteenth century chanced to be born under the Sign of the Dog, the Dog being one of the twelve celestial signs of the Japanese Zodiac. For this reason, the Emperor had as great an esteem for dogs as the Roman Emperor Augustus is reported to have entertained for rams. When he ascended the throne, he willed and ordained that dogs should be held as sacred animals ; and, from that time, more puppies saw the light, and were permitted to live in Japan than in any other country on the face of the earth, Turkey, perhaps, excepted. These dogs have no masters, but lie and prowl about the streets, to the exceeding great annoyance of passengers, especially if they happen to be foreign travellers, or Christians in Christian dresses. If they come round you in packs, barking, snarling, and showing their teeth, nay, even if they fall upon you and bite you, you must on no account take the law into your own hands, and beat them off or shoot them. To kill one of them is a capital crime, whatever mischief the brute may have done you. In every town there are Guardians of the Dogs, and to these officers notice must be given in case of any canine misdemeanour, these guardians alone being empowered to punish the dogs. Every street must keep a certain number of these animals, or at least provide them with victuals ; huts, or dog-hospitals, stand in all parts of the town, and to these the animals, in case of sickness, must be carefully conveyed by the inhabitants. The dogs that die must be carried up to the tops of mountains and hills, the usual burying-places of men and women, and there be very decently interred. Old Kämpfer says :—" The natives tell a pleasant tale on this head. A Japanese, as he was carrying the carcase of a dead dog to the top of a steep mountain, grew impatient, grumbled, and cursed the Emperor's birthday and whimsical command. His companion bid him hold his tongue and be quiet, and, instead of swearing, return thanks to the gods that the Emperor was not born under the Sign of the Horse, for, in that case, the load would have been heavier."

We give the pleasant tale as we find it, but we do not believe that it points to the real origin of the superstitious regard for dogs, which many of the Mongol race share with the Japanese and Turks. That superstition had its origin in the wilds of Tartary, or in whatever other part of the world it was that served as the cradle and great starting point of the wide-spread Mongol race. The dog must have been in a manner deified, when they first put him among their celestial signs. And it is not to be wondered at. The dog is the best conquest that man has made amongst the brute creation. He is the first element of progress in society. Without the dog man would have been condemned to vegetate everlastingly, a mere unmitigated savage. The Dog changed Man from a *savage* to a *patriarch* when he gave man a flock, and took care of it for him. Without the dog there is no flock : without the flock, no certain maintenance, no " leg o' mutton," no wool, consequently, no time to lose—no time for astronomical observations—no time for science—no industry. The dog first enabled man to enjoy a moment of leisure—made a gentleman of him—*civilized* him. [*]

Among some of the Mongolian tribes, the dog is the indicator of fate, the harbinger of death ; among others, he is an object either of dread or devotion[†]

But our learned German is not always so facetious

---

[*] See Toussenel's admirable remarks on the dog, in his recent work, *L'Esprit des Bêtes*, ed. 1858, p. 149, *et seq.*

[†] A very curious specimen of this superstition has been traced in

about this monstrous annoyance of street dogs. On reaching Nagasaki, he says, "The dogs also deserve to be noticed among the inhabitants of this city, they being full as well, nay, better maintained and taken care of than many of the people, and although the imperial orders on this head are not regarded and complied with at Nagasaki with that strictness as they must be in other parts of the empire which are not so remote from court, yet the streets be full of these animals, leading a most easy and independent life, giving way neither to men nor horses. The town is never without a great deal of noise from those animals." *

The Japanese have no dogs of superior breed, but they have cats of a peculiarly beautiful kind. These are of a whitish colour, with large yellow and black spots, and a very short tail : the ladies carry them about as lap-dogs.

In the islands are found deer, wild boars, and hares, but apparently in no great numbers. There are also monkeys, wild dogs, foxes, some curious animals that look like a cross between the fox and the wolf, and a few small bears in the secluded parts of the northern provinces. The fox bears not the very best of characters among the Japanese ; the peasantry believe him to be in league with all evil spirits or devils, and to be himself the very incar-

India among the Pársis. With these people a dead body cannot be buried or removed, unless a dog be brought in to look upon it.

"The 'Sag-did,' that is, *dog-gaze*, is the ceremony of bringing a dog to look upon the dead body ; for, according to some superstitious notions of the Pársis, evil spirits are driven away by the presence of the dog, and the fate of the deceased's soul may be, they think, guessed at, by the manner in which he regards the corpse. This usage they do not willingly make known."[1]

* The nocturnal noise made by the dogs of Constantinople can never be forgotten by those who have heard it. Such as have had the felicity of passing a long dreary winter in that comfortless city, are apt to have their dreams disturbed, years after, by the yelling of dogs, and the nightly cry of *yang-in-war !* fire ! fire !

---

[1] *Illustrations of the Languages called Zend and Pahlavi,* by John Romer, Esq., late Member of Council at Bombay, M.R.A.S.; *Journal of the Royal Asiatic Society,* vol. iv. p. 352.

nation of craft, malice, and wickedness ; " but," says old
Kämpfer, " the fox-hunters are expert in conjuring and
stripping this animated devil, his hair and wool being
much coveted for writing and painting pencils." The
weasel and ferret are found. Rats and mice swarm
throughout the country, for the beautiful cats, being pets,
have no turn for mousing. The rats are tamed by the
natives, and taught to perform several tricks, and form a
common diversion for the poorer people. We find mention made of two small animals of a red colour, that live
under the roofs of the houses, and are very tame. They
are called the *itutz* and the *tin*.

The destructive white ant, that great annoyance of
most parts of the East Indies, is very common. The
Japanese call them *do toos*, or piercers, a name they well
merit, for they perforate whatever they meet, stones and
metals only excepted ; and when once they get into a
merchant's warehouse, they in a very short compass of
time can destroy or ruin an amazing quantity of his best
goods. Nothing has been yet found that will keep them
off, except salt laid under the goods and spread about
them. The common European ants are their mortal
enemies, and wherever these have been introduced, the
do toos have rapidly disappeared, like the original English
rat before the invasion of the Norwegian.

The islands, however, may be said to be remarkably
free from insects and noxious reptiles. There are but few
snakes, and hardly any of them appear to be venomous.
One of these is of a beautiful green colour, with a very
flat head. Japanese soldiers cook it and eat its flesh, in
the belief that it imparts courage and audacity. The
natives also calcine the flesh in an earthen pot hermetically sealed, and derive from it a powder, which they
believe to possess the most extraordinary medicinal virtues.* There is a water snake of monstrous size, and
another very large snake, of a black colour, but quite in-

* The bite of this snake is, however, considered very dangerous.

offensive, is found in the mountains.   Both are very
scarce, and when taken are shown about for money.

Birds are numerous.   Of tame poultry they keep only
fowls and ducks.   They sell them sometimes to foreigners,
but never eat them.   Cocks are highly prized by the religious orders, because they mark the time, and foretell
changes of the weather.   Indeed, they are chiefly kept up
as *time-keepers.*

The crane is the chief of the wild birds of the country;
but like the heron and the stork, which also abound, they
can scarcely be called wild, for they are held as sacred
birds, and nobody must injure or molest them.   They
thus become quite familiar, and mix with the people, and
throng the market-places, just as the storks do in all
towns, villages, and bazaars in Turkey, where they are
equally objects of affection and veneration.   No doubt
this feeling also had its rise in the Tartarian regions.
When the conquering Turks first came into Europe, they
were accustomed to say that the stork had a singular
affection for their race, and that whithersoever they might
carry their victorious arms, the stork would follow them
and live with them.   In Japan the country people never
call the crane by any other name than that of *O Tsuri-
sama,* "My great lord crane."   There are two sorts of
them : one white as snow, and the other grey.   They
portend good fortune and long life.   For this reason the
imperial apartments, the walls of temples, and other happy
places, are commonly adorned with figures of them.
Cranes are also painted on dishes and drinking-cups, and
reproduced on articles of domestic furniture.   The native
paintings of these birds are exquisitely beautiful, true and
correct in drawing, beautiful in finish and colouring.
They are among the very best specimens of Japanese art.

The winged tortoise, the porpoise, or dolphin of the
ancients, are favourite designs in all their decorations,
whether of wood-carving or painting, in the various
buildings.*

* *United States Expedition to Japan.*

Wild geese and wild ducks are very abundant, and very tame. There are several species of both. One kind of duck is of immense size, and of wonderfully brilliant and beautiful plumage. Pheasants, wild pigeons, and woodcocks are very common birds. Hawks, also, are common. Ravens are scarce. Our common European crows, as also parrots, and other Indian birds, are never to be met with.

Of singing birds, Kämpfer mentions only larks and nightingales; but he says that both of these sing more sweetly than with us. The natives highly prize the nightingale, and large sums are paid for a caged one with a good voice.

They have plenty of bees, and, consequently, honey and wax are produced.

The shrill cicada, or winged-grasshopper, peoples the pines, and fills the woods and mountains with its endless song. Butterflies and beetles are numerous and diversified, some of both kinds being very beautiful. Among the night-moths there is one sort which the Japanese ladies keep in little cages, as pets and curiosities. This moth is about four inches long, slender, round-bodied, with four wings, two of which are transparent, and concealed under the other pair of wings, which shine like polished metal, and are most curiously and beautifully adorned with blue and gold lines and spots. The following graceful fable owes its origin to the matchless beauty of this moth. All other night-flies fall in love with it; and, to get rid of their importunities, it maliciously bids them, as a trial of their devotion and constancy, to go and fetch it fire. The blind lovers, obedient to command, fly to the nearest lamp or candle, and never fail to get burned to death.

The sea all about Japan is plentifully stocked with all sorts of fish, and the natives are very expert fishermen. In the time of Charlevoix and Kämpfer, and earlier travellers, the whale fishery was carried on to a great extent, particularly in the sea which washes the southern coasts of the great island, Niphon. The common way of catch-

E

ing them was by harpooning, in the manner of our Greenland fishermen ; but the Japanese boats seemed to be fitter for the purpose than ours, being small, narrow, tapering at each end into a sharp point, and rowing with incredible swiftness. "About 1680 a rich fisherman, in the province of Omura, found out a new way of catching whales with nets made of strong ropes, about two inches thick. This method was afterwards followed with good success by another man of the country. They say that as soon as the whale finds its head entangled in a net, he cannot, without great difficulty, swim away or dive, and may be very easily killed with the harpoon in the common manner. The reason why this new method hath not been universally received is, because it requires a greater and much more expensive set of tackle than common fishermen can afford."*

They enumerate six kinds of whales, differing in name, form, and size. Of all these several kinds nothing was thrown away by the Japanese as useless. They boiled the fat or blubber into train oil ; they pickled, boiled, roasted, or fried the flesh, and ate it ; they even reduced the cartilaginous bones into food ; they made cords, ropes, and strings for their musical instruments out of the nerves and tendons ; they made a great use of the fins ; and out of the jaw-bones, and other solid bones, they manufactured numerous articles, particularly their fine steelyards for weighing their gold and silver.

The Japanese fishermen attribute to the flesh of the whale, their favourite food, their strength and hardihood, and their extraordinary capability of enduring exposure to cold and foul weather.

It was in pursuing the whale to the coast of Japan that the American ships met with those disasters, and that inhospitable treatment, which first made the government of the United States turn its attention in this direction.

Turtles of enormous size are said to abound on the southern and eastern coasts. Salmon, soles, turbot, a sort

* Kämpfer.

of cod, smelts, and other delicious sea-fish, together with all sorts of lobsters, crabs, shrimps, oysters, mussels, &c. are taken in surprising abundance ; and there are other

JAPANESE FISHERMEN.

fish of species unknown to us, and of which some are said to be delicious. It is fortunate for the natives that their prejudices and superstitions allow them to eat fish. In

E 2

the larger islands every part of the coast is thickly
strewed with buildings, and at every second or third mile
are populous villages, from which extensive fisheries are
carried on.*   In fact, the Japanese are essentially fish-
eaters, or *ichthyophagi.*   Aided by a good growth of
potatoes, or an adequate supply of rice, the sea alone
would support a vast population.

Without going into further detail, enough has been
said to convey to the reader an adequate notion of the
natural riches and ample resources of this beautiful and
healthy country.

MINERAL WEALTH, PEARLS, PRECIOUS STONES.

However great may be estimated the treasures which
the Japanese archipelago formerly gave to Europe, we
have reason to believe that it contains veins of the
precious metal as rich as those of California and Australia.   From Yedso to the Lioukiou group, across the
maze of oriental isles towards Indo-China, there are
continuous veins of gold and silver.   All the primary
formations of the south-east of Asia are more or less
metallic.   But the mines of Japan are now scarcely
worked at all.   Is it because in their peculiar political
and social system the Emperors and guides of the people
do not think that the abundance of those metals is necessary or even conducive to the well-being or the happiness
of their subjects and the prosperity of their country?   If
so, they stand in a wonderful contrast of philosophical
opinion with us of the Western world.   But, perhaps, it
may be owing to their ignorance, not having as yet become initiated in the mysteries, or listened to the revela-

* Golownin.—As this Russian captain and fellow-captives, tied
to a plank or tray, were conveyed along the coast, they were fed
with rice and broiled fish, the natives putting the food into their
mouths with their little sticks, which are like the chop-sticks of the
Chinese.

tions, of Geology,—that wonderful science which alarmed religious faith, enlarged the bounds of intellectual speculation in the glorious works of God, and condescended to tell us where to look for and find the mammon of iniquity.

But in the absence of precise, unerring Geology, the Japanese have incomprehensible traditions, which, handed down from father to son through ages, tell them of hidden treasures somewhere in the country. They talk mysteriously of the Isle of Gold and the Isle of Silver, situated in the most distant regions of the north-east. They say that their learned geographers have designedly omitted to mark the locality in their maps. They call them respectively Kinsima and Yinsima. Of course the Spaniards and the Dutch fitted out numerous and fruitless expeditions in search of these fortunate islands. The Spaniards claimed them beforehand as theirs exclusively, by virtue of the famous political Bulls of Popes Martin V. and Alexander VI.

At Yedso there are numerous mines of the precious and other metals. Auriferous sand accumulates abundantly in the beds of rivers and on the shores of the ocean. This fact was noticed by Father Jerome des Anges, the first European who visited the island ; but the Japanese government, doubtless apprehensive lest Yedso, undefended as it is, should be torn from the empire in consequence of that everlasting European temptation, has abstained from verifying the discovery.

"These islands," says a Spanish writer of the seventeenth century, "are excessively rich in gold and silver. The abundance of these metals is scarcely credible. In Jeddo, the capital, not only the palace of the Emperor, but also many houses of great lords, are covered with rich plates of gold."* "The greatest riches of the Japanese soil," says the careful and accurate Kämpfer, "and those wherein this empire exceeds most known countries, consist in all sorts of minerals and metals, particularly

* Don Pedro Hurtado de Mendoza, "Espejo Geographico."

in gold, silver, and copper." On this point all the old writers are agreed.

Gold is dug out of the mines in many provinces. The greatest quantity of it is melted out of its own ore. Some is washed out of gold sand, and small quantities are said to be contained in the copper. The richest gold ore, and that which contains the finest gold, is mined in one of the northern districts of the great island Niphon ; the Emperor reserving two-thirds of the product as a royalty. There is also a very rich gold sand in the same part of the island. But gold ore, or gold in dust, appears to be found in innumerable parts of the Japanese archipelago.* Deterred by superstitious fears, the native miners have seldom penetrated far into the earth, but have rested satisfied with the gold found near the surface.

In a memorandum laid before the Dutch Governor-General at Batavia, in 1744, is a calculation showing that in the beginning of the seventeenth century, when the trade with Japan was an open one, the export of gold and silver was ten millions of Dutch florins, or about £840,000 per annum. This export was first contracted, and, in 1680, entirely forbidden. The same calculation goes on to prove that, in the course of sixty years, the export of gold and silver must have amounted to the enormous value of from twenty-five to fifty millions sterling.

In a good many old accounts of India (both French and English), we find frequent mention made of "the gold lingots of Japan." About the middle of the seventeenth century these lingots appear to have abounded in Bengal. But at an earlier period, or between 1545 and 1615, it is notorious that the Portuguese obtained in Japan, in exchange for merchandise, enormous quantities of the precious metals.†

---

* " We have seen some gold articles of Japanese manufacture, in which the precious metal was uncommonly pure and beautiful,— thoroughly virgin gold. The same may be said of some of their silver, which we have examined."—MacFarlane, *Japan.*
          † T. Rundall, *Memorials.*

Silver mines are described as being quite as numerous as the gold mines, and their produce as excellent in quality. In one year we find the Portuguese exporting 2,350 chests of this fine silver, valued, in round numbers, at £587,500 sterling. To the east of Japan lie two islands, called, *par excellence*, the "gold and silver islands." These have never been touched by Europeans.

Copper abounds all through the group, and some of it is said to be the finest in the world. It is refined and cast into small cylinders about a foot long and an inch thick. It was formerly one of the chief commodities purchased in Japan by the Dutch, who brought it into Europe, and carried on a great trade in it. There is also a coarser kind of copper, which is cast into large roundish lumps or cakes.

The Dutch have in some years carried off from thirty to forty thousand pekuls of this copper, each pekul being about 133 pounds weight English. Alarmed at the amount, the Japanese Government decreed that instead of two yearly ships, only one should be allowed to carry off copper, but, in 1820, the restriction was mitigated, and the number of vessels and amount of copper were again increased. It may be said that all the Japanese metals are everywhere esteemed for their high degree of purity. If they have exhausted their old copper mines, there can be little doubt that new ones would easily be found, if the restrictive and tyrannical native Government did not interfere with, and almost entirely check, private enterprises.

Both lead and quicksilver are said to be abundant.

Tin, so fine and white, that it almost comes up to silver, is found in small quantities. As this metal is not much used or prized by the natives, it has probably not been much sought after.

Iron is dug up only in three of the provinces, although it may very likely exist in many other parts of the islands. The Japanese smelt it on the spot, and cast it into small bars or cylinders. It is of admirable quality, as is also the steel which they make from it. Although they have great ingenuity in smelting and refining metals, and in working them, there can be little doubt that modern European science would turn all these mines to an incomparably greater account.

Coal, which gives wings and life to steam navigation, and so tends to unite together all portions of the globe, is the mineral for which the Americans profess to have the greatest desire. Indeed, they declare that their main object in fitting out their Japan expedition is to obtain from the Emperor permission to purchase from his subjects the supplies of coal which their steamers, in their out and inward voyages, may require.* "They have no want of coals in Japan," says Kämpfer, "they being dug up in great quantities in the province of Sikusen, and in most of the northern provinces." Von Siebold speaks of coal as being in common use in the country. At Koyanose, in very cold weather, he found a comfortable coal fire. At Wuku-moto he visited a coal mine, and although he was not permitted to descend quite to the bottom of the shaft, he saw enough to convince him that the mine was skilfully worked. The upper strata were only a few inches thick, but he was told that the lower beds measured many feet, and he saw some very thick blocks which had been brought up. It appears that, for domestic uses, the natives convert this coal, which is very bituminous, into coke. The value of these beds can scarcely be over-estimated. They will contribute wonderfully to the interests of commerce, and may, indeed, be considered "a gift of Providence, deposited by the Creator of all things in the depths of the Japanese islands for the benefit of the human family."† Without free access to this coal, the chain of steam navigation must remain broken. In this sense, it is to be considered of more value than all the mines of gold, silver, and copper, that the islands may contain.

* See Instructions to Commander Aulick, as given in the *Times* newspaper, of May 12th, 1852.

† Mr. Webster's Letter of Instruction to the Commodore of the American Expedition.

Pearls are fished up on nearly all parts of these coasts, and they are frequently of great size and beauty. The native Japanese put little or no value upon them, till they found that the Chinese were ready to pay high prices for those of the finest qualities. Mother-of-pearl, of great size, transparent and beautiful, is found in abundance, as are also corals, corallines, sea-fans, and other submarine productions. Naphtha, ambergris, and sulphur (the last in inexhaustible quantities) are to be numbered among the exports of the islands, which abound in volcanoes, extinct or in action. Fine pure native sulphur is found at many of these volcanoes, in broad deep beds, and may be dug up and removed with as much ease as sand. One small volcanic island renders, or rendered, by its sulphur, a considerable annual revenue to the Government.

At comparatively recent dates, volcanic islands have been projected from the depths of the sea. It seems that some of these have disappeared, like the volcanic island which rose so suddenly off the coast of Sicily some twenty years ago ; but others have not only remained, but have gradually increased in size. Adjoining to the department of Satsuma is an island covered with sulphur. Kämpfer states that the Japanese did not venture there more than a hundred years before his time. "The island was thought to be wholly inaccessible, and by reason of the thick smoke which was observed continually to rise from it, and of the several spectres and other frightful apparitions which people fancied to see there, chiefly by night, it was believed to be a dwelling-place of devils ; but, at last, a resolute man obtained permission to go and examine it. He chose fifty bold fellows for this expedition ; upon going on shore they found neither hell nor devils, but a large flat piece of ground at the top of the island (the crater originally), which was so strongly covered with sulphur, that wherever they walked a thick smoke issued from under their feet. Ever since that time this island brings in, to the prince of Satsuma, about twenty chests of silver per annum."

Agates, cornelians, jaspers, fine variegated marbles, and other precious or valuable stones, are brought down from many of the mountains. Some of the agates are uncommonly fine, of a bluish colour, and not unlike sapphires. Of diamonds we find no mention. It is rather singular, in a people so keenly alive to all that is rich and beautiful, that the Japanese have entirely neglected the arts of the lapidary, and hold jewels in hardly any esteem. All the precious stones of which travellers speak appear to have been found by them in the rough, unpolished, uncut state. It is conjectured that some properly skilled men might drive a very profitable trade in this line.

We have the testimony of Tavernier to the size, purity, and value of the pearls of Japan, and we could hardly look for a better authority on such a point, as Tavernier was a thorough proficient, and gained a great estate by trading in gems and jewels.*

SCENERY OF JAPAN.

Gold is brilliant, silver is useful, the precious stones have their attractions, their price, and their temptations. Japan has her ample share of these allurements—the perverted gifts of God; although from time immemorial thus degraded from their uses, they have been made to represent the glories 'of Heaven and the ravishments which await the well-tried soul admitted to her reward in the realms of everlasting bliss.

---

* *Travels in the East,* &c. The first edition of this valuable work appeared at Paris, in 1676. The author of it, a traveller of the right stamp, and one who, according to Gibbon, united the soul of a philosopher with the pursuits of a jeweller, died, on his way to Moscow, in July, 1689, in the eighty-fourth year of his age.

The reader may also be referred to Captain Alexander Hamilton:— *A New Account of the East Indies,* &c. &c. Two Vols. 8vo, Edinburgh, 1727. This Hamilton spent his time, from the year 1688 to 1723, in trading and travelling by sea and land in most of the countries between the Cape of Good Hope and the islands of Japan. On matters of trade his book is worthy of consultation. It has been republished in *Pinkerton's Collection of Voyages and Travels.*

'Tis pleasanter to contemplate the thousand beauties of nature adorning the islands of Japan.

'Tis more refreshing to tear ourselves for awhile from the painful calculations of material wealth, the bone of the world's contention, " the root of all evil," and fix our ravished eyes on the inexhaustible attractions of nature enthroned on the mountains, the hills, the shores, the seas of these beautiful islands.

THE KIRISIMA, JAMMA.

The deep blue sea, in admirable contrast with the verdure of the hills—with the green fields obedient to the will of man—the brilliant whiteness of the sands on the shore, transformed into diamond-dust by the Eastern sun —the noble masses of rose-coloured granite, through which the everlasting waves have carved fantastic and majestic grottoes—towering arches which, when illumined by the rays of the sun, bring to mind, in their religious gloom and silence, the sublime Gothic cathedrals of the Western world.

Beautiful limpets and mussels of a thousand hues cling to the rocks of the life-giving ocean. The pearl-shell is there—suffering that disease, or, at all events, abnormal secretion, which shall produce the gem much prized by

THE PORT OF SIMONESEKE.

Beauty; and there also is the coralline—the indefatigable mound-builders of the deep—whose petrified branches, with their tints so rich and varied, seem anxious to conceal their mysterious beauty beneath the flowing drapery of the waves.

The hand of God is in the marvels of those abysses. It is also on the land, where the luxuriant vegetation of the

East blooms, fades, dies, and is renewed in eternal Spring —life and death hand-in-hand united.

"As we moved out past the promontory of Urága," says Bayard Taylor, "the western shore opened on the left, showing a broad deep bay, embosomed by hills covered with the greenest and most luxuriant foliage, and with several large villages at their base. We approached within three miles of the eastern shore, which is loftier and wider than the western, rising into a range of rugged mountains, which showed no signs of habitation or cultivation. But the lower slopes, which undulated gently to the water, charmed me by the rich beauty of their scattered groves, and the green terraces and lawns into which centuries of patient cultivation has formed them. Outside of England there is nothing so green, so garden-like, so full of tranquil beauty."

FIRANDO, OR FIAANGO.

CHAPTER II.

ALL the primitive races of men that have been enabled by their superior endowments to advance in the career of beings, have invariably claimed a specific Divine origin, an heroic descent, or a special providence which presided over their creation—making them thus " different from other men"—segregated by a wall of separation which opinion, manners, and customs have always kept standing, and which Nature herself has seemed to protect by the everlasting seal which she stamps on " the children of men," indicative of their origin and descent.

The Japanese claim a descent from the gods—scorning the idea of any connexion with any other race, especially the Chinese, whom they despise and abhor.*

Their legendary descent is consecutive enough. They refer to the existence of a primal Chaos, whence were produced all things that exist—the gods included. There were two species of gods—Celestial Spirits, altogether disengaged from the mixture of matter, who ruled over Japan during a succession of ages which it is impossible to compute; and Terrestrial Spirits, or god-men, who,

---

* " A curious illustration of their dislike to the Chinese, who are greatly inferior to them in propriety and elegance òf manner, occurred while they were on board. One of the interpreters, noticing some of the Chinese deck-hands, who had been shipped at Shanghai, asked with a face expressive of great contempt and disgust, ' Is it possible that you have Chinese among your men ?' The sequel is equally significant and characteristic. Mr. Portman, *with much readiness, but not entire candour* (!) replied, ' These men are *the servants of our sailors,*"—and thereby reinstated us in the good opinion of the Japanese."—Bayard Taylor, *India, &c.* p. 434.

having succeeded to the first, also held the sceptre for a very long period, until at last they engendered the third Race, which now inhabits Japan, but which retains nothing of the purity and perfections of their divine ancestors.*

Kämpfer could not see the reasonable myth of this legend, and invented another decidedly incomprehensible to the Japanese. He says :—" As the Japanese language has no resemblance to that of any other Oriental nation, and seems to be perfectly pure, it is perhaps one of those primitive languages which Providence infused into the mind and memory of those who undertook to build the Tower of Babel ; and that the first Japanese were some of those foolhardy builders." Moreover, he actually traces the route they must have journeyed to reach Japan.†

It is a matter of no little wonder that there appears to be amongst this most intelligent nation, no historical monuments worthy of consideration dating beyond the thirteenth century of the Christian era. Their chronicles are little more than a bare list of names and dates, with some legendary statements interwoven, the historical importance of which is insignificant.‡

Altogether unknown to the Greeks and Romans of the ancient world,—to the modern world it was first mentioned, under the Chinese name of Zipangu, by that truly illustrious traveller, Marco Polo, who was in China, and engaged in the service of the great conqueror Kublaï-Khan at the close of the thirteenth century.

It is to be noted that Marco Polo did not visit the country in person. He collected his information in China, at the court of the great Khan. This is his brief description :—

" Zipangu is an island in the Eastern Ocean, situate at the distance of about fifteen hundred miles from the mainland or coast of *Manji*. It is of considerable size ; its inhabitants have fair complexions, are well-made, and

---

* *Hist. Gén. des Voy.*, p. 557.
† *Ubi suprà*, 559 ; Kämpfer, p. 139 *et seq.*
‡ Hildreth, *Japan*, &c.

are civilized in their manners. Their religion is the worship of idols. They are independent of every foreign power, and governed only by their kings. They have gold in the greatest abundance, its sources being inexhaustible; but as the king does not allow of its being exported, few merchants visit the country, nor is it frequented by much shipping from other ports. To this circumstance we are to attribute the extraordinary richness of the sovereign's palace, according to what we are told by those who have had access to the place. The entire roof is covered with a plating of gold, in the same manner as we cover houses, or more properly churches, with lead. The ceilings of the halls are of the same precious metal; many of the apartments have small tables of pure gold considerably thick, and the windows also have golden ornaments. So vast, indeed, are the riches of the palace, that it is impossible to convey an idea of them. In this island there are pearls also in large quantities, of a red (pink) colour, round in shape, and of great size; equal in value to, or even exceeding, that of the white pearls. It is customary with one part of the inhabitants to bury their dead, and with another part to burn them. The former have a practice of putting one of these pearls into the mouth of the corpse. There are also found there a number of precious stones.

" Of so great celebrity was the wealth of this island, that a desire was excited in the breast of the Grand Khan Kublaï, now reigning, to make the conquest of it, and to annex it to his dominions."*

The Khan Kublaï failed in his expedition against the islanders; but it is remarkable that the fact should give occasion to Marco Polo to record it in his *Oriental Travels*, which evidently suggested to Columbus his fixed idea of discovering Cipango by a western course. It was at that period supposed that China was " fifteen hours," or 225 degrees to the east of Europe, and consequently

* *Travels of Marco Polo*, as edited by the late William Marsden, Esq. An invaluable work to all who are engaged in studying the remote countries of the East.

that Zipangui or Cipango was still further. Columbus, therefore, naturally concluded that he would shorten his voyage by directing his course towards the *west*.* Certain it is that on arriving at Hispaniola he thought he had discovered the true Zipangui or Cipango.

If this conjecture be founded on fact, how significant it is that the record of a failure at invasion, and the enslavement of one nation by an Eastern barbarian, should definitively lead to the utter destruction of another people by the civilized Christians of the western world.

GOVERNMENT, LAWS, POLICE, TAXES, ETC.

The government of Japan is an absolute despotism, yet far from being altogether arbitrary. Everything and everybody are under a system of ancient, unchanging laws. No individual in the whole empire, however elevated in rank, is above the law. Both sovereigns, the spiritual and the temporal, are as completely enthralled by Japanese despotism as the meanest of their subjects, if not more so. This despotism is in the law and custom of the land, and operates by and through them. Law and custom press upon all with the same tyrannous weight. Scarcely an action of life is exempt from their rigid and inflexible control ; but he who complies with the dictates of law, and with the established usages, seems rarely to have cause to apprehend any other arbitrary power or capricious tyranny. In times of successful usurpation, some of the laws have been set at nought, and occasionally the court and great Council of State, who, in reality, administer the government, have been irregular and arbitrary ; but the number of these exceptional cases is said to be inconsiderable.

This singular double-headed monarchy is not the least remarkable of the "manner and custom" of Japan. It originated as follows.

* *Hist. Gén. des Voy.* 560.

F

All Japan was formerly under one monarch, whose title was Voo or Daïri. Two great lords or captains managed his affairs ; they were his two arms, his lieute-

A VASSAL PRINCE.

nants, his viceroys, and rejoiced in the title of Cubes or Kubos.

About seven or eight hundred years ago, according to the ancient annals of Japan, these two Cubes were Guenei and Fryin. One of them, observing that the Daïri "addicted himself to his private delights" like another Sardanapalus, became virtuously indignant thereat, murdered his companion in office, and resolved to depose his sovereign lord and master.

The great lords and princes of the kingdom cried out against the usurper of another's right, and rushed to arms—not only to punish him for his ungrateful treason, but, as the result showed, to follow his example. " Thus," observes Father Solier, the historian of Japan, "thus doth bad example lead the heart of men oftener than the zeal of virtue."

A dreadful civil war ensued : it lasted long, with the usual varying fortune of war on both sides ; but at length the enterprising Cube, who began with virtuous indignation, like our own glorious Oliver Cromwell, managed to crush all his enemies by a "crowning victory"—made himself master of almost all Japan—stripped the Daïri, his Charles I., of all his inheritance, but did not cut off his head. And he contented himself with sending all his antagonists home " to their lands," where they consoled themselves by assuming the empty title of kings or princes—in Japanese, *Yacatis*. Thus began the division of Japan into so many petty princedoms, vassals of the Empire—according to one account.

The successful " Mayor of the Palace"—the traitor Cube—assumed the title of Cubozana, which many of his successors have also borne, and conceded to the unfortunate Daïri and his posterity the honorary title of Universal Lord of Japan ; but strictly confined his prerogative to the distribution and arrangement of grades and titles of honour amongst the princes, lords, and knights of Japan whom the Cube had driven " to their lands"—in the words of old Purchas, "leaving the Daïri a bare title and a Herald's Kingdom."

This explanation of the binary government of Japan is sufficient for the fact : but the difficulty is to imagine—in our western way of thinking—how the Japanese could adopt such a solution in the matter of misgovernment.

In deposing our kings we have either sent them packing, or knocked them on the head ; but here is a people who, after fighting it out, have quietly "split the difference," and contented themselves with insinuating to the negligent monarch, that as he was unfit to rule a kingdom, he might do very well as a "Master of the Ceremonies."

Was it not, however, merely a compromise between the contending parties, leaders and followers—an arrangement on terms, and "for a consideration ?" Did it not result in the usual expectation of sharing "the loaves and fishes ? "

That the institution has lasted so many centuries only shows that it must have its advantages in the estimation of those who uphold it—like some of our own time-honoured institutions, the abolition of which would only strike off one more human absurdity from the shoulders of men, produce much inconvenience to all parties concerned, necessitate pensions and "compensations," and, finally, set our minds upon saddling ourselves with some other absurdity, but much more onerous from its novelty.

The Jesuit Solier offered an elucidation of this apparently incongruous arrangement, by observing that it was the ambition of the Cubozama and his Yacatis that preserved this empty title of the Mikado, whom they had unjustly dispossessed of his kingdom. "For, as they are pre-eminently ambitious, and huge worshippers of honour, being anxious that theirs should be the most exquisite and the most legitimately acquired, they came to the conclusion, in their political consultation on the subject, that it was incomparably more honourable to leave the award and distribution of honour and dignity in the hands and at the disposal of him who represented the natural sovereign Lord of all Japan, than to arrogate and assume them to themselves." *

Under this view, the institution is merely an embodiment of the gracious "Fountain of Honour," which metaphorically gushes from the breast of our own sove-

* *Hist. Eccles. du Japon.*

reigns. Besides, the Mikado is unquestionably the spiritual head, the "Defender of the Faith" of the Church of Japan—at all events quite as much in that predicament as is the sovereign of England.

It is impossible, however, to be satisfied with this early view of the subject. Later investigations have thrown some little light on the political history of Japan. The country is utterly deficient in historical monuments. Coins and idols are in Japan what pyramids are in eternal Egypt. The perpetual earthquakes of this volcanic centre has always prevented the development of that constructive genius which is evidently one of the national endowments. They have had no mendacious "poets" like the Greeks, who stole, mystified, and debased significant Egyptian symbols, myths, and allegories.

The authentic history of Japan begins with the first mortal sovereign of the land, *Zin-mo-ten-woo*, or "the divine warrior"—the "divine conqueror." Whence he issued we know not : we infer that he conquered Niphon. The annals of Japan give him a reign of nine and seventy years : he it was who built the *daïri* or "*temple-palace*," dedicated to the sun-goddess, and founded the dynasty of the *Mikado*. He may have been a native, or he was perhaps a Chinese William the Conqueror : all we know is, that the Japanese annals refer the establishment of his absolute sovereignty, as *Daï-Niphon*—"Great sun-source-king or kingdom," to the year B. C. 660, about forty years before Draco gave his proverbial sanguinary laws to Athens.

We are told that for some centuries these Mikados governed the land by right divine and hereditary, absolute sovereigns ; and that their sovereignty was completely acknowledged even after they ceased to command their armies, and had confided this dangerous function to their sons or their relatives ; and that their authority received its first shock from the custom established by these Mikados, of abdicating at so early an age, that their sons became kings in their childhood, although they constituted themselves regents during the minority. No reason is given for this incomprehensible custom ; but we shall find, in the sequel, that early abdication of authority, in all ranks, is still the custom of Japan.

At length, a Mikado, whose queen was the sister of a powerful prince, abdicated in favour of his son, only three years old ; whereupon that princely brother seized the regency from the abdicating monarch.   A civil war ensued, during which appeared on the scene *Yoritomo*, one of the most famous and important personages of Japanese history, himself remotely allied to the Mikado-blood royal.   He took the field against the usurper, and after many years of struggle, he succeeded in restoring the regency to the abdicating Mikado.   It appears that the latter was then called *Fowo*, that is, " emperor consecrated priest of Buddha ;" and that he retained the regency only nominally, conceding all power to his champion, Yoritomo, whom he created *sio i daï Siogoun*, that is, " generalissimo fighting against the barbarians."

At the death of the ex-Mikado, Yoritomo assumed the reins of Government under the guise of lieutenant or deputy, and managed ultimately to establish himself in power, so that at his death, in the year A.D. 1199 or 1200, he was quietly succeeded by his son in all his royal prerogatives, apparently still masked under the title of lieutenant or deputy.

Meanwhile, it appears that Mikados existed, reigned, and constantly abdicated in favour of infant sons—thus consolidating the power of the Siogouns, who, in like manner, transmitted their function, which became so decidedly hereditary, that the annals of the empire tell of abdicating Siogouns, of infant Siogouns, and rival heirs " fighting for the crown."

It is stated that this serious modification of the political institutions of Japan became so fully established, that even the widow of Yoritomo, the first " generalissimo," who at the death of her husband had become a nun of Buddha (strange reminder of our European Middle Ages !) afterwards left her convent, mounted the throne, and governed—in the name of her infant, Siogoun—as

" Regent." She held the reins of Government till her death, and she is called, in the annals of the Daïri, or Court, *Ama Siogoun* ; that is, the Nun-Siogoun." This is said to be the only instance of a female Siogoun.

Meanwhile, however, all apparent authority, and much real power and prerogative, remained in the hands of the Mikado—his was the important prerogative to name and invest his lieutenant, the Siogoun.

Thus, the Government of Japan, under an autocrat emperor and a sovereign deputy, continued to the latter part of the sixteenth century, at which period the Siogoun was the real and supreme monarch of a powerful empire, and not what they seem to be at the present time, insignificant puppets, displaying their magnificent and idle irresponsibility in a gilded palace, totally under the control of a " President of the Council."*

Such is the modern version that accounts for this double sovereignty of Japan—which, however, turns out to be really no sovereignty at all—excepting in the constitutional sense of the word, as in England.

It is clearly a misnomer to talk of " Spiritual and temporal Emperors" of Japan, if this version be correct. The Mikado is evidently the hereditary supreme ruler, absolute alike in spiritual and temporal affairs. The Siogoun is an hereditary commander-in-chief, professedly the mere lieutenant or vicegerent of the Mikado, although constitutionally more powerful, as it were " viceroy over him." Klaproth says, that when the meaning of the title Emperor was explained to the Japanese, they were indignant at its application to the Siogoun, declaring that there was no Emperor in Japan but the Mikado.† In the recent treaty with Japan, we read that it engages in the first place " that there shall be perpetual peace and friendship between her British Majesty and the *Tycoon* of Japan." This word " Tycoon" must be merely the great " imperial" title *Taiko*, as in *Taiko-Sama*, and cannot designate

---

* Jancigny, *Japon, &c.*
† *Manners and Customs of the Japanese.*

royalty, as implied, contradistinguished to that of the
Queen of England. Sama signifies "lord," and the Japanese say *Dairisama*, that is, "lord of the daïri," or
court (*dai* signifying "great"), when speaking of the
Mikado. The Europeans dropped the *sama*, and erroneously
applied the word *daïri* to the person.*

The descriptions given in the books concerning the
Mikado almost warrant disbelief. We are told that the
Japanese revere him as a god, considering themselves
as unworthy to approach him even in thought. He is the
lineal descendant of the gods—identified with the gods—
since the "solar goddess" is believed to be incarnate in
each Mikado. He deifies or canonizes great men after
death, at the proposal of the Siogoun. The dignitaries
who surround him, and who constitute a true spiritual
hierarchy, are considered to be of such exalted rank, that
the princes, the ministers of the Siogoun, and the Siogoun
himself, are ambitious to obtain the purely honorary titles
of these great officers of the Daïri, or Court of the Mikado.
It is affirmed, indeed, that the Siogoun, as a grand dig-
nitary, is but the *fourth* personage in the empire!

What are the privileges which hold the second and
third rank? According to Fisscher, Klaproth, and Siebold they are the *dai-sio-dai-sin*, "greatest saint," or the
President of the Council of the Mikado ; or the *kwanbak*,
the regent of the empire, in case of an infant Mikado
(kwan-bak means "holy person") ; and the *sa-dai-sin*, or
"the first servant of the left hand." The son or daughter
whom the autocrat destines to ascend the throne when he
mounts to heaven, must, it seems, rank higher than the
Siogoun.

The functions of the Mikado are various. He alone
determines the days when the moveable festivals must be
celebrated, the proper colours of the garments in which
certain religious actions must be performed—in a word, all
the ceremonial of religion. He nominates or confirms the
superiors of the different monastic orders of Japan—for

* Jancigny *ubi suprà.*

there are monks in Japan, as will appear in the sequel—original monks, and not imitations or suggestions. He decides without appeal all theological questions : his Bulls are implicitly obeyed.

But the most solemn, the most extraordinary, and most incredible manifestation of the Mikado's influence is that which, in the belief of the Japanese, identifies him with the Sun-goddess before mentioned—the goddess who presides over human destinies. Every day the Mikado passes a certain number of hours seated on his throne in a state of perfect immobility. By that absolute immobility he maintains the stability and the peace of his empire. Should his head unluckily turn either to the right or the left, that part of the empire *towards* which it turns, or the part *from* which it turns, is threatened with the greatest dangers, or even vowed to destruction. The august head should not turn either to the right or the left, or anyhow whatever.

We are assured that this ceremonial is no longer performed; but it is significant of the race, and should be recorded.

The gods themselves honour the Mikado—pay him a monthly visit. During this month, which is called " the absence of the gods," the temples are supposed to be deserted, and no one goeth there to pray : the gods have left heaven above and their temples below to visit their representative on earth.

He must never touch the ground with his feet. He would be deposed if he did. He must be carried, if he wants to move, on the shoulders of men. No profane eye may see him—his wives are of course excepted—and consequently he never leaves the interior of his palace. I suppose the men who carry him shut their eyes, or keep custody thereof, else how can they avoid seeing him?

His hair, his beard, the nails of his fingers and his toes are never cut excepting when he is asleep—or rather, I should think, whilst he pretends to be asleep—otherwise how is the thing possible, unless he drugs himself for the purpose ?

Sun-light may not touch him, some affirm, lest it should defile him; but this must be false, else how can he have anything to do with the sun-goddess?

Everything that he uses daily in any way must be new. He never wears the same garments twice; the cups, plates, kitchen utensils, are renewed at every meal of the Mikado; and, moreover, none of these things must be subsequently used by any one else. To wear his cast-off garments, to eat from his plates, to use his kitchen utensils, to eat the remnants of his meal, are crimes of divine treason that will bring down upon the delinquent the vengeance of the gods. Everything that he has used is utterly destroyed, broken, torn to pieces or burnt up as soon as he has done with it. We are assured that with an economical eye to this tremendous daily destruction of the useful, the Siogoun (who has to pay the costs) takes care that the Mikado is supplied in every way with the coarsest articles, "dirt-cheap."

Of course the reader has all along been reminded of the Tartar god-priest Dalai-Lama. I have omitted some particulars, as I should in the case of the Dalai-Lama—too disgusting, although in a religious point of view considered meritorious. And it is said, that once admitting the principle, we must admit all the consequences ; but I venture to hope that when the promised intelligent Japanese ambassador shall come and live amongst us, he will tell us that all we have read about this Mikado is an old woman's tale, a Middle-age legend, a myth—downright humbug—such as Herodotus would have repeated from his informants, adding—"but I don't believe it." And yet are there not those amongst us who believe things quite as absurd and ridiculous ?*

Abdication is not unusual with the Mikado in his wearisome dignity, if not his sinecure. In this case the whole empire is informed of the fact without delay, but quietly ; but when he dies his death is kept a secret

* The accounts of the Mikado differ in all the books. For instance, Solier says he goes a-hunting, and Thunberg says he walks in his garden.

THE MIKADO, OR SPIRITUAL EMPEROR, AND HIS WIVES.

until the enthroning of his successor—male or female—
and then they announce to the people that their Mikado
has " disappeared," has "vanished"—vanished into heaven
to watch over the safety of the empire.

In order to secure the direct transmission of this divine
dignity, the Mikado has no less than twelve lawful wives;
but they are divided into two ranks, and one of them is
called *kisaki,* importing that she is the queen-Mikado.
He selects these wives from the ladies of the daïri, or
court. According to some avouchers their garments are
splendid, and subject to the same destructive rule as the
things used by their lord and master. They never appear
before the Mikado without letting down their hair in its
ample profusion. All the members of the Court affect
very wide garments, which are imitated by all the
various religious orders of the empire.

In striking opposition to these vain ceremonies, superstitious practices, monotonous etiquette of the daïri, we
are assured that this very Court is the seat of the highest
Japanese literature, the centre of all Japan's national
poesy, her philosophy. It is said that Jeddo's academy
may be more scientific, but it is in the daïri that we shall
find Japan's theologians, historians, poets, moralists; and,
moreover, that the women there are equally distinguished
for their intelligence and acquirements.

It appears, however, that the Siogoun has reason to
look with apprehension on this intellectual development
of the Mikado's Court, lest its mental speculations might
superinduce political combinations. The Siogoun has
consequently stationed at Meaco a functionary called
Syosï-daï, or " grand judge," to watch the march of the
human intellect, and to report its revolutionary manifestations. This spy is in an awkward position : he is
known to be such; he may therefore offend both the
Mikado and the Siogoun, and thus be placed in the unpleasant necessity (as *we* should feel it) of " ripping up
his abdomen"—the mode of suicide customary in Japan.*

* Jancigny, *ubi suprà.*

Napoleon the Great denounced literary men—whom he called "idealogists,"—his successor is following his example, and may point to the Siogoun of Japan for a precedent—if such a ruler, and in such circumstances, can be expected to look for "precedents" to justify his measures.

Finally, the Mikado distributes honours, decorations, and coats-of-arms, according to the birth of the recipients, their exploits in battle, the extent of the landed property they may acquire, the services they may render to the State by their intellectual acquirements and civic administration—all which reminds us of *our* "Fountain of Honour."* Their titles are, as with us, Lord, Highness, Excellence ; and they have a perfect blazonry—coats-of-arms, heraldic devices, quite as extensive, and—judging from the engravings before me—quite as fantastic as ours.† I am but little conversant with *azure* and *gules*, *chevrons*, *fusils*, and *frets*—" the noble study of heraldry," yet I fancy that some of these Japanese most honourable devices might be adopted by our ambitious *parvenus*, together with some such motto as *Quid nunc ?* to figure in the Park during the season.

The Japanese grandees change their heraldric devices repeatedly, according to the price fixed upon them by the Mikado, " whence he raiseth great revenue." The Jesuits say that the King of Bungo changed his signet and coat-of-arms thirty-four times, in less than ten years. *Grande vanité*, great vanity ! exclaims Father Solier, the historian of Japan.

To procure these titles and honours, the grandees maintain and fee certain agents at the Court, make rich presents to the Mikado every year, send embassies to him, never empty-handed.

The Mikado wears a black tunic (black is not mourning in Japan), a red robe, and over this a veil of crape, the fringes of which conceal his hands. His head-gear is a cap orna-

---

* Father Solier, *Hist. Eccl. du Japon.*
† See *Hist. Gén. des Voyages*, x. 569.

mented with various tufts or knobs, after the manner of the ancient priests of Rome.

The numbers of the grand Council of State, or of those who govern in the Siogoun's name, are variously given by different writers ; but the best, or the latest, authority makes them thirteen : to wit, five councillors of the first class, selected from the princes of the empire, and eight of the second class, selected from the old nobility.* There appears good reason to doubt whether all these high offices are not hereditary ; in which case there can be no selection or election. Under these, in regular, and apparently interminable gradations, are other state functionaries ; as lords or guardians of the temples, commissioners of foreign affairs, ministers of police, superintendents of agriculture, etc. It appears that all the offices of Government are filled, not by the relatives of the Mikado, but by those of the temporal Siogoun. Personal interviews happen very rarely between the two potentates : the Siogoun is now said to visit the Mikado only once in seven years. It seems, however, that the Siogoun frequently sends embassies and rich presents to the Holy Court at Meako, in return for which the Mikado sends back his blessing and prayers. This, it has been observed, is no more than an equitable arrangement ; for the Siogoun has the revenues of the whole country in his hands, whereas the Mikado must be content with the revenues of his limited principality of Kioto and his "fees." There he governs, or is governed for, as an independent Prince, or Damjo, as the Japanese call them, only with this difference, that the Princes, or Damjos, maintain their military at their own expense, whilst the Mikado is not allowed to have any soldiers.†

The dignity of both the rulers is inherited by the eldest of their male descendants. In default of male issue, they now adopt the eldest son of some Prince of the Empire, who is nearest to them in blood : formerly, it is

* Siebold. Kämpfer gives a different number ; but there may have been some slight change since his time.

† Golownin, *Recollections of Japan.*

said, the Mikado had some male child placed by a tree, and then it was declared to be god-descended, and installed accordingly. There appears to be a head councillor of state, with functions and powers corresponding to those of the grand vizier in Turkey. He is called the " Governor of the Empire," and all the other councillors are strictly subordinate to him. No public affair of any consequence can be undertaken without him. The councillor of state, as we have said, transacts the whole business of Government, decides upon every measure, sanctions or reverses every sentence of death, wherever it may be pronounced, appoints to all offices and employments, and corresponds with all the chief authorities of the empire. Whenever law or usage is not perfectly clear, he must be consulted before anything can be done. The council, collectively, have the power of dethroning the Siogoun. When they adopt any important resolution, it is laid before the Siogoun for his approval. This is usually given as a matter of course, without any delay, or any inquiry into the matter : like the royal consent to our Acts of Parliament. But if, by any extraordinary accident, he should trouble himself about the concerns of his empire, attempt to examine for himself, and then withhold the expected fiat, the measure is referred to the arbitration of three princes of the blood, the nearest kinsmen of the monarch, and their decision is final, and very often attended with melancholy and fatal circumstances. Should their verdict coincide with the sentiments of the council, the Siogoun must forthwith abdicate in favour of his son, or other legal heir. This despotic sovereign, as Europeans have considered him, has not, in these State cases, the liberty of retracting an opinion.

On the other hand, should the three arbitrating princes pronounce the monarch to be in the right, and the council in the wrong, the consequences are still more serious. The minister who proposed the obnoxious act must die the death ; the ministers who most warmly seconded him must frequently die also, and, occasionally, all the members of the council, with the vizier or governor of the empire at their head, must rip open their bowels. Under such responsibility, men must be little disposed to attempt new laws, or any sort of innovation. When to this we add, that the whole council, collectively and individually, is perpetually surrounded by spies (some known, and some unknown), employed by superiors, inferiors, rivals, and by themselves, the one against the other, it will be evident that these seemingly absolute ministers cannot venture upon the slightest infraction of the law without fear and trembling.

If we turn to the vassal princes of the empire, we find that they are the objects of as much caution as the members of the supreme council. It is, indeed, against these princes that the jealousy of the Siogoun and council is chiefly directed.

There were, originally, sixty-six or sixty-eight principalities, which had previously been so many independent kingdoms. As principalities, they were hereditary, but subject to forfeiture in case of rebellion or other treason. As many of the princes incurred this penalty of forfeiture, advantage was taken of the circumstance, by splitting the forfeited principalities into many fragments; and instead of sixty-six, or sixty-eight, there are now said to be six hundred, and four distinct administrations, including great and small principalities, lordships, imperial provinces, and imperial towns.

The vassal princes still govern with all the outward forms and appearances of actual sovereignty, and each, by means of the nobles who are his vassals, keeps up his own army. But this sovereignty is little more than an appearance : the princes can do nothing, can propose nothing, without the consent and concurrence of the Siogoun and his council ; they are entangled in a most intricate web of policy and statecraft, they are kept under the perpetual surveillance of spies and informers, who watch their private and domestic, as well as their political or public conduct. The real administration of every principality is conducted, not by the prince himself, or by ministers of his own choice, but by two secretaries, appointed by the Supreme Council. Of these two secretaries one resides in the principality, and the other at Jeddo, where the family of the absent secretary is detained in hostage for his fidelity. Duality is a leading characteristic of Japanese policy. These double appointments extend to all high provincial posts, and it is only by the annual alternation of the situation of two official colleagues, that men holding such posts ever see their families ; for, the functionary on duty for the year in the provinces must leave his family in the capital, and when, at the expiration of the term, he returns thither, his colleague must go to the provinces and leave his family behind him.

Each alternate year the vassal princes are allowed, or rather compelled, to reside at Jeddo, near the Siogoun's palace. They are then reunited to their families, but continue under the same surveillance as ever. In fact, so long as they retain their principalities, their life is one of constant inquietude and restraint. Hence the very prevalent practice among them of abdicating in favour of a son or other lawful heir. It has been remarked, that a reigning prince, of advanced age, is rarely seen in Japan. They vacate the throne, or they die prematurely upon it, of grief or ennui. Whatever it may be for the governed, the Japanese system seems to be a wretched one for the governors. Mikado, or Siogoun, vizier or vassal prince, supreme councillor or provincial secretary, all are " cabined, cribbed, confined," and condemned to a state of existence, which would be, to a European, about as insupportable as ·that of a galley-slave.

The government of the lordships (which are merely small inferior principalities) is managed and controlled upon the same jealous system as that of the principalities themselves ; and the same may be said of the provinces and cities called Imperial, and which have been retained as imperial domains. To the government of each of them two governors are appointed, who live alternately at their posts and at the capital, where their wives and children must always be in hostage. These governors of imperial provinces, or imperial cities, are not named by hereditary right, but are selected from among the nobility by the Jeddo vizier and council, who appoint their secretaries, sub-secretaries, police officers, spies, and all their official establishment. At Nagasaki, where European observations have been most frequently made, only the treasurer, the military commandant, and the inferior police-officers, are allowed to have their families with them. All the rest, so long as they are in the service of Government, must leave their wives and children either at Jeddo or at the capital of the province or principality. in which they are stationed. Whether at Nagasaki, or in any other place, the functionaries who are allowed the comforts of domestic life are perpetually surrounded by spies—one spy watching another, one delator informing against another. It may well be called " a government of spies."

These spies are said to be of every rank in life, from the lowest to the highest, beneath that of a prince. The proudest of the nobility have been known to undertake the office, either out of the ambitious hope of succeeding to the places and emoluments of those whom he might denounce, or in dread of the consequences of a refusal. Where a man, if nominated, must be a spy, or rip open his own bowels, it is not wonderful that there should be so many spies, of all classes, ages, and conditions.

Complaints of the governor of Matsmai were remitted to the court at Jeddo, where the council resorted to its usual method for ascertaining the truth. The obnoxious governor was soon displaced, but it was not without astonishment that the people recognised, in his successor, a journeyman tobacco-cutter, who, a short time before, had suddenly disappeared from his master's shop. The journeyman tobacco-cutter had been personated, for the nonce, by a noble of the land, who had assumed that disguise in order to perform the office of a spy, for which he had been sent to Matsmai by the court.*

Yet, living under such a governmental system, the

---

* Meylan.

G

people of Japan are almost always described as frank in their manners, free and open in speech, and most sensitively alive to the point of honour. We should have much difficulty in believing the fact if we had not ourselves seen precisely the same thing in the Ottoman empire.* There, nearly every Turk unconnected with Government may be described as a frank, honest, truth-loving, honourable man; while every Turk at all connected with Government (with remarkably few exceptions) may be, with equal safety, set down as the very reverse— as a man capable of playing the spy, or of resorting to any other iniquity or baseness. And, let the most honest-hearted Turk, by ambition or by accident, or by the caprice of some great man, only once get involved in the governmental meshes, and at once his nature is changed. With our experience of this seeming anomaly, we can give credit to the favourable reports of the character of the Japanese people.

Savary, and Fouché himself, might have taken lessons from the Japanese in that art and mystery of spying.

"Not only," says M. Meylan, "is the head of every family answerable for his children, his servants, and the stranger within his gates, but, the city being divided into collections of five families, every member of such division is responsible for the conduct of the others,† and, in consequence, that which, according to European ideas, would be the height of indiscretion, becomes here the duty of every man; for every extraordinary occurrence which falls out in a household is reported by four several witnesses to the members of the civil administration. House-arrest is usually the penalty of the irregularities thus reported; and a severe one it is. The doors and windows

---

* MacFarlane, *Japan.*

† This will remind the reader of our ancestral "frank-pledge" during the Middle Ages,—"The responsibility of ten men, each for the other, throughout every village in the kingdom; so that if one of the ten committed any fault, the nine should produce him in justice, where he should make reparation by his own property or by personal punishment."—Hallam, *Mid. Ages,* ii. 289.

of the offender's house are closed, generally for a hundred days; his employments are suspended; salary, if any, stopped; and the friend and the barber alike forbidden entrance.* Every household is held bound to produce a man capable of bearing arms; a division of five constitutes a company; twenty-five such companies are arrayed under an officer, and constitutes a brigade of six or seven thousand men; and thus the force of the city, apart from the regular military or police, can be presently mustered. Guard-houses are established in every street, in which a guard is on duty every night, and on occasions of festivity, or other cause of popular concourse, by day. Each street has a rail or barrier at its issues, and can consequently be cut off from communication with the rest of the city at a moment's notice."

As every street of every town has its officers and police regulations, and as each street has its gate at both ends, we may be sure that there is little difficulty in securing an offender. The chief officer is called Ottona; he sees that the guard patrols the street during the night, and keeps a register in which are inscribed the names of all the occupants of every house. He registers births, deaths, and marriages; the names of those who go on their travels, those who change their residence, with their class, rank, religion, and trade. He arbitrates in all disputes, but may not enforce his decision. He can punish small derelictions by imprisonment. He compels the inhabitants to aid in the pursuit of an offender. In a word, he is responsible for everything that happens within his jurisdiction. He holds his office by public vote or election—confirmed by the Government—and his salary is

---

* This system of house arrest is very common among the Turks. In Constantinople, in 1828, and again in 1848, we frequently saw a house having all its windows blocked up with deal boards, roughly nailed on the outside. It was the konak or town residence of some pasha, bey, or other official, who had fallen into disgrace. So long as those boards remain up, the man is cut off from all society. If his nearest relative has courage enough to visit him, he does so under cover of night, and by stealing in at the back door.—MacFarlane, *Japan*, &c.

one-tenth of the street's revenue; at Nagasaki it is levied on foreign merchandise.

All the street-gates are closed every night, and for the slightest reason during the day. During the progress of Lord Elgin, on the late occasion, the gates of each street were closed successively to keep back the crowd. At Nagasaki they are closed at the departure of the foreign ships, to prevent the flight of the inhabitants or frauds on the "custom-house," and are not opened until the ships are out of sight, having previously examined every quarter to see if any one is missing : the searcher calls every one by name, and every one must answer to the call. In suspicious times, a passport from the ottona is required to go from one street to another, and the party must be accompanied by one of the guard. To change residence, a petition must be sent to the ottona of the street, explaining the reason; and the petition must be accompanied with a present of fish. I must state that a present of fish, with the Japanese, exactly corresponds to our present of "compliments," as will appear in the sequel. Before the ottona of the street to which he would remove replies, he inquires into the profession, the character, and the general conduct of the petitioner ; he asks every inhabitant of the street if they consent to receive the applicant. Any serious opposition, founded on any objectionable or scandalous vice, is fatal to the petition ; but even when obtained, the applicant must get from the inhabitants of the street he is leaving a certificate of good life and morals—in fact, " a character," and a permit to depart. One would think that here the matter ended; but Japanese precaution and punctilio go much further. The patient street-emigrant carries his " character," &c., to his new ottona, who takes him under his protection, incorporates him in the street, and begins to answer for his conduct. He must then give a treat to all the inhabitants of the street. He then sells his old house—but only with the consent of all the inhabitants of the street in which it stands—and they may effectually object to an unknown purchaser, or one of a bad reputation. An indispensable condition of the sale is that the purchaser must pay a duty of eight, and sometimes twelve per cent. to the common treasury of the street—one part of the proceeds is distributed equally to the inhabitants, and the other is applied to the general outlay of the street.

The same formalities are necessary if any one wishes to travel. The certificate must state the particular reason and the length of absence. All the officers of the street must affix their seal to it gratuitously, but the paper must be paid for at a charge fixed by Government.

Should a fight arise in the street, the nearest inhabitants must separate the combatants. Should a man kill another, of course he shall lose his head, even if he did it only in self-defence ; but the three nearest families are by law and custom compelled to keep within doors for many months : time is given them to lay in a stock of provisions for the period of their domiciliary imprisonment, and then their doors and windows are closed upon them. Besides, all the inhabitants of the street are also punished by public labour in proportion to their negligence in preventing the murder ; the chief men of the street are more rigorously punished than the rest, for whom they are responsible.

Every Japanese of a certain rank wears a sword and poniard ; if, in a quarrel, he merely lays his hand on his sword or poniard—without even touching his adversary —he is condemned to death if denounced. At the death of the humblest individual, the inhabitants of the street must attest that he died a natural death. At Nagasaki, and elsewhere, the corpse is examined, with the double object of discovering if there be any marks of violent death or any sign of Christianity—perhaps any medal or other devotional amulet common amongst Catholics.*

The result of this minutely ramified organization is said to be, that the whole empire affording no hiding-place for a criminal, there is no country in the world where so few robberies are committed. It is even said

* *Hist. Gén. des Voy.* x.

that, with valuable property within, the doors of the house may be left open all night with impunity.

Although not divided, like the Hindoos and other Oriental peoples, into castes, the Japanese may be said to be nearly, if not strictly, divided into hereditary classes. To be respected, every man must remain through life in the class in which he was born, unless exalted by some very rare merit, or very peculiar circumstance. Generally, the Japanese abhor *parvenus.* But it is very discreditable to sink below one's original class. These classes are eight in number.

Class I. is that of the hereditary vassal princes.

Class II. consists of the hereditary nobility under the rank of princes. The nobles hold their lands in fief, by military service, due to the several princes, or, in the imperial provinces, to the Siogoun. The number of fighting men to be furnished by each lord is regulated by the size and value of the estate he holds. Each lord has generally sub-vassals under him, who are bound to furnish their quotas. This closely resembles our old feudal system ; but assuredly the condition of a feudal lord in England or in Normandy was one of independence, freedom, and happiness, compared with that of the Japanese prince or noble. It is from this second class that the officers of state, governors, generals, and the like, are selected. Wherever they may be employed, they are all subjected to long separations from their families. They are also compelled to live a part of their time in the capital, and there to incur heavy expenses, it being the policy of this suspicious government to keep all its officers and servants out of the way of accumulating wealth ;—for wealth is power as well in Japan as elsewhere.

Class III. comprises the priests (apparently indiscriminately) of all the religions and sects that flourish in the empire.

Class IV. consists of the military, or the vassals furnished as soldiers by the nobility.

All these four classes, who constitute the higher orders of Japanese society, enjoy the envied privilege of carrying two swords, and of wearing a sort of loose petticoat trousers, which none beneath them dare ever put on. Thus, unless he be disguised to do spy work, the way to tell whether a man belongs to the upper classes, is to look at his sword-belt and breeches.

Class V. appears to comprehend what we call the upper portion of the middle classes; consisting of medical men, government clerks, and other professionals, and employés.

Class VI. consists of the more considerable shopkeepers and of merchants, who, whatever may be their wealth or intelligence, are held at a very low price by the Japanese. According to Kämpfer, the very gods they worship are rated as sordid, inferior divinities. The gentleman, or even the common soldier, that should engage in any trade or traffic, would be thereby disgraced for ever. Yet among these trading classes are to be found the only very rich men in the country. Speaking of his residence at Jeddo, M. Doeff says—" There is here an extensive dealer in silks, by name Itsigoja, who has large establishments besides in all the other great cities of the empire. Any customer who conveys his purchase to another of these cities, Nagasaki for example, and there tires of his acquisition, may give it back, and receive the price in full. The wealth of this man must be enormous, as the following will show :—During my residence at Jeddo, there occurred a vast fire, which consumed everything within a space three leagues in length and a mile and a half in breadth ; among the rest our lodging. Itsigoja lost his entire shop, and a warehouse containing more than a hundred thousand bales of silk thread, which loss was unmitigated, for the Japanese know nothing of insurance. He nevertheless sent to our assistance forty of his servants, who stood us in great stead ; and on the second day he was already actively engaged in rebuilding his premises, paying every carpenter six florins per diem." *

Nor is such a case of commercial wealth by any means

* *Recollections of Japan.*

rare in the great cities of the empire. A merchant or an aspiring shopkeeper of London, Paris, or other European capital, may spend his money as fast as he gets it—or faster than that—by taking a house in a fashionable quarter, by setting up fashionable equipages, by giving costly entertainments, and by imitating in all things the style and magnificence of the wealthiest and most profuse nobleman. But the Japanese merchant can do nothing of the sort : his style of living is strictly regulated by sumptuary laws, which he dare not infringe. He cannot even have the satisfaction of wearing the single sword, unless he attach himself in a menial capacity to the household of some great lord. It appears, however, that not a few of them take this degrading course, and that the impoverished nobility are generally very ready to swell the number of their nominal retainers upon considerations given and paid.* But no amount of money or patronage can procure for the merchant the inestimable honour of wearing *petticoat trousers,* of which more in the sequel.

Class VII. is composed of retail dealers, little shop-keepers, pedlers, mechanics, and artisans of all descriptions. It also includes painters and other artists, who might have been expected to occupy a somewhat higher grade in the social scale.

Class VIII. consists of the peasantry, agricultural labourers, and day-labourers of all kinds. The mass of the peasantry are said to be little better than serfs or villeins attached to the soil, and the property of the landholder. There is, however, a class who hire and cultivate land on the *metayer* system, so common in many parts of

---

* Something like the system obtained in England down to "the happy days of Good Queen Bess." The retainers of the Earl of Leicester, as painted by Sir Walter Scott in his *Kenilworth,* were living realities. The practice continued in the reign of Charles I., and many traces of it are found in the reign of Charles II., and down to the Revolution of 1688. It appears, however, that though these Japanese sometimes pay for the privilege of wearing a sword, they rarely use the weapon ; that they are not brawlers and fighters, as the retainers of our nobility in the olden time were wont to be.

the European continent—that is, they divide the produce of the estate and farm with the landed proprietor, according to certain proportions previously agreed upon between them. Unfortunately, it is added, that the Japanese landlords take the lion's share, and leave so little to the farmers, that they are generally found as indigent as the serfs.

There is another class, which is held to be so vile, that it is not even enumerated or set down in the list. They are the very *pariahs* of Japan. All tanners, curriers, leather-cutters, and, in fact, every man connected in any way with the preparation of leather, or the leather trade, lie under ban and interdict. They are not permitted to dwell in any town or village with other classes of men ; but they live in detached huts, or in hamlets exclusively their own. They are not even numbered in the census of the population, which appears to be taken with considerable care at certain intervals. They may not enter an inn, public-house, tea-house, or any place of public entertainment. If they are travelling, and in want of food or drink, they must wait humbly outside the wall, and be there served in their own bowl or platter ; for no one but a man or woman of their own class would ever use the vessel out of which they have eaten or drunk. They are the public executioners and gaolers in most parts of the empire. It is conjectured that this banning of a whole class originated in the Sintoo doctrine of defilement by contact with any dead body. In India, the arts of the currier and cordwainer are practised only by the despised aborigines—a large branch of the unhappy pariahs. They are excluded from all towns and villages, and can keep only dogs and asses. Nearly every conceivable degradation is put upon these Indian aborigines ; and yet, according to excellent authorities, they are the honestest fellows in the country, most faithful servants, and ready and brave soldiers. The best part of our native forces, in the campaign of Seringapatam, was composed of them.

Although the Japanese have been so long at peace,

internally as well as externally, and although they govern
rather by spies, policemen, and other civilians, than by
soldiers, it appears, from all accounts, that a very considerable standing army is kept up in the empire.   It is,
however, very difficult, from the data before us, to come
to any conclusion as to the actual number of this force.
It is divided into two classes :   1. The imperial guards,
or the troops of the Siogoun.   2. The vassal soldiers of
the nobility.   It has been asserted by Balbi that the first
of these amount to 100,000 foot and 20,000 horse.

Varenius, in the middle of the seventeenth century, from
the best authorities, estimated the standing army maintained by the princes and governors at 368,000 infantry,
and 38,000 cavalry, whilst the Siogoun maintained
100,000 foot and 20,000 horse ; thus constituting in all a
regular force of 468,000 infantry and 58,000 cavalry.

As, by the military tenure, every prince, sub-prince, or
lord, must furnish his full contingent of able-bodied men
whenever called upon by the lay emperor so to do, we
might form some estimate of the number of combatants
that could be brought into the field if we only knew the
total amount of the population of the empire.   But
although the census is taken, it is kept a state secret,
and, as we have stated, there is a great difference of
opinion on the question of population.   The Siogoun's
own troops are far superior in appearance to those furnished by the vassal princes and lords.   The fact is mentioned in one of the early Dutch accounts.   This old
writer, after speaking of the military tenure, and of so
many armed men being raised and maintained for so
much land, praises the order, *discipline*, dress, and *silence*
of the imperial guards, and concludes by calling them
"all chosen brave fellows, clad in rich black silks." *
Golownin at first mistook all the privates for officers.
In ancient times they were highly esteemed for their
valour in actual combat, for their celerity on the march,
and for their perseverance and cheerfulness under fatigue

* *A Collection of Voyages*, &c. 6 vols. folio.   London, 1732.

and privation; and, with a very few exceptions, they may probably be found at this day the bravest of Asiatic nations.

Anterior to 1615, Japanese served as soldiers of fortune in many of the neighbouring countries, and were highly esteemed by the princes who retained them. On more than one occasion they fought side by side with Spanish and Portuguese troops, at that time as good soldiers as any in the world. As for *discipline*, as we now understand that word, we may believe, with due deference to the old Hollander sea-captain, who wrote his account 200 years ago, that they have none of it. Their formations, their manœuvres, their tactics, would no doubt excite the derision of the least martial of European nations. Apparently they know next to nothing of military architecture, or of the art of defending or attacking fortresses or fortified positions. Their gunnery is said to be of the very worst sort, although their guns are beautifully made.* Their portable fire-

* Yet the following very interesting incident seems to show that the Japanese gunner is not "a bad shot." *Visit of English Mutineers to Japan.*—The confession of William Swallow, *alias* Captain Waldon, one of the convicts who ran away with the brig *Cyprus*, on its voyage to the penal settlement at Macquarrie Harbour, New South Wales, in August, 1829, several of whom had been sent home in the *Charles Grant* from Canton, and tried at the Old Bailey, contains the following particulars of their visit to Japan:—After running some distance up the coast of Japan, he anchored in a convenient bay. A boat came off from the shore with a mandarin or person in authority, and desired to know what brought him there, and desired him to give in writing what he wanted, which he did in English, and said they were in want of wood and water, and would give anything in the vessel in exchange. At that time they were in great distress. They had been cruising about nearly five months; all the sails were split, and there was no canvas to mend them. In four hours the letter was returned, with the seal broke, and they were told to be off by sunset, or they would be fired upon, and a large ball was shown them as earnest of the intentions of the natives. At that time it was a dead calm, and it continued so until after sunset, and they could not get away. The Japanese, to frighten them, then opened a fire from the batteries with musketoons. They made every attempt to get away, but could not, and the Japanese fired upon them from the guns of the batteries. One shot knocked his spy-

arm is the old long slow matchlock, which, from prejudice, or the absence of *flint* in Japan, they will not change
for our modern muskets and rifles, with which they are
well acquainted, and with which they could be well supplied by their own native artisans.   But even the matchlock appears to have a very confined range, for bows and
arrows, awkward spears, long and weak in the shaft,
javelins, and even wooden clubs, are often mentioned as
common Japanese arms.   Their sword-blades, however,
are of admirable temper, and many of the Siogoun's
picked men are said to be expert swordsmen.   But, in
modern battles, the *armes blanches* of chivalry really count
for little.

In the old times the Japanese made use of curious
chain armour, and occasionally their officers are still seen
wearing these coats of mail over their silk jerkins, having
below their jerkins the wide silk petticoat or petticoat-
trousers.

Notwithstanding the 200 years of profound peace
(which *may* have deteriorated the military virtues of
the nation), the military profession is held in great
honour.   In conversation, the common people, and even
the rich merchants, give the common soldier the title of
Sama, or my lord, and address him with all possible respect.   To turn a soldier out of his profession is considered the greatest punishment that can be inflicted on
him.   Every soldier, whatever may be his rank, has the
right to wear two swords, or a sabre and dagger, like the
first lord of the empire.   It is said that the common men
have such a keen sense of the point of honour, that they
frequently resent affronts by fighting duels with one
another, or by ripping themselves up, in order to show
that they prefer death to dishonour.*   If they really retain this mettle, they are troops that will assuredly stand

---

glass out of his hand, and another struck the vessel under the counter
betwixt wind and water.   At ten o'clock a breeze sprung up from
off the land, which enabled them to depart and make sail from the
shore, and the Japanese ceased firing."—*Asiatic Journal*, 1830.
   * Golownin, *Recollections of Japan.*

and fight. Beaten they must be by men such as those who marched from the United States into Mexico ; but we cannot, without emotion, think of the numbers that may be slaughtered before any surrender, capitulation, or military or political settlement whatsoever can take place.

Apparently they have no condensed, written code of laws. Their laws consist of edicts issued in the name of the emperor, from time to time. They are said to be exceedingly simple in their construction, and to possess the somewhat rare merit of being intelligible to the commonest capacity. On the issue of every new edict, the magistrates, in the first instance, assemble the people, and proclaim, by word of mouth, the will of the emperor. Next, the edict is extensively circulated in a printed form, and, as nearly every man or woman in the empire is said to be able to read, the law must thus become well known. But they have yet another method of giving it publicity : the edict is placarded, for a permanency, in a public hall or place appropriated to the purpose, in every city, town, or village, throughout the empire.

If arbitration fail to settle a dispute amongst the Japanese, their princes, magistrates, and even the fathers of families, decide the matter, without appeal. Common sense supplies the accidental deficiency of the laws, or imperial edicts, or ukases. These frequently leave the penalty at the discretion of the magistrates. The Japanese look with admiration on the concise terms of these edicts—as did the ancient Romans on the Laws of the Twelve Tables, so incomprehensibly bepraised by Cicero ; and the least doubt on the justice and discernment of the emperor would be a crime deserving of punishment.

" I have often admired," says Kämpfer, " while travelling through this country, the shortness and laconism of these tables, which are hung up on the roads, in places especially appointed for the purpose, to notify to the public the emperor's pleasure, and to make known the laws of the country ; for it is mentioned, in as few words

as possible, what the emperor commands to be done or
omitted by his subjects. There is no reason given how it
came about that such and such a law was made : no mention of the lawgiver's views and intention ; nor is there any
certain determined penalty put upon transgression thereof.
Such conciseness is thought becoming the majesty of so
powerful a monarch."*

The Japanese have laws and lawgivers, but no professional practising barristers, or lawyers of any kind.
Every man is considered competent to be his own lawyer
or pleader. Mr. Thomas Rundall, who has consulted and
condensed all the best authorities, says :—

" *The proceedings under the laws* are as simple as the
laws themselves.

" The Japanese system does not admit any technical
and complicated forms ; and, consequently, there is no
professional class required to elucidate, or, as the case may
be, further to perplex what is already obscure. In the
empire, a party feeling himself aggrieved appeals direct
to the magistrate. The case is stated in presence of the
accused, and he is heard in reply. Witnesses are examined. Sentence is then passed, and generally carried
into execution *instanter*. In trivial cases, the parties are
usually ordered to retire and settle the difference, either
between themselves, or with the assistance of mutual
friends ; and the matter may be considered to be ad-
justed.

" It is perfectly well understood that persisting in the
dispute would lead to unpleasant consequences. Should
both parties appear to be blameable, the judge makes his
award accordingly, and neither escapes without censure.
When false accusations are preferred, the false accuser is
punished ; and should malice be apparent, the punishment is augmented in proportion.

" In cases of great intricacy and importance, the magistrate has the option of referring the matter to the Chief
Justice at Meaco, or to the Emperor in Council ; but

* *History of Japan.*

when a decision is once given, there is no appeal.* Towards the conclusion of the seventeenth century, Kämpfer makes the following remarks on the Japanese system of administering justice. He says :—' Some will observe, that the Japanese are wanting in a competent knowledge of the law. . . . But I would not have the reader imagine that the Japanese live entirely without laws. Far from it. Their laws and constitutions are excellent, and strictly observed.'

"Coming down to the present century, competent authorities concur in bearing testimony to the purity with which justice is administered in the empire—to the great solemnity and strict decorum with which the proceedings are conducted before the tribunals—to the ardent desire manifested by the magistrates to elicit the truth—and to the remarkable acumen they display in detecting false-hood." † If the representations on the subject be not overcharged, the judicial institutions of the empire appear to realize, in a great degree, the maxim propounded by one of our most profound thinkers, that " *Truth is but justice in our knowledge, and justice is but truth in our practice.*" ‡

" In the theory of Punishment, it is not considered ' *qu'un homme pendu est un homme perdu,*' that to hang a man is to lose a man. § As a principle, *death* is the punish-ment for all offences.

" It does not, however, appear to have been adopted either from caprice, or through wanton disregard of human life, but may be traced rather to an erroneous conception

* No superior court hath it in its power to mitigate the sentence pronounced in another, though inferior. . . . Although it can-not be denied but this short way of proceeding is liable to some errors and mistakes in particular cases, yet I dare affirm that, in the main, it would be found abundantly less detrimental to the parties concerned than the tedious and expensive lawsuits in Europe.— Kämpfer, Appendix, vol. ii. p. 64.

† Doeff, Fischer, Siebold, &c., quoted in *Manners and Customs of the Japanese in the Nineteenth Century.*

‡ Milton, *Answer to Eikon Basilike.*

§ Voltaire, *L'Homme aux Quarante Ecus.*

of the means of doing equal justice. It is maintained, that justice would be violated unless all persons, whatever their rank, guilty of similar offences, were punished in an equal manner ; and it is conceived that death is the only penalty that affects alike prince and peasant. 'Justice,' says William Adams, ' is very severe, having no respect to persons.' Accordingly, the only favour exhibited in regard to the man of rank, is that of his being permitted to anticipate the act of the executioner by the commission of suicide.

" But though sanguinary in principle, the laws are greatly modified in practice.

" The power of inflicting death appears to be permissive, not compulsory, on the magistrate ; and accordingly, a very wide discretion is exercised. From this discretion murder alone is excepted, including homicide of any kind, even in its least aggravated form. This appears to have arisen from the disposition of the population, represented to have been originally, but probably now tempered by altered circumstances, ' no less fiery and changeable than the neighbouring sea is stormy and tempestuous.' On the principle of equal justice, *pecuniary fines* are not tolerated. Recourse is had to *imprisonment* as a punishment, which is rendered more or less severe according to the place in which incarceration takes place. One description of prison is called *raya* or *cage*. Here due provision is made for cleanliness and ventilation, and a fair proportion of wholesome food is provided. The other description of prison is denominated *gokuya*, or *hell*. It is a dungeon, generally within the walls of the governor's house, into which from fifteen to twenty persons are usually thrust, or at least more, ordinarily, than the place can conveniently accommodate. The door is never opened but for the admission or release of a prisoner. A hole in the wall serves as the means of ejecting the filth, and of receiving food. Except from a small grated window at the top, there is neither light nor ventilation. Books, pipes, all kinds of recreation, are prohibited. No beds are allowed, and, as a mark of disgrace which is acutely felt, the prisoners are deprived of their silk or linen waist girdles, for which bands of straw are substituted. A singular regulation is connected with these hells. The diet is limited in quantity, and execrable in quality; but on a certain condition, prisoners who have the means, or who have friends willing to assist them, are allowed to be provided with good and sufficient food. *The condition on which this indulgence is granted, is, that it shall be shared equally by all the inmates of the dungeon.* It is utterly repugnant to the Japanese notions of justice, that a criminal of wealth or influence should fare better than those who may be destitute. *Banishment* seems not to extend beyond the persons of the nobles attached to the imperial court, with some political offenders of high rank. These parties are deported to certain barren islands, from whence escape is impracticable. Food is provided for them, but they must work for their living. Their usual employment is the manufacture of silk goods, which are represented to be of an exceedingly fine description, and to be highly prized.

" *Corporal punishment* is inflicted frequently, and with great severity. *Torture* is resorted to but rarely, principally in cases of religious apostasy or political delinquency.

"The substance of the following proceeding, derived by Titsingh from a native source, is given in his ' Illustrations of Japan,' and will afford an idea of the manner in which the discretionary power vested in the magistrate may be exercised.

" A man was charged by his master, a trader in Osacca, with having robbed him of five hundred kobans, equivalent in sterling value to about £700. The charge was made before the governor. The accused solemnly protested his innocence; and the accuser, supported by the testimony of other servants, as solemnly maintained the truth of the charge. Circumstances were against the prisoner; but the evidence was of that doubtful nature, that the magistrate did not feel himself warranted in convicting or discharging the man. He, therefore, to use a familiar phrase, remanded him. At the end of some days

the magistrate called the parties before him again, and he
remonstrated with the accuser, but ineffectually. At
length he required the charge, and the demand of the
accuser, to be submitted to him in writing. This was
done in the following terms:—'Tchoudjet, servant to
Tomoya, has robbed his master of five hundred kobans.
This we attest by this writing, and we demand that, by
way of example, he be punished with death.' 'We, the
servants and relatives of Tomoya-kiougero, have confirmed
this writing, by affixing our signatures and our seals, the
second month of the first year *Geu-boun* (1736).' The
governor, Kavatche-no-kami by name, read the paper
attentively, and then said to Tomoya: 'Good. Now am
I absolved from responsibility. Depart. Be assured justice shall be done.' So Tomoya and his party went away
rejoicing. A short time afterwards a convicted felon
confessed himself guilty of the robbery with which
Tchoudjet had been charged; and Tomoya, with all his
people, were straightway summoned into the presence of
the governor. 'What is this thing ye have done?' said
the governor, addressing the party sternly. 'Know ye
not that your false accusation hath tended to cause the
death of an innocent man? Know ye not the law, that
ye have put your own lives in jeopardy? that thou thy-
self, Tomoya, thy wife, and thy people, may be delivered
over to the executioner? And behold me, should I not
die the death, because I have not looked with greater care
into this matter. Prepare for doom.' Thunderstruck, the
terrified wretches threw themselves on their knees, and
implored for mercy. The magistrate beheld their abject
state for some time in silence. He kept them in agoniz-
ing suspense, willing to give them a lesson they should
not speedily forget. At length he exclaimed:—'Be of
good cheer. The man is not dead. I doubted his guilt, and I
have kept him in concealment, hoping that, in process of
time, his innocence might be brought to light. Most
sincerely do I rejoice that my precaution hath proved of
avail. Let Tchoudjet be brought in.' The order was
obeyed, and the governor, resuming his address, said:

'Tomoya, behold an innocent man, who might have fallen a victim to thy unjust accusation. A grievous injury hast thou inflicted on him. Thy life I spare, because his has not been taken; but for what he has suffered through thy injustice, thou owest him reparation. Pay unto him, then, the sum of five hundred kobans, and henceforth cherish him as a faithful servant. Go thy ways. Justice is now done.' In due course this proceeding was reported to the Emperor. What had been done by Kavatche was approved, and he was in a short space of time appointed to the lucrative and high posts of Inspector of the Chamber of Accounts, and Governor at Nagasaki, where his good qualities endeared him to the people, his memory being held in reverence in the time of the European narrator of the transaction."*

According to some writers, torture is very common where the crime is heinous, or where the evidence is deficient; but we may believe, with Mr. Rundall, that it is now but rarely resorted to. We may also perhaps doubt some other horrible, revolting stories which have been told by travellers, and which seem to be opposed to the character given to the Japanese by these very travellers themselves. It has been said, for example, that public executions, not by one merciful stroke, but by slow torture, are by no means unfrequent; that the young nobles are accustomed to lend their swords to the torturing executioner, in order that the edge and temper of the blade may be tried; that they take great delight in witnessing tortures, particularly when the criminal is enveloped in a thick, close-fitting garment or shirt made of reeds, and to which fire is applied; that they laugh and applaud, as at a dance in the theatre, when the poor victim feels the flames, and runs and leaps about in his agony, and that this they call by the pleasant name of the "Death-dance." It must be admitted, however, that the modes of torture, degradation, and death, invented and applied to their wretched Christians during the perse-

* *Memorials of the Empire of Japan*, &c. Printed for the Hakluyt Society. London, 1850.

H 2

cution, indicate a refined as well as a brutal cruelty, quite
equal to that of the ancient Romans, the Spanish Inquisi-
tion, and our own persecution under Mary and Elizabeth.

Several executions witnessed by the Dutch near Nagasaki were conducted with decency and humanity. The
prisoner was carried to the place of execution—a large
open field outside the town—on a horse, his legs and arms
being bound with cords. On his way thither any person
might give him refreshment. At the appointed spot
were the judges, with their assistants and insignia of
office. Here the victim to the laws received from the
executioner a cup of cheering saki, with its usual
accompaniments, dried fish, fruit, and pastry, which he
was allowed to share with his relatives and friends. He
was then seated upon a straw mat between two heaps of
sand, and his head was struck off with a sharp sword.
The severed head was set upon a stake, to which was
affixed a placard, indicating the crime for which he had
died. At the end of three days the relations were allowed
to take down the head, and bury it and the body in their
own way.

The severity of the Japanese laws is Draconic. They
may really be said to be written in blood, as death is the
allotted punishment for every offence, and, not unfrequently, whole families are involved in the fate of a single
offender. Death, by decapitation at the hands of the
common executioner, or by instant self-murder—and
nothing short of death—is considered an atonement of the
slightest breach of the law or of public tranquillity, or of
disobedience to any order or instruction of Government.
Imprisonment, exile, or relegation in distant, cold, and
desolate islands appears to have fallen out of use since the
troubles of the seventeenth century. In the rare occasions
on which they are now resorted to they seem to be extended not only to the offender, but to his wife and children, however innocent and however young.

Crucifixion is or was in vogue. Old Purchas says :—
" Crucifying is common, the bodies still hanging and
putrifying by the highways : their crosses have two cross-

timbers fastened to the main post, which is set into the ground, the one for the expansion of the hands, the other of the feet, with a shorter piece in the middle to bear up the weight of the body. They bind them thereto, and run a lance into the right side of the crucified, sometimes two across. Heading is usual, which in solemnity is thus performed : one goes before with a mattock, another follows with a shovel ; a third with a board or table containing the crime, which also he himself following next, holdeth in a stick, to which is fastened a paper made like a vane, the end whereof is in his hands tied behind him—by which cord the executioner leads him—on each side a soldier with his lance resting on him ; at the dismal place, without show or scare [fear] he sits down and holds out his head, presently wiped off, others mangling him, as is said."

It seems, however, that crucifixion is confined to regicides ; but the *Hari-kari*, or "Happy dispatch," is still practised by the Japanese. This consists in ripping open their own bowels with two cuts in the form of a cross— after the artistic dissector's fashion.* Officials resort to it under the fear of the punishment which they may expect, for it is a leading principle that it is more honourable to die by one's own hands than by another's. Princes and the high classes receive permission to rip themselves up as a special favour, when under sentence of death : their entire family must die with the guilty. Sometimes, by favour, the nearest relative of the condemned is permitted to perform the function of executioner in his own house. Such a death is considered less dishonourable than by the public executioners, who are the tanners before-mentioned, aided by the servants of those who keep disreputable houses.

But the Japanese, for the most part, always ask permission to rip themselves, and they set about it with astonishing ease, and not without evident ostentation. The criminal who obtains this favour assembles all his

* *United States Expedition,* i. 487.

family and his friends, puts on his richest apparel, makes an eloquent speech on his situation, and then, with a most contented look, he bares his belly, and in the form of a cross rips open the viscera. The most odious crimes are effaced by such a death. The criminal thenceforward ranks as a brave in the memory of men. His family contracts no stain, and his property is not confiscated.

It is curious that the Romans and the Japanese should hit upon crucifixion as a mode of punishment. These coincidences often startle us in reviewing the manners and customs of men. Vainly we strive to conjecture how such a mode of punishment could have suggested itself to the mind of man. The *in terrorem* object scarcely accounts for it. Constantine abolished it amongst the Romans, in honour of Him who was pleased to make that mode of dying honourable in the estimation of men.

The Hari-kari, or happy dispatch, is still more incomprehensible. We shudder at the bare idea of it. To commit suicide by hanging, by drowning, by poison, by fire-arms, by a train in rapid motion—all these modes are reasonable in their madness; but to rip open our bowels! —and with *two* cuts! We are totally at a loss to imagine how such a mode of self-murder could have been adopted; we cannot but wonder at the strength of nerve which enables it to be accomplished : but we feel no doubt of the everlasting force of national custom—especially amongst the Orientals—in the continuance of this practice. Montesquieu said, " If the punishments of the Orientals horrify humanity, the reason is, that the despot who ordains them feels that he is above all laws. It is not so in Republics, wherein the laws are always mild, because he who makes them is himself a subject." This fine sentiment, thoroughly French, is evidently contradicted by the institutions of Japan, where the Emperor himself, the despot, is a subject; besides Montesquieu would have altered his antithesis had he lived to see the horrors of the Reign of Terror in the glorious French Republic.

The vigorous enforcement of these punishments amongst the Japanese is more effective than a long code of laws in restraining all orders of the nation ; but it is evident that there must exist a peculiar mental organization in the people who have prospered, and are contented and happy under such a system. To suppose that they would be better off with our mode of procedure and governmental arrangements is not more reasonable than would be *their* opinion, that theirs would solve our terrible problem—the suppression of crime. When we shall have studied and thoroughly comprehended the distinct characteristics of the various races of men, as Nature has fashioned them, we shall assuredly cease to err in our hopes—refrain from Quixotic battling with Nature—and repent for the frightful evils which we have inflicted on human natures otherwise characterised than ourselves—but always with very " good intentions."

It is stated, though not upon the very best authority, that in certain cases, involving the honour of wives or daughters, the Japanese may take the law into their own hands, and that fathers have the power of life and death over their refractory wicked children. Although the contrary has been stated, it does not appear—except in very peculiar cases—that the lord has the power of life and death over his serf. We have somewhere seen it stated that he cannot even inflict any severe punishment unless he previously take the serf before a magistrate.

To return from criminal to civil jurisprudence or practice, it is said that the law of primogeniture is so thoroughly recognised and established, that family disputes about property very rarely occur. The younger sons have small portions, regulated according to usage, and of which, if old enough, they are put in possession during their father's lifetime. If of noble birth, they are regarded with respect, however poor they may be. The pride of birth seems to be very strong among all the upper classes. As a general rule, the daughters, even of the high nobility, have no fortunes or dowry on marriage. On the contrary, if they are considered very handsome, amiable in temper, and very accomplished, the parents expect the bridegroom to pay down to them a handsome sum of money, or to make over to them some other valuable property.

Whatever may be the extent of his harem, the Japanese can have only one lawful wife at a time ; and she must be of the same rank as her husband. Her issue alone can inherit family property, titles, and honours. It appears, however, to be very easy for a man to put away his wife and take another—at least, as far as any law exists to the contrary. But this tendency to divorce is said to be checked by serious financial considerations. If he sends one wife back to her home, he does not recover the money he paid for her ; and if he gains the evil reputation of being a capricious, inconstant husband, the price in the matrimonial market is raised upon him, and he must disburse largely before he can get another wife.

There are, of course, some lingering remains of the old Mongol barbarism ; but, whether it be by law or by usage, by the edicts of emperors, or by a natural gallantry in the people, the position of women in Japan is far higher and better than in any other essentially Asiatic country. A lady at Jeddo enjoys a hundred times more real liberty, and is treated with immeasurably more respect, than a Turkish lady at Constantinople,—and this, after all the reforms or innovations of Sultans Mahmoud and Abdul-Medjid.

The government of Japan is unquestionably a pure despotism, in which policy and force combine to support a throne which owes to policy and force its establishment and conservation ; but if we—in this Western world— see in the establishment and development of an European despotism the inevitable preparation of anarchy and the vengeance of Western humanity, then may we rest assured that if we attempt to meddle and reform and " revolutionize" the Orientals in their peculiar institutions, we shall merely render them instrumental to their own destruction without in the least fructifying our very " good intentions."

The mode of raising the revenue of this singular government is very simple. The Japanese have had to pay a

property-tax for centuries before we thought of it in
England.   It is assessed on all the houses and lands
within the precincts of the towns, and it is regulated
according to the *length*, not the value of the property.
Length of houses or lands under ninety feet are exempt,
like our incomes under £100 ; but the slightest extension
of that length entails a double assessment.   There is no
income-tax for the general public, but there is a "voluntary contribution"—which, however, nobody dares to
refuse—corresponding to our "benevolences" of revolutionary remembrance.   This benevolence or present to
the Government falls also on the proprietors of lands and
houses.   At Nagasaki the proceeds are applied "in
honour of the gods ;" but if this should remind us of a
church-rate, it differs in this respect, that in Japan it is
perfectly voluntary, no one being obliged to pay it.   The
property-tax is levied annually, but the benevolence
comes round only once in seven or eight years, because
only a certain number of streets have to pay each year in
rotation ; each street being a sort of ward or district.   A
tax is also annually levied on the proprietors of disreputable houses.   The city of Meako is by privilege
totally exempt from taxes.   The villages and hamlets are
otherwise assessed.   An annual tax is there raised on
wheat, rice, and all the produce of lands in cultivation.
Fruit-trees are paid for in silver equivalent to one-half of
the crop.   The farmer's crops are inspected and valued
by proper officers, and he is bound to carry to the imperial
warehouse the specified quantity of his annual increase.
Woods and forests pay a property-tax according to their
length.*

The revenues of the empire, as calculated by Varenius,
according to princes and provinces, made up the sum total
of 2834 tons of gold, on the Flemish mode of computation ;
and taking the ton at only £10,000 sterling, the amount
would be £28,340,000 sterling, besides the provinces and
cities which are immediately subject to the Siogoun.

* Kämpfer, *Hist. Gén. des Voy.*

These revenues must not be considered as national, being only yielded in coin to the various princes. The Siogoun, however, besides the large revenues of his provinces, has a considerable treasure in gold and silver, disposed in chests of 1000 *taels*, each being nearly in value equal to a Dutch rix-dollar, or about four shillings and fourpence English money. As the greatest expense of the public revenue is generally in the support of the army, the real amount of the Japanese resources may be estimated from the numerous army supported. Thunberg computes the revenue of the crown-lands at more than 44,000,000 of sacks of rice, each sack weighing about twenty pounds. But this calculation implies nothing to an European reader. Balbi gives it £12,000,000.

The navy, like that of other Oriental Powers, is very trifling. The Japanese vessels are, for the most part, open at the stern, so that they cannot bear a boisterous sea. They are all made according to certain dimensions settled by edict, like everything else in Japan. They have the mariner's compass, like the Chinese, but it is inconceivable how they could in former times make voyages, as is asserted, to Formosa, and even to Java. Captain Cook observes :—" If the Japanese vessels are, as Kämpfer describes them, open at the stern, it would not have been possible for those we saw to have survived the fury of this storm ; but as the appearance of the weather all the preceding part of the day foretold its coming, and one of the sloops had, notwithstanding, stood far out to sea, we may safely conclude that they are perfectly capable of bearing a gale of wind. Spanberg describes two kinds of Japanese vessels, one answering to the above description of Kämpfer ; the other, which he calls *busses*, and in which, he says, they make their voyages to the neighbouring islands, exactly corresponding to those we saw."*

The reasons assigned for requiring the sterns of all vessels to be constructed in the way alluded to, has been to render more convenient the management of the rudder,

* *Voyages,* vii.

which is large and unwieldy, and is hoisted up or lowered by means of runners worked by a windlass fitted in the cabin. Kämpfer and others ascribe it to the suspicious policy of the Government, which forbids any of its vessels to visit foreign countries; and the punishment of death was adjudged against all who, by design or accident, were thrown upon a strange land; and hence they very naturally assumed that the navigators of these frail and open-stern craft would not venture beyond the sight of land. It is known, however, that the Chinese junks usually have sterns and rudders somewhat similar, and a presumption may be reasonably advanced that this description of rudder was the first substitute for the paddle, oar, or sweep used in early times for steering, and the recess in the stern has been left for the sole convenience of taking the rudder out of the water.

The same writer says :—"We saw nothing remarkable in the manner or workmanship of the Japanese ship-builders. It is doubtful whether they have any scientific rules for drafting or modelling, or for ascertaining the displacement of their vessels; nor, perhaps, has it been necessary, as the law confined them all to one model and size. The tools with which they work are of primitive description, and the finest of their work is not remarkable for its neatness; copper is preferred to iron in fastening when it can be advantageously used, and this doubtless owing to the great abundance of the former as a native production.

"It is a singular fact, strongly illustrative of the effect produced upon the people of this strange country by our friendly and social communications with them, that the law already mentioned, which restricted the construction of their vessels to one particular model, and that inflicting death upon those of their nation who should return to the empire after having once left it, no matter how, were both suspended,—whether annulled or not, I cannot say.

"Kayama Yesaiman, the Governor of Uraya, was authorized, as we have heard, and instructed to build a vessel after the model of the store-ship *Supply*, a very

pretty vessel, and the Japanese commissioners who negotiated with me, invited a native we had on board the
flag-ship to land and rejoin his family, pledging themselves in my presence that he should be treated kindly
and provided for, under the immediate protection of one
of them. Since then there has been, as I understand,
no objection made to the return of any of the shipwrecked
Japanese; but how far they have improved in shipbuilding I have not heard.

"We saw no war-junks, and it is probable they have
none of any size, the country not having been engaged
for a long period in war. They content themselves, most
likely, in putting light swivels or howitzers on the larger
of their boats, whenever they cannot depend entirely
upon their many land batteries."*

More than a thousand of these vessels—nearly all of
the same dimensions in burthen, corresponding to about
a hundred tons of our measurement—are occasionally
seen at one time at anchor in the port of Hakodadi.†

* *United States Expedition.*
† Ibid.

CHAPTER III.

PALACES, TEMPLES, CASTLES, TOWNS, HOUSES, GARDENS, VEHICLES, ETC.

THE description of Jeddo by Don Roderigo de Vivero y Velasco, in 1608, tallies with that given by our own countrymen who have recently opened the gates of Japan.* Don Roderigo, however, was received as a friend before the Europeans inspired the Japanese with suspicion and hatred, and had an opportunity of seeing and describing far more than we shall probably find described even in the more extended details that may be expected from the country into which we have intruded under the present arrangements.

" I should think myself fortunate," he says, " if I could succeed in affording an exact idea of all the wonders I saw there, as well in respect to the material of the edifices at this royal residence, as to the pomp and splendour of the Court. I think I may affirm that, from the entrance to the Prince's apartment there were more than 20,000 persons—not assembled for the occasion, but constantly employed and paid—for the daily service of the Court."

The principal wall which encloses the palace, he says, is composed of immense blocks of freestone, put together without cement, with embrasures at equal distances for

* Don Roderigo was a favourite of Anne, wife of Philip II. of Spain. He filled important posts, in which he distinguished himself, and subsequently obtained the place of Governor and Captain-General of the Philippines. On his return voyage to Spain he was shipwrecked, and cast on the shores of Japan, and most kindly treated by the Emperor, who loaded him with presents, concessions, and despatches for the King of Spain, on his departure in 1610. The Emperor requested the King of Spain to send him fifty miners to work his mines ; but no notice was taken of his presents, his concessions, and his request,—apparently one of the first provocations received by the government of Japan.

artillery, of which there is no small quantity. At the foot
of this wall is a very deep wet ditch; the entrance is by a
drawbridge of a peculiar and extremely ingenious construction. The gates were very strong. Don Roderigo
passed through two ranks of musketeers, about 1000
strong, to the second gate in the second wall, about 300
paces from the other. Here was stationed a body of 400
lancers and pikemen. A third wall, about twelve feet
high, was guarded by about 300 halberdiers. At a short
distance from this wall was the palace with the royal
stables, containing 300 saddle-horses on one side, and the
arsenal, filled with armour and arms for 100,000 men, on
the other.

The first apartment of the palace was entirely covered
with rich ornaments, carpets, stuffs, velvets, and gold.
The walls were hung with pictures representing hunting
subjects. Each apartment excelled the preceding in
splendour, until he reached that in which the prince was
seated on a superb carpet of crimson velvet, embroidered
with gold, placed upon a kind of alcove raised two steps,
in the centre of the apartment.

At Meako he was shown the tomb of Taiko-Sama, the
great warrior, in a magnificent temple, the *Dai-Bods*, and
the colossal image of Buddha, an idol of bronze, and a
superb building which contains the images of all the gods
of Japan. This Dai-Bods, he thought, was worthy of
being classed amongst the wonders of the world. Its
dimensions rendered him mute with astonishment. " I
ordered," he says, " one of my people to measure the
thumb of the right hand of the idol, and I perceived that
although he was a man of large size, he could not embrace
it with his two *arms* by two palms ! But the size of this
statue is not its only merit : the feet, hands, mouth, eyes,
forehead, and other features, are as perfect and as expressive as the most accomplished painter could make a
portrait." This praise of Japanese art, from a native of
the land of painters, is noteworthy. Roderigo continues :—" When I visited this temple it was unfinished ;
more than 100,000 workmen were daily employed upon

it. The devil could not suggest to the Emperor a surer expedient to get rid of his immense wealth."

The temple and tomb of Taiko-Sama is magnificent, and Roderigo, like a good Catholic, deplores the dedication of such an edifice to the remains of one " whose soul is in hell for all eternity." The entrance was by an avenue paved with jasper, 400 feet by 300. On each side, at equal distances, were posts of jasper, on which were placed lamps, lighted at night. At the end of this passage was the peristyle of the temple, ascended by several steps, and having on the right a monastery of priests. The principal gate was encrusted with jasper, and overlaid with gold and silver ornaments skilfully wrought. The nave of the temple was supported by lofty columns. There was a choir, as in European cathedrals, with seats and a grating all round. Male and female choristers chanted the prayers, much in the same manner as in our churches ; the costume of the former reminded Roderigo of the prebends of Toledo, except that the train of their robe was excessively long, and their caps were much wider at top than at the bottom. Four of these priests accosted him, and gave him much uneasiness, apparently, by conducting him to the altar of their " infamous reliques," surrounded with an infinite number of lamps. The number of persons, their silence and devotion, surprised him. After raising five or six curtains, covering as many gratings of iron and silver, and the last of gold, a kind of chest was exposed, in which were contained the ashes of Taiko-Sama ; within this sacred enclosure none but the chief priests could enter. All the Japanese prostrated themselves, but Roderigo quitted the " accursed spot," and proceeded, accompanied by their priests, to see their gardens, which were more tastefully laid out, he says, than those of Aranjuez in New Castile.

This pantheon was the largest building he had seen in Japan ; it contained 2600 gilt bronze statues of gods, each in his own tabernacle, decorated with emblems, doubtless Buddhas and Bodhisatras.*

* *Asiatic Journal*

Curiously corresponding with Roderigo's reminiscences is the observation of the Americans at Hakodadi. " The temples, chiefly Buddhist, are beautifully situated in the suburbs. The entrance to them leads generally through rows of elegant trees and wild camellias. They are large plain structures, with high peaked roofs, resembling the houses pictured on Chinese porcelain. In the space immediately in front is a large bell for summoning the faithful, a stone reservoir of holy water, and several roughly-hewn stone idols. The doorway is ornamented with curious-looking dragons and other animals, carved in wood. Upon entering, there is nothing special about the buildings worth noting, the naked sides and exposed rafters having a gloomy appearance. The altar is the only object that attracts attention. It so much resembles the Roman Catholic, that I need not describe it. Some of the idols on these altars are so similar to those I have seen in the churches in Italy, that if they were mutually translated, I doubt whether either set of worshippers would discover the change. The priests count beads, shave their heads, and wear analogous robes, and the service is attended by the ringing of bells, the lighting of candles, and the burning of incense. In fact, except that the cross is nowhere to be seen, one could easily imagine himself within a Roman Catholic place of worship." Paulus Samfidius, the companion of St. Francis Xavier, in his mission to Japan, made a similar announcement three hundred years ago.*

Kämpfer visited the Buddhist temple and convent, where the emperor lodges when he visits the Daïri at Meako. The approach to this temple was a broad, level gravel walk, half a mile in length, lined on both sides with the stately dwellings of the ecclesiastics attached to it. He passed a lofty gateway, and ascended to a large terrace, finely gravelled and planted with trees and shrubs. Passing two handsome structures, he ascended a beautiful stairway to a magnificent building, with a

---

* *Epist. Japan.* 16. Preces spherulis precariis quæ centum et octo signis constat, ut nos, rosariis vocatis, numerant, &c.

front superior to that of the imperial palace at Jeddo.
In the middle of the outermost hall was a chapel, containing a large idol with curled hair, surrounded with

BUDDHIST TEMPLE.

smaller idols.   On both sides were some smaller and less
elaborate chapels ; behind were two apartments for the
emperor's use, opening upon a small pleasure-garden at

I

the foot of the mountain, clothed with a beautiful variety of trees and shrubs. Behind this garden, and on the ascent of the mountain, was a chapel dedicated to the predecessor of the reigning emperor, who had been deified.

Up the hill, near a quarter of a mile distant, was a large bell, which Kämpfer describes as rather larger than the smaller of the two great bells at Moscow; rough, ill cast, and ill-shaped; but it was a bell, nevertheless, cast by the Japanese for a religious purpose. It was struck on the outside by a large wooden stick. The pagan prior, who, with a number of his pagan monks, to be described in the sequel, received and entertained the Dutch visitors, was an old gentleman of an agreeable countenance and good complexion, clad in a velvet or dark purple-coloured gown, with an alms-bag in his hand, richly embroidered with gold.

Kämpfer saw the completed temple mentioned by Roderigo—the *Dai-Bods*—the largest and most remarkable of the temples at Meako. It was enclosed by a high wall of freestone, the front blocks being nearly twelve feet square. A stone staircase of eight steps led up to the gateway, on either side of which stood a gigantic image, nearly twenty-four feet high, with the face of a lion, but otherwise well-proportioned, black, or of a dark purple, almost naked, and placed on a pedestal six feet high. That on the left had the mouth open, and one of the hands stretched out. The opposite one had the mouth shut, and the hand close to the body. They were said to be emblems of the two first and chief principles of nature, the active and the passive, the giving and the taking, the opening and the shutting; in fine, generation and corruption, corresponding to the Brahmanic primitive and continuous world-destruction and renewal—the *avatars* or incarnations of Vishnou.

The temple itself had a double roof, supported by ninety-four immense wooden pillars, of at least nine feet diameter, some of them of a single piece, but others of several trunks, put together after the manner of the

masts of our large ships, and all painted red. The floor
was paved with square flags of freestone. There were
many small narrow doors running up to the first roof,
but the interior, forming but one room up to the second
roof, was very badly lighted, owing to its great height.
There was nothing within except an immense idol, sitting—not after the Japanese, but after the Brahmanic
manner—with the legs crossed before, on a lotus-flower,
supported by another of which the leaves were turned
upwards, the two being raised about twelve feet from the
floor. The idol, which was gilt all over, had long ears,
crisped, in fact woolly, negro hair; according to one
authority, a crown on the head, which appeared through
the window over the first roof, with a large spot not gilt
on the forehead :—this is the *thika* of the Hindoos, showing
clearly its Indian origin.* The shoulders, so broad as
to reach from one pillar to another, a distance of thirty
feet, were naked. The breast and body were covered
with a loose piece of drapery. It held the right hand
up, and the left rested edgewise on the belly. Such is the
Dai-Bods, the great god of Japan.

The temple of Quanwon is not less remarkable. In
the midst is a gigantic image of Quanwon, an adopted
Chinese divinity, called in Batavia, Quanum, Quarlva,
and Santea, a secondary divinity, revered as the master of
the air; hence his thirty-six arms, typical, I suppose, of
the points whence the wind blows, although our compass
designates but thirty-two. Sixteen black images, bigger
than life, stand around it, and on each side two rows of
gilt idols, with twenty arms each. On either side of the
temple, running from end to end, are ten platforms, rising
like steps, one behind the other, on each of which stand
fifty images of Quanwon, as large as life, a thousand in
all, each on its separate pedestal, so arranged as to stand

---

* This image was set up in the year 1576 by the Emperor Taiko.
The temple was destroyed by an earthquake in 1596, but was commenced rebuilding in 1602. The colossus was seriously injured by
another earthquake during the same year. It was then melted
down, and a substitute made of wood covered with gilt paper.

in rows of five, one behind the other, and all visible at the same time, each with its twenty hands. On the hands and heads of all these are placed smaller idols, to the number of forty or more ; so that the whole number, thirty-three thousand three hundred and thirty-three, according to the Japanese, does not appear exaggerated. Japanese Guide-books, sold to the visitants, explain all these particulars.

At a short distance is a chapel called Mimitsuka, or "tomb of ears." Here are buried the ears and noses of the Coreans who fell in the war waged against them by the renowned Taiko-Sama, who had them salted and carried to Japan. The grand portico of the outer wall of the temple is called Ni-wo-mon—that is, "gate of the two kings." On entering this vast portico, which is eighty-three feet high, on each side appears a colossal figure, twenty-two feet in height, representing the two celestial kings, Awoon and Jugo—the usual porters at the Buddhist temples.

Another edifice placed before the apartment of the great Buddha contains the largest bell known in the world. It is seventeen feet two and a half inches high, and weighs one million seven hundred thousand pounds English : its weight is consequently five times greater than the great bell at Moscow, and fifty-six times larger than the great bell at Westminster.*

The castles of the Japanese nobility are built with the same grandeur of design, expense, and magnificence. Their site is either on some great river, upon hills, or rising grounds. They commonly consist of three different fortresses, or enclosures, which cover and defend, or, if possible, encompass one another, over a vast expanse of ground. Formerly they had no guns ; but probably they have them now, as at Nagasaki and other ports. The principal and innermost castle or enclosure is called the *Fourmas*—that is, the true or chief castle. It is the resi-

---

* Klaproth, *Ann. des Emp. du Jap.* ; *Asiatic Journal*, Sept. 1831 ; Hildreth, *Japan*, &c.

dence of the prince or lord in possession, and as such it is distinguished from the others by a square, large white tower, three or four stories high, with a small roof encompassing each story, like a crown or garland. In the second enclosure, called *Nimmas*—that is, second castle—are lodged the gentlemen of the prince's bedchamber, his stewards, secretaries, and other chief officers, who are to give a constant attendance about his person. The empty spaces are cultivated, laid out in gardens, or sown with rice, according to the locality. The third and outermost enclosure is called *Sotogamei*, or third castle. It is the abode of a numerous train of soldiers, courtiers, domestics, and other people, this portion being open to the public. Viewed at a distance, the white walls, bastions, gates, each of which has two or more stories built over it, and above all the beautiful tower of the innermost castle, are extremely pleasant to behold. There is commonly a place without the castle designed for a rendezvous and review of troops.

Hence it appears, that considering the absence of guns in the internal warfare of Japan, these castles are well enough defended, and might hold out a long siege. The proprietors are bound to keep them in constant repair ; but if there be any part going to ruin, it cannot be rebuilt without the knowledge and express leave of the emperor, who will not permit new ones to be built in any part of his dominions. These castles are generally situated at the extremity of some large town, which forms a half-moon around them. In a Japanese map brought to Europe by Kämpfer, the number of castles in the whole empire is set down at a hundred and forty-six.

By the same authority, the number of towns in the empire is more than thirteen thousand. Most of them are very populous and well built. The streets are, generally speaking, regular, running straightforward, and crossing each other at right angles, as if they had been laid out at one time, and according to one general ground-plot. The towns are not surrounded with walls and ditches, as in Europe in the olden time. There are two gates, however, which are shut at night, similar to those previously mentioned, in every street. In large towns, where some prince resides, these two gates are somewhat handsomer, and kept in better repair, and there is commonly a strong guard mounted, all out of respect for the residing prince. The rest of the town generally lies open to the fields, and is but seldom enclosed even with a common ditch or hedge.

The number of shops astonished Kämpfer—in every town whole streets being scarcely anything but continued rows of shops on both sides. " I own, for my part," he says, "that I could not well conceive how the whole country is able to furnish customers enough to make the proprietors get a livelihood, much less to enrich them." According to the Spaniard before quoted, all the streets of Jeddo "have covered galleries, and are occupied each by persons of the same trade ; thus, the carpenters have one street, the tailors another, the jewellers another, and so on, including many trades not known in Europe : the merchants are classed together in the same way. Provisions are sold in places appropriated for each sort. I remarked," he says, "the market where game is sold : there was a vast quantity of rabbits, hares, wild-boars, deer, goats, and other animals which I never saw before. The Japanese rarely eat any flesh but that of game, which they hunt. The fish-market is immense, and extremely neat and clean. I observed more than a thousand different kinds of fish, sea and river, fresh and salt. Large tubs contained, besides, a vast quantity of live fish. The inns are in the same streets, adjoining those where they let and sell horses, which are in number that the traveller who changes horses, according to the custom of the country, every league, is only embarrassed where to choose. The nobles and great men inhabit a distinct part of the city. This quarter is distinguished by the armorial ornaments, sculptured, painted, or gilt, placed over the doors of the houses. The Japanese nobles attach much value to this privilege." It is, in fact, their Belgravia—only with us, exclusiveness is secured by the high figure of the rental—the result being that Belgravia does not *necessarily* answer for the nobility, gentility, or even respectability of the inhabitants. The convenience of classifying tradesmen into distinct streets seems to recommend itself to our attention ; although I have heard a selfish tradesman wish that Parliament would enact a law to prohibit every tradesman from setting up his shop near another of the same kind already established. Not to dwell upon its obvious advantages, it must form a striking feature in the general beauty of the towns and cities.

The frequency of earthquakes has compelled all ranks in Japan to circumscribe the size and magnificence of their houses. Constructed of wood, the houses of private persons never exceed six *kins*, or forty-four feet three inches in height; indeed, they seldom build them so high, unless they are designed also for warehouses. Even the palace of the Daïri, of the secular monarch, and of the princes and lords, are not above one story high. The upper story in general is very low, and used chiefly for stowing away household goods.

But if the houses of the Japanese be not so large, lofty, or so substantially built as ours, they are, on the other hand, remarkable for their exquisite neatness, cleanliness, and for their curious furniture and ornaments, which they have admirably adapted in size and design to the dimensions of their apartments. Instead of partition-walls to divide their rooms, they have folding screens, made of coloured or gilt paper, and laid into wooden frames, which can be put up or removed at pleasure, to enlarge the rooms or make them narrower, according to their fancy or convenience.

The floors are somewhat raised above the level of the street, and are all made of boards, neatly covered with mats, made of rushes and rice straw, three or four inches thick, the borders curiously fringed, embroidered, or otherwise neatly adorned. By imperial edict establishing the custom of the land, all mats are of the same size in all parts of the empire ; namely, one kin, or seven feet four inches and a half in length, and half a kin, or three feet eight inches and a quarter in width. All the lower part of the house, the staircase leading up to the second story, if there be any, the windows, posts, and passages are curiously painted and varnished. The windows are of light frames, which may be taken out, and put and slid behind each other at pleasure, and are divided into squares like our panes of glass, and covered with oiled paper, mica, and shells; glass windows are unknown. The ceilings are neatly covered with gilt or silver-coloured paper, embellished with flowers; and the screens which serve as partitions are often curiously painted. As furniture is cheap, and the people take a delight in adornment, every part of the house is pleasing to the eye as well as convenient for the purposes intended.

A case, with latticed or wire doors, to contain the fine articles of earthenware, a framework with hooks and shelves to suspend iron utensils or wooden ware, or a moveable case of drawers to hold silks, fine lacquered ware, or similar goods, constitute nearly all the furniture of the shops. Apothecaries' shops are hung with gilded signs and paper placards setting forth the variety and virtues of their medicines, some of which are described as brought from Europe. The partition which separates the shop from the dwelling is sometimes closed, but more usually open; and a customer has, generally speaking, as much to do with the mistress as the master of the establishment. When he enters, his straw-sandals are always left on the ground as he steps on the mats and squats down to look at the goods, which are then spread out on the floor. A foreigner had need of some thoughtfulness in this particular, as it is an annoyance to a Japanese to have his mats soiled by dirty feet or broken through by coarse shoes.

The signs of the shops are inscribed on the paper windows and doors, in various well-known devices and cyphers, either in Chinese or Japanese characters. "The shopmen at Hakodadi," says the narrator of the American Expedition, "were at first very shy, and showed but little disposition to sell their goods to the Americans; but when they became somewhat more familiar with the strangers, the characteristic eagerness of tradesmen developed itself to the full, and the Hakodadi merchants showed themselves as clever at their business as any Chatham-street or Bowery salesman with us. They bustled about the raised platform upon which they were perched, pulled out the drawers arranged on the walls, and displayed their goods to the greatest advantage when they thought there was a chance of catching the eye and pleasing the taste of a passing American. They were always very jealous, however, of their prerogatives, and were exceedingly annoyed if any of their purchasers stepped upon the platform, which was their trading sanctum, and as carefully guarded against intrusion as the 'behind the counter' of a New York shopman. The purchaser ordinarily stood under the roof, on the ground, in the space which intervened between the side walk and the elevated shop-floor. Some of the more impatient and intrusive Yankees, however, would occasionally spring up, and pulling out the goods, handle them very unceremoniously ; not, however, without a serious protest on the part of the sellers, who sometimes were so annoyed that official complaints were made by them to the authorities. The shopkeepers had always a fixed price for their goods, and all attempts to beat them down were useless, and were generally rebuked by an expression of displeasure."

The roof is covered with planks, shingles of wood, very thick, and heavy brown tiles laid in a gutter form. When shingles are used, they are fastened by means of pegs made of bamboo, or kept in their places by long slips of board, which have rows of large pebbles put upon them to prevent their removal. The stones, however, are intended to have the additional advantage of hastening the melting of the snow in winter. For a similarly provident reason, the roof rests upon thick, strong, and heavy beams, as large as can be procured, and the second story is generally built stronger and more substantial than the first. "This they do by reason of the frequent earthquakes which happen in this country ; because they observe that, in case of a violent shock, the pressure of the upper part of the house upon the lower, which is built much lighter, keeps the whole from being overthrown." If experience has convinced them of this fact, our established theory of stability in connexion with the position of the centre of gravity is clearly at fault. On the other hand, the sudden shock of an earthquake would cause the lighter story to yield, and so preserve the building ; but this does not explain the necessity for making it top-heavy. The outsides of the houses are commonly covered with plaster. The rear of the building is appropriated to the family. Here the domestic operations are all carried on ; here the family take their meals in the day ; here, on the same mats, do they sleep at night. It is the " drawing-room " for visitors and the nursery for children, and sometimes the kitchen.

In almost every house there is a room set apart for the purpose of bathing, with a tub in it. This generally looks towards the yard ; and, as cleanliness is one great characteristic of the Japanese, they are constantly washing in the most open manner—the women quietly sitting in tubs in front of their doors, washing themselves with the utmost unconcern, traffic and the business through the street going on past them as usual. In Jeddo and all the large towns there are large bathing establishments, in which men, women, and children enjoy the bath promiscuously, decently, and without shame. The doors are open to the passer-by, and present a curious spectacle, more especially if the inmates of both sexes rush to it to gaze at him, as he rides blushingly past—not being a Japanese.

We cannot say here that in the times of innocence morals are so pure that nothing is indecent. We cannot refer to the simplicity of the ancients—Telemachus, for instance, at Pilos, undressed, bathed, and perfumed by the King's daughter ; or to Ruth approaching Boaz, as mentioned in the Bible. Yet it is curious to note that nakedness in some countries is the proof of modesty. In some

country of India I have read of, only courtezans put on
garments by way of allurements to men. The arts,
sculpture and painting, know not shame, and are, it seems,
above the laws of modesty. Venus, the Graces, and the
Greek Slave (that " white thunder," I think it was called
by a strong-minded woman), may be viewed without a
blush. Helvetius was of opinion that we are ashamed
to be naked because we are accustomed to dress. But
clearly the Japanese, in this particular, are not modest.
The promiscuous mingling of the sexes, whilst bathing, in
Japan need not remind us of scenes at Boulogne, Rams-
gate, and Margate exactly ; indeed, as with us, it is said
not to be a general practice throughout the country, but
it seems certain that the Japanese of the lower orders are,
notwithstanding their moral superiority to most Oriental
nations, a lewd people. Apart from the bathing scenes,
there is enough in the popular literature, with its ob-
scene pictorial illustrations, to prove a licentiousness
of taste and practice among a certain class of the population that is not only disgustingly intrusive, but disgrace-
fully indicative of foul corruption.* I suppose, in connexion with this fact, we must remember our own
Holywell-street and other "institutions" included or not
in the provisions of Lord Campbell's Act, and the curious
discussion which it provoked.

The gable-ends, as in Dutch houses, face towards the
street, and the roofs, projecting to some distance, serve as
a cover and shade to the doors. All the roofs of the
houses in front are topped with what at first might be
supposed to be a curious chimney wrapped in straw, but
which upon examination turns out to be a tub, protected
by its covering of straw from the weather, and kept constantly filled with water, to be sprinkled upon the shingled
roof in case of fire, by means of a broom, which is always
placed at hand to be ready for the occasion. In addition
to the tubs, there are wooden cisterns ranged along the
streets, and fire-engines in constant readiness. These are

* *United States Expedition.*

constructed much on the plan of ours, but are deficient in that important part of the apparatus, the air-chamber, and consequently they throw the water, not with a continuous stream, but in short, quick jets.

Fire-alarms, made of a thick piece of plank, hung on posts at the corners of the streets, and protected by a small roofing, which are struck by the watchman in case of a fire breaking out, show the anxious fears of the inhabitants.*

Trusty and numerous watchmen are stationed at all places early in the evening. "The watch was double at Jeddo," says Thunberg, "that is, one of them only gave intelligence with respect to the hour, which was done by striking two pieces of wood against each other. These strokes were given very frequently, and almost at every house, by the watch as they went their rounds. The two last strokes followed very quick upon each other, for a token that no more were to be expected. Such a watch was kept for the most part in every street. The other watch is particularly appointed for the prevention of fires, and is known by the circumstance of his dragging along the streets a cleft bamboo, or an iron bar, in the upper part of which there is an iron ring that produces a singular and disagreeable sound. At the end of every street, where it can be shut with gates, there is always a high ladder, on which the watch can mount, to see if there be anywhere an appearance of fire. In a great many places are erected, near the houses, store-rooms of stone that are fire-proof, in which merchandize and furniture may be saved. On the sides of these I observed several large iron hooks fixed in the wall, which served to hang wet mats on, and by that means to moderate the force of the fire.

"As the houses are very liable to take fire, conflagrations very often happen in Jeddo which lay waste whole rows of houses and entire streets. During our stay here

* *United States Expedition,* corresponding in every way with the old descriptions in all the details above given.

fires broke out several times, but were very soon extinguished. Our ambassador gave us the history of a terrible fire which happened during his stay here in the month of April, 1772. The fire broke out at twelve o'clock at noon, and lasted till eight in the evening of the following day, insomuch that the devastation made by it extended six leagues in length and three in breadth." These figures must be exaggerated, as the whole city of Jeddo is stated to be about sixteen miles long by twelve in breadth.

The houses of country people and husbandmen consist of four low walls, covered with a thatched or shingled roof, the thatch being often overgrown with a fertile crop of vegetables and grass, the seeds of which have been deposited by vagrant crows. In the back part of the house the floor is somewhat raised, and there is placed the hearth, the rest is covered with neat mats, as in all other houses. Indeed the mat is everything to the Japanese. Upon the mat people sit to take their meals, to sell their wares, to smoke their pipes, to converse with their friends, and lie down at night, without undressing themselves, to go to sleep ; adding, however, a quilted mat for a coverlid, and the equivocal comfort of an oblong lacquered piece of wood, or hard box, for a pillow.

Behind the street-door the rich hang a barred lattice of bamboo, the poor suspend rows of coarse ropes, made of straw, to hide the inmates from passing observation. "As to household goods," says Kämpfer, speaking of the poor country people and husbandmen, "they have but few. Many children and great poverty is generally what they are possessed of; and yet with some small provision of rice, plants, and roots, they live content and happy."

As squatting, not sitting, is almost the invariable practice, there seems no occasion for chairs, although they are sometimes found, and invariably supplied on state occasions. These are, however, clumsy contrivances, with coarse leathern seats, and a framework like that of the common camp-stool, which is readily folded up when not used. At the recent American conferences with the Japanese, the subordinate officers, both American and Japanese, were seated on sedans or benches, covered with red crape, whilst the Commodore and the highest native dignitaries were honoured with stools, which occasionally had the comfortable addition of arms and backs to them.

The national posture of all classes, however, in Japan, when at rest, is crouching, either upon the knees, or on the haunches, with their legs crossed. The latter is common among the lower classes, and is pronounced by the fashionables as decidedly vulgar.

Tables are not generally used, but on the occasion of public entertainments given to the American officers, the narrow red crape-covered benches were appropriated for the spread of the feast, the dishes being raised to the proper height for the guest by means of the ordinary lacquered stands of a foot in height and fourteen inches square. The Japanese eat from these raised trays while squatting on their mats, and the apparently unsocial mode thus obtains of each person taking his food by himself.

Some lacquered cups, bowls, and porcelain vessels, the invariable chopsticks—after the manner of the Chinese—and an occasional earthenware spoon, comprise the ordinary utensils used in eating. They drink their soups directly out of the bowl, as a hungry child—seizing with their chopsticks the pieces of fish which are generally floating in the liquid. Their teakettles, which are always at hand, simmering over the fire in the kitchen, are made of bronze, silver, or fire-proof earthenware.

There are no fireplaces and chimneys in the houses of the Japanese. In the centre of the common sitting-room there is a square hole, built in with tiles and filled with sand, in which a charcoal fire is always kept burning, and suspended above is the teakettle, supported by a tripod. There is thus constantly a supply of hot water for making tea, which is invariably handed to the visitor on his arrival—for the Japanese are moderate eaters, but great drinkers, though generally a sober nation. "*Tem-*

peratè cibum sumunt, largiùs bibunt," said St. Francis
Xavier of them three hundred years ago.*

Their tea is prepared as with us, but very weak, and
not ordinarily sweetened.   The cup is generally of porcelain, with a wooden lacquered cover.

The better houses are warmed, but very imperfectly,
by metal braziers, placed on lacquered stands, containing
burning charcoal, which are moved readily from room to
room, as they may be required. They have, therefore,
much to learn of us in this important matter—the construction of a chimney and the hearth—inventions peculiar
to the western branch of the great and dominant race to
which we belong.

In the cottages of the poor there is but little ventilation, from their small size—no issue for the smoke—
and the burning charcoal in the fixed central fireplace
becomes a great nuisance.   In the more pretentious establishments, where there is plenty of space, and holes in
the roof or in the walls for the escape of smoke, while
the charcoal is not brought in until it is perfectly ignited,
this mode of heating the apartments is more endurable.

It is obvious that the poorer classes must suffer much
from the wintry weather—indeed, we are assured that
they keep much within doors, huddled about their meagre
fires in their hovels, which, without chimneys, and with
but a scant light from the paper windows, are exceedingly
cold, gloomy, and comfortless.   The rich strive to make
themselves comfortable by enveloping their bodies in
numerous warm robes ; but, nevertheless, they constantly
complain of the severity of the weather.

It is by the charcoal fires, in the centre of the sitting-
apartment, where the water for tea is boiled, sundry
small dishes cooked, and their *saki* heated.   The saki is
their ale, an intoxicating liquor, fermented from rice instead of malt : the Americans call it " a sort of whisky."†

* *Epist. Jap.*, 27.
† Whether the western races invented ale for themselves I know
not : certain it is that the ancient Egyptians made and drank it,
using lupines instead of hops for the flavour and the keeping.

In large establishments there is a kitchen besides, where the family cooking is effected; these are generally provided with a stove, like an ordinary French cooking apparatus, in which wood is often burned; but this is an article which they are very economical in using.

Contiguous to the houses they have large fireproof warehouses, used for the storage of valuable goods. They are built with a great deal more care than the ordinary shops and other buildings, and have walls two feet thick, made of dried mud and pebbles, and faced with stone, whilst their roofs are securely constructed of earthen tiles. These warehouses are generally two stories high, the upper one having window-shutters of wood, sheathed with iron. Their exterior is sometimes covered with a coat of fine plaster, which, with their substantial structure, gives them a neatness and solidity of aspect which contrast greatly with the flimsy, stained look of the ordinary houses. They are used for the storage of valuable goods to be protected from fire.*

After what has been previously said, the reader will not be surprised to find that the Japanese consider a garden as indispensable to their comfort—if they can afford it. The love of plants and flowers, like that of dumb animals, is acknowledged to be a good human characteristic; the Japanese are largely endowed with this propensity. If there be not room enough for a garden, they have at least an old engrafted plum-tree, cherry or apricot-tree; and the older, the more crooked and monstrous, the greater value they put upon it. They let the branches grow into the rooms, and make a pet of it fondly. They trim and check it to two or three branches, to make it bear larger flowers—caring nothing for the fruit.

Like many or most of our poor and even well-to-do suburbans, who have not room enough for a garden or trees, they have at least an opening or window, before which they place a flower-pot or two, and a small "tub" of gold and silver fish.

---

* *United States Expedition,* Kämpfer, and others.

A garden of thirty feet square is with us, for the most part, not worth inspection; but the Japanese transform such a space into a very curious panopticon. First, you see the ground covered partly with round stones of different colours, gathered from the rivers or the seashore,

COUNTRY HOUSE.

well-washed and cleaned, and those of the same kind laid together in beds or with gravel, which is swept daily, and neat to admiration; the large stones being laid in the middle as a path to walk on without injuring the gravel— the whole "in a seeming but ingenious confusion." Perhaps you perceive some few flower-bearing shrubs, apparently planted all in confusion, but upon minute examination, you discover that certain rules of contrast in colour or other peculiarities have really made a design of

K

the distribution. In the midst of the clump there is probably a *Saguer,* that is, some outlandish, or scarce, or dwarf tree worthy of observation. Yonder is a small rock, or a hill, made in imitation of nature, curiously adorned with birds and insects cast in brass, and placed between the rock-work; or perhaps it is the model of a temple, built, as it were, on a remarkable eminence, or the brink of a precipice, or in some very pleasant spot—as are all their temples—and a small rivulet is made to gush and run down the stones with a pleasant murmur, all well contrived and proportioned, and in accurate imitation of nature. A small thicket or miniature forest on the side of a hill or mountain startles you with its resemblance to the scenes you have admired at a distance; and yet the gardener has done it all by merely selecting such trees as will grow close together, and planting and cutting them according to their size, nature, and the colour of their leaves and flowers, so as to make the whole very accurately imitate a natural wood or forest. Lastly, there is a cistern or pond stocked with various fishes, surrounded with appropriate plants in equal variety. It need not be mentioned that to effect all this there are professed gardeners in Japan who make a study of their business, and who, by such proficiency, would be invaluable amongst us to make the most of the useless "gardens" said to be attached to our suburban "villas."

Before interminable, useful, and disastrous railroads changed "Merry England" into one huge electric rod or conductor—and thereby decidedly influencing all her inhabitants, physically, and therefore socially and morally —hostelries and inns were indeed something pleasant to think of. We journeyed to enjoy them. Now-a-days we rush to our "destination," as we obey our "destiny"— Heaven only knows how—but certainly comfortless and blindly—seeing nothing but what the eye, however interested, is not permitted to enjoy; hearing nothing but a clatter which makes deafness a blessing. Hostelries and travelling in Japan are a curious study.

In all the chief villages and hamlets you will find a

post-house, which is the monopoly of the lord of the manor.   Here at all times are kept in readiness, at fixed prices, horses, footmen, porters, and norimons—the portable carriage of Japan.   The norimon is, in fact, a small room, of an oblong square figure, big enough for one person conveniently to sit or lie in, curiously platted of fine, thin, split bamboos, sometimes "japanned" and finely painted, with a small folding-door on each side, sometimes a small window before and behind, the roof being covered with varnished paper.   Occasionally it is fitted up for the convenience of sleeping in it during a journey.   It is carried by two, four, eight, or more men, according to the quality of the traveller.   If the traveller be a prince or lord of a province, the porters carry the pole on the palms of their hands ; otherwise they lay it upon their shoulders.   These porters, or norimon-men, are all clad in the same livery, with the coat-of-arms or insignia of their masters—a subject on which more anon.   They are at intervals relieved by others, who, meanwhile, walk by the side of the vehicle.   Of course there is a style in the appointment, according to rank, as amongst ourselves— sumptuous or magnificent, or plain and simple.   *Kango*, or " basket," being the name of the latter : norimon signifying " a place to sit in."   Both sorts, however, vary by such insensible degrees, from the plainest to the most curious, that a fine kango can scarcely be distinguished from a plain and simple norimon, except by the pole—the pole of the former being massy and uniform, whilst that of the latter is larger, curiously adorned, and hollow— being formed of four thin boards, neatly joined together in the form of a wide arch, and much lighter than it appears to be.   Princes and great lords show their rank and nobility in other respects, but especially by the length and width of the poles of their norimons.   As amongst us, snobs and upstarts affect " a grand set out," and elongate their poles preposterously ; but then Japanese custom and prescription may be set in motion against the " swell"—the magistrate, if called upon, will enforce the abbreviation of the pole—not without a severe reprimand, and perhaps considerable punishment in the bargain. As the punishment is left to the discretion of the magistrate, perhaps the least he would do would be to place one of the porters within the vehicle, and make the pretender tackle to the pole, or condemn him to use a kango. These are not unlike a basket with a round bottom and flat roof. They are used for carrying travellers over rocks and mountains which are not easily passed on horseback. Three men are appointed for every kango, and they have enough to do.*

The nature of the country does not admit of other vehicles for general use. Loads are sometimes conveyed on cars, but oftener on the backs of men, horses, and oxen. It is only in the environs of Meako and a few other places that such cars or carts are seen; they have only three wheels, two behind and one before, which probably suggested our Bath or invalid chairs, latterly imitated by the "perambulator," which is voted a nuisance by "the public," but found to be extremely convenient to nursemaids. Some of these carts have but two wheels; and, for the preservation of the roads, they must travel only on the lower part of the thoroughfare; and to prevent all "stoppages," they must start in the morning and return during the afternoon. The princes and most distinguished people have carriages which resemble our old-fashioned ones, and were introduced into Japan by the Dutch. They are often drawn by horses, but for the most part by oxen.

The Japanese mode of using the horse is very singular. In the first place, like the porters, he is shod with straw-slippers instead of iron. These horse-shoes are merely twisted straw, provided with ropes, likewise of straw, to tie them about the horse's feet. Of course they are soon worn out on the stony and slippery roads, and must often be changed for new ones. For this purpose, the men that look after the horses always carry a competent stock of such shoes tied to the baggage. Poor children on the

* Kämpfer.

road, however, offer them for sale, a mode of begging
which has its correspondences in our own country.
Kämpfer ventures a piece of wit anent this matter :—
" Hence," says he, " it may be said that this country hath
more farriers than perhaps any other, though in fact it
hath none at all."

The saddle is of wood, very plain, with a cushion
underneath, and a caparison behind, lying upon the horse's
back, with the traveller's coat of arms stitched upon it.
Another piece of cloth hangs down on each side, as a
safeguard to the horse, to keep it from being daubed with
dirt, both pieces being tied together loosely under the
horse's belly.   The head is covered with a network of
small strings to defend it, particularly its eyes, from the
flies, which seem to be as troublesome in Japan as in
England.   The neck, breast, and other parts are hung
with small bells.   The saddle, not unlike the Swedish
pack-saddle, is girded on the horse with a poitral or
breast-leather, and has a crupper.   As two pormanteaus
must be carried, there are latchets on each side of the
saddle to secure them, or rather, the trunks are tied
together and flung on the horse's back, one on each side,
both being further secured by means of an *adofski*, that
is, a long box or trunk laid over them, and tied to the
saddle with thongs.   Over the whole they spread a
covering, or rather bedding, with broad sashes, the middle
cavity being filled with some soft stuff, as the traveller's
seat, where he sits, as it were upon a table, tailor-fashion,
cross-legged, or extending his continuations along the
horse's neck, just as he pleases or finds most convenient.
Of course, under such circumstances, the rider must sit
right in the middle, and not lean too much on either side,
which would either upset the horse or himself and his
baggage ; in going up-hill or down, the footmen and
grooms support the trunks for fear of an accident.

The Japanese mode of mounting a horse is peculiar.
The rider mounts and alights, not on one side, after our
fashion, but by the horse's breast, a mode which is said
to be very troublesome for stiff legs ; indeed one cannot

form an adequate notion of the feat at all. The Japanese
say that their object in thus mounting is to do honour to
the noble animal. Truly he is one of the best friends of
man, and the worst used ; but if he be selfish like ourselves, he has the consolation to see, if he can observe,
that man treats man, his human horse, quite as badly.
The horses are unsaddled and unladen in an instant ;
having removed the upper covering, they need only untie
a latchet or two, at which they are very expert, and the
whole baggage falls down at once. The latchets, thongs,
and girths are all broad and strong, made of cotton, and
very neatly worked, with small oblong cylindrical pieces
of wood at both ends, which are of great use to strain
the latchets and tie the load securely.

The Japanese traveller wears very wide breeches,
tapering towards the end, and slit on both sides to tuck
in the ends of their large long gowns, which would otherwise be troublesome in walking and riding. Some wear
a short coat or cloak over the breeches. Instead of
stockings they tie a broad ribbon round their legs. Ordinary servants, the norimen-bearers and pikemen, wear
no breeches, and tuck their gowns up to their belt,
thereby exposing their naked bodies, which they say
they have no reason to be ashamed of.

A Japanese on horseback, tucked up after this fashion,
makes a very comical figure at a distance. He is naturally short and thick ; but when he gets on his large hat,
wide breeches and cloak, and perches cross-legged on his
seat, he appears broader than long.

Upon the road they ride one by one. Merchants have
their horses, with their heavy baggage packed up in two
or three bales, led before them. As to the bridle, the
traveller has nothing to do with that ; the horse is led
by one of his footmen, who walks at the horse's right
side, close to the head, and together with his companions
sings some merry songs to divert themselves and to ani-
mate the horses.

Our European mode of sitting on horseback and holding
the bridle is, they say, warlike, and properly becoming a

soldier, and therefore unfit for travelling—for this reason they seldom or never use it in their journeys. It is more frequent among persons of quality in cities, when they go on a visit. But even then the rider—who makes but a sorry figure when sitting after our manner—holds the bridle merely for form, the horse being still led by one, and sometimes two footmen, who walk on each side of the horse's head, holding it by the bit.* Their saddles on such occasions resemble those of the Germans more closely than those of any Asiatic nation. A broad round leather flap hangs down on both sides, after the fashion of the Tartars, to defend the legs. The stirrup (*abumi*) is made of iron or *sowa* (sappan wood), very thick and heavy, not unlike the sole of a foot, and open on one side, in order that the rider may get his foot loose easily, in case of a fall, commonly of an exceedingly neat workmanship, and inlaid with silver. The stirrup-leathers are very short, and the reins (*tasuna*) are not of leather, but of silk.†

Golownin says—" We once saw the governor of Matsmai ride on horseback to a temple, where thanksgivings were to be celebrated, and where he must go once every year in spring. The high priest, the priests and officials, and officers who were obliged to be present, were gone there before. He rode alone, without ceremony ; a small train attended him on foot. To the horse's bit there was fastened, instead of the bridle, two light blue girdles, which two grooms held fast on each side of the horse's mouth ; the two ends of these girdles were held by two

---

* This is not unlike the style of riding now in fashion among the fat and dignified pashas and effendis of the Ottoman Empire, where equestrianism and every other manly exercise or manly virtue seems dying out. The horse of the pasha is not led ; the great man holds the reins himself, but two grooms walk on foot at the horse's head, while two other grooms, one on each side, walk on a line with the stirrup-irons, to prop up his greatness, by catching him under the arm-pits, in case the horse should fall or stumble,—no uncommon event where the roads are execrable, and good horses an exceeding great rarity.—MacFarlane, *Japan.*

† Kämpfer, Thunberg, Titsingh, *var. loc.*

other grooms, who went at a little distance from the others ; so that these four men occupied almost the whole road.   The tail of the horse was covered with a light silk bag.   The governor, dressed in his usual clothes, in which we had often seen him, sat without his hat, upon a magnificent saddle, and held his feet in wooden japanned stirrups, which resembled little boxes.   The grooms who

AN EQUESTRIAN PARTY.

held the horse at the bit continually cried, "*Chai, chai,*" that is, softly, softly ; however, they pushed on the horse, and made it jump and go quick ; the governor, therefore, stooped, and held fast to the saddle with both hands.   At a short distance before him went some soldiers in a row, with two sergeants, and though nobody was in the way, they continually cried, 'Make room ! make room !'   Behind the governor followed the armour-bearers, who carried all the insignia of his dignity in japan cases. This was to signify that the governor was *incognito.*" *

Incognito or not, this certainly looks very much like a decay in the noble art of horsemanship. Perhaps, however, it may be found that gentlemen, remote from court and great cities, and not puffed up with the pride of office, may still delight in the saddle, and ride like men, instead of being carried like bales of silk or satin. It is to be hoped that such may really prove to be the fact ; for no nation that is not equestrian can pretend to be a nation of gentlemen, which is the proud claim of the Japanese.

The Japanese never go out without fans in their hands ; these correspond to gloves amongst Europeans, being in constant requisition. No respectable man goes without his fan, not even the soldiers. These fans are a foot long, and sometimes serve as parasols, at others as memorandum-books ; they are adorned with paintings of landscapes, birds, flowers, or nicely-turned sentences. The etiquette to be observed with regard to the use of the fan requires profound study and close attention. At feasts and on ceremonial occasions, the fan is stuck in the girdle, on the left hand, behind the sword, with the handle downward. Their travelling-fan has the map of the road printed upon it, indicating the number of miles, the inns on the route, and the prices of refreshments. Still they have road-books, hawked about by poor children begging along the road. The Dutch are not permitted to buy any of these fans—at least publicly.

The traveller's cloak is made of double-varnished oiled paper, and large enough to cover and shelter at once man, horse, and baggage from the rain. Kämpfer supposed that the Japanese learned the use of a cloak from the Portuguese, the name being *kappa* ; but this seems improbable, although he might have heard that name given to it. They have two names for cloak—*hawori* and *toi,*

* *Recollections of Japan.*

the latter being applied to the cloak in question. It is probably made of the same paper which is used as a handkerchief (*te-no-goi*) for blowing their noses withal, of which they have two sorts—common nose-paper (*fanaganni*) and large nose-paper (*sitkusumi*).

To shade them from the sun they have a large hat (*kasa*), made of split bamboos or straw, very neatly and artfully twisted, in form an extensive Spanish sombrero or an umbrella. It is tied under the chin with broad silk bands, lined with cotton. It is transparent and exceedingly light, and yet after one wetting it becomes perfectly waterproof. The women in cities and villages wear such hats at all times and in all weathers, and it is said they are not unbecoming ; doubtless they will one day become fashionable at our watering-places, at least; and, still more than the recent very pretty style so fascinating, add to the thousand charms of our naiads and hamadryads—waternymphs and wood-nymphs wild, in their innocent simplicity—fancy free.

JAPANESE MERCHANT.

CHAPTER IV.

A JOURNEY BY LAND AND WATER FROM NAGASAKI TO JEDDO.
INCIDENTS OF TRAVEL IN JAPAN.

I.

DOUBTLESS the time will come when the great Magician of Egyptian Hall will fling himself amongst "the Sons of the Sun," and return to us with a budget of facts and scraps—as now he cometh with John Chinaman in his pocket. Meanwhile, hoping for better things, we must do our best, borrowing the eyes and ears of old Dr. Kämpfer,

Dr. Thunberg, Captain Golownin, Heer Izaak Titsingh, Siebold ; in fact, of all who have visited or described these fortunate isles—all who have seen and admired this wonderful nation.

We set sail in the good ship *De Toren van Babel* from Batavia, in the island of Java—for there is no direct commercial intercourse between Holland and Japan. After a voyage of some five or six weeks, touching at the other Dutch settlements by the way, we neared the coast of Japan, making for the port of Nagasaki.

As we drew close to the land we were not long before we became impressed with the peculiarities, physical and moral, of the unknown country to which we were bound. The first aspect of both is unprepossessing. The rocks and reefs that render so large a part of the coast inaccessible, and the frequent fogs that obscure, and storms that sweep, the neighbouring seas—making these rocks formidable even to the experienced mariner—are hardly more inhospitable than the offensive precautionary rules to which the ship and every individual on board are subjected, ere permission can be obtained to anchor in the Bay of Nagasaki.

It may be a question whether in this life we oftener suffer or profit by the misfortunes of others. On the present occasion the wreck of a Japanese junk turned out greatly to our advantage. Unable to carry the smallest sail, she was driving before the wind further and further from land. We lay to, and, stiff as was the gale, high as was the sea, lowered a boat to offer our assistance to the unfortunate crew in their desperate situation. The Japanese received us as their deliverers ; and seeing the impossibility of making the land in their dismasted, leaky vessel, resolved to leave it for our ship.

It may seem that, under such circumstances, no great deliberation as to adopting the means of escape tendered could be requisite; but when we reflect on the inexorable stringency of the laws of the land against all contact with foreigners, and the life-and-death responsibility weighing upon the officers and constituted authorities, we must wonder that any degree of danger could induce a Japanese sailor to quit his own vessel and seek safety on board a foreigner.

Meanwhile the *Onderneming* had rejoined us, and her gallant captain, Lelsz, also hastened with his boat to the rescue. The Japanese sailors, twenty-four in number, were divided between the two boats. Some provisions—as rice, salt pork, saki—their beer, and the only fermented liquor in Japan—tobacco, as well as arms and clothes, were taken out, and the wreck was abandoned, after being scuttled at the urgent prayer of her crew. Their crime would have been unpardonable, had their deserted bark by any chance drifted to the coast of Japan. She must sink, in order to palliate, in some measure, the step which the unfortunate men had hazarded for safety.

In highly excited expectation we stood on the deck, watching our stout sailors as they battled with the mountain-billows. The boat was soon rowed to our side ; and curiously did we gaze at the strange guests as they successively appeared on deck. They greeted us courteously, but stood amazed ; and, sailor-like, they first admired the ship that had braved a storm so fatal to their own.

They were the first Japanese we had seen, and greatly were we struck with their staid appearance and modest behaviour. Their dress, arms, implements—in short, all they brought on board—drew our attention, and we were soon engaged in pantomimic conversation with reference to their position. They were indeed tranquillized, and the unhoped-for change in their condition seemed gratifying to them ; but the frighttul images of past danger, and traces of long days of painful exertion, still spoke distinctly in their features. Their neglected dress, their whole carriage, all bore the stamp of the despair whence they had so unexpectedly escaped.

They were, however, quickly reconciled to their lot, seemed to relish their *saki* and tobacco, and chatted away with great animation. They spread their mats on the deck, each fetched his box, and a scene new to us began ;

namely, a Japanese toilet.   Nothing can exceed the dexterity with which a Japanese shaves his own head.   The
Japanese shaves his beard and the crown of his head,
omitting so to do only in misfortune—as captivity, death
of friends, and the like.   In the appropriate coiffure of
the Japanese, the newly-washed bristly hair left round
the shaven crown gives him a wild aspect, which had here
passed into the comic, every individual having cut off his
tuft of hair as a sacrifice to his patron divinity, in acknowledgment of his deliverance from imminent danger—a
Japanese seaman's vow.   Cleanly dressed, they now
walked the deck, and seemed transported to a new world.
Every object awakened their curiosity, and offered matter
for conversation.

The wreck proved to be a vessel belonging to the
Prince of Satzuma, employed in the trade with the
Loo-Choo Islands, dependencies of the Japanese empire,
but more especially of his principality.   It may here be
observed, that the danger of their deserted wrecks floating home was not the only one against which the impe-
rilled mariners had to guard in accepting foreign assistance.   Had the Dutch been bound elsewhere than to
Nagasaki, the involuntary absence of the Japanese from
home could hardly have been so short as not to subject
them to imprisonment, and a severe judicial examination
before they could be allowed to resume their station, low
as it might be, amongst their countrymen ; whilst anything of a distant voyage would have inevitaby incurred
the absolute forfeiture of all their rights as natives of the
empire.   Another incident of the same nature will still
more forcibly illustrate the stringent system of the Japanese government, in this matter of absolute interdic-
tion to foreign contact in any way whatever.

About seventy-eight years ago, a Japanese vessel was
wrecked on one of the Aleutian Islands belonging to
Russia ; the crew were saved and conveyed to Irkutzk,
where they were detained about ten years, well treated,
and instructed in the Russian language, by order of the
great Empress Catherine.   On sending these Japanese

back to their native country, Catherine directed the governor of Siberia to endeavour to establish such friendly
relations as might tend to the mutual benefit of both
countries. For this purpose he was directed to despatch
an envoy, in his own name, with credentials and suitable
presents, taking especial care to employ no Englishman
or Dutchman. The governor of Siberia fixed upon a
lieutenant named Laxman, who, embarking in the *Catherine* transport, sailed from Okotzk in the autumn of
1792. Laxman soon made a harbour or bay on the
northern coast of the Japanese island of Matsmai, where
he passed the winter. In the following summer he went
round to the southern coast of the same island, and entered the harbour of Chakodade, still having with him
the natives whom the Russians had rescued from
shipwreck. The officers of the Japanese government were
exceedingly courteous; but all that Laxman could obtain from them was a declaration in writing to the following effect :—

" 1. That although their laws inflict perpetual imprisonment on every stranger landing in any part of the
Japanese empire, the harbour of Nagasaki excepted, yet,
in consideration of the ignorance of these laws, pleaded
by the Russians, and of their having saved the lives of
several Japanese subjects, they are willing to waive the
strict enforcement of them in the present instance, provided Lieutenant Laxman will promise, for himself and
his countrymen, to return immediately to his own country, and never again to approach any part of the coast,
but the harbour aforesaid.

" 2. That the Japanese government thanks the Russians
for the care taken of its subjects ; but at the same time
informs them, that they may either leave them or carry
them back again, as they think fit, as the Japanese consider all men to belong to whatever country their destiny
may carry them, and where their lives may have been
protected."

During his stay, Laxman had been treated with the
greatest civility ; at his departure he was provided, with-

out charge, with everything he wanted, and was finally dismissed with presents.

"On approaching the port of Nagasaki, being about to set foot for the first time upon the prohibited shores of Japan, our excitement was raised to the highest pitch, as we gazed in unspeakable admiration at the lovely panorama spread before us. Hills clothed with fresh green, and cultivated to the very summit, adorn the foreground, behind which arise blue mountain-peaks in sharp outlines. Dark rocks here and there break the crystal surface of the sea, and the precipitous wall of the adjacent coast glittered with ever-changing hues in the bright beams of the morning sun. The mountain side of the nearest island, cultivated in terraces; tall cedars, amongst which white houses shone, and insulated temple roofs jutted magnificently forth, with numerous dwellings and huts bordering the strand and the shores of the bay, gave delight to the eye, and filled the mind with admiration.

"We did not neglect the opportunity of obtaining information and explanations from our Japanese guests, and learned with surprise that the pretty houses which we had taken for the mansions of grandees, were nothing but storehouses, warehouses, the walls of which are coated, as a precaution against fire, with mortar prepared from shell-chalk.

"Sailing vessels and fishing boats enlivened the mouth of the bay. At the call of our Japanese guests, many fishermen approached and offered us their fish, with a liberality and affability truly astonishing in their rank of life. They were most friendly, and evidently enjoyed presenting to us and their rescued countrymen the fruit of their toil. They refused gold and gifts of value, but begged some empty wine bottles. Common green glass bottles are much prized in Japan. Bottle-blowing seems one of the few arts and trades which they have as yet to learn from Europeans. These fishermen were as nearly naked as was compatible with decency.

"It is here, without the mouth of Nagasaki Bay, that the annoyances resulting from Japanese law and Japanese suspicion begin to try the patience of the traveller. Guards, stationed on the coast, keep a constant look-out for ships, and as soon as the approach of one is reported at Nagasaki, a boat is despatched thence to demand her name, country, equipage, and every other necessary particular.

" The business of interrogation is accomplished without the exchange of a word or any personal intercourse, by papers drawn up from the boat, and returned, after inserting the proper answers. This done, the ship must wait for further orders where she is, on pain of being considered and treated as an enemy.

" We occupied the interval in packing up bibles, prayer-books, pictures or prints representing sacred subjects—in short, everything connected with Christianity, and our money in a chest, which was duly locked and sealed. Indeed, it should seem that latterly all books had to be locked up, since certain missionaries in China piously smuggled into Japan Christian tracts and religious engravings.

" When the Governor of Nagasaki received the answers, a boat was again sent to demand hostages, and when these were delivered and conveyed to their destined temporary abode, a Japanese deputation, headed by a police officer of the highest rank, called a *gobanyosi*, and accompanied, at the express request of the Governor of Nagasaki, by one or two members of the Dutch factory, visited the ship, in order finally to ascertain that she was one of the two lawful, annual merchantmen. Should the ship, at any stage of the proceedings, prove to be an interloper, she is at once ordered to depart ; if in distress of any kind, she is supplied with whatever she may need, and that gratuitously, the more strongly to mark the determination to suffer no trade ; but she is not permitted to enter the bay, or to hold any communication with the shore, beyond asking for and receiving the necessaries of which she is in want.

" On the present occasion the investigation proved satisfactory, the Dutchmen returned home, the gobanyosi took possession of the guns, arms of all kinds, ammunition, &c., which, together with the chest containing religious objects, he removed to an appointed place on shore, where they remain in deposit during the stay of the ship, to be restored at her departure. On board ship the same official placed a seal on the ship's sails, and sent away the rudder." During this part of the proceedings the officials conducted themselves with considerable disdain towards our sailors, and even the ship's officers ; they used the stick, and struck them as dogs.*

Dr. Siebold, who was on board, said the Japanese

---

* Van Diemen, writing in 1642. Jacigny gives a curious note on this incident. "Certainly Kämpfer had reason to exclaim at the abject submission of the Dutch in their commercial relations with the Japanese,

> Quid non mortalia pectora cogis
> Auri sacra fames !

> Oh thirst of gold ! what dost thou not compel
> The soul of man to bear !

But the Dutch are not the only people who have preferred, in the same circumstances, the interests of commerce to their honour. And without going further to seek examples in past ages, or amongst fallen nations, have we not seen the English, that nation so haughty and so powerful, opposing for so many years but timid and respectful representations to the insults and humiliations of all kinds with which the Chinese rabble (canaille), titled or not titled, drenched them at Canton ? Was it not on the 1st of February, 1835, that Captain Elliot (then third commissioner (surintendant) of the English trade at Canton) the bearer of a written remonstrance to the Chinese authorities, a just and moderate remonstrance, if ever there was one, suffered himself to be collared, thrown violently on the ground, insulted with impunity, both by words and gesture, by the vilest soldiery at the gate Yiulam? This, we repeat it, took place on the 1st of February, 1835, and it was only at the end of 1839 that the English Government felt the necessity to exact by force reparation for the past and guarantees for the future. Read the correspondence of the English agents in China with the ministry, published by order of Parliament, and judge for yourself! Foreign commerce is doubtless useful, an inevitable result of the development of civilization ; but we must confess that the history of this commerce seems too often to justify that contempt which the higher classes of the population profess (at least in the farthest East, and chiefly in China and Japan) for the mercantile spirit and ignoble avidity of European speculators."—*Japon*, &c., 33.

interpreters spoke better Dutch than himself, and immediately declared their disbelief of his being a native of Holland ; but, as various accents and dialects prevail in the different districts of Japan, he got over the difficulty by stating that he was a Yamma Hollander, or Dutch mountaineer ; literally, a Dutch mountain. Similar mistrust had been excited in the last century by the accent of the Swede Thunberg.

Our shipwrecked Japanese sailors had to undergo a long and careful examination, to justify the suspicious and illegal step of going on board a foreign ship. This also proved satisfactory, and the vessel being declared spiritually and physically innoxious by the removal of her bibles and her guns, was towed by Japanese boats into the inner harbour, and led to her regular anchorage.

The bay became more animated as we approached the town, and presented on both sides the most delightful variety of objects. How inviting are the shores, with their cheerful dwellings ! What fruitful hills ; what majestic temple-groves ! How picturesque those green mountain-tops, with their volcanic formation ! How luxuriantly do those evergreen oaks, cedars, and laurels clothe the declivity ! What activity, what industry, does nature, thus tamed as it were by the hand of man, proclaim ! As witness those precipitous walls of rock, at whose feet corn-fields and cabbage-gardens are won in terraces from the steep ; witness the coast, where Cyclopean bulwarks set bounds to the arbitrary caprice of a hostile element !

A superior police-officer is now stationed at Desima (the Dutch residence adjoining Nagasaki), to watch the unloading and subsequent loading of the vessel, towards which not a step may be taken except under his immediate superintendence. Nay, not a soul is permitted to land without undergoing a personal search in this officer's presence ; a new chief or president (*opperhoofd*) of the factory being the only individual exempt from this annoyance.

This offensive custom originated probably in the

stratagem long employed to facilitate the immoderate smuggling carried on. We were told, that formerly every captain of the annual ships was wont, whilst the bibles and other things were in process of packing, to clothe himself in loose attire, which was made to fit him in external appearance, by internal waddings. Thus enlarged, he presented himself to the visiting Japanese officers. When about to land, he exchanged his waddings for the contraband articles intended to be introduced, wore his waddings during his stay, and repeated the former operation prior to re-embarking for departure.

This practice has now been rendered impossible; but it seems that, in spite of Japanese suspicion and vigilance, other modes of introducing and bringing off prohibited goods have been adopted, since all the members of the factory agree that such prohibited goods are brought on shore, and secretly sold or bartered for such Japanese wares as the Dutch wish, but are forbidden to acquire. Of these last, many specimens are even now extant, in proof of the fact that they can still be exported, as well as purchased, in the Royal Museum at the Hague; whilst the possibility of introducing prohibited articles into Desima, at least, further appears from President Doeff's statement—that the factory have bibles and psalm-books, the possession of which, President Meylan observes, is now connived at. It may, perhaps, be inferred that the Japanese dread of Christianity has very much subsided during the long period that has elapsed since the last missionary endeavours to convert the empire.*

But to return to the annoyances connected with landing. The indispensable necessity of searching the persons of new comers, as well as the inexorable rigidity of the Japanese system of exclusion, may be illustrated by an incident that could hardly have occurred elsewhere. It appears that, in the year 1817, Doeff's successor in the presidentship of the factory, Heer Blomhoff, threw the whole town of Nagasaki, population and government,

---

* *Manners and Customs of the Japanese.*

into consternation, by bringing with him, not an armed force, but his young wife, their new-born babe, and a Javanese nurse—a contravention of Japanese law, the heinousness of which was enhanced by its having been imitated; inasmuch as the mate of the ship had likewise brought his wife with him, less criminally, indeed, than Heer Blomhoff, the mate intending to take his family away again when the vessel sailed, whilst the new head of the factory meditated the atrocious offence of obtruding his wife, child, and nurse upon Nagasaki, or at least upon Desima, during all the years of his presidentship.

The governor at once objected to the lady's even landing. Heer Doeff, kindly desirous to procure for his successor—perhaps for all future opperhoofds or presidents, and the whole factory—the solace of virtuous female and domestic society, entered into a negotiation upon the subject, the course and issue of which he thus narrates :—

" I appealed to the precedent of 1662, when the Chinese pirate, Coxinga, having taken Formosa from the Dutch, as many women and children as fled thence to Japan were admitted into Desima; and I solicited the self-same favour now. The governor replied that the cases were not alike; that, on the occasion cited, the women had come *through necessity*, as fugitives—but now, *by choice*. In the first case, the Japanese could not refuse an asylum to a friendly nation, the second was altogether different. He promised, however, to submit my request to the Court at Jeddo, and to allege the precedent in question in its support. Meanwhile, Mevrow Blomhoff was allowed provisionally to land at Desima, with her child and servant, there to await an answer. Still a great difficulty remained. No one who sets foot in Japan is exempt from an examination of his whole person—the opperhoofd alone excepted; the governor himself has no power to dispense with this search. I took it upon myself, nevertheless, to arrange this affair in regard to the women, as well as with the superintending *gobanyosi* on board, as on shore, at Desima; and, although the examination could not be omitted, it was managed with the utmost forbearance and decency. . . . .

"After an interval of two months, the answer to Heer Blomhoff's petition, for leave to keep his wife and child with him, came ; it was a refusal. The husband was naturally much dissatisfied and dejected, but all our efforts to soften this determination were vain ; against the presumed decision of the Emperor, the Governor durst not offer any fresh remonstrance or representation. This severity of exclusion was not directed expressly against all Hollanders, or even foreign *women*, but against all persons who are not *positively necessary to carrying on the trade*. The general principle of the Japanese is, that no one must enter their country *without cause*, so that not even to a Dutchman is access allowed, unless he belongs to the ship's crew, or to the counting-house. Thus when, in 1804, Captain van Pabst, a military officer, accompanied his friend, Captain Musquetier, of the *Gesina Antoinetta*, from Batavia to Japan, being entered on the ship's muster-roll as ' passenger,' we were obliged, in spite of all I could say against it, to enter him on *our* muster-roll as ' clerk,' or ' mate ' (I forget which), before he could come ashore. The amiable character of Heer van Pabst caused his presence to be winked at ; yet might he not bear the name of ' passenger.'

"It may easily be imagined how affecting was the parting of the wedded pair, now condemned to a long separation. On the 2nd of December, Heer Blomhoff conducted his wife, child, and nursemaid on board the good ship *Vrouw Agatha*, in which I was to return with them to Batavia."

The first Japanese whom we saw impressed us favourably. They have all the organic characteristics of Mongol or Tartar conformation, the obliquity of the eye included ; but they are manifestly a superior race in every human endowment. They have greater energy, are more muscular, and decidedly more intellectual than any other nation referred exclusively to that type of mankind. They are generally well-made, strong, alert, and fresh-coloured—

at least amongst the higher classes—and the young of both sexes are smooth-faced, rosy, and graced with an abundance of fine black hair. We were particularly struck with the beauty of the young women. The gait of both sexes is awkward, and that of the women particularly so, in consequence of their bandaging their hips so tightly as to turn their feet inwards.

The ordinary dress of both sexes and all ranks is in form very similar, differing chiefly in the colours, delicacy, and value of the materials. It consists of a number of loose, wide gowns, worn over each other—those of the lower orders made of linen or calico, those of the higher generally of silk—with the family arms woven or worked into the back and breast of the outer robe; and all fastened at the waist by a girdle. The sleeves are enormous in width and length, and the portion that hangs below the arm is closed at the end, to answer the purpose of a pocket, subsidiary, however, to the capacious bosoms of the gowns, and to the girdles, where more valuable articles are deposited; amongst these are, whilst clean, neat squares of white paper, the Japanese substitutes for pocket-handkerchiefs, which, when used, are dropped into the sleeve, until an opportunity offers of throwing them away, without soiling the house. This description applies to both sexes, but the ladies usually wear brighter colours than the men, and border their robes with gay embroidery or gold. Gentlemen wear a scarf over the shoulders; its length is regulated by the rank of the wearer, and serves in turn to regulate the bow with which they greet each other, inasmuch as it is indispensable to bow to a superior until the ends of the scarf touch the ground.

To this, upon occasions of full dress, is superadded what is called the garb of ceremony.* It consists of a frock (*kamisamo*) generally of a blue stuff, with white flowers, about half the length of the gown, and made much in the same way, but carried on each side back over the shoulder, so as to give a very broad-shouldered

---

* *Manners and Customs of the Japanese.*

appearance to the wearer. With this frock is worn by
the higher classes a very peculiar sort of trousers, called
hakkama, which may be called an immensely full-plaited
petticoat sewed up between the legs, and left sufficiently
open on the outside to admit of free locomotion.

The difference of rank signalized by these petticoat-
trousers is only apparent on occasions of ceremony : the
constant criterion turns upon the wearing of swords.
The higher orders wear two swords, the next in rank
wear one ; and, whether two or one, the swords are never
by any chance laid aside.   To the lower orders it is strictly
forbidden. These swords, or rather sword and dirk, are
called respectively *ken* and *kattan*—the latter being used
in their self-disembowelling operation, or ".happy dispatch."

All their gowns are fastened about the waist by a belt,
which for the men is about the breadth of a hand, and
for the women of twelve inches, and of such length as to
go twice round the body, with a large knot or rose.   The
knot worn by the fair sex, which is larger than that worn
by the men, shows immediately whether the woman is
married or not, as the married women wear the knot
before, and the single behind.   The men fasten to this
belt their swords, fan, tobacco-pipe and pouch.   The
swords are stuck into the belt on the left side, a little
cross-wise, and with the edge turned upwards.   When
a person is seated, the longer sword is taken from the belt
and laid on the mat beside him.*

Young girls have the sleeves of their gowns so long as
frequently to reach quite down to the ground.   I may
remark that, on account of the width of their garments,
the Japanese are soon dressed and undressed, as they have
nothing more to do than to untie their girdle and draw
in their arms, when the whole of their dress instantly
falls off of itself.   The gowns serve also for bed-clothes.

---

* Thunberg notices an odd mistake by the engravers, in Kämpfer's
History of Japan, in representing the Japanese as wearing their
swords as we do, edge downward—their custom being just the
reverse, edge upwards.   The swords were left in the cabin, on board
the American ship.

The common people, when at work, are frequently seen naked, with only a girdle about them, or with their gowns taken off the upper part of their bodies, and hanging down loose from the girdles. All the gowns, of all classes and both sexes, are rounded off about the neck, without a cape, open before, and show the bare bosom, which is never covered, either with a kerchief or anything else.

Within doors, socks are the only covering of the feet. Abroad, shoes are worn, but of the most inconceivably inconvenient kind. They are little more than soles of straw, matting, or wood, mainly kept on by an upright pin or button, held between the two principal toes, which, for this purpose, project through an appropriate aperture in the socks, or by a horn ring. The impossibility of lifting a foot thus shoed in walking, may amply account for the awkward gait ascribed to the Japanese. Upon entering any house, these shoes are taken off.

The head-dress constitutes the chief difference, in point of costume, between the sexes. The men shave the whole front and crown of the head; the rest of the hair, growing from the temples and back of the head, is carefully gathered together, drawn upwards and forwards, and so tied as to form a sort of tuft on the bald skull. Some professions, however, deviate from this general fashion; Buddhist priests and physicians shaving off all the hair, while surgeons retain all theirs, gathered into a knot at the top of the head.

The abundant hair of the women is arranged into the form of a turban, and stuck full of pieces of lacquered wood, or fine tortoiseshell, fifteen inches long, of the thickness of a man's finger, highly wrought, and polished to look like gold. They are extremely costly; and the more of them project from a lady's hair, the better she is dressed. They wear no jewellery or other trinkets. Vanity has not suggested to them the use of rings or other ornaments for the ears. Women who are separated from their husbands shave the head like men. We saw one of the sort at Jeddo, and she made with her bald pate a droll and singular appearance. They wear flowers in their hair

instead of pearls and diamonds, which they do not value
for their own use in Japan.   Sometimes the hair stands
out like wings, and thus distinguishes single women and
servant-maids from the married.* The face is painted red
and white, to the utter destruction of the complexion;
the lips purple, with a golden glow; in addition to this,
the teeth of a Japanese married lady are blackened and
her eyebrows extirpated.

Neither men nor women wear hats, except as a protection against rain : the fan is deemed a sufficient guard
from the sun; and, perhaps, nothing will more strike the
newly-arrived European than this fan, which he will
behold in the hand or the girdle of every human being.
Soldiers and priests are no more to be seen without their
fans than fine ladies, who make of theirs the use to which
fans are put in other countries.   Amongst the men of
Japan, it serves a great variety of purposes; visitors
receive the dainties offered them upon their fans; the
beggar, imploring charity, holds out his fan, for the alms
his prayers may have obtained.   The fan serves the dandy
in lieu of a whalebone switch ; the pedagogue instead of a
ferule for the offending schoolboy's knuckles; and, not to
dwell too long upon the subject, a fan, presented upon a
peculiar kind of salver to the high-born criminal, is said
to be the form of announcing his death-doom : his head is
struck off at the same moment as he stretches it towards
the fan.†

It may be readily imagined that we were but too glad
to be allowed to escape from our prison-house of Desima.

When the Japanese Government began to entertain
jealousy and dislike of foreigners, the first measure they
took, at the instigation of those feelings, was so to situate
them as that they could be conveniently watched.   Na-·
gasaki and Firando were the two ports thus circumscribed
to the Portuguese and the Dutch respectively.   But the
Portuguese were greater objects of suspicion, required

* Thunberg.   Charlevoix says the ladies wear pearls on the
hair-pin.
† Siebold, Thunberg, *Manners and Customs*, Jancigny, &c.

closer watching to be kept always in sight. And so they built for them the prison of Desima*—raised an island from the bottom of the sea, or added to a previous islet. The Emperor's pleasure being asked as to the form of the future island, he significantly unfolded the ever actively-employed *fan*—the fan which is always before their eyes and in their hands—and, accordingly, in the shape of a fan, without the sticks upon which a fan is mounted, was the island constructed. When the Portuguese were finally expelled, the Dutch were transferred from Firando to their prison-house.

Distant but a few yards from the pleasant town of Nagasaki, we were utterly secluded from the busy hum of men. The stone-bridge which connects Desima with the town is indeed "a Bridge of Sighs" to the traveller; a high wall prevents the dwellers on either side from seeing each other. We had the fine view of the bay, teeming with life and bustle, but the view was a distant one only; no Japanese boat being permitted to approach the island within a certain prescribed distance, marked by a stockade.†

For upwards of a century the Dutch head of the factory at Desima repaired annually, with a large retinue of Dutch as well as Japanese, to Jeddo, and offered his tribute and his homage at the foot of the throne; but gradually the trade between Japan and Batavia fell off, and these annual journeys were felt to be burthensome. Since the year 1790 they have been limited to every fourth year.

But the presents of the Dutch being esteemed of more value than their homage, were not so easily dispensed with; and these are duly transmitted during the three intermediate years by means of the interpreters at a

* See p. 17 of this work.

† The word *Desima* is variously written in all the books. It is derived from *de* "fore," (*ante*) and *dzima* or *sima* "island;"—that is, it means *fore-island*. Sometimes the Japanese call it *Desimamatz*, that is, "the *street* of the fore-island," because it is included in the streets of Nagasaki, and is subject to the same police-regulations.

much less expense. Since the restoration of Java to the Dutch upon the general peace, however, it seems that the trade of the factory has much revived; whereupon President Blomhoff solicited permission to visit Jeddo every alternate year; but his request was rejected by the Siogoun's government.

The preparations for the Jeddo journey are long and formal. When the regular time of departure draws near, the President makes a communication to the governor of Nagasaki, through the proper official channel, respectfully inquiring whether a visit from him will be acceptable at Jeddo. The governor replies that the President's homage will be accepted, and desires him to provide for the maintenance of order in the factory during his absence. The warehouse-master, as next in rank and authority to the President, is always the person selected to supply the place of the absent head; and, as deputy-manager of the factory, always is presented to the governor by the Dutch official, at his audience of leave, prior to his departure.

Originally, the head of the factory was attended to Jeddo by twenty of his countrymen; a goodly train, which, it is needless to say, can no longer be supplied by a factory reduced to its present scale. The numbers of the retinue have been gradually reduced, probably in proportion with the factory; and, since the journey has been rendered quadrennial instead of annual, the Dutch visitors have been limited to three, namely, the President himself, his secretary, and his physician.

The numbers of the Japanese who accompany the Dutch are not thus confined. At the head of the whole is a principal police-officer—the gobanyosi—with whom rests, in every respect, the whole conduct of the expedition. The purse, however, is not in his hands, but in those of the chief interpreter, who receives a sum of money intended to defray the whole expense of the expedition, which sum is, like other factory debts, deducted from the proceeds of the next sale, or rather from that of a lot of goods specifically appropriated to this object, but never producing what is sufficient to cover the expense;

the remainder is supplied by the Japanese Government
—a circumstance that may explain the refusal to admit
of more frequent visits to Jeddo.

Of persons of inferior rank, there are under-police
officers, under-interpreters, clerks, baggage-masters, superintendents of porters, and others ; in all about thirty-five
persons, every one individually appointed by the governor. Then there are attendants to wait upon the
Dutch and Japanese ; namely, three cooks—two for the
Dutch, one for the Japanese, two upper and five under-
servants, besides thirty other servants, of whom six are
likewise for the Dutch, and these are commonly called
" spies"—as if there were no others attached to the expedition. In addition to these, and to the native attendants
allotted them, each of the three Dutchmen may, if he
pleases, at his own especial charge, take a Japanese physician, a private interpreter, and more servants. Accordingly, Dr. von Siebold, when, in the year 1826, he
accompanied *Opperhoofd* Colonel van Sturler to Jeddo,
added to the train a young native physician, an artist,
and six servants, to aid his naturalist researches. A Japanese pupil of the German doctor's not being permitted
to attend his instructor in that character, followed him as
a servant to one of the interpreters. In fact, no restrictions appear to exist respecting the number of Japanese
that may, upon this occasion, be engaged and supported
by the foreign traders ; but the name of every individual
must be previously submitted for the Governor of Nagasaki's approbation : one object of which arrangement may
probably be to insure there being a due proportion of unsuspected spies amongst the servants.

Every sort of convenience and comfort required by the
principal travellers during the journey they must take
with them—such as linen, bedding, tables and chairs for
the Europeans, table-service, kitchen furniture—in a
word, every requisite for those who carry everywhere
their wants and necessities. Provisions, such as wine,
cheese, butter, and the like, which, not being in use in
Japan, are sent from Batavia to the factory ; also sweet-

meats, cakes, and liqueurs, of which an immense stock appears to be requisite to entertain Japanese visitors. When to these indispensables are added the wardrobe of the whole company, the presents destined as well for the Siogoun as for the several great men entitled to such a tribute of respect, and the goods carried for underhand trading with the natives ; and when it is further understood that the Japanese roads not always admitting of wheel carriages, carts are not used for the conveyance of this baggage, but everything is carried by men, or on packhorses and oxen—some idea may be formed of the immense number of porters, attendants upon the beasts of burthen, grooms, and hands of every description required for this journey.

Part of the baggage is indeed sent by sea from Nagasaki to a port of the larger northern island, Niphon, in which are situated the residences of both the autocrat by right divine, the mikado, and his vicegerent, the Siogoun ; but when the Dutch deputation likewise lands on Niphon, this portion of the baggage joins the rest ; and, upon the subsequent land-journey to Jeddo, the train often amounts to two hundred persons.

Such a retinue sounds abundantly grand and cumbrous to English ears, and may induce a reader to think that the position and dignity of the factory-president has been unduly depreciated in the account given of " life " in Desima, and the general treatment of the Dutch. Far different is the effect of his travelling-array to Japanese eyes. The trains with which the princes of the empire visit Jeddo amount in number to ten thousand men for those of the lowest rank, and twenty thousand for those of the highest ; whence it will be seen that his retinue of two hundred persons does not very extravagantly exalt the mercantile foreigner.* But more on this topic will appear in the sequel.

All our arrangements being made—every formality complied with—we found ourselves comfortably seated in

* *Manners and Customs of the Japanese,* Jancigny, Siebold, Fisscher.

our first-class norimons, beautifully appointed within, and in which we found that we could either sit or repose —at all events recline—at our pleasure. Our President had a norimon of the kind confined to very high rank, beside which was borne his tea-equipage—an indulgence restricted nearly, if not wholly, to Japanese personages sufficiently exalted to deserve that honour.*

A journey of seven weeks, over more than one thousand miles, was before us, and yet we were very far from feeling that sort of desolation in which the traveller sometimes sets out for a distant destination. Imagination had been warmed, Memory had summoned all her treasures respecting this singular country and its singular people, and we felt convinced that every hour of our long journey would gratify the intensest curiosity, and make us forget every inconvenience at which the traveller is privileged to grumble.

I must describe the order of our procession—our right royal "progress," in point of fact—for, as we were honoured with permission to visit the Siogoun of Japan, all whom we met on the journey, or with whom we had to deal, treated us with the utmost deference and civility.

The presents intended for the Siogoun lead the way, duly escorted and followed by the baggage. Then at a proper interval, went the procession.

First went our baggage-master and the superintendent of the porters, followed by the inferior police-officers, or *banyoos*, making themselves comfortable in norimons of the lowest class—indeed, kangos—nevertheless each had his servant and two porters carrying his clothes-chests. I need not state that each norimon or kango was accompanied by all the servants belonging to its occupant, and bearers of clothes-chests and rain-cloak baskets.

Then come a clerk of the interpreters, the vice under-interpreter, and the under-interpreter, in their kangos, properly attended.

The Dutch physician, preceded by his medicine-chest,

---

* See p. 131 of this work.

and borne in a norimon of somewhat superior character to those before-mentioned.

The secretary in a similar norimon.

A superintendent of norimons.

Two superintendents of bearers.

The Dutch president, with eight bearers, who relieve each other, and whose dresses are adorned with the initials of the United Netherland (*i.e.*, Dutch) East India Company, U.N.O.C.

A servant, carrying shoes and slippers in a leathern box.

The *Tchao-binto*, or tea equipage.

A bearer with a seat.

The president's counting-house, as it is called ; a sort of cabinet, or scrutoire, of black lacker work, ornamented with silver, and covered with a red cloth, upon which the initials of the Dutch East India Company are embroidered in gold. Originally the charter granted by the Siogoun to the Dutch was carried in this cabinet ; but that document is now left at Desima (thus does change occur even in the immutable East), and its former sacred receptacle serves for the president's papers or other valuables. It is borne by three men.

Two couple of clothes-chests, containing the changes of raiment required by the president upon the road.

Two couple of the same for the secretary and the physician.

Two bearers with rain-cloak baskets.

The chief interpreter in his norimon, followed by his money-chest, his clothes-chests, and his rain-cloak baskets.

The *gobanyosi*, in his norimon, with his attendants.

A pike-bearer.

A chest of armour.

Clothes-boxes and cloak baskets.

The third *banyoos*, who, with some servants, either in kangos or on foot, and the rest of the luggage, closes the train.*

In this order of march we proceeded through the three

---

* *Manners and Customs of the Japanese.*

REPRESENTATION OF DOMESTIC LIFE IN JAPAN.

stages of our journey—first by land through the island of
Kewsew, which occupied seven days; then by water
through an archipelago of small islands to Niphon, occupying another week. I may observe, that the length of
this voyage is at the mercy of the winds and waves, or
depends upon the inclination of the travellers, who may
feel disposed to loiter at their nightly island-quarters;
lastly, across Niphon to Jeddo, which cannot be accomplished in less than twenty-two days of actual travelling,
besides those spent at Osacca and Meako.

We were not alone on the journey; there were plenty
of travellers besides those who were merely going on a
visit of ceremony. In no country is travelling so frequent,
so constant, as in Japan. Governmental policy has much
to do with it; for the numerous princes must annually
go to and return from the capital on the appointed days
of the Court Kalendar. They must go to the Emperor's
levee—a long and costly journey—but with ample room
and verge enough to keep them in good temper and benefit
their constitutions.

These princes do the thing in a grand style. They are
preceded by their pikemen, their archers, their musketeers, all in their best appointments.

At Osacca, the half-way halting-place, the general
entrepot of inland commerce, we fell in with the merchants
congregating there from all points of the empire, to "buy
or sell," but without a trace of the Jew in them in look,
gesture, or his proverbial dishonesty.

And throughout the journey we met with pilgrims—
pilgrims of the old sort, in piety, and faith, and devotion
—but pilgrims of Buddha and Sintoo. All the numerous
religions of Japan—some five-and-thirty—religious sects
without any Bossuet to denounce their "variations"—
inculcate the importance, the necessity of pilgrimages.
The followers of Sintoo—the primitive, the national
Church of Japan—no idolaters, though acknowledging
"divinities"—must go on a pilgrimage once a year, or at
least once in their life, to Isje or Ixe, a central province
in the south-coast of Niphon, at which spot the special

M

patron divinity of Japan was born—the ancestor of the Mikado, and the God of Japan, Ten-sio-daï-zin.

All the pilgrims who go to Isje must travel over part of the great road to Jeddo.   The pilgrimage is made at all times of the year, but particularly in the spring, when vast multitudes throng the roads.   Both sexes, young and old, rich and poor, undertake this meritorious journey, generally on foot, in order to obtain at this holy place indulgences and remissions of their sins.   Some of these pilgrims are so poor that they must live wholly upon what they get in charity from the great lords and princes whom they beset on the journey, saying :—" Great Lord, be pleased to give the poor pilgrim a seni [about one eighth of a penny] towards the expense of his journey to Isje."   Children apprehensive of severe punishment for their misdemeanours, will run away and go to Isje, and thence bring back an *ofarri* or indulgence, which is deemed sufficient expiation of their crime, and will effect a reconciliation.   Multitudes of these pilgrims must pass whole nights lying in the open fields, exposed to the injuries of wind and weather, some for want of room in the inns, others out of poverty, having left their employments for the sake of this act of their religion. And many are found dead upon the road.   In this casualty the passers-by see if they have an *ofarri* about them, in order to hide it carefully in the next tree or bush.

Others fructify the pious pilgrimage after the manner of our strolling players, acrobats, mountebanks, or Punch and Judy.   They form themselves into companies, generally of four, clad in white linen, after the manner of the Kuge or persons of the holy ecclesiastical court of the Daïri.   Two of them walking a grave, slow, deliberate pace, and standing often still, carry a large barrow adorned with fir-branches, and cut white paper, on which they place a resemblance of a large bell, made of some light substance, or a kettle, or of something else alluding to some old romantic history of their gods and ancestors ; whilst a third, with a commander's staff in his hand, adorned, out of respect to his office, with a bunch of white paper, walks or dances before the barrow, singing with a dull, heavy voice a song relating to the subject they are about to represent. Meanwhile, the fourth goes begging before the houses, or addresses himself to charitable travellers, and receives their donations.

We fell in with others; amongst the rest, pilgrims running naked along the roads in the hardest frosts, with nothing but a little straw about their waists. Their object is the accomplishment of a religious vow which they have made to visit certain temples in case they should obtain, from the bounty of their gods, deliverance from some fatal distemper under which either they themselves, their parents, or relations, may labour, or from some great misfortune that may impend. These live very poorly and miserably upon the road, receive no charity, and proceed on their journey by themselves, almost incessantly running.

We were struck with the singular appearance and conduct of the begging nuns of Japan, so quaintly described by old Kämpfer :—" To this shaved begging tribe belongs a certain remarkable religious order of young girls, called Bikuni, which is as much as to say nuns. They live under the protection of the nunneries at Kamakura and Meako, to which they pay a certain sum a year of what they get by begging, as an acknowledgment of their authority. They are, in my opinion, by much the handsomest girls we saw in Japan. The daughters of poor parents, if they be handsome and agreeable, apply for and easily obtain this privilege of begging in the habit of nuns, knowing that beauty is one of the most persuasive inducements to generosity. The Jomabo, or begging mountain priests (of whom I shall presently speak), frequently incorporate their own daughters into this religious order, and take their wives from among these Bikuni. Some of them have been bred up as courtesans, and having served their time, buy the privilege of entering into this religious order, therein to spend the remainder of their youth and beauty. They live two or three together, and make an excursion every day some few miles from their dwelling-house. They particularly watch

M 2

people of fashion, who travel in norimons or in kangos, or on horseback. As soon as they perceive somebody coming, they draw near and address themselves, though not altogether, but singly, every one accosting a gentleman by herself, singing a rural song ; and if he proves very liberal and charitable, she will keep him company and divert him for some hours. As, on the one hand, very little religious blood seems to circulate in their veins, so, on the other, it doth not appear that they labour under any considerable degree of poverty. It is true, indeed, they conform themselves to the rules of their order, by shaving their heads, but they take care to cover and wrap them up in caps or hoods made of black silk. They go decently and neatly dressed, after the fashion of ordinary people. They wear also a large hat to cover their faces, which are often painted, and to shelter themselves from the heat of the sun. They commonly have a shepherd's rod or hook in their hands. Their voice, gestures, and apparent behaviour are neither too bold and daring, nor too much dejected and affected, but free, comely, and seemingly modest. However, not to extol their modesty beyond what it deserves, it must be observed that they make nothing of laying their bosoms quite bare to the view of the charitable travellers all the while they keep them company, under pretence of its being customary in the country ; and for aught I know, they may be, though never so religiously shaved, full as impudent and lascivious as any public courtesan."

If this institution strikes us as something very singular and strangely characteristic of the nation, there were others still more curious and interesting which challenged attention on the journey.

Another religious begging order is that of the Jamado, as they are commonly called, that is, the mountain priests, or rather Jamabuo, mountain soldiers, because at all times they go armed with swords and scimitars. They do not shave their heads, but follow the rules of the first founder of this order, who mortified his body by climbing up steep high mountains ; at least they conform themselves thereunto in their dress, apparent behaviour, and some outward ceremonies, for they are fallen short of his rigorous way of life. They have a head or general of their order residing at Meako, to whom they are obliged to bring a certain sum of money every year, and who has the distribution of dignities and of titles, whereby they are known among themselves. They commonly live in the neighbourhood of some famous Kami, or national god, which is worshipped there, making a short discourse of his holiness and miracles with a loud coarse voice. Meanwhile, to make the noise still louder, they rattle their long staffs, loaded at the upper end with iron rings, to take up the charity money which is given them ; and, last of all, they blow a trumpet made of a large shell. They carry their children along with them upon the same begging errand, clad like their fathers, but with their heads shaved. These little bastards are exceedingly troublesome and importunate with travellers, and commonly take care to light on them as they are going up some hill or mountain, where, because of the difficult ascent, they cannot well escape, nor indeed otherwise get rid of them without giving them something. In some places they and their fathers accost travellers in company with a troop of Bikuni, and, with their rattling, singing, trumpeting, chattering, and crying, make such a frightful noise as would make one almost mad or deaf. These mountain-priests are frequently applied to by superstitious people, for conjuring, fortune-telling, foretelling future events, recovering lost goods, and the like purposes. They profess to be of the Kami religion, as established of old, and yet they are never suffered to attend or take care of any Kami-temple.

Others are shaved and clad like the Budsdo priests, standing two together, each with a book, which contains part of their Fokekio or bible, and which they pretend to read, having got a portion by heart ; for reciting it they expect your charity.

Others were seen sitting near some river or brook, performing a *siegaki*, literally, a ceremony for the relief of departed souls. They take the green branch of a certain tree called *fauna skimmi*, and murmuring certain words in a low tone, they wash and scour it with wood shavings, having previously written upon them the names of the deceased. " This they believe to contribute greatly to relieve and refresh the departed souls confined in purgatory." Any one wishing to purchase the benefit of this washing for himself prospectively, or for his relatives and friends, has only to throw a *seni* upon the mat, which is spread out near the beggar, who does not condescend to give thanks for the offering, " thinking his art and devotion deserve still better." Besides, it is not customary amongst beggars of note to thank people for their charity.* It is evidently one of the " institutions" which make up the felicity of Japan.

Another sort we met as we went along were differently clad, some in ecclesiastical, others in secular habit. These stood in the fields, next to the road, and commonly had a sort of altar standing before them, upon which they placed the idol of their Briareus or Quanwon, as they call him, carved in wood and gilt ; or the pictures of some other idols, scurvily done, as, for instance, the picture of Amida, the supreme judge of departed souls ; of Semaus, or the head-keeper of the prison, whereunto the con- demned souls are confined ; of Dsisoo, or the supreme commander in the purgatory of children, and some others, wherewith, and by some representations of the flames and torments prepared for the wicked in a future world, they endeavour to stir up in passengers compassion and charity.†

There were others, similarly dressed and with staff in hand ; these we were told had made a vow not to speak during a certain time ; they expressed their wants and desires by a sad, dejected, woful countenance.

There were in fact beggars of all kinds, but evidently not beggars in our sense of the word, although it seems a distinction without a difference. Religious motives

---

* Kämpfer.   † Ibid.

were constantly appealed to, or the fancy was amused. We could not be otherwise than struck with this evidence, that there is in the Japanese mental organization a very strong religious sentiment, combined with a sense of the ludicrous and the histrionic art, since such a large portion of the people is entirely supported by appeals to them. Whether stout and lusty, diseased or lame, it mattered not, the charitable trifle was always forthcoming. A strange national substitute was this for poor-rates, workhouses, and unions. Some sang, some played on fiddles, guitars, or other instruments, whilst juggler's tricks of a kind precisely similar to that which amuses us in Europe elicited applause from the multitude.* One of these performances was especially deserving of notice. A young boy, with a sort of wooden machine hanging from his neck, and a rope, with eight strings attached to it, from which hang down eight bells of different notes, turned round in a circle with a swiftness scarcely credible, in such a manner that both the machine, which rests upon his shoulders, and the bells turn round him horizontally ; the boy in the meantime, with great dexterity and quickness beating them with two hammers, making a strange, odd sort of melody. To increase the noise, two others sitting near him beat, one upon a large, the other upon a smaller drum.

The great majority of these beggars, or rather pilgrims, presented a well-to-do appearance. Amongst the rest there was a woman well-dressed in silk, with her face well painted, leading a blind old man, and begging before him. This we thought a very extraordinary sight.

This reminds me of a fact, noticed by all travellers, that there are a great many blind in Japan. I have nowhere found any cause alleged for the prevalence of this misfortune, nor can I suggest one, unless it be their peculiar diet, being largely vegetable and of fish ; they drink almost incessantly either tea, saki, or hot water—indeed, hot drinks seem necessary to aid the digestion of their

---

* See wood-cut, p. 1.

vegetable food. It may be, that this large quantity of fluid keeps up too great an action in the kidneys, the excessive action of which weakens, and may finally destroy the sight—for there is a well-known sympathy between those organs and the eyes. Whatever may be the cause, the fact is certain, and it has given rise to two institutions for the blind, the history of which is not a little interesting. These are ancient and numerous bodies, composed of persons of all ranks and professions. Originally they made up but one society. In process of time, however, they split into two separate bodies, one of which is called " Bussets-Sado," or the blind Bussets, and the other " Feki-Sado," or the blind Fekis.

The original founder of this " Order of the Blind " was the son of an Emperor, who reigned in very remote ages. " This young prince," say the Japanese historians, " wept himself blind for the loss of his beautiful beloved princess ; and thereupon, with his father's leave, and under an imperial charter, he erected a society, wherein none were ever to be admitted but such as had the misfortune to be blind." The society prospered exceedingly, and was held in great repute at court, and all over the empire, for many centuries.

The native annalists relate a characteristic, thoroughly Japanese legend to account for the rise of the Feki-Sado. During the dreadful civil wars between the great families of the Feki and Gendzi, Kakekiko, a very renowned general of the Feki party, was defeated and made prisoner by the celebrated Joritomo, who had slain the generous prince to whom Kakekiko had been devotedly attached. Instead of putting his prisoner to death, according to the usual practice in those times, Joritomo treated him with the greatest kindness, allowed him much liberty, and endeavoured to persuade him to enter his service. One day, when he was pressing him in this manner, and offering him whatever conditions he might please to demand, the captive general said, " I was once a faithful servant to a kind master. He is dead, and none other shall ever have my faith and friendship. You have laid me under obligations; I owe to you my life; yet can I never set my eyes on you without a design of avenging my dear dead master by slaying you. These, therefore, these designing instruments of mischief, I will offer up to you, as the only acknowledgment for your generous behaviour towards me, that my unhappy condition allows me to give." And having thus said, he plucked out both his eyes, and presented them on a plate to Joritomo, who, astonished at so much magnanimity and resolution, forthwith set him at full liberty. The dramas of the Japanese seem chiefly made up of incidents like these, in which the passion of revenge stands out most prominently. The blind general retired into a distant province, where he learned to play upon the bywa, or Japanese lute, and gave birth to the society of the Feki blind, of which he himself was the first head. These Feki do not live upon charity, but make a shift to get a livelihood for themselves, and contribute to the maintenance of their convents, by following various professions or callings not altogether inconsistent with their unhappy condition of total blindness. The greater number of them apply themselves to music, and find employment in the houses of princes and great men, as also at weddings, festivals, processions, and all public solemnities. It appears that the orchestras of all the theatres in the empire are filled by members of the Feki society. At least, travellers tell us that all the musicians they saw in th theatres were blind men.

The crowd upon the roads is not a little increased by numberless small retail traders, and children of country people, who run about from morning to night, following travellers, and offering for sale their poor (and for the most part eatable) merchandise, such as cakes and sweetmeats, wherein the quantity of sugar is so small as to be scarcely perceptible; other cakes of different sorts, made of flour, roots boiled in water and salt, ropes, strings, toothpicks, road-books, straw shoes for horses and for men, and a multitude of other trifles, made of wood, straw, reed, and bamboos.

For the convenience of travellers, there are inns enough in Japan where everybody travels. The best are in those villages where there are post-houses—distinct establishments from the inn. I may observe, with regard to the latter, that they are admirably organized in every way—under the control, indeed in the possession, of the governing prince, who regulates all the prices for man, beast, and vehicle—not according to distances, but the goodness and badness of the roads, price of victuals, forage, and the like. A horse to ride, with two portmanteaus and an *adfoski* or valise, may cost about eight *seni* a mile, that is, about one farthing ; a horse only saddled, without men or baggage to carry, costs six *seni* a mile ; whilst porters and kango-men may be had for five—both of these prices being evidently less than a farthing—the *seni* being about one-eighth of a farthing.* As a man may live comfortably in Japan at threepence a-day, these prices are strictly proportionate, though ridiculously small, according to our cost of travelling.

It is at these post-houses that the imperial post is managed. Messengers are waiting, day and night, at all these post-houses, to carry the letters, edicts, and proclamations of the Emperor and the princes of the empire, which they take up the moment they are delivered at the post-house, and carry to the next with all speed. They are kept in a small black, varnished box, bearing the coat of arms of the Emperor or prince who sends them, which the messenger carries upon his shoulder, tied to a small staff. Two of these messengers always run together, that in case any accident should befal either of them upon the road, the other may take his place, and deliver the box at the next post-house. All travellers, even the princes of the empire and their retinues, must retire out of the way, and give free passage to these messengers or postmen of the Emperor, and they accordingly give notice of their approach by ringing a small bell at a due distance.

Like other well-built houses, the inns are but one story

---

* The money of Japan will be considered in the sequel.

high, or if there be two, the second is but a lumber-attic. Of the same length of frontage as other houses, they extend considerably deeper—sometimes forty kin, or about two hundred and ninety feet—being provided with a *Tsubo*, or small pleasure-garden, behind, enclosed with a neat white wall. The front has only lattice windows, which in the daytime are kept open; the folding screens and moveable partitions which divide the several apartments, are also so disposed as to lay open to travellers, as they go along, a very agreeable perspective view across the house into the garden; unless there happens to be a man of rank with his retinue in the house. The floor is raised about three feet above the level of the street, and projects towards the street and the garden, so as to form a gallery, with a roof; here the traveller may sit or walk and smoke, or otherwise while away his leisure. They use this gallery as a stepping-stone in mounting their horses, for fear of soiling their feet by mounting in the street.

Distinctions of rank make a difference of inn-treatment in Japan as elsewhere. In some of the great inns there is a passage contrived for the convenience of the "quality," so that they may step out of their norimons and walk directly to their apartments without passing through the fore-part of the house, which is commonly not over clean, and makes but an indifferent figure, being covered with poor, sorry mats, and the rooms divided by ordinary screens. The kitchen, too, is in this part of the house, and often fills it with smoke, as they have no chimneys to discharge the smoke.* Here foot travellers and ordinary people live amongst the servants. Persons of quality and fashion are accommodated in the back part of the house, which is kept clean and neat to admiration. Not the least spot is to be seen upon the walls, floors, carpets, window-screens, in short, nowhere in the room, which looks as if it were quite new and but newly furnished. There are no tables, chairs, benches, or other furniture in

* See p. 127 of this work.

these rooms.   The Japanese are a nation of squatters on mats, and their taste, corresponding to our love of fine cabinet-work, lies in a different direction; it is called *miseratsie*, and may really have its representative in our picture-galleries and curiosity-shops.   The items of the collection may be a paper neatly bordered with a rich piece of embroidery, instead of a frame, either with the picture of a saint, done apparently with a coarse pencil, and by means of three or four strokes the proportions and resemblance have been so accurately observed, that no one can mistake the likeness, nor help admiring the skill and ingenuity of the artist ; or perhaps you will see a " wise saw" or moral sentence of some noted philosopher or poet, written in his own handwriting, who had a mind to show his skill by a few hasty strokes or characters, but still very ingeniously drawn, and such as will afford sufficient matter of amusement and speculation to a curious and speculative observer ; and lest any one should question its authenticity, these sentences are commonly signed, not only by the writer himself, but have the sign-manual and seals of some other witnesses.   They are hung up nowhere but in the toko, or most honourable place in the room, and are very much prized by the Japanese.   There are also pictures of Chinese, birds, trees, landscapes, and the like, on white screens ; flower-vases, filled with all sorts of curious flowers such as the season affords—all curiously arranged according to certain rules of Japanese art; for it is as much an art in Japan to arrange a flower-vase as it is in Europe to carve at meals or to lay out a table.

Sometimes it is a perfuming pan of excellent workmanship, cast in brass or copper, resembling a crane, lion, dragon, or other strange animal.

Amongst a collection of such *miseratsie* we observed an old Cologne earthen pot, such as is used for spa-water, with all its cracks and fissures carefully mended, and used as a flower-vase; it was esteemed a very great rarity because of the distant place whence it came, the clay of which it was made, and its uncommon shape.   Curious specimens of wood, beautiful network, a piece of rotten root, or an old stump of a tree, remarkable for their deformed shape; in short, Japanese fancy runs riot in such collections.

The small gallery before-mentioned leads to the outer offices, and a bath-house, which contains either a sweating-

ORNAMENTAL CANDLESTICKS.

stove or a warm-bath, and sometimes both. It is warmed every evening; for the Japanese usually bathe or take a sweating after their day's journey. The floor of these sweating-houses consists of small planks, a few inches apart, for the admission of the rising vapour and the discharge of the water : they are otherwise constructed much according to our plan as to valves and furnace. The vapour is rendered fragrant by certain plants put into the water. There are always two tubs, one of warm, the other of cold water, for bathing.

Besides the large inns, there are numberless small ones

—cook-shops, saki, or ale-houses, pastrycooks' and confectioners'-shops, all along the road, even in the midst of woods and forests, and on the top of mountains, where the weary foot traveller and the lower sort of people find at all times, for a few *seni*, something warm to eat, or hot tea, or saki, or something else of the kind to refresh themselves withal. Compared to the large inns, these are but poor and sorry houses, being kept by poor people ; yet, even in these there is always something or other to amuse passengers, and to draw them in—either a garden, an orchard, beautiful flowers, or the agreeable view of a stream of clear water falling from a neighbouring hill, either natural or artificial, or by some other curious ornament adapted to tempt the traveller to enter and enjoy himself. Sometimes, however, the attraction is a handsome waiting-maid, or a couple of young girls well dressed, who with great civility invite the traveller to enter.

The eatables—such as cakes—are kept before the fire, sticking to skewers of bamboo, so that passengers as they go along may take them and pursue their journey without stopping. The landladies, cooks, and maids, as soon as they see any one coming at a distance, blow up the fire to make it look as if the victuals had been just got ready. Some busy themselves with making the tea, others prepare soup, others fill cups with saki, or other liquors, to present them to passengers, all the while talking and chattering, and commending their wares with a voice loud enough to be heard by their next neighbours of the same trade and " calling," as it may well be named in Japan in both senses of the word.

The eatables constitute a pretty extensive and varied bill of fare. You may have *mansél*—a sort of round cake, borrowed from the Portuguese, as big as a hen's egg, and filled with black bean-flower and sugar,—cakes of the pith of a root found in the mountains, cut into round slices, like carrots, and roasted ; snails, oysters, shell-fish, and other fish, roasted, boiled, or pickled ; Chinese *laxa*—a thin sort of pap or paste, made of fine wheat-flower, cut into small thin slices of some length,

and baked ; all sorts of vegetables which the season
affords, and innumerable other dishes peculiar to Japan,
made of seeds and powdered roots, and dressed in many
different ways. The common sauce for these and other
dishes is *soy* mixed with saki. They garnish their dishes
with the leaves of the plant sansio, or thin slices of ginger
or lemon-peel. They flavour their soup with powdered
ginger, sansio, or a root peculiar to the country. They
colour their sweetmeats as we do, but these are, for the
most part, far more agreeable to the eye than pleasing to
the taste, being deficient in sugar, and so tough that
strong teeth are required to chew them. The printed
road-books, which the travellers always carry with them,
tell them where and at what price the best victuals of the
kind required are supplied.

Tea is almost the only drink of travellers on the
road. It is made of the coarsest and largest leaves which
remain upon the plant after the youngest and tenderest
have been gathered twice, for the consumption of the rich.
These large leaves are not rolled up and curled as the
best sort, but simply roasted in a pan, and continually
stirred whilst roasting, lest they should get a burnt taste.
When done enough they are packed in straw baskets, and
placed under the roof of the house, near the place where
the smoke escapes. In preparing them for drinking,
they merely take a handful and boil them in a large iron
kettleful of water. The leaves are sometimes put into a
small bag, or in a little basket swimming in the kettle.
Half a cup of this decoction is mixed with cold water
when presented to the traveller. Tea thus prepared
smells and tastes like water infused with wood-ashes ; yet
the Japanese consider it much more wholesome for daily
use than the finer sorts, prepared in the Chinese manner,
which they say affect the head too strongly—though even
these lose a great part of their narcotic quality when
boiled. The common tea of Japan is an inferior article,
not suited for exportation.

At all these inns, great and small, and the tea-houses,
there are numberless women, whose position, to say the

least of it, is very equivocal. About noon, when they have done dressing and painting themselves, they make their appearance, standing under the door-way of the house, or sitting upon the small gallery around it, whence, with a smiling countenance and good word, they invite the traveller to come into their inn in preference to others. In some places, where there are several inns standing together, they make, with their chattering and rattling, no inconsiderable noise, and prove not a little troublesome. These women commonly occupy the handsomest houses in the place, and these are sometimes situated near their idol's temples : sometimes a single house contains eighty of them.

Amazed at such a vicious institution amongst a people in other respects so sensible and judicious, I was at some pains to find out from the interpreters when, and on what occasion, this institution had originated, and afterwards became diffused all over the country. In answer to my inquiries, I was informed that this dissolute institution had not subsisted in ancient times, but had first taken its rise during the civil war which was carried on, when the Siogoun, or generalissimo of the army, dispossessed the Mikado of the imperial power. At that time the Mikado, according to this informant, was obliged, being as yet very young, to flee with his foster-mother and his court to Simonoseki. The Mikado's domestics consisted then, as now, of none but the fair sex, and he is even now considered so holy that no male may approach him. In this flight over sea, being pursued by the enemy, his foster-mother leaped with him into the sea, where they both perished. His female servants, who arrived at Simonoseki, and had nothing left to subsist on, were under the necessity of adopting a rather dishonourable mode of getting their livelihood. This, as several people assured me, gave rise to houses of this kind, the number of which gradually increased during the civil war and disturbances of many years. The interpreters told me likewise that these women are not called by the same name everywhere, or alike regarded. In Simonoseki they are still more peculiarly called *jorcessi*, this being actually the name given to the twelve wives of the Mikado! Others elsewhere are called *keise* or *kese*, which signifies a castle that is turned upside down.*

These tea-houses are the resort of the Dutch in the vicinity of Nagasaki; they are licensed places of entertainment for drinking and music. It is impossible to pass over in silence an institution so extraordinary in many points, and altogether peculiar to the Japanese as an enlightened nation, the thinking part of whom, according to Thunberg, allow that it is indecent and a scandal to the nation. The proprietors of the tea-houses are also licensed to purchase female infants of indigent parents, for purposes of infamy. These girls act during their childhood as the servants of the full-grown inmates, but are, at the same time, educated with the utmost care; they are not only rendered skilful in every accomplishment that can enhance the effect of their personal charms, but their minds are sedulously cultivated, and enriched with all the stores of knowledge that can make their conversation attractive and agreeable. Thus, the whole body of these victims of the vices of others bear considerable resemblance to the few celebrated individuals amongst the courtesans of ancient Greece; and the resemblance holds good in another point, the consequence of the first. As we are told that Athenian husbands took their wives into the society of the notorious Aspasia, to share in the instruction they themselves derived from her, so in Japan do husbands invite their wives to join their party to the tea-houses, there to partake of the amusement afforded by the music, singing, dancing, and conversation of their intellectual and highly accomplished, but unfortunate and dishonoured sisters.

But the most extraordinary part of the whole is the position in the moral scale assigned to these degraded

---

* Thunberg, iii. 125, *et seq.* Kämpfer says that the Siogoun indulged his soldiers in this matter in order to keep them from their families.

women by the Japanese, who are, in the general relations
of life, to the full as tenacious of female purity as the
nations by whom wives and daughters are kept under
lock and key. Whilst their worthless purchasers, those
shameless speculators in human depravity, the tea-house
proprietors, are universally despised as the very scum of
the earth, far more lenient is the appreciation of the
purchased thralls, who may, indeed, be held guiltless of
their own pollution, being destined to a temporary career
of sin without their own concurrence :—a temporary
career only, however, inasmuch as these girls are purchased
for a term of years, and may be considered rather as
apprentices than slaves for life. When the period for
which they are bound to their disgraceful trade expires,
they may return to their families, and are received into
society in any station of which they show themselves
worthy. Many enter the order, as it may be called, of
Mendicant Nuns ; still greater numbers are said to find
husbands, and to emulate all the good qualities of the
most immaculate Japanese wives and mothers. But
whatever be the new condition of these ex-courtesans, it
is solely by their conduct in the character of their choice
that they are thenceforward judged, without any reference
to their past compelled occupation.

The number of tea-houses appears to be beyond all
conception. The Dutch writers state that at Nagasaki, a
town with a population of from sixty to seventy thousand souls, there are no less than seven hundred and fifty.
It is from these houses that the Dutch factory obtain their
female servants or companions.*

* *Manners and Customs of the Japanese.* The Abbé Raynal seems
to throw some light on this singular and deplorable institution :—"On
ne voit pas que la secte du Sintos ait eu la manie d'ériger en crimes,
des actions innocentes par elles-mêmes ; manie si dangereuse pour
les mœurs.   Loin de répandre ce fanatisme sombre, et cette crainte
des dieux, qu'on trouve dans presque toutes les religions ; le Sintos
avait travaillé à prévenir ou à calmer cette maladie de l'imagination
par des fêtes, qu'on célébrait trois fois chaque mois.   Elles étaient
consacrées à visiter ses amis, à passer avec eux la journée en festins,
en rejouissances.   Les prêtres du Sintos disaient que les plaisirs

Whatever may have been the origin of this strange institution, abject want, as one of the causes in all European communities—the political expediency of the sovereign, which is very improbable—the peculiar views of Japan's primitive religion inculcating such action as meritorious, a cause possible enough, seeing that other ancient nations have thus been deluded—certain it is, that in its present aspect it has all the moral guilt and deformity of its similitude in Christian Europe, whilst it is totally exempt from the frightful social evils and penalties everlastingly incurred by the latter. To *us* this is incomprehensible, like many other matters in the manners and customs of Japan.

Such were the scenes and observations of our journey. Everywhere we found the roads excellent, in admirable order, lined with trees on each side, and carefully swept by persons appointed for this purpose by the farmers in the vicinity—for the Japanese know the value of manure, and do not lose a particle of it.* Everywhere we saw small shops, where the peculiar straw-shoes for man, bullock, and horse are manufactured. This trade gives employment to multitudes of poor persons throughout the empire. How many will be made wretched if we teach them the superiority of iron for horses and leather for men? Yet may this calamity be in store for the Japanese

innocens des hommes étaient agréables à la divinité ; que la meilleure manière d'honorer les camis, c'était d'imiter leurs vertus et de jouir, dès ce monde, du bonheur, dont ils jouissent dans l'autre. Conformément à cette opinion, les Japonais, après avoir fait la prière dans des temples, toujours situés au milieu d'agréables bocages, allaient chez des courtisanes qui habitaient des maisons ordinairement bâties dans ces lieux consacrés à la devotion et à l'amour. Ces femmes étaient des *religieuses, soumises à un ordre de moines, qui retiraient une partie de l'argent qu'elles avaient gagné* par ce pieux abandon d'elles-mêmes au vœu le plus sacré de la nature. Dans toutes les religions les femmes ont influé sur le culte, comme prêtresses ou comme victimes des dieux, &c.—*Hist. Polit. des deux Indes*, i. 240, *et seq.*

* In every street in Japan there are public conveniences of a portable nature—merely tubs—probably for the purpose of using the contents as manure. Travellers complain of the nuisance.

in the working out of this grand revolution in the policy
of their Government.

THE TEA-PARTY.

The highways are so broad that two companies of
travellers, however numerous, may pass each other without hindrance. There is a law or rule of the road in
Japan as well as in England. The travellers who "go

up," that is, towards Meako, take the left side of the way, and those who come from Meako take the right ; on all occasions, in fact, their rule of the road is like ours—keep to the left and you're sure to be right. All the highways are divided into measured miles, which are all marked, and begin from the great bridge at Jeddo, as the common centre of the empire. This bridge is by way of pre-eminence called Nipon-bas, that is, the bridge of Japan. It is two hundred and fifty-two feet in length, built on piles like our bridge at Battersea, and without any other pretension to architectural skill or design. By means of this common centre of mile measurement, the traveller, in whatever part of the empire he may be, knows at any time how many miles he is from Jeddo. The miles are marked by two small hillocks thrown up one on each side opposite each other, and planted at the top with one or more trees. At the end of every tract, province, or smaller district, a wooden or stone pillar is set up in the highway with characters upon it, showing what provinces or lands are here bounded, and to whom they belong. Similar pillars are erected at the entry of the branch-roads, show-ing what province they lead to, and the distance in leagues to the next remarkable place. The natives, as they im-prove every inch of ground, plant firs and cypress-trees in rows along the roads over the ridges of hills, mountains, and barren places. No firs or cypress-trees can be cut down without leave of the magistrate of the place; and then young ones must be planted to replace the felled timber, as before mentioned.

As soon as we approached any town or village, the landlord of the inn to which we were proceeding came out to meet us, just as he would do at the arrival of the princes and lords of the empire. Dressed in his *kamisino*, or ceremonial costume, wearing his kattan stuck in his girdle, he made us his compliments with a low bow; so low, indeed, that he touched the ground with his hands, and almost with his forehead—a ceremony which he repeated at our entrance into the inn.

On arriving, we were immediately ushered into the

apartments destined for us, glad to escape from the
number of spectators and the petulant scoffing of the
children thronging around us.   Here we were confined,
having no liberty but to walk into the small garden
behind the house.   All other avenues, all the doors,
windows, and holes which opened any prospect towards
the streets or country, were carefully shut and nailed up,
in order—as they would fain persuade us—to defend us
and our goods from thieves ; but in fact to watch and
guard us as thieves and deserters.   It must be owned,
however, that this superabundant care and watchfulness
was considerably lessened upon our return, when we found
means to insinuate ourselves into their favour, and by
presents and otherwise to procure their connivance.*   To
talk of connivance seems strange to those who consider
the strict letter of Japanese law ; but we may rest assured that human nature is human nature all the world
over, and that nature will " out" as well, or even more so
than " murder."   I shall have occasion to relate an incident in point, showing how the strictest regulation was
evaded.

As soon as we had taken possession of our apartment,
the landlord entered with some of his chief male domestics,
each with a dish of tea in his hand, which they presented
to us, according to our rank and dignity, and repeating,
with a submissive, deep-fetched voice, the words " ah ! ah !
ah !" This done, the necessary apparatus for smoking was
brought in, consisting of a board of wood or platter of
brass, upon which were placed a small firepan with coals,
a pot or dish to spit in, a small box filled with tobacco,
cut small, and some long pipes with small brass heads.
We were also presented with *socaro*, that is, " something
to eat," refreshment, consisting of several sorts of fruits,
figs, nuts, several sorts of cakes, mansie, and rice-cakes.

Other travellers were served by the housemaids, who
took the opportunity to engage their guests otherwise ;
but it was quite different with us, for even the landlords

---

* Kämpfer.

themselves and their male domestics, after they had presented us with a dish of tea, were not suffered on any account to enter our apartments.

Some peculiar contrivances attracted our attention. In the deficiency of regular spittoons, they substitute pieces of bamboo hollowed out between the knots. Their candles are hollow in the middle ; the wick, which is of paper, ,being wound about a wooden stick before the tallow is laid on. The candlesticks have a punch or pin at the top, on which the candles are fixed. These candles burn very rapidly, with much smoke and smell, the tallow being made of bay-tree berries, camphor-wood, and other kinds of resinous substances. Instead of lamps, they make use of small flat earthen vessels, filled with train-oil or the oil of cotton-seeds. The wick is a rush, and the vessel stands in another filled with water, or in a square lantern, as a precaution against setting the house on fire.

The Japanese are very jovial on all occasions, and on their journeys enjoy themselves to the utmost. They sit down to table thrice a day, besides eating between meals. They begin early in the morning, before they set out, with a good substantial breakfast ; then follows dinner at noon, and the day is concluded with a plentiful supper at night. It is contrary to law to play at cards, and they pass their time after meals in drinking and singing ; or they propose riddles round, or play at some other game. He who cannot explain the riddle, or loses the game, is obliged to drink a glass of saki.

On our departure from each inn, the landlord was called in, and our president, in the presence of the two interpreters, paid him the reckoning in gold, laid upon a small salver. He draws near in a creeping posture, kneeling, holding his hands down to the floor ; and when he takes the salver with the money, he bows his forehead almost quite to the ground, in token of submission and gratitude, uttering with a deep voice the words "ah ! ah ! ah !" by which, in Japan, inferiors show their deference and respect to superiors.

One curious feature deserves to be mentioned in connexion with our departure. It is a custom in Japan that
guests, before they quit the inn, should order their
servants to sweep the room they have been occupying,
not to leave any dirt or dust behind them. We complied
with the rule, in return for the civility which we received ; indeed, every traveller must confirm the opinion
expressed by Kämpfer—" The behaviour of the Japanese,
from the meanest countryman up to the greatest prince
or lord, is such, that the whole empire might be called
a school of civility and good manners. They have so
much sense and innate curiosity that, if they were not
absolutely denied a free and open conversation and correspondence with foreigners, they would receive them with
the utmost kindness and pleasure. In some towns and
villages only, we took notice that the young boys, who
are childish all over the world, would run after us,
calling us names, and cracking some malicious jest or
other, levelled at the Chinese, whom they take us to be.
One of the most common, and not much different from a
like sort of compliment which is commonly made to
Jews in Germany, is ' *Toosin bay bay ?*' which, in
broken Chinese, signifies, *Chinese, have ye nothing to
truck ?*"

It may not be amiss to observe, that in Japan it is of
importance to travellers to set out on a lucky day.   For
this purpose, there is a special table printed in all the
road-books, which, it is affirmed, has been observed to
hold good in the experience of many ages.   This table
gives all the unlucky days of every month.   The most
intelligent of the Japanese have but little regard for this
superstitious table, but it is held in credit by the common
people, the mountain priests and monks, just like our
astrological almanacs, annually published and bought at
the present day, and, doubtless, implicitly obeyed.

The invention of this table is connected with a myth
of Japan.   It is said to have been invented by the
astrologer Seimei, a man of great quality, and very
eminent in his art.   King Abino Tassima was his father,

and a fox was his mother, to whom Abino Tassima was married on the following occasion :—He once happened with a servant of his to be in the temple of Inari, who is the god and protector of the foxes. Meanwhile some courtiers were hunting the fox without doors, in order to make use of the lungs for the preparation of a certain medicine. It happened upon this that a young fox, pursued by the hunters, fled into the temple, which stood open, and took shelter in the very bosom of Tassima. The king, unwilling to deliver up the poor creature to the unmerciful hunters, was forced to defend himself· and the fox, and to repel force by force, wherein be behaved himself with so much bravery and success that, having defeated the hunters, he set the fox at liberty. The hunters, ashamed and highly offended at the courageous behaviour of the king, seized, in the height of their resentment, an opportunity which offered to kill his royal father. Tassima mustered up all his courage and prudence to revenge his father's death, and with so much success that he killed the traitors with his own hands. The fox, to return his gratitude, appeared to him, after the victory which he obtained over the murderers of his father, in the shape of a lady of incomparable beauty, and so fired his breast with love that he took her to his wife. It was by her he had this son, who was endowed with divine wisdom, and the precious gift of prognosticating and foretelling things to come. Nor did he know his wife had been that very fox whose life he saved with so much courage in the temple of Inari, till, soon after, her tail and other parts beginning to grow, she resumed by degrees her former shape. Seimei not only calculated the table in question by the knowledge he had acquired of the motion and influence of the stars, but, as he was at the same time a perfect master of the "cabalistic" sciences, he found out certain words which he brought together into an *uta* or verse, the repetition of which is believed to have the infallible virtue of keeping off all those misfortunes which, upon the days determined in the table to be unfortunate, would otherwise befall

travellers. This verse is for the use and satisfaction of
poor ordinary servants, who have not leisure to accommodate themselves to the table, but must go when and
wherever they are sent by their masters.*

Corresponding to the god Terminus of the ancient
Romans, the Japanese have their idol Dsisos. If Terminus presided over bounds and limits, Dsisos protects
the roads and travellers. He stands three feet high, on
a stone pillar of six feet, and is adorned with flowers.
Two smaller stone pillars, hollow at the top, stand before
the idol, upon which are placed lamps, which travellers
light to his honour ; at some distance stands a basin of
water, in which they wash their hands before lighting the
lamps.

In concluding this portion of my narrative, it may be
interesting to state the charges at these inns on the road.
We paid the landlord two kobangs for dinner, and three
for supper and lodgings for the night. For this money
he provided victuals for the whole train, excepting the
horses, the grooms, and porters ; this sum is equivalent
to about £6 10s. sterling, a very small expenditure con-

---

* Here is the table showing what days of the month are unfortunate and improper to begin a journey, invented by the wise and
experienced astrologer, Abino Seimei :—

Months.		Unfortunate days are the
January and July	. . . .	3rd, 11th, 19th, 27th.
February ,, August	. . .	2nd, 10th, 18th, 26th.
March ,, September	. .	1st, 9th, 17th, 25th.
April ,, October	. . .	4th, 12th, 20th, 28th.
May ,, November	. .	5th, 13th, 21st, 29th.
June ,, December	. . .	6th, 14th, 22nd, 30th.

I have now before me a modern English book, entitled *The Complete
Book of Knowledge*, treating of all manner of occult and wise prog-
nostications, amongst the rest " Of the Evil and Perilous Days in
the different Months of the Year." " Whosoever beginneth a journey on any of these days shall be in danger of death before the
return." Some of the days correspond with those of the Japanese
table. Here is the Japanese couplet which puts the illiterate in a
better position than their betters, by keeping off their misfortunes :—

Sada Mejesi Tabiaatz Fidori Josi Asijwa.
Omojitatz Figo Kitz Nito Sen.

sidering our numbers; but the fact was, that the poor landlord had agreed upon the five kobangs long ago, when our train was not so bulky as it became. It seems that a contractor has not, in Japan, the right to insist on the original terms of his agreement, at all events in his dealings with the Dutch embassy to Jeddo.

II.

THE first twelve miles of our journey gave us a taste of mountain-travelling in Japan; upwards, however, the sturdy porters carried us,—their usual "stage" is seventeen miles! And gaily went the horses and the oxen on their straw shoes. Will they ever get used to hard iron after enjoying their gentlemanly slippers?

We reached the shores of Omura, whose bay lay before us, the town on the right, and beyond it a smoking volcano. The Bay of Omura is famous for its pearls. The Japanese tell us that as to one particular kind, if you put them in a box full of a peculiar face-powder, made of another shell, one or two young pearls will grow out at the sides; and when they come to maturity, which they do in two or three years, they will drop off. We shall wait for future scientific experiments before we believe this assertion, which, however, reminds us of our boyish experiment of reviving a drowned fly by imbedding it in powdered chalk.

The Bay of Omura is too shallow for vessels of any size, and the prince of the district furnished us with boats, each rowed by fourteen watermen: they rowed the distance across, thirty miles.

On the following day we passed the old Camphor-tree first noticed by Kämpfer; it was in full bloom: a very beautiful sight—a giant of a tree, fifty feet in circumference.*

* In 1822 Fisscher saw a fir-tree, in the vicinity of Fimesi, which was 983 years old: it grew near a temple.

We dined at Swota, a seaport in the Gulf of Simabara remarkable for a manufactory of large earthen pots or jars used by vessels as water-casks, and also china-ware made of a whitish clay abundant in the vicinity. We also visited a hot-spring, much frequented for its medicinal virtues, and provided with accommodation for bathing : there are several others in the neighbourhood.

At Tsuka-sake is a celebrated hot-spring, with a bathing establishment for invalids. We were permitted to bathe in the Prince of Fitzen's own bath, and were much struck by the superlative cleanliness of the whole ; as an instance of which, we may state that the water, although clear as crystal, was made to pass through hair sieves into the bath, to guard against the possible introduction of any impurity. Whilst speaking of princely establishments, it may be added that we passed a night in a country-palace of the Prince of Tsikuzen, where his highness's own apartment was assigned to us. This apartment consisted only of an anteroom and a bed-chamber, which last, like most others in Japan, became a sitting-room when the bedding was stowed away in a chest for the day—an operation of no great difficulty, the said bedding consisting only of a thin mattress for each person ; except, indeed, a wooden pillow, or rather bolster, upon which a wadded pillow or cushion is laid. This bolster is fashioned into a tiny chest of drawers, the established receptacle of small and highly-valuable articles. The walls of the Prince of Tsikuzen's rooms are of cedar-wood, highly-polished and coloured ; the division between them is made by screens of gilt paper, in gilt and lackered frames, removable at pleasure. The apartment opens into a garden, containing, as usual, a small *miya*, or chapel. But the chief peculiarities of the apartment were, first, a cleanliness and neatness perfectly luxurious; and next, its great modesty and smallness, considered as destined for the occupation of a reigning prince ; but principally, a large closet, more resembling a cage, formed out of a corner of the anteroom, in which the chamberlain in attendance is condemned habitually to pass his

hours alone—there, unseen and unobtrusive, waiting and
watching for his highness's commands.*

The hot-springs of this entirely volcanic province have
a melancholy notoriety : their boiling-hot water was
used to torture the poor Christians during the persecution
in Japan.

Janga, our next stage, is the capital of Figen, a province in which the women have the reputation of being
the handsomest in all Japan.   They are certainly handsomer than their sisters of any other Asiatic country,
but—adorning their rose and painting their lily—they
are so much bedaubed with colouring cosmetics that they
might be taken for wax-dolls rather than living creatures;
they are, however, well-shaped, though short, as are the
men also.   We noticed women who seemed little more
than girls, yet evidently the mothers of several children.

This province is reputed to be the most fertile in all
Japan, being particularly famous for its rice, of which it
produces ten different sorts, one of which is reserved for
the special use of the Siogoun.   The rice-fields were
bordered with tea-shrubs, about six feet high ; they had
been stripped of their leaves, and therefore, like plucked
geese, made a sorry appearance—all, however, for the use
and comfort of man, the lord of all creation, who is
privileged to do as he likes with his own.

But perhaps the most important object in Kewsew is
its coal.   At Koyanose we saw a coal-fire, which was
most acceptable, as the journey is always begun in
February, when the country wears its winter garb, and
bristles with frost.   We visited a coal-mine at Wuku-
moto, and though not allowed to descend the shaft more
than half-way, or about sixty steps, we saw enough to
satisfy us that the mine was well and judiciously worked.
The upper strata, which we saw, were only a few inches
thick, but we were told that the lower beds were of many
feet, and the blocks of coal drawn up confirmed the statement.   The coal, being bituminous in its nature, appears

* *Manners and Customs of the Japanese.*

to be made into coke for use ; and, perhaps, independent of this reason, it may be more agreeable in that form to persons whose more general fuel is charcoal.

At Kokura, the capital of the province of Buigen, once a large town, but now much decayed, there is a large castle of freestone, with a few cannon, and a tower of six stories—the usual sign of princely residences. A river flowed through the town, crossed by a bridge nearly two hundred yards long, but it is too shallow to admit vessels of any size. At least a hundred small boats were drawn up on the banks.

On leaving our inn of this town, we found the square in front of it, as well as the bridge, crowded with upwards of a thousand spectators, chiefly of the lower orders, who had collected to see us; and who knelt in profound silence, without motion or noise.

Nothing in the journey through Kewsew impressed us more than our visit to a Buddhist temple of the Ikko-seu sect, at Yagami. It was the rare instance of a Buddhist temple that might be said to be exempt from idols : it contained only a single image, designed to represent the one only god, Amida. The bonzes of this sect are the only Buddhist priests in Japan allowed to marry and eat meat. Their faith is pure monotheism.*

At Simonoseki, also in Niphon, there is a temple dedicated to Amida. It was built to appease the ghost of a young prince of the family of Feiji—so celebrated in the legendary annals of Japan—whose nurse, with the boy in her arms, is said to have thrown herself headlong into the straits, to avoid capture by his father's enemies, at the time of the ruin of his family.

The voyage from Simonoseki to Osacca, in Niphon, affords little worth dwelling upon—except, indeed, the means which—the winds being contrary and tempestuous —the Japanese sailors adopted in order to obtain favourable weather. These and their result are too national to be omitted. The mariners flung overboard a small barrel

* Siebold.

of *saki*, and a certain number of copper coins, as a sacrifice to the god Kampira. The money, of course, sank, and thus it is to be hoped found its intended way to the deity it was destined to propitiate ; but the barrel floated, and was picked up by some fishermen. Does the reader suspect that the finders drank this favourite and intoxicating liquor ? He would do them great injustice. They well knew the meaning of the act, and honestly carried the offering to the proper temple !

Where else shall we find such national devotion ? . . . The French naturalists absurdly classify man as " a kingdom by himself" amongst animals.: "a race by itself" seems certainly to be the designation of the Japanese.

The voyage occupied six days—the distance being one hundred and thirty-four Japanese miles. We anchored every night in good harbours, which are numerous on the coast. The voyage lay first through the strait between Ximo and Niphon, and then through the strait or sea between Niphon and Sikokf, dotted with numerous islands, some cultivated, others mere rocks. On the main land we beheld, on either side, snow-clad mountains towering in the distance.

At length we reached Osacca, one of the five imperial cities. It is pleasantly situated in a fruitful plain, on the banks of a navigable river. At the east end is a strong castle ; and at the western, two strong, stately guard-houses, which separate it from the suburbs. The river Jodogawa runs on the north side, and falls into the sea below the city. This river rises a day and a half's journey to the north-east, out of the midland lake in the province of Umi, which was formed in one night by a violent earthquake. The stream washes one-third part of the city, and thence its waters are conveyed by a broad canal to supply the south part, which is the largest, and is the residence of the richest inhabitants. Several small channels, cut from the larger, pass through the chief streets, deep enough to be navigable for small boats, which bring goods to the merchants' doors. Upwards of a hundred bridges, many extraordinarily beautiful, span these channels.

The main river is narrow, but deep and navigable. From its mouth upwards as far as Osacca there are seldom less than a thousand boats going up and down, some with merchants, others with the princes and the lords, from the eastward, on their way to and from Jeddo. The banks are raised on both sides into ten or more steps, coarsely hewn out of freestone, so that they look like one continued set of stairs, and you may land wherever you please. Stately bridges are laid over the river at every three or four hundred paces' distance. These are built of cedar-wood, and are raised on both sides, some of the rails being adorned at top with brass knobs or buttons. We counted in all ten such bridges, three of which were remarkable for their length, being laid over the great arm of the river where it is broadest.

The streets are for the most part narrow, but regular, cutting each other at right angles, and are very neat, though not paved. For the convenience of walking, there is a small pavement of square stones along the houses on each side of the street. We observed the strong gates, at the end of every street, which are shut at night, when nobody is suffered to pass from street to street without special leave and a passport from the Ottona, or street officer. There was also in every street a place railed in, where were kept all the necessary instruments in case of fire. The houses, built of wood, and coated with lime and clay, presented to the eye the uniform aspect of houses built in strict accordance with the "Building Act of Parliament" in Japan—two stories high, each of nine or twelve feet—flat roof, covered with black tiles. The shops exhibited some fine patterns of their wares, or showed us the various artificers openly exercising their trade :—from the upper end of the room hangs a piece of black cloth, partly for ornament and partly to defend them in some measure from the wind and weather.

Within doors all the houses were kept neat and clean to admiration—the staircases, rails, and all the wainscoting varnished—the floors covered with the neat national mats, with all the other appointments as previously described.*

Osacca is extremely populous : as before stated, the Japanese boast that it can raise an army of 80,000 men. It is certainly the best trading town of Japan, being well situated for carrying on commerce both by land and water. Here wealthy merchants abound, skilful artificers ply their trade, and manufacturers of all kinds produce their wares. Called by the Japanese themselves the universal theatre of pleasure and diversion, as before stated, whatever tends to promote luxury, and to administer to sensuality, may be had at Osacca at as easy a rate as anywhere. Besides the daily plays, both in private and public-houses, mountebanks, jugglers, who perform some clever tricks,† and all the proprietors of some wonderfully clever or monstrous animal, real or fictitious, resort thither from all parts of the empire, being sure to get a better penny here than anywhere else. Some years ago, the Dutch East India Company sent over from Batavia a casuar—a large bird said to swallow stones and hot coals—as a present to the emperor. The bird having had the bad luck not to please the rigid imperial censors, the Governors of Nagasaki, the Dutch were ordered to send him back to Batavia. Whereupon a rich Japanese assured them that if he could have obtained leave to buy him, he would have willingly given a thousand *taels* (about £280), as being sure within a year's time to get double that money by showing him at Osacca.

The Japanese seem particularly fond of the marvellous, the strange, the monstrous, and anything of the sort is sure to succeed amongst them. Their clever geniuses turn this propensity to account, as appears by the following anecdote of a Japanese fisherman :—

He contrived to unite the upper half of a monkey to the lower half of a fish so neatly as to defy ordinary inspection. He then gave out that he had caught the

---

* See page 125 of this book.
† See woodcut, p. 1.

O

creature alive in his net, but that it had died shortly
after being taken out of the water ; and he derived considerable pecuniary profit from his cunning in more ways
than one.   The exhibition of the sea-monster to Japanese
curiosity paid well; but yet more productive was the
assertion that the half human fish, having spoken during
the few minutes it existed out of its native element, had
predicted a certain number of years of wonderful fertility,
and a fatal epidemic, the only remedy for which would be
possession of the marine prophet's likeness.   The sale of
these pictured mermaids was immense.   Either this com-
posite animal, or another, the offspring of the success of
the first, was sold to the Dutch factory, and transmitted
to Batavia, where it fell into the hands of a speculating
American, who brought it to Europe, and here, in the
years 1822-3, exhibited his purchase as a real mermaid at
every capital, to the admiration of the ignorant, the perplexity of the learned, and the filling of his own purse.*
Indeed, the mermaids exhibited in Europe and America,
to the great profit of enterprising showmen, have been of
Japanese manufacture.†

Osacca is the Paris of Japan, to which thousands resort
daily, chiefly the rich, as a place where they can spend
their time and money with much greater satisfaction than
perhaps anywhere else in the empire.   The western princes
and lords to the south of Osacca have houses in this city,
with a suite to attend them in their passage through ; yet
they are not permitted to stay longer than one night in
the city, and upon their departure they must follow a road
entirely out of sight of the castle.

The water drunk at Osacca is somewhat brackish ; but
in lieu of it they have the best saki in the empire.   It is
brewed in great quantities in the neighbouring village of
Tenusii, and the right good liquor of these Japanese Basses
and Barclays is exported into most other provinces ; nay,
by the Dutch and Chinese out of the country.   Doubtless

* *Manners and Customs of the Japanese.*
† Hildreth.

the time will come when, improved by its voyage across the ocean, it will rival amongst us the choicest brewings of Edinburgh or Burton.

On the east side of the city, in a large plain, lies the famous castle built by the renowned siogoun, Tiko Sama. We took half an hour in walking round the edifice, which is square, and strongly fortified with round bastions, according to the military architecture of the country. The moles or buttresses which support the outer-wall are of uncommon thickness, I believe at least forty-two feet thick. They are built to support a high, strong brick wall, lined with freestone, which, at its upper end, is planted with a row of firs or cedars.

The day after our arrival, we were admitted to an audience of the governor of the city, to which we were carried in kangos, attended by our whole train of interpreters and other officers. Just before the house we stepped out of our kangos, and put on each a silk cloak, which is reckoned equal to the garments of ceremony which the Japanese wear on these occasions. Through a passage thirty paces long we came into the hall or guardhouse, where we were received by two of the governor's gentlemen, who very civilly desired us to sit down. Four soldiers stood upon duty on our left as we came in, and next to them we found eight other officers of the governor's court, all sitting upon their knees and ankles, or squatting. The wall on our right was hung with arms, ranged in a proper order; fifteen halberds on one side, twenty lances in the middle, and nineteen pikes on the other; the latter were adorned at the upper end with fringes. Hence we were conducted by two of the governor's secretaries through four rooms (which, however, upon removing the screens, might be enlarged into one) into the hall of audience. I took notice as we passed that the walls were hung and adorned with bows, with sabres and scimitars, as also with some fire-arms, kept in rich black varnished cases.

In the hall of audience, where there were seven of the governor's gentlemen sitting, the two secretaries sat down at three paces' distance from us, and treated us with tea, carrying on a very civil conversation with us till the governor appeared, as he soon did, with two of his sons, one seventeen, the other eighteen years of age, and sat down at ten paces' distance in another room, which was laid open towards the hall of audience by removing three lattices, through which he spoke to us.

He seemed to be about forty years of age, middle-sized, strong, active, of a manly countenance and broad-faced; very civil in his conversation, and speaking with a great deal of softness and modesty. He was but meanly clad in black, and wore a gray garment of ceremony over his dress. He wore, also, but one ordinary scimitar. His conversation turned chiefly upon the following points:—That the weather was now very cold; that we had made a very great journey; that it was a singular favour to be admitted into the emperor's presence; that, of all nations in the world, only the Dutch were allowed this honour.

He promised us, that since the chief-justice of Meako, whose business it is to give us the necessary passports for our journey to court, was not yet returned from Jeddo, he would give us his own passports, which would be full as valid, and that we might send for them the next morning. He also assured us that he was very willing to assist us with horses and whatever else we might stand in need of for continuing our journey.

On our sides, we returned him thanks for his kind offers, and desired that he would be pleased to accept of a small present, consisting of some pieces of silk stuffs, as an acknowledgment of our gratitude. We also made some presents to the two secretaries or stewards of his household; and, having taken our leave, were by them conducted back to the guard-house. Here we took our leave of them also, and returned through the above-mentioned passage back to our kangos, and returned to our inn.*

On the following day we started early, and after about two hours' riding we arrived, at two in the afternoon, at

* Kämpfer.

Fusimi. This is a small open town, or rather village of a few streets, of which the middle and chief reaches as far as Meako; and is contiguous to the streets of that capital, insomuch that Fusimi might be called the suburbs of Meako, the rather since this last city is not at all enclosed with walls. It was to-day *Tsitats* with the Japanese, that is, the first day of the month, which they keep as a Sunday or holiday, visiting the temples, walking into the fields, and following all manner of diversions. Accordingly we found this street, along which we rode for full four hours before we got to our inn, crowded with multitudes of the inhabitants of Meako, walking out of the city to take the air, and to visit the neighbouring temples. Particularly the women were all on this occasion richly apparelled in variously coloured gowns, wearing a purple-coloured silk about the forehead, and large straw hats to defend themselves from the heat of the sun. We likewise met some particular sorts of beggars, comically clad, and some masked in a very ridiculous manner. Not a few walked upon iron stilts; others carried large pots with green trees upon their heads; some were singing, some whistling, some fluting, others beating of bells. All along the street we saw multitudes of open shops, jugglers and players diverting the crowd.

The temples which we had on our right as we went up, built in the ascent of the neighbouring green hills, were illuminated with many lamps, and the priests, beating some bells with iron hammers, made such a noise as could be heard at a considerable distance. I took notice of a large, white dog, perhaps made of plaster, which stood upon an altar on our left, in a neatly adorned chapel or small temple, which was consecrated to the Patron of the dogs.

I have before stated, that the princes and lords of the empire, as also the governors of the imperial cities and crown lands, must go to court once a year, to pay their homage to the Siogoun. I will now describe their magnificent "progress" in all its details.

The train of some of the most eminent amongst the

princes of the empire fills up the road for some days.
Accordingly, though we travelled pretty fast ourselves,
yet we often met the baggage and fore-troops, consisting
of the servants and inferior officers, for two days together,
dispersed in several troops, and the prince himself followed
on the third day, attended with his numerous court, all
marching in admirable order.   The retinue of one of the
chief Daimios, as they are called, is computed to amount
to about 20,000 men, more or less ; that of a Sjomio, to
about 10,000 ; that of a governor of the imperial cities
and crown-lands, to one or several hundreds, according
to his revenues.

If two or more of these princes and lords, with their
numerous retinue, should chance to travel the same road
at the same time, they would prove a great hindrance to
one another, particularly if they should happen at once to
come to the same siuku or village, forasmuch as often
whole great villages are scarce large enough to lodge the
retinue of one single Daimio.   To prevent these incon-
veniences, it is usual for great princes and lords to bespeak the several siukus they are to pass through, with
all the inns, some time before ; as, for instance, some of
the first quality a month, others a week or two before
their arrival.   Moreover, the time of their future arrival
is notified in all the cities, villages, and hamlets they are
to pass through, by putting up small boards on high poles of
bamboos, at the entry and end of every village, signifying
in a few characters what day of the month such or such a
lord is to pass through that village, to dine or to lie there.

To satisfy the reader's curiosity, it will not be amiss to
describe one of these princely trains, omitting the forerunners, baggage, led-horses, kangos, and palanquins,
which are sent a day or two before.   But the account
which I propose to give must not be understood of the
retinue of the most powerful princes and petty kings,
such as the lords of Satzuma, Cango, Owari, Kijnokuni,
and Mito, but only of those of some other Daimios, several
of which we met in our journey to court, the rather as
they differ but little, excepting only the coats of arms,

and particular pikes, some arbitrary order in the march, and the number of led-horses, lackered chests, norimons, kangos, and their attendants.

1. Numerous troops of forerunners, harbingers, clerks, cooks, and other inferior officers, begin the march, they being to provide lodgings, victuals, and other necessary things for the entertainment of their prince and master, and his court. They are followed by

2. The prince's heavy baggage, packed up either in small trunks, such as I have above described, and carried upon horses, each with a banner, bearing the coat of arms and the name of the possessor, or else in large chests covered with red lackered leather, again with the possessor's coat of arms, and carried upon men's shoulders, with multitudes of inspectors to look after them.

3. Great numbers of smaller retinues, belonging to the chief officers and noblemen attending the prince, with pikes, scimitars, bows and arrows, umbrellas, palanquins, led-horses, and other marks of their grandeur, suitable to their birth, quality, and office. Some of these are carried in norimons, others in kangos, others go on horseback.

4. The prince's own numerous train, marching in an admirable and curious order, and divided into several troops, each headed by a proper commanding officer : as—
1. Five, more or less, fine led-horses, led each by two grooms, one on each side, two footmen walking behind.
2. Five or six, and sometimes more porters, richly clad, walking one by one, and carrying fassanbacks, or lackered chests, and japanned neat trunks and baskets upon their shoulders, wherein are kept the gowns, clothes, wearing-apparel, and other necessaries for the daily use of the prince ; each porter is attended by two footmen, who take up his charge by turns. 3. Ten, or more fellows, walking again one by one, and carrying rich scimitars, pikes of state, fire-arms, and other weapons in lackered wooden cases, as also quivers with bows and arrows. Sometimes, for magnificence sake, there are more fassan-back bearers, and other led-horses follow this troop.
4. Two, three, or more men, who carry the pikes of state,

as the badges of the prince's power and authority, adorned at the upper end with bunches of cock-feathers, or certain rough hides, or other particular ornaments, peculiar to such or such a prince. They walk one by one, and are attended each by two footmen. 5. A gentleman carrying the prince's hat, which he wears to shelter himself from the heat of the sun, and which is covered with black velvet. He is attended, likewise, by two footmen. 6. A gentleman carrying the prince's sombrero or umbrella, which is covered in like manner with black velvet, attended by two footmen. 7. Some more fassanbacks and varnished trunks, covered with varnished leather, with the prince's coat of arms upon them, each with two men to take care of it. 8. Sixteen, more or less, of the prince's pages, and gentlemen of his bed-chamber, richly clad, walking two and two before his norimon. They are taken out from among the first quality of his court. 9. The prince himself sitting in a stately norimon or palanquin, carried by six or eight men, clad in rich liveries, with several others walking at the norimon's sides, to take it up by turns. Two or three gentlemen of the prince's bedchamber walk at the norimon's side, to give him what he wants and asks for, and to assist and support him in going in or out of the norimon. 10. Two or three horses of state, the saddles covered with black. One of these horses carries a large elbow-chair, which is sometimes covered with black velvet, and placed on trappings of the same stuff. These horses are attended each by several grooms and footmen in liveries, and some are led by the prince's own pages. 11. Two pike-bearers. 12. Ten, or more people carrying each two baskets of a monstrous large size, fixed to the ends of a pole, which they lay on their shoulders in such a manner, that one basket hangs down before, another behind them. These baskets are more for state than for any use. Sometimes some fassanback bearers walk among them, to increase the troop. In this order marches the prince's own train, which is followed by

5. Six or twelve led-horses, with their leaders, grooms, and footmen, all in liveries.

6. A multitude of the prince's domestics, and other officers of his court, with their own very numerous trains and attendants, pike-bearers, fassanback-bearers, and footmen in liveries. Some of these are carried in kangos, and the whole troop is headed by the prince's high-steward, carried in a norimon.

If one of the prince's sons accompanies his father in this journey to court, he follows with his own train immediately after his father's norimon.

It is a sight exceedingly curious and worthy of admiration, to see all the persons who compose the numerous train of a great prince, the pike-bearers the norimon-men and liverymen alone excepted, clad in black silk, marching in an elegant order, with a decent becoming gravity, and keeping so profound a silence, that not the least noise is to be heard, save what must necessarily arise from the motion and rustling of their habits, and the trampling of the horses and men.

On the other hand, it appears ridiculous to an European to see all the pike-bearers and norimon-men, with their clothes tucked up above their waists, exposing their nakedness to the spectators' view, with only a piece of cloth about their loins. What appears still more odd and whimsical is to see the pages, pike-bearers, umbrella and hat-bearers, chest-bearers, and all the footmen in liveries, affect, when they pass through some remarkable town, or by the train of another prince or lord, a strange mimic march or dance. Every step they make, they draw up one foot quite to their backs, stretching out the arm on the opposite side as far as they can, and putting themselves in such a posture, as if they had a mind to swim through the air. Meanwhile the pikes, hats, umbrellas, chests, boxes, baskets, and whatever else they carry, are danced and tossed about in a very singular manner, answering to the motion of their bodies. The norimon-men, who have their sleeves tied with a string as near the shoulders as possible, so as to leave their arms naked, carry the pole of the norimon either upon their shoulders, or else upon the palms of their hands, holding it above their heads. Whilst they hold it up with one arm, they stretch out the other, putting the hand into a horizontal posture, whereby, and by their short, deliberate steps and stiff knees, they affect a ridiculous fear and circumspection. If the prince steps out of his norimon into one of the green huts which are purposely built for him at convenient distances on the road, or if he goes into a private house, either to drink a dish of tea or for any other purpose, he always leaves a kobang with the landlord as a reward for his trouble.* At dinner or supper the expense is much greater.†

Half-way between Meako and Jeddo, on the western coast of a deep bay with a harbour (and not on a lake, according to Fisscher), stands the town of Aray, the station of the great Jeddo guard. So important is this post esteemed, that the prince in whose dominions it lies, and whose troops furnish the guard, is almost invariably a member of the Council of State. No one may pass Aray towards Yedo without the grand judge's passport. No woman can pass without the most especial permission; and, therefore, besides the examination of their papers and baggage to guard against the introduction of contraband goods, travellers are obliged to submit to a personal inquest, lest a woman should be smuggled through in male attire; a crime, the perpetration of which would infallibly cost the lives of the offending woman, of her male companions, and of the guards whose watchfulness should have been thus deceived. Why such watchfulness is exercised upon persons going to Jeddo, is, however, nowhere explained; the avowed object of the regulation being to prevent the escape of the wives of princes, governors, and other men high in office, whose families are detained at court as hostages for the fidelity of the husband and father.‡ Probably government does not wish to augment, without sufficient cause, the number

---

* The kobang is about twenty-six shillings sterling.
† Kämpfer.
‡ *Manners and Customs of the Japanese,* from Fisscher; corrected by Jancigny, *Japon.*

already so considerable, of families under special and constant surveillance, since neither the wife nor daughters of the high functionaries may leave the capital.

When every form has been gone through, a vessel belonging to the prince, but bearing for this occasion the Dutch flag, carried the whole party across the lake. The next day we were ferried over the rapid river Tenriogawa, the sand of which is full of gold dust, which, Fisscher says, the Japanese do not understand the art of separating from the baser matter. A strange piece of ignorance in a nation whose skill in metallurgy is highly praised!

But a river that, without gold-dust, is much more renowned in Japan, is the Oyegawa, which we crossed the following day. The river has too much of the torrent character to bear a bridge or a ferry boat. It is accordingly passed by fording; an operation rendered dangerous, as well as difficult, by the unevenness of the bottom, which is thickly strewed with large blocks of stone. Upon the banks are stationed persons, whose business it is to conduct travellers across. These people answer with their lives for the safety of man, beast, and baggage; not the slightest accident must happen to the traveller; and the number of guides to attend upon each, as well as their remuneration, is fixed by law, according to the depth of the water. The bed of the river is about a quarter of a mile broad, of which, when we crossed, the stream occupied not more than fifty feet, whilst the water reached to a man's breast. It need scarcely be stated that, after heavy rain, this river is often unfordable, and travellers are delayed very many days upon its banks. Our party experienced no such inconvenience, but even then from twelve to sixteen men were required for their *norimons*, and the pedestrians were carried over on the shoulders of the guides.*

Nothing can exceed the comical appearance of this operation. The whole stream is agitated by human beings in every direction, ladies sitting on a sort of

* *Ubi suprà.*

stretcher with hand-rails, the men, or rather the gentlemen, in a like position, or perched on the shoulders of
the sturdy porter, with his legs stuck out at a right angle,
and firmly grasped by the brawny arms engaged in this
" life and death" struggle with the Styx or infernal river
of Japan.*

The Japanese, endowed as they are with an exquisite
eye for the beauties, the contrasts, the sublimities of
nature, as well as the comicalities of life and its occasionally queer and unexpected positions, could not fail to
find abundant illustrations in this their renowned river.
It supplies to their painters their favourite landscapes ;
to their poets and aphoristic novelists their endless
metaphors, similes, and illustrations.†

But the mighty extinct volcano, Fousi Yamma, seen
shortly before coming to the banks of the river, rivals in
the Japanese mind the attractions of the latter. Fousi
stands up in the midst of his confraternity of mountains,
like Goliath over David. For more than a century and
a half he has been taking his rest—putting on his snowy
garments in winter, and clothing himself in nature's
favourite green in summer. Contemplatively he seems
to look down and around upon the fertile region beneath
him, now teeming with a rejoicing population, who no
longer fear him—who have practically forgotten that he
once was as Shiva, the Destroyer—heeding not that
there may be still mischief in him. Should he get tired
some day of " doing nothing"—should he—like the deep
designing villain who, after a long interval of close observation, preparation, and plotting, seizes the moment of
attacking, ruining, killing you unawares—blaze forth, as
of old : but God forfend it ! And indeed the realities
of human suffering, in mind and body, are sufficient for
the day ;—to anticipate evil is neither wise nor grateful

---

* In the *United States Expedition,* i. 493, there is a Japanese
picture of this scene.

† As a specimen of our ignorance of the true Japanese names, I
may state that this river is variously called in the books, Ohoegawa,
Ogingawa, Oïngawa, Ojegawa, Oyugawa, and, as above, Oyegawa.

to that Providence which we are forced sometimes to believe *special* in our deliverance.

Abraham built his altar on a moutain. Mountains have always held a conspicuous place in the religions of antiquity. From their awful majesty, and because they seem to touch the heavens, and are difficult of access, and because in fair weather their summits appear either cloud-covered or light-illumined, and in foul weather are the centre of the gathering storm, they have been made by infant nations the dwelling-place of the gods. Merou is the mountain home of the Hindoo deities ; Albordj was the habitation of the Persian Ormuzd ; on Olympus the Grecian Jupiter was wont to hold his court ; and on Sinai Jehovah first appeared to Moses, as also in the temple on Zion afterwards He dwelt. Nay, even the negroes of the Gold Coast imagine that the highest mountains—those whence they behold the lightning flash —are the dwellings of their gods. Not only are they, to the mere uneducated eye, nearer to heaven, and there- fore nearer to God, but they do seem, as it were, natural altars which the Earth herself has raised to the Deity. It is everywhere the same. The "high places" have always been consecrated to religious uses. In China they have set apart four mountains for divine service. In India there is scarcely a mountain with a well or spring that is not surmounted by some temple. Had not the Greeks the lofty hill of Jove everywhere ? Had not the Hebrews their Bethel—the house of God—where the people went up ?* And so is Fousi Yamma to the Japa- nese the object of "superstitious" veneration. How can they help it ? Those who can reach the summit, amidst the whirlwinds that riot in the everlasting snow, believe that they have performed a holy pilgrimage to the natural temple of the god of storms, and to that top they mount to put up their prayers to the idols which their ancestors placed there, in the hollow of the rocks. It requires

---

* Priaulx, *Quœstiones Mosaicœ*, 288, ed. 1854. A wonderfully elaborate, thoughtful, and conscientious book.

three days to mount it; but it is said that you may
descend, if you like, in three hours by means of a sort
of sledge made of reeds or straw, and fixed to the waist ;
thus prepared you may roll or slide down over the snow
in winter, or the sands in summer, the mountain being
wonderfully smooth in its gentle slope. Fousi has his
priests, or monks—the *yammabosis*—the sacred Order of
Æolus, and they are "mendicants," begging with the
words, "For Fousi Yamma"—that is, "for the Lord
Fousi."   It is one of their special duties to visit the
" high places."*

The mountain is strikingly beautiful, as well as bold
in aspect, and commands admiration from the first moment
that it is fairly seen—at a distance of two days' journey.
Kämpfer says that those who have been at the top report
that they found there a prodigious hole, which formerly
emitted smoke, until at last there arose a small hill on
the highest points, but that at present it is full of water.
The road running along its foot affords, during a considerable time, a view of its sublime beauties ; and at
the village Motoitsiba, whence it is seen to peculiar advantage, a peasant hospitably offers the traveller an entertainment, the principal dish of which is a preparation of
saki, with *snow from Fousi*, bearing some resemblance to
the ice-creams of Europe.   The peasant's hospitality is
rewarded by the present of a kobang.

Soon after leaving the vicinity of this, often-painted
and often-sung, extinct volcano, we began the toilsome
ascent of another mountain, or mountainous ridge, which
must be crossed.   It is called Fakone, and likewise offered
splendid views of mingled fertility and savage nature.

The villages are inhabited by the best turners, carvers,
and artificers in lacker-work ("japanning"), and they
sell their wares at very moderate prices.   The princes
and nobles of the land congregate at an establishment a
few miles from Fakone, where tea, confectionary, and
other dainties are served up by beautiful damsels.

* More of these rigorous ascetics in the sequel.

The village itself is situated near a small fresh-water lake, whence we procured a dish of salmon. Nothing could excel the beauty of the maples round about: the brilliant *Gardenia florida* was planted as a hedge-bush, by the rich, near their dwellings. The seed-vessels of the latter were sold in the shops, and used for dyeing yellow.

The lake is a league in length and three-quarters broad. That it was produced by an earthquake, which sunk the land, as was stated, seems evident from the fact that from its bottom the divers still bring up large cedar-trees which must have sunk with the land itself.

We left this beautiful spot, and proceeded on our journey down the mountain. We saw a great many pretty artificial cascades and aqueducts from the lake, made by the inhabitants; but before we reached the foot of the mountain, we were narrowly searched in presence of the sitting imperial commissioner.*

The duty of the commissioner is, particularly, to take great care that no weapons are carried this way up the country, nor women downwards—especially such as are kept at Jeddo. This post is more important than Aray, before mentioned, and here all travellers must show their passports, or be detained. A curious anecdote is told of a trick put upon this Fakone guard, and of the combined artifice and violence by which the extensively fearful consequences of that trick were obviated.

An inhabitant of Jeddo, named Fiyosayemon, a widower with two children, a girl and a boy, was called to a distance by business. He was poor; he knew not how to provide for his children during his absence, and resolved to take both with him. Accordingly, he dressed his daughter in boy's clothes, and thus passed the Fakone guard unsuspected. He was rejoicing in his success, when a man, who knew what children he had, joined him, congratulated him on his good luck, and asked for something to drink. The alarmed father offered a trifle; the man demanded a sum beyond his means; a quarrel

* Thunberg.

ensued, and the angry informer ran back to the guard to make known the error that had been committed. The whole guard was thunderstruck. If the informer spoke truth, and the fact were detected, all their lives were forfeited ; yet, to send a party to apprehend the offenders, and thus actually betray themselves, was now unavoidable. The commanding officer, however, saw his remedy. He delayed the detachment of reluctant pursuers sufficiently to allow a messenger with a little boy to outstrip them. The messenger found Fiyosayemon and his children refreshing themselves at an inn ; he announced the discovery made, and the imminent danger ; offered the boy as a temporary substitute for the disguised girl, and told the father that, when the falsehood of the charge should have been proved by both the children appearing to be boys, he might very fairly fly into such a rage as to kill his accuser. The kind offer was, of course, gratefully accepted. The wilfully dilatory guard arrived, surrounded the house, seized upon Fiyosayemon and the children, and gladly pronounced that both the latter were boys. The informer, who well knew Fiyosayemon's family, declared that some imposition had been practised, which the accused indignantly resenting, drew his sword, and struck off the informer's head. The delighted guard exclaimed that such a liar had only met his deserts, and returned to their post ; while the father, receiving back his daughter instead of the substituted boy, went his way rejoicing.*
I give this anecdote as related, without vouching for its consistency or credibility : both may be questioned.

On the banks of the Lake of Fakone there were five small wooden chapels, in each of which a priest was seated, beating a gong and howling a namada—that is, a prayer to the god Amida. This prayer, or invocation, unintelligible to the Japanese, is, as modern orientalists have discovered, good Sanscrit.† All the Japanese foot-travellers of our retinue threw some small pieces of money

* Titsingh, *Japanese Annals ; Manners and Customs of the Japanese.*
† Hildreth, *Japan.*

into the chapel, and in return received each a paper, which they carried, bareheaded, with great respect to the shore, in order to throw it into the lake, having first tied a stone to it, that it might be sure to go to the bottom, which they believe is the purgatory for children who die before seven years of age. So their priests tell them, and for their comfort assure them that as soon as the water washes off the names and characters of the gods and saints written upon the papers, the children at the bottom feel great relief, if they do not obtain a full and effectual redemption.*

At another place in the vicinity there lived in a cell an old gray monk, eighty years old, who had spent the greater part of his life in holy pilgrimages, running up and down the country, and visiting all the temples. The people had canonized and reverenced him as a saint in his lifetime, and worshipped his statue which he had caused to be carved in stone—thus beating Alexander the Great, who received no divine honours during his life.†

After escaping from this critical police-net, we journeyed on to the Banningawa, another large, rapid, and dangerous river of Japan. No bridge can be built over it ; and we crossed in flat-bottomed boats constructed for the purpose. Here ended the mountainous tracts, and a level plain lay open before us, as far as the eye could see.

At length the last day's journey began—ten leagues from the object of our eager expectations—the great city of Jeddo. On this, and on the preceding day, we travelled through an extremely well inhabited and cultivated country, where one town or village almost joined another, and where travellers in large troops, near the capital, as it were, jostled each other, eager to enter.

The coast, in different parts, is well supplied with oysters and various shells : the people were engaged in collecting green and brownish sea-weed, which serves them for food. After these weeds—naturally not a little tough—have been well washed, and freed from salt, sand,

* Kämpfer.   † Idem.

P

and other impurities, they are cut into pieces, which are again washed and squeezed, until they are fit to be made into small cakes, and eaten.   It is probably the trace of iodine contained in this sea-weed that accounts for the absence in Japan of scrofula and other skin diseases affecting the glands.

At Sinagawa, one of the suburbs of the imperial city, we rested, took some refreshment, and enjoyed the delightful view presented to us by the largest town in the empire, and probably on the whole face of the earth, and by its beautiful harbour.

With the same curiosity with which we beheld the town, harbour, and adjacent country, the Japanese beheld us ; and making up to us in shoals, formed around us, shut up, as it were, in our norimons, a kind of encampment.   Amongst the rest were several ladies of distinction, who had been carried to the spot in their norimons, and seemed displeased when we at any time let down the curtains.   The norimons, when set down on the ground around us, seemed to form a little village, whose moveable mansions a short time afterwards disappeared.*

Having passed through the suburbs of Sinagawa and Takanava, our train went forward, preceded and accompanied by soldiers belonging to the town, chiefly for the purpose of preserving order.   The streets were so thronged with men, that we could scarcely see anything of the houses ; and although our escort resolutely endeavoured to repel the people, still they could not prevent our bearers from being inconveniently crowded.   We passed along wide streets, paved on both sides with stone, and, as in other towns, formed by regularly built houses, large edifices and shops, the latter protected by awnings.   In front of these shops, and of every place where goods were on sale, stood a number of boys, who recommended the goods, emulously clamouring, in order to draw the attention of passers-by.   Here, as in England, much is thought of signs and inscriptions over shops ; dragons and

* Thunberg.

other imaginary animals always figure over the doors throughout the East—amongst Mahometans in Arabia and Persia, as well as in China and Japan—according to the Mahometans, to prevent the envious from disturbing the peace of families. Although there are here no carriages to increase the noise and tumult, I can compare the hurly-burly of Jeddo to nothing but that of London.

Long before we entered Sinagawa, we were moving amidst the thronging of an unnumbered multitude, and along wide streets, all of which may be reckoned as part of the town; and, from the suburb to our residence, we were full two hours on our way, proceeding at a steady pace, rather faster than usual.*

Immediately on our arrival at Jeddo, we were visited by great numbers of the Japanese, although we were not suffered to go out before the day of audience at the court of the Saogoun. No one, however, had liberty to pay us a visit except such as had received express permission from the Government. At first we were visited by the learned and great men of the country, afterwards even merchants and others were numbered amongst our visitors.

Five physicians and two astronomers were the very first to visit us, and express their satisfaction at our arrival. We had several hours' conversation with them on scientific questions, to which they requested satisfactory answers and illustrations.† It was evident that they had considerable mathematical learning. The Japanese astronomers have made decided progress since the time of Thunberg, who gave an unsatisfactory account of them in 1776. One of these astronomers understood the Copernican system, was acquainted with the orbit and satellites of Uranus, knew the nature and doctrine of sines and tangents, and was familiar with the difference between the old and new styles. He assured us that the Japanese can calculate eclipses with much exactness.‡

---

* Fisscher.   † Thunberg, in 1776.
        ‡ Hildreth, from Golownin.

P 2

The names of the physicians were Okada Jeosin, a man above seventy years of age; he generally took the lead of the conversation, and, amongst other things, particularly requested me to give him some information concerning cancer, broken limbs, bleeding at the nose, boils, ulcerated throat, &c., toothache and the piles. Amano Reosjun and Fokusmoto Dosin were the names of two others, who in general were only listeners. All these did not often repeat their visits; but two of the doctors not only visited me daily, but sometimes stayed till late in the night, in order to be taught and instructed by me in various sciences, for which they evinced great ardour—such as natural philosophy, rural economy, and more especially botany, surgery, and physic. One of these gentlemen, Katsragawa Fosju, was the emperor's physician; he was very young, good-natured, acute, and animated. He wore the imperial arms on his clothes, and was accompanied by his friend Nakagawa Sunnan, who was somewhat older, and was physician to one of the first princes of the country. These two, particularly the latter, spoke Dutch tolerably well, and had some knowledge of natural history, mineralogy, zoology, and botany, collected partly from the Chinese and Dutch books, and partly from the Dutch physicians who had before visited the country; both of them were inexpressibly insinuating and fond of learning.*

The doctors were distinguished from others by the cir-

---

* Thunberg thus continues :—"And they were the more desirous of engaging me in conversation, as in me they found that knowledge which had been sought for in vain in others ; and as the interpreters had long before our arrival spread the report that this year a Dutch doctor would arrive much more learned than those who usually came thither, and who frequently were very little better than farriers. . . . . Although I was often wearied out by their questions, yet still I cannot deny that I have spent many an hour in their company with equal satisfaction and advantage. . . . Their principal books in botany were Johnston's *Historia Naturalis*, and Dodonæus's *Herbal*, and in physic Woyt's *Treasury* (*Gazophylacium*), which books they had purchased from the Dutch. In surgery, they had Heister translated into Dutch, and I sold to them at this time, amongst other books, a very fine edition of Muntingius's *Phytographia*."

cumstance that they sometimes shaved their heads all over, and sometimes kept their hair on, without taking, like others, part of it off.*

The third day after our arrival we witnessed one of the common but dreadful calamities which seem intended to prepare the minds of the Japanese for their periodic volcanic visitations—a fire at Jeddo.

At ten o'clock in the morning of the 22nd of April, 1806, we heard that a fire had broken out in the town, at the distance of about two leagues from our quarters. We heeded not the news, so common are fires at Jeddo ; a fine night never passes without one ; and as they are less frequent during rain, a lowering evening is a subject of mutual congratulation to the Jeddoites. But the flames came nearer and nearer ; and about three o'clock in the afternoon, a high wind driving the sparks towards our neighbourhood, four different houses round about us

---

* Thunberg, in 1776. Siebold, in 1826, gave a still better account of the Japanese men of science, "who are anxious to make the most of the opportunity of acquiring information respecting the latest scientific discoveries, an appreciation of the superiority of European knowledge which strikingly distinguishes the Japanese from the self-sufficient Chinese." Siebold (whose testimony is, from his own character for learning, most satisfactory) says that the questions of both physicians and astronomers discovered a proficiency in their respective sciences, which, considering their deficient means of acquiring information, actually astonished him. And it may be added, in proof of the acuteness and cultivation of the Japanese intellect, that the objections and difficulties started by the priests in their arguments with the first missionaries are reported to have been singularly astute and logical. The most acceptable present that can be offered to the physicians and astronomers is a new scientific publication in the Dutch language. Many of those given them they have translated into Japanese ; some of Laplace's works included.

"These scientific men are members of the Jeddo College. Such colleges, which the Dutch writers compare to their own high schools, are said to exist in many of the great cities, but the most distinguished for the excellency of their scientific professors are the colleges of Jeddo and Meako, though the latter, indeed, seems more akin to an academy of sciences."[1]

---

[1] *Manners and Customs of the Japanese.*

caught fire. Two hours before this occurred we had been sufficiently alarmed to begin packing; so that now, when the danger had become imminent, we were prepared to fly. On coming into the street, we saw everything blazing around us. To run with the flames before the wind appeared very dangerous; so, taking an oblique direction, we ran through a street that was already burning, and thus reached an open field, called *Hara*, behind the conflagration. It was thickset with the flags of princes, whose palaces were already consumed, and who had escaped hither with their wives and children. We followed their example, and appropriated a spot to ourselves by setting up a small Dutch flag used in crossing rivers. We had now a full view of the fire, and never did I see anything so frightful. The horrors of this sea of flame were yet enhanced by the heart-breaking cries and lamentations of fugitive women and children.

Here we were, for the moment, safe, but had no home. The Governor of Nagasaki, then resident at Jeddo, Fita-Boengo-no-Cami, had been dismissed; and the house of his successor, appointed that very day, was already in ashes. We had quarters assigned us in the house of the other governor, then resident at Nagasaki, which stands quite at the other side of the town; thither we were led at half-past ten in the evening, and were received, and all our wants supplied, in the most friendly manner, by the son of the absent governor.

About noon next day a heavy rain extinguished the fire. We learned from our Nagasakkya landlord, who paid us a visit, that the flames had caught his house within five minutes after our departure, and had consumed everything, neither goods nor furniture being saved. To afford him some relief, our Government charitably gave him, for three successive years, twenty *kanassars* of sugar; the *kanassar* being equal to sixty or seventy Amsterdam pounds. He likewise told us that thirty-seven palaces of princes were destroyed, and about twelve hundred persons (including a little daughter of the Prince of Awa) were burnt to death or drowned.

This last misfortune was caused by the breaking down of the celebrated bridge *Nippon-bas*, under the weight of the flying multitude, whilst those in the rear, unconscious of the accident, and wild to escape from the flames, drove those in front forward, and into the water.[*]

The official audience of the Siogoun can only take place on the twenty-eighth day of the current month—a holiday appropriated to the paying of compliments and making visits—after the performance of religious rites.

A sort of full dress is ordered for this occasion. That of the Dutch president is composed of velvet, the doctor's and secretary's of cloth, trimmed with gold or silver lace, or embroidered with gold or silver. All three wear cloaks —the president's is of velvet, those of the others of black satin—but these are not put on until they enter the interior of the palace. The president alone enjoys the privilege of having his sword borne behind him in a black velvet bag; no other foreigner is suffered even to retain his side-arms in Japan.

On the appointed day, the 28th of the 3rd Japanese month (which then answered to the 3rd of May), we repaired in state to the palace at six o'clock in the morning, to the end that we might be there prior to the arrival of the state counsellors. We were carried in our norimons into the castle, and to the gate of the palace, where even princes are obliged to alight, except only the three princes of Owari, Kiusiu, and Mito, who, being princes of the blood, are carried as far as the gate opposite to the *guard of a hundred men*. To this guard we proceeded on foot, and there awaited the coming of the counsellors of state. We were desired to sit on benches covered with red hangings, and were offered tea and materials for smoking. Here also we saw the Governor of Nagasaki, and one of the chief spies, or general commissioners of strangers (an odd title that seems to denote an office analogous to the French *Ministère de Police*), who, after congratulating us upon our prospect of immediate happiness in ap-

[*] Doeff.

proaching the Emperor, entered the palace. Then came
the commandant of the guard to visit the President;
and here it is necessary to stand rigidly upon one's rank.
The commandant required that I should come from the
innermost room, which is held the most honourable, into
the first, or outer room, because his inferior rank did not
authorize him to enter the inner room.   I, on my side,
asserted the impossibility of leaving the upper place
assigned me.   The commandant advanced, but paused at
the distance of two mats (about twelve feet), whence he
saluted me.   By thus resolutely maintaining my place
(which must always be done in Japan, when one is in the
right), I insured the observance of old customs, the restoration of which, if through goodnature one ever gives
way, is exceedingly difficult.

When all the state counsellors had arrived, we were
invited to cross yet more courts, and enter the palace,
where we were received by persons who, except for their
shaven heads, might be compared to pages. They conducted us to a waiting-room, where we sat down on the
floor, in a slanting direction, and covered our feet with
our cloaks ; to show the feet being in Japan an act of
gross rudeness.   This hall is a remarkably handsome
waiting-room, where several imperial spies kept us company, and divers great men visited us.   After remaining
some time here, the Governor of Nagasaki and the commissioner of foreigners led us into the audience-hall,
where we were desired to rehearse the required ceremonial, as the governor would pay the penalty of any
imperfection.   We were then led back to the waiting-
hall.   Some time afterwards, we accompanied the governor
to the real audience, from which we saw several grandees
returning.   We were led along a wooden corridor to the
Hall of a Hundred Mats—so named, because it actually
is carpeted with a hundred mats, each six feet by three.
These are made of straw, are about two inches thick, and
over them are laid others of finer workmanship, orna-
mentally bordered : such mats cover all handsome sitting-
rooms.   There we left the chief interpreter, and I alone,

with the Governor of Nagasaki, went into the audience-hall, where I saw the presents arranged on my left hand. Here we found the Siogoun, or Emperor, whose dress differed in no respect from that of his subjects. I paid my compliment in the precise form in which the princes of the realm pay theirs, whilst one of the state counsellors announced me by the shout of *Capitan Horanda !** Hereupon, the Governor of Nagasaki, who stood a step or two behind me, pulled me by the cloak, in token that the audience was over. The whole ceremony does not occupy a minute.†

The whole ceremony consists in making the Japanese compliment upon the appointed spot, and remaining for some seconds with the head touching the mats, whilst the words *Capitan Horanda* are proclaimed aloud. A stillness, as of death, prevails, broken only by the buzzing sound used by the Japanese to express profound veneration. The Governor of Nagasaki and the chief interpreter are the only persons who accompany the President, and give him the signal of retreat, which, like his entrance, is performed in a very stooping attitude; so that, although the presence of numbers may be perceived, it is impossible, without violating the laws of Japanese courtesy, to look round for what should attract attention or excite curiosity.‡

We then had to pay a complimentary visit to the Misnomor, or Crown Prince, in his palace. He is never at home on such occasions, and the deputation is received in his name by the state counsellors appointed for the purpose. His palace is finely situated upon a hill, whence some idea of the extent of the palace-grounds may be formed, and perhaps of the size of the town, since from that height its limits cannot be discovered in any direction.

We had also to visit the ordinary and extraordinary state counsellors, to present them with gifts—all in their absence, however, leaving their secretary to represent

---

* The Japanese convert the sound of *l* into *r*.
    † Doeff.   ‡ Fisscher.

them, according to Japanese etiquette—at least, as far as concerned the Dutch " traders."

We were everywhere politely received by a secretary, and entertained with tea and confectionary. This last was set before us on wooden trays, but not touched ; it was neatly folded up in paper, secured with gold or silver cords, and carried to our lodgings, in lackered bowls, by the under interpreter and our landlord. Behind the screens we heard the wives and children of the counsellors, who were curiously watching us. That they did not show themselves in the room was not from any Turkish custom of secluding women, but because it might have led to too great familiarity with strangers.*

We were everywhere presented with pipes and tobacco. In some houses permission was asked to examine our watches, and the President's hat and sword ; whilst at every visit I had the irksome task of writing with red lead upon several sheets of paper, which, after the fatigues of the day, together with the inconvenience of the posture, sitting on the ground, became at last exceedingly trouble-some, and almost intolerable. It was half-past nine in the evening before we got home from these honourable ceremonies, and then we had to receive a number of con-gratulatory visits, as though the object had been, by dint of compliments, to put our health and strength to the test, for it became at last a feverish agitation, under which many persons might have fainted.†

More than three or four days are seldom suffered to elapse, after the first compliment and tribute-paying audience, ere the Dutch deputation is summoned to an audience of dismissal. This did not differ from the former, excepting in being far less honourable. The Siogoun does not receive the deputation in person. His state counsellors receive the President in the Hall of a Hundred Mats, where the Governor of Nagasaki reads to him the proclamation, which is annually read to him at Nagasaki, detailing the stringent conditions on which

* Doeff.   † Fisscher.

the Dutch are permitted to trade with Japan. After these commands have been communicated, the Dutch President withdraws for a short time, and on his return receives the Siogoun's present, consisting of thirty robes of state. He withdraws again, and on his return receives twenty from the Crown Prince. He then goes home, and in the afternoon the secretaries of the state counsellors and other dignitaries bring him their master's leave-taking compliments, thanks for the presents received, and return-presents, consisting of silk robes, but inferior in quality to those given by the Siogoun. Each bearer of these gifts receives a present of sweetmeats, a paper of Dutch tobacco, and two gilt pipes.*

This is the whole of the ceremonial now practised at the court of Yedo, in the reception of foreigners, as given by writers of the present century. It differs not much from the forms described by Kampfer, as observed nearly one hundred and fifty years ago ; but the modern relations want the second part of the earlier narrative. A comparison of the two accounts, including this second part, which seems to be now obsolete, can hardly be uninteresting. Kämpfer, though admitted to the imperial presence, was, like his successors, excluded from the tribute-presenting audience, his description of which agrees with Fisscher's. Still, as the quaint and somewhat prolix old German physician is both more explicit and more graphic, the extract about to be taken from his book may as well begin with this audience.†

" As soon as the resident entered the hall of audience, they cried out, '*Horanda Capitan!*' which was the signal for him to draw near and make his obeisances. Accordingly, he crawled on his hands and knees to a place shown him, between the presents ranged in due order on one side, and the place where the Emperor sat on the other ; and there, kneeling, he bowed his forehead quite down to the ground, and so crawled backwards like a crab, without uttering a single word. So mean and short a thing is

---

* *Manners and Customs of the Japanese.*   † Ibid.

the audience we have of this mighty monarch. Nor are there any more ceremonies observed in the audience he gives, even to the greatest and most powerful princes of the empire. For, having been called into the hall, their names are cried out aloud, then they move on their hands and feet humbly and silently towards the Emperor's seat, and having showed their submission, by bowing their forehead down to the ground, they creep back again in the same submissive posture.

"In the second audience (seemingly an extra audience, and immediately following the first), the Emperor and the ladies invited to it, attend behind screens and lattices, but the counsellors of state, and other officers of the court, sit in the open rooms, in their usual and elegant order. As soon as the captain had paid his homage, the Emperor retired to his apartment, and not long afterwards we three Dutchmen were likewise called up, and conducted through galleries, &c."

But it is hard for modern patience to extract the circumstantial detail ; and we must be allowed to proceed at once to the more private audience-hall, where every one, Dutch and Japanese, is at length arranged in his proper place, Bengo, the Emperor's favourite and prime minister, sitting on a raised mat, between them and the Emperor.

"After the usual obeisances made (bowing and creeping towards the lattice, behind which sat his Majesty), Bengo bade us welcome in the Emperor's name ; the chief interpreter received the compliment from Bengo's mouth, and repeated it to us. Upon this, the ambassador made his compliment in the name of his masters. . . . This the chief interpreter repeated in Japanese, having prostrated himself quite to the ground, and speaking loud enough to be heard by the Emperor. The Emperor's answer was again received by Bengo, who delivered it to the chief interpreter, and he to us. . . . The mutual compliments over, the succeeding part of the solemnity turned to a perfect farce. We were asked a thousand ridiculous and impertinent questions. Thus, for instance, they desired to know, in the first place, how old each of us was, and what was his name? which we were commanded to write on a bit of paper, having for these purposes taken an European ink-horn along with us. This paper, together with the ink-horn itself, we were commanded to give to Bengo, who delivered them both into the Emperor's hands, reaching them over, below the lattice. The captain, or ambassador, was asked concerning the distance of Holland from Batavia, and of Batavia from Nagasaki? Which of the two was the most powerful, the Director-general of the Dutch East India Company at Batavia, or the Prince of Holland? As for my own particular the following questions were put to me :—What external and internal distempers I thought most dangerous and the most difficult to cure? How I proceeded in the cure of cancrous humours and imposthumations of the inner parts? Whether our European physicians did not search after some medicine to render people immortal, as the Chinese physicians had done for many hundred years? Whether we had made any considerable progress in this search, and which was the remedy most conducive to long life that had been found out in Europe? . . . . To which I returned in answer, that very many European physicians had long laboured to find out some medicine, which should have the virtue of prolonging human life, and preserving people in health to a great age; and having thereupon been asked, which I thought the best? I answered, that I always took that to be the best which was found out last, till experience taught us a better : and being further asked, which was the last? I answered, a certain spirituous liquor, which could keep the humours of our body fluid, and comfort the spirits. This general answer proved not altogether satisfactory, but I was quickly desired to let them know the name of this excellent medicine, upon which, knowing that whatever was esteemed by the Japanese, had long and high-sounding names, I returned in answer, it was the Sal volatile Oleosum Sylvij. This name was minuted down behind the lattices, for which purpose I was commanded to repeat it several times. The next question was, who it was that found it out, and where it was found out? I answered, Professor Sylvius in Holland. Then they asked, whether I could make it up? upon this our resident whispered me to say, No; but I answered, Yes, I could make it up, but not here. Then it was asked, whether it could be had at Batavia? and having returned in answer, that it was to be had there, the emperor desired that it should be sent over by the next ships. The emperor, who hitherto sat among the ladies, almost opposite to us, at a considerable distance, did now draw nearer, and sate himself down on our right behind the lattices, as near us as possibly he could. Then he ordered us to take off our cappa, or cloak, being our garment of ceremony, then to stand upright, that he might have a full view of us; again to walk, to stand still, to compliment each other, to dance, to jump, to play the drunkard, to speak broken Japanese, to read Dutch, to paint, to sing, to put our cloaks on and off. Meanwhile we obeyed the emperor's commands in the best manner we could; I joined to my dance a love-song in High German. In this manner, and with innumerable such other apish tricks, we must suffer ourselves to contribute to the Emperor's and the court's diversion. The ambassador, however, is free from these and the like commands, for as he represents the authority of his masters, some care is taken that nothing should be done to injure or prejudice the same. Besides that he showed so much gravity in his countenance and whole behaviour as was sufficient to convince the Japanese that he was not at all a fit person to have such ridiculous and comical commands laid upon him. Having been thus exercised for a matter of two hours, though with great apparent civility, some servants shaved came in, and put before each of us a small table with Japanese victuals, and a couple of ivory sticks, instead of knives and forks. We took and ate some little things, and our old chief interpreter, though scarce able to walk, was commanded to carry away the remainder for himself. We were then ordered to put on our cloaks again and to take our leave, which we gladly, and without delay, complied with, putting thereby an end to this second audience. We were then conducted back by the two commissioners to the waiting-room, where we took our leave of them also.

"It was now already three o'clock in the afternoon, and we had still several visits to make to the counsellors of state, of the first and second rank, as I have set them down above under the 25th of March. Accordingly we left the Fonmar forthwith, saluted as we went by the officers of the great imperial guard, and made our round a-foot. The presents had been carried beforehand to every one's house by our clerks, and because we did not see them in our audiences, I conjectured that they had been actually presented to the persons to whom they belonged. They consisted in some Chinese, Bengalese, and other silk stuffs, some linen, black serge, some yards of black cloth, gingangs, pelangs, and a flask of tent wine. We were everywhere received by the stewards and secretaries with extraordinary civility, and treated with tea, tobacco, and sweetmeats, as handsomely as the little time we had to spare would allow. The rooms, where we were admitted to audience, were filled behind the screens and lattices with crowds of spectators, who would fain have obliged us to show them some of our European customs and ceremonies, but could obtain nothing excepting only a short dance at Bengo's house (who came home himself a back way), and a song from each of us, at the youngest counsellors of state, who lived in the northern part of the castle. We then returned again to our kangos and horses, and having got out of the castle through the northern gate, we went back to our inn another way, on the left of which we took notice that there were strong walls and ditches in several places. It was just six in the evening when we got home, heartily tired."

It may be interesting to know the total cost of each of these embassies to the Dutch. In round numbers the sum may be set down as £4000, or rather £4500, taking the rix-dollar at 4*s.* 6*d.*. The following is old Kämpfer's curious summary of the various items :—

	Rix dol.
For victuals and lodging at 50 rix dollars a day, in our journey by land, makes in two months' time	3000
For 40 horses, and so many men, to carry our baggage from Osacca to Jeddo, which number is greater in going up to court and less upon our return, at 15 thails a horse, and 6 thails a man, as hath been agreed on of old (half of which money the interpreters put in their pockets), amounts to	3000
A sum of money divided among our retinue, to bear some extraordinary expenses of the journey, of which every Dutchman receives 54 thails, and the others more or less, according to their office and quality, amounts to about	1000
For hiring a barge (or if she be ours, for building her) 420 thails, to the sailors 50 thails : for the cabin-furniture and tackle 90 thails ; for maintaining and repairing the said barge 40 thails ; amounts in all to 600 thails, or	1000
For victuals, drink, tea, tobacco, and other necessary provisions for our voyage by sea	1000
For the usual presents in money; as for instance, to the bugjo, or commander-in-chief of our train, 300 thails (or 500 rix dollars), and much the same to the inn-keepers, their sons and domestics, at Osacca, Meako, and Jeddo, in all	1000
Hire for the norimon-men, as also for the kangos we make use of instead of horses, in order to be carried over mountains and bad roads, as also to visit certain temples and pleasure-houses : for passage-money to be ferried over rivers and harbours ; for some extraordinary expenses and presents, whether necessary, or for our diversion, may amount in all to	2000
Presents to be made to his Imperial Majesty, of little value indeed for so powerful a monarch, but what, if sold, would bring in a sum of at least	2500
Presents to be made to fourteen of the prime ministers, and chief officers of the imperial court at Jeddo ; to the two governors of that city, to the chief judge at Meako, as also to the two governors of that city, and of the city of Osacca. These presents consist in some foreign commodities, and are but a trifle to every one of them, but bring us to an expense of at least	3000
Presents to the two governors of Nagasaki, which they receive before our departure in raw silk and stuffs, which they sell again to very good advantage, make to us the sum of	2500
Sum total of all the expenses of our journey	20,000

FAMILY WORSHIP.

CHAPTER V.

RELIGION; RELIGIOUS INSTITUTIONS.

An old Dutchman says, "There are twelve several religions in Japan, and eleven of them are forbidden to eat
meat." If sects be counted, the number will greatly exceed twelve or twenty; indeed, it has been stated to be
five-and-thirty—a proof that there exists a spirit of inquiry
and freedom of interpretation in the Paganism of Japan
as well as in the Christianity of Europe and America.

Liberty of conscience, so far as it did not interfere
with the interests of Government, or affect the peace and
tranquillity of the empire, was, for a long time, allowed
in Japan, and (exception being had to Christianity) may
be said still to obtain to a very remarkable degree.

Q

There were, no doubt, preceding and ruder forms of faith ; but what is now considered the original, national religion of Japan, is called *Sinsyn ;* from the words *sin* (the gods) and *syn* (faith) ; and its votaries are denominated *Sintoos.**

All primitive mythologies are coupled with, and made to rise out of, cosmogony. The cosmogony of the Japanese is of the wildest sort, as I have before shown. From primeval Chaos there sprung a self-created, supreme God, whô fixed his abode in the highest heaven, and could not have his tranquillity disturbed by any cares. Next there arose two plastic, creative gods, who framed the universe out of chaos. The universe was then governed, for myriads of years, by seven gods in succession. They are called the Celestial Gods. The last of them was the only one that had a wife, and to him the earth we inhabit owes its existence. Once upon a time he said to his wife, "There should be, somewhere, a habitable earth. Let us seek it under the waters that are seething beneath us." He plunged his spear into the water, and as he withdrew it, the turbid drops that trickled from the weapon, congealed, and formed a great island.† This

---

* Dr. Von Siebold, however, says that the proper native name of this religion is *Kami-no-Mitsi,* signifying "the way of the Kami," or gods ; that the Chinese translated this compound word into *Shin-Tao,* and that the Japanese adopted the Chinese term, and, according to the genius of their language, softened it into *Sintoo.*

† Although the existence of a chaos—any state of things without form, and void, and dark—cannot be conceived by the mind, nor admitted excepting as by Revelation ; because all things, everywhere, in all time, must have borne the mighty impress of God's plastic hand, perfectly regulated according to a pre-established harmony ; yet it is certain that this belief prevailed amongst all the superior races of antiquity, and everywhere *water* plays a principal part. "I do not remember," says Burnet, "that any of the ancients that acknowledged the earth to have had an original, did deny that original to have been from a chaos. We are assured of both from the authority of Moses, who saith that in the beginning the earth was *tohu-bohu,* without form and void, a fluid, dark, confused mass, without distinction of parts, but without order or any determinate form." By the Brahmins it is believed that this All once existed in darkness, imperceptible, undefinable, undiscoverable, and undis-

island was Kewsew, the largest of the eight which then constituted the world—for Japan was then all the world. Eight millions of gods were then called into existence, and the ten thousand things necessary to mankind were created. The plastic divinity then committed the government of the whole to his favourite daughter, Ten-sio-dai-sin, the Sun Goddess, whose reign was shortened to the space of 250,000 years. She was succeeded by four other gods, who altogether reigned two million and odd years. These are the Terrestrial Gods. The last of them, having married a terrestrial wife, left a mortal son upon earth, named Zin-mu-ten-wou, the ancestor and progenitor of every Mikado that has ruled in Japan.

Of all these Gods of Sintoo mythology, none seem to be objects of great worship except the Sun Goddess ; and she is too great to be addressed in prayer, except through the mediation of the inferior Kami, or of her lineal descendant, the Mikado. The Kami consist of 492 born gods, and 2640 canonized or deified mortals. All these are mediatory spirits, and have temples dedicated to them.

We must speak doubtingly of this ancient faith, for it has evidently been mixed up with other worships and superstitions, and the amount of the foreign admixture

covered, as if wholly immured in deep. According to Sanchoniatho, we infer that the Phœnicians supposed that the "beginning of all things was a wind of black air, and a chaos dark as Erebus, and that they were boundless and for many ages without bound." And although the Chinese books nowhere directly speak of a chaos, yet, as they speak of the Heaven (Tien) and the Earth as the father and mother of all things, they imply that God and matter are co-eternal, and, as Tien, is also creator of chaos. But see Priaulx, *Quæstiones Mosaicæ*, p. 7, *et seq.* There is another version of Japanese cosmogony which speaks of "chaos," under the form of an egg, containing the *breath* [of life] self-produced, including the germs of all things. The word "breath" happens to be the true meaning of the Hebrew *ruah*, which our version renders by "spirit of God ;" and Milton inferred the idea of an "egg," as do some of the other translations :—

"Thou from the first
Wast present, and with mighty wing outspread,
Dove-like sat'st *brooding* on the vast abyss,
And mad'st it pregnant."

Q 2

seems very much to vary in different parts of the country. In all probability the Sintoos have nowhere preserved its original simplicity. The only decorations of the old temples consisted of a mirror, the emblem of the soul's purity, and a *gohei*, which is formed of many strips of white, spotless paper, another emblem of purity. The temples now possess images of the Kami to whom they are dedicated ; but it is assumed that these idols are not set up to be worshipped, that they are kept in secret recesses, and exhibited only upon particular festivals. Private families are said to keep images of their patron Kami in shrines and chapels. Meylan asserts that every Mya, or temple, was originally dedicated to one supreme divinity. This pure theism in such a state of society as that of the early Japanese may be questioned. Siebold considers every idol or image as a corrupt foreign innovation. He is of opinion that, originally, the Sun Goddess alone was worshipped, that the Kami was analogous to Roman Catholic saints, and that no images of them existed prior to the introduction of the Buddhist idolatry.* It appears that the Sintoo worship is now thoroughly permeated with Buddhism.

* This system of Kamis reminds us of both the *lares* and *penates* of the Romans, as also of the apotheosis of their emperors ; but it is a curious fact that the primitive islanders of the west not only had a similar system, but gave them a very similar name. "I could discover," says Columbus, "neither idolatry nor any other sect among them, though every one of their kings, who are very many, as well in Hispaniola as in all the other islands and continent, has a house apart from the town, in which there is nothing but some wooden images carved, by them called *Cemies ;* nor is there anything done in those houses but what is for the service of those cemies, they repairing to perform certain ceremonies, and pray there, as we do to our churches. . . . They also give the image a name, and I believe it is their *father's* or *grandfather's*, or both ; for they have more than one and some above ten,—all in memory of their *forefathers*, as I said before."—*History of Columbus*, by his son. (Churchill's collection, ii. 543.) This curious coincidence will add to the belief of those who infer that the Japanese, in early times, voyaged to America, because in modern times a junk or two have been blown out to sea, and driven to the north-west coast of America ; but like many coincidences in the manners, and customs, and words in the languages

According to Dr. Siebold, the Sintoos have some vague notion of the immortality of the soul, of a future state of existence, of rewards and punishments, of a paradise, and of a hell. " Celestial judges call every one to his account. To the good is allotted paradise, and they enter the realms of the Kami; the wicked are condemned, and thrust into hell." The duties enjoined by this ancient religion are :— 1. Preservation of pure fire, as the emblem of purity and means of purification. 2. Purity of soul, heart, and body. The purity of the soul is to be preserved by a strict obedience to reason and the law; the purity of the body, by abstaining from everything that defiles. 3. An exact observance of festival days. 4. Pilgrimage. 5. The worship of the Kami, both in the temples and at home.

External purity is most rigidly enforced; and, in too many cases, stands in lieu of everything else. Impurity is contracted in various ways; by associating with the impure, by listening to impure language, by eating certain meats, by coming in contact with death or with blood. Whosoever is stained with his own, or with the blood of another man, is *fusio* for seven days; that is, *impure*, and unfit to approach holy places. If, in building a temple, a workman should happen to cut or hurt himself so as to bleed, it is reckoned a very great calamity, and the man is thereby rendered altogether incapable of working for the future on that sacred edifice. If the same accident should happen in building or repairing any of the temples of the Sun Goddess, at the holy town of Isye, the misfortune does not affect the workmen alone, but the temple itself must be pulled down and built anew. With this inculcated abhorrence of blood, it is curious to see the Japanese Government so much addicted to blood-shedding, as it is, indisputably. Whosoever eats the flesh of any four-

of totally distinct nations, the fact proves nothing to the purpose, being otherwise unsupported. There must necessarily be points of resemblance in the various races of men all the world over, because they all belong to one *genus*, and therefore must present the general characteristics of "kind ;" *species*, or *race*, or *type*, is quite a different question, which I cannot here discuss.

footed beast, deer only excepted, is *fusio* for the term of thirty days. On the contrary, whoever eats a fowl, wild or tame (water-fowls, pheasants, and cranes excepted), is *fusio* for only one Japanese hour, which is about equal to two of ours. Whoever kills a beast, or is present at an execution, or attends a dying person, or comes into a house where a dead body lies, is *fusio* that day. But, of all the things which make us impure, none is reckoned so contagious as the death of parents and near relations. The nearer you are related to the dead person, so much the greater the impurity is. All ceremonies which are to be observed on this occasion, the time of mourning and the like, are determined by this rule. By not observing these precepts, people make themselves guilty of external impurity, which is detested by the gods, and they become unfit to approach their temples.* In serious cases of impurity, the *fusio* is not to be removed without a long course of purification, consisting of fasting, prayer, and the solitary study of devotional books. All the period appointed for mourning on the death of a relation is supposed to be thus spent.· When purified, they throw aside their mourning dress, which is not black, but white, and return to society in festal garments.

The religious observances on festival days appear to be very simple and very short. The worshipper, clad in his best clothes, approaches the temple, performs his ablutions at a tank, kneels in the veranda opposite a grated window, through which he can fix his eyes on the mirror; he then offers up his prayers, and a sacrifice of rice, fruit, tea, saki, or the like; deposits a little money in a box, and takes his departure, to spend the rest of the day in sports and pastimes, or in the manner he thinks best. According to Kämpfer, they conclude their ceremonies at the temple by striking three times upon a bell, which is hung over the door, believing the gods to be highly

---

* Kämpfer. Dr. Von Siebold, M. Fisscher, and other recent writers, appear to agree very closely with Kämpfer, and not unfrequently to follow that excellent old observer.

delighted with the sounds of musical instruments. " All this being done, they retire, to divert themselves the remaining part of the day with walking, exercises, sports, eating and drinking, and treating one another to good things." The temple must not be approached with a downcast spirit or a sorrowful countenance; for that might disturb the placid beatitude of the Kami. This ancient religious rule appears to have had an effect on the national character. The early Dutch writers observed that the Japanese hardly ever betrayed any outward emotion of sorrow or grief; that they had a wonderful degree of resignation under misfortune; that they were hardly ever heard to murmur or complain, and that they went even to execution and a horrible death with placid and even cheerful countenances.*

At home in every Sintoo house, each meal is preceded by a short prayer, and in nearly every garden or courtyard attached to such house there is a miniature mya, or temple. The Sintoo priests are called *Kami-Nusi*, or the hosts or landlords of the gods: they dwell in houses built within the grounds attached to the temples. The money deposited by the worshippers goes into their purse, and the oblations of rice, fruit, tea, and the rest, go to their kitchen and table. They have thus the means of hospitality, and are said to exercise it liberally to strangers. The Dutch, however, always found that in their case a return in solid cash was expected, and that these temple-visits were very expensive. Celibacy is no tenet of the Sintoos : the Kami-Nusi marry, and their wives are priestesses, to whom specific rites and duties are allotted. It appears that they act as godmothers-general to all the female children of their sect that are born in Japan, giving them their names, sprinkling them with water, and performing other ceremonies.†

But pilgrimage is the grand and most sanctifying act

* Arnold Montanus. *Remarkable Embassies of the East India Company of the United Netherlands to several Emperors of Japan*, &c. Amsterdam. 1670.

† Siebold.

of Sintoo devotion.   There are no fewer than twenty-two
shrines in different parts of the empire, which are frequented annually or more frequently by the devout.   The
most conspicuous and most honoured of all—the very
Loretto of the Japanese—is Isye, with its ancient temple
of Ten-sio-dai-sin, or the Sun Goddess.   The principal
temple is surrounded by nearly a hundred small ones,
which have little else of a temple than the mere shape,
being, for the most part, so low and narrow that a man
can scarcely stand up in them.   Each of these temples, or
little chapels, is attended by a priest.   Near to them live
multitudes of priests and functionaries, who call themselves the messengers of the gods, and who keep houses
and lodgings to accommodate travellers and pilgrims.
Not far off lies a considerable town, which bears the same
name (Isye) as the temple, and is inhabited by inn-
keepers, paper-makers, printers, book-binders, turners,
cabinet-makers, and such other artisans whose business is
in any way connected with the holy trade carried on at
the place.   The principal temple itself is a very plain,
unpretending edifice, and evidently of great antiquity,
though not quite so old as the priests and devotees pretend.   According to the latter, the Sun Goddess was born
in it and dwelt in it, and on that account it has never
been enlarged, improved, or in any way altered.   Among
the priestesses of the temple, there is almost always a
daughter of a Mikado.

"Orthodox Sintonists," says Kämpfer, "go in pilgrimage to Isye once a year, or at the very least once in
their lifetime ; nay, it is thought a duty incumbent on
every true patriot, whatever sect or religion he otherwise
adheres to, and a public mark of respect and gratitude
which every one ought to pay to the Sun Goddess, as to
the protectress, founder, and first parent of the Japanese
nation. . . . .   This pilgrimage is made at all times of
the year ; but the greatest concourse of people is in their
three first months, March, April, and May, when the
season of the year and the good weather make the journey
very agreeable and pleasant.   Persons of all ranks and

qualities, rich and poor, old and young, men and women, resort thither ; the lords only of the highest quality, and the most potent princes of the empire excepted, who seldom appear there in person.

"An embassy from the Emperor is sent there once every year, in the first month, at which time also another with rich presents goes to Meako, with presents to the ecclesiastical hereditary monarch. Most of the princes of the empire follow the emperor's example. As to the pilgrims, who go there in person, every one is at liberty to make the journey in what manner he pleases. Able people do it at their own expense in litters, with a retinue suitable to their quality. Poor people go on foot, living upon charity, which they beg upon the road. They carry their beds along with them on their backs, being a straw mat rolled up, and have a pilgrim's staff in their hands, and a pail hung by their girdle, out of which they drink, and wherein they receive people's charity, pulling off their hats much after the European manner. Their hats are very large, twisted of split reeds. Generally speaking, their names, birth, and the place from whence they come, are writ upon their hats and pails, that in case sudden death, or any other accident should befal them upon the road, it might be known who they are, and to whom they belong. Those that can afford it, wear a short white coat without sleeves over their usual dress, with their names stitched upon it before the breast and on the back. Multitudes of these pilgrims are seen daily on the road. It is scarcely credible what numbers set out only from the capital city of Jeddo, and from the large province Osju. It is no uncommon thing at Jeddo for children to run away from their parents, in order to go in pilgrimage to Isye. The like attempt would be more difficult in other places, where a traveller that is not provided with the necessary passports would expose himself to no small trouble. As to those that return to Isye, they have the privilege, that the ofarria which they bring from thence, is allowed everywhere as a good passport."

This ofarria, or " capital purification," is considered equivalent to the absolution and remission of their sins, and is given to the pilgrims by the priests " for a small consideration." It appears to be nothing more (in its cheap or ordinary shape) than a scrap of paper with a few Japanese characters written upon it—not unlike the things which are sold by the wandering dervishes in Turkey and Persia, and the fakirs in India. But the superstitious believe that, coupled with the pilgrimage they have performed, these vouchers secure them health, prosperity, and children in this world, and a happy state in the world to come. The priests drive a great trade in the article. As there are very many who stay at home, and think it sufficient for the ease of their conscience to purchase these indulgences, great quantities of ofarrias are sent every year from Isye to all parts of the empire.

The Mikado did not always get the pilgrimage performed vicariously. At one period both he and the lay emperor went in person to the shrine, at least once or twice during their lives. Motives of economy are thought to have put an end to those journeys, and to those of the great lords and princes, from whom great donations were expected ; but it is probable that the disuse has in part arisen from a decline in Sintoo piety, or from an addiction to other forms of worship.

Anchorites and hermits are numerous, but they appear to hold rather loosely to the ancient Sintoo creed. One set, called *Jammabos,* or " mountain soldiers," lead a very secluded, austere life, spending most of their time in going up and down holy mountains, and washing themselves in cold springs or rivers. The poorer sort of them go strolling and begging about the country. The order is said to have been founded more than twelve hundred years ago, by a strange adventurous man, who consumed nearly all his days in wandering through deserts, mountains, and wild uninhabited places, which, in the end, proved of considerable service to his country, as he thereby discovered the situation and nature of such places, which nobody before him had ventured to visit, and thus found out new, easier, and shorter roads from district to district, to the great advantage of travellers.

They burn incense or perfumes on a table raised like an altar, opposite their idols ; they light candles as a species of sacrifice ; they make the sign of the cross—but a St. Andrew's cross—very often, especially at rising in the morning, with the express object of driving away the devil. The King of Satsuma, who received St. Francis Xavier, had a cross on his escutcheon—a strange fact in a country where the cross is held in such contempt. They use a rosary or chaplet, consisting of one hundred and eighty beads, strung on a long string, and not united, as those of the Catholics, though Kämpfer thus represents it in his engraving. They chime a bell at certain hours of the day, like the *Angelus* in Catholic countries ; then the people kneel and invoke the name of their favourite god. Pilgrimages for the pardon and remission of sins I have mentioned. They carry their gods, images, and relics in procession. They make vows and have public prayers during public calamities. Their temples are places of sacred asylum, which may not be invaded. They practise canonization, and have a regular hierarchy. These might be taken for Christian traditions, if we could show, with any amount of probability, that these practices were not indigenous to India and Buddhism.*

I have already described the "mendicant nuns" of Japan,† as they have been styled by travellers. The members of this society appear to be of no particular faith, and of very doubtful morality. Besides what they pay to their "nunneries" for protection, they are obliged to bring so much a year of their collections to the temple of the Sun Goddess at Isye, by way of tribute.

There are numerous nunneries or societies of females, who appear to follow the Buddhist religion, without any intermixture of the Sintoo, or old national faith.

Buddhism, the most widely diffused of all Eastern

* Kampfer, and *Hist. Gén. des Voy.*
† Page 163.

creeds,* seems, from all the accounts we have read, to be, at present, the prevalent faith in Japan. Yet it cannot be called *dominant,* and it may be doubted whether it exists anywhere in the remoter parts of the country without an admixture of the old Sintoo. It is not necessary to our present purpose to give any detailed account of doctrines so well known (particularly through our connection with India) as those of Buddhism. Some excellent recent notices of the religion as it exists among the Chinese, Tartars, and Thibetans, will be found in that most amusing of books, "Huc's Travels in Tartary," &c., and in the recent work of Mr. T. Prinsep.† It will be enough for the reader to remember here, that the leading dogma of Buddhism is the metempsychosis ; from which belief arises the prohibition to take animal life ; that the Buddhist believes that man, after going through a variety of animal forms, as an elephant, a dog, a horse, or so on, will, in the end, when purged of all his sins upon earth, be absorbed into the divine essence ; that they worship a countless number of uncouth idols ; that they have the notion that the Dalaï Lama, or high-priest king, never dies ; that their priests form a distinct order in the state, and are bound to celibacy. There is a difference of opinion as to the dates of the introduction and establishment of Buddhism in Japan ; but the probability is, that the faith was first brought into the country from India or from Corea, at the close of the sixth century of our era.‡ The government appears to have tolerated it from the beginning ; but the people several times rose in tumult, killed the bonzes, burned their idols, and levelled their temples with the ground. But as this spontaneous

* It has been calculated that there are in the world 252,000,000 Mahometans, 111,000,000 followers of Brahma, and 315,000,000 of Buddhists.

† *Tartary and Thibet.* 1 vol. 8vo. London. 1851.

‡ Those who are curious on this subject may be referred to the publications of Klaproth and Von Siebold, who both give their statements upon the authority of Japanese writers. Yet the same two learned Europeans differ as to the dates.

popular persecution passed away, and as Buddhism gradually blended itself with some of the old national faiths,
it became an established religion, and gained innumerable
converts.   It should seem that, at least in the maritime
parts of the empire, there are twenty Buddhist to one
Sintoo temple.   In Japan, as in every other country
where it exists, Buddhism is divided into a high, pure,
mystic creed for the learned, and a gross idolatry for the
unlearned and common people.

One of the four Buddhist temples at Hakodadi is called
the Zhiogen-zhi, that is, "the country's Protector," a
good specimen of Japanese architecture, but otherwise
worthy of notice.   On either side of the avenue leading
to the temple there are pairs of stone candelabras, and
near by, the statue of a goddess with a child in her arms;
a copper nimbus or "glory" surrounds the head of all the
idols, and reminds the Christian visitor of what he may
have seen in some churches of his own country.*

The temples of Japan, as in China, are often used for
places of concourse and entertainment, indeed of revelry
and debauch.   On such occasions the altars and shrines
are covered or removed, which so changes the aspect of
the interior that no one would suspect that he was in a
house of worship.   On the visit of the American squadron
one of the temples was appropriated for a bazaar, a
worldly use that the ecclesiastics, so far from objecting
to, highly approved of, as it added considerably to their
revenue, the rent of the apartments being the perquisite
on the occasion.†

The Japanese are not content with devout prayers,

---

* *United States Expedition.*   The Buddhist temples have very
fanciful names : the largest is called Rio-shen-zhi, or Buddha's obedient monastery ; and there are Daian-zhi, or great peace monastery ;
the Hon-gaku-zhi, or source of knowledge monastery ; the Too-den-
zhi, or rice-field monastery ; the Ri-gen-zhi, or source of reason
monastery, &c.   Twenty-five priests and a few acolytes are attached
to these temples, and are supported by fees bestowed by devotees
for burial services and the various offices peculiar to Buddhism
(Simoda).

† Ibid.   Kampfer, &c.

pilgrimages, prostrations, offerings to the gods in order to secure blessings here and hereafter; they also pray by machine, by *wheel and axle.* There is a square post, nearly eight feet in length, and near the centre, at a convenient height to be reached by the hand, is fixed vertically a wheel, which moves readily on an axle passed through the post. Two small rings are strung upon each of the three spokes of the wheel. Every person who twists this instrument in passing is supposed to obtain credit in heaven for one or more prayers inscribed on the post, the number being graduated according to the vigour of the performer's devotion, and the number of revolutions effected. The jingle of the small iron rings is believed to secure the attention of the deity to the invocation of the devout, and the greater the noise, the more certain of its being listened to.* Some of the inscriptions on this post are worth remembering :—" The great round mirror of knowledge says, ' wise men and fools are embarked in the same boat;' whether prospered or afflicted, both are rowing over the deep lake; the gay sails lightly hang to catch the autumnal breeze; then away they straight enter the lustrous clouds, and become partakers of heaven's knowledge."

" He whose prescience detects knowledge, says :—As the floating grass is blown by the gentle breeze, or the glancing ripples of autumn disappear when the sun goes down, or as the ship returns home to her old shore, so is life : it is a smoke, a morning tide."

" Others are more to the point—as to the machine— " Buddha himself earnestly desires to hear the name of this person (who is buried), and wishes he may go to life."†

The Tartars of Thibet have a similar substitute for prayer and pilgrimage. On the roads you see at certain distances pasteboard barrels, fixed on an axle, and inscribed with choice prayers. The devout give the

* *United States Expedition.*

† *United States Expedition,* where the machine is figured, i. p. 445, and in *Americans in Japan,* p. 327.

barrel a turn, and it revolves for a long time, according to the force applied ; meanwhile he may go and drink, eat, and sleep, and the barrel prays for him as long as gravitation and friction will permit. They sometimes fight for the privilege of turning the barrel.* All this is, of course, very ridiculous, sadly benighted ; but are not very many of us in Christian Europe accused of re- sorting to analogous mechanical devices with the vain hope of fooling heaven into granting our petitions ? What do we mean by "lip-service?" Does not even the habitual repetition of set forms of prayer at last find its repre- sentative in the revolving-wheel or the spinning-barrel ? 'Tis human nature all the world over. Beings superior to us, exempt from all our infirmities, may laugh at us, may scoff at us ; but a comprehensive meditation of the manners and customs of all nations would convince us that nations, like individuals, have no reason to scoff and to laugh at each other. I need not remind the reader of the sacred proverb about the beam and the mote in the visual organ.

"We believe," says Mr. Macfarlane, "that none of these creeds in Japan have now any great hold on the popular mind, and what has been said by an able writer of the Chinese, may with equal justice be said of the Japanese:"—

"It is rather extraordinary that foreigners, though conversant with every part of Chinese literature, know so little about their religious writings. One reason may be found in their being written in a style almost unin- telligible to the common reader. The Buddhist works are full of expressions from the Pàli, of which the sound is clumsily imitated in Chinese characters. Even few priests of that sect know the true meaning, and the same set of phrases are chanted by the votaries, over and over, for ages, without a single thought being bestowed upon their import. The religion of Taou, which is a national superstition, has clothed its votaries in mysterious

* Huc, *Voy. dans la Tartarie.*

laconism ; many sentences admit five or six different versions, and when the student imagines that he has caught the real signification, he finds himself puzzled by a new maze of vagaries. Only truth can show her face unveiled, error requires the fanciful and dark envelope of unmeaning language, for, if seen in its nakedness, it would be loathsome. The religious works of the literati are mere treatises on ceremony, dry and uninteresting to the general reader, and only of value to the master of rites to exercise himself in the prescribed prostrations, genuflexions, and bows. The work before us* is intended as a comprehensive statistical account of the gods, including all the fables that have been propagated about them, and describing their various offices and functions, nature, attributes, &c., without regard to connexion and system. The author first treats upon that large class of beings known under the name of genii, who are the special objects of adoration amongst the Taou sect. He then expatiates upon Buddha and his fellows, and finally treats upon the sages and worthies that claim the veneration of scholars. It is a very pantheon—a labyrinth through which, even with the clue of Ariadne, it is difficult to thread our way.

" To understand the book thoroughly, one ought to be intimately acquainted with the absurdities suggested by a disordered fancy, one ought to study the deviations from common sense, and hear patiently the ravings of a diseased mind.

" We frankly confess that we have not yet come to a satisfactory conclusion regarding the religious opinions of the Chinese as a nation.

" The general division of their creed into the sects of Taou and Buddha, and the religion of the state, holds only true regarding the initiated, the priests, and their immediate adherents, whilst the mass of the people, devoid of religious instruction, combine all in one, and

---

* *Shin Seën Tungkeen,* a general account of the gods and genii ; in twenty-two Chinese volumes.

individuals are either entirely indifferent towards all
superstitions, or each cherishes his own peculiar tenets.
All religious persons are stigmatized with popular contempt, and viewed in no other light but as mountebanks
and quacks, who practise their unhallowed arts in order
to gain a scanty livelihood. Under such circumstances,
it is extraordinary to see so many temples and shrines,
some of them richly endowed. But it ought never to be
forgotten that the Chinaman loves show, and that he
must have a public house, where he may occasionally
spend an idle hour, consult his destiny, burn incense, and
offer sacrifices, upon which he afterwards may feast. We
do not think that many of these edifices were erected
from religious motives, but are mere matters of convenience, and are always viewed in that light.

" But there is none so poor that he fits not up a little
shrine, or corner, with an inscription, or a bit of an idol,
before which he every day burns incense.

" You may find these in the very sheds of beggars, and
the small boats of Tanka-women are never without this
appendage. It must be confessed, on the other hand,
that the majority of the people view these images in no
other light than as a child its doll, which old custom has
taught them to have always at hand. We have never
yet heard a pagan Chinese pray ; he considers it is the
business of the priest to rattle off a few unmeaning
sentences, and that it is quite sufficient that he should
just utter a few pious ejaculations. If you discourse
with him about his religious opinions, he will always
come forward with Heaven and Earth, the two grand
objects of his veneration. There is no work exclusively
upon religion to which he may refer. If he consult the
classics, he will be told that filial piety and loyalty constitute true religion ; but no hint is given him that there
is an omnipotent Creator and Preserver to whom he owes
his first and most sacred duty. It has again and again
been asserted, without a shadow of truth, that the Chinese
acknowledge one Supreme Being ; if such a confession is
ever made, it is by men who have come in contact with

R

foreigners, and are anxious to avoid the ridicule which
attaches to a votary of idols. Nor are the impressions
of polytheism so very easily removed from the mind;
and though the absurdity may be fully admitted, the son
of Han cleaves tenaciously to his ancient superstition.
God alone can change this state of things, and open the
heart of their understanding to perceive the truth." *

With regard to the Japanese, however, we must remember that they are a very different race : the unanimous character given to them as to religious susceptibility
by the ancient missionaries, and by recent travellers
—with reference to the mass of the population—can
scarcely have disappeared from the minds of those whom
their magnanimous apostle Xavier called "the delight
of his heart." We cannot forget the incident of the
barrel of saki—which, consigned to the deep by one
crew, picked up by another, was, instead of being drunk,
carried religiously to the temple of the god to whom it
was offered.† Everything seems to prove that the Japanese is a "God-fearing" man.

Suto, meaning "the way of philosophers," is always
called another leading Japanese religion, although it is, in
reality, much rather a philosophic school or sect, inculcating no particular faith, and being compatible with almost
any faith, whether true or false. It is evidently an importation from China, consisting almost entirely of the
moral doctrines taught by Confucius, and of some high
Buddhist mystic notions concerning the final condition of
the human soul. It is totally unconnected with any
mythology, and it has no religious rites or ceremonies.
Probably *Sintoo* never made much progress among
the vulgar, but it is very generally followed by the
nobility and all the educated classes, who may therefore be described as men of no religion. This *philosophy*, as Kämpfer correctly calls it, may be reduced to
five points, which they call *Dsin, Gi, Re, Tsi,* and *Sin.*

---

* *Chinese Repository,* vol. vii. p. 505. Canton. 1839.
† Page 191 of this work.

Dsin teaches them to live virtuously ; *Gi*, to do right and act justly with everybody ; *Re*, to be civil and polite ; *Tsi* sets forth the rules for a good and prudent government ; and *Sin* treats of a free conscience and uprightness of heart. They have no metempsychosis, but, although they do not admit the transmigration of souls into mortal bodies, they believe in a universal soul, spirit, power, or real essence, which is diffused throughout the universe, which animates all things, which reassumes the departing souls of men, as the ocean receives the rivers and waters that flow into it from all parts of the globe. This universal spirit is not our Supreme Being, but what we may call Nature. They thank Nature for the food on their tables, and for all the necessaries and blessings of life. Kämpfer, whose account of this sect has never been improved, says :—

"Some among them, whom I conversed withal, admitted an intellectual, or incorporeal being, but only as governor and director, not as the author of nature ; nay, they pretended that it is an effect of nature produced by *In* and *Jo,*—heaven and earth, one active, the other passive ; one the principle of generation, the other of corruption : after the same manner, also, they explained some other active powers of nature to be spiritual beings. They make the world eternal, and suppose men and animals to have been produced by *In* and *Jo*—the heaven and five terrestrial elements. Admitting no gods, they have no temples, no forms of worship. Thus far, however, they conform themselves to the general custom of the country, in that they celebrate the memory of their deceased parents and relations, which is done by putting all sorts of victuals, raw and dressed, on a *Biosju*, as they call it, or table purposely made with this view ; by burning candles before them ; by bowing down to the ground, as if they were yet alive ; by monthly or anniversary dinners, whereto are invited the deceased's family and friends, who appear all in their best clothes, and wash and clean themselves by way of preparation, for three days before, during which time they abstain from all impure

things ; and by many other tokens of respect and gratitude. As to the burial of their dead, they do not burn
them, but keep the corpse three days, and then lay it on
the back in a coffin, after the European manner, with the
head raised. Sometimes the coffin is filled with spices
and sweet-scented herbs, to preserve the body from corruption, and when everything is ready, they accompany
it to the grave, and bury it without any further ceremony.

" These philosophers do not only admit of *self-murder*,
but look upon it as an heroic and highly commendable
action, and the only honourable means to avoid a shame-
ful death, or to prevent falling into the hands of a victorious enemy. They celebrate no festivals, nor will they
pay any respect to the gods of the country, any more than
common civility and good manners require. The practice
of virtue, a free conscience, and a good and honest life, is
all that they aim at. They were even suspected of secretly favouring the Christian religion, for which reason,
after the said religion had been entirely abolished by
cross and fire, and violent means taken to prevent its ever
reviving again, they also were commanded to have each
an idol, or at least the name of one of the gods, worshipped in the country, put up in their houses, in a conspicuous and honourable place, with a flower-pot and in-
censory before them."

Nearly all our early writers assert that by far the
greater part of the Japanese men of learning follow this
doctrine ; and that, notwithstanding the infinity and variety of gods or idols introduced into the country, most
of the grandees are either free-thinkers or downright
atheists, if such a thing can exist.

An industrious and accurate writer sets down the
number of religions or sects, quite distinct from Buddhism,
at *thirty-four*.* It would be difficult to find in any other
country (not England or the United States of America)
such striking instances of religious toleration. As far as
regards the State, all these sects indulge their several

* **T.** Rundall, Esq., *Memorials of the Empire of Japan*, &c.

opinions without restraint. The fact is, the Japanese government exhibited a rare and wonderful indifference to mere matters of doctrine, so long as they did not interfere with the public tranquillity. When the bonzes of all the sects concurred in a petition to the emperor Nobunanga that he would expel the Jesuits and all the Romish monks from Japan, that prince, annoyed by their importunities, inquired how many different religions there were in Japan? " Thirty-five," said the bonzes. " Well," said the emperor, " where thirty-five religions can be tolerated, we can easily bear with thirty-six : leave the strangers in peace."*

In emoluments and dignities all sects are pretty nearly on an equality. On these points causes for dissension cannot often arise. Occasionally (but not recently), when disputes on doctrinal points were running rather high, the Government decided them in a summary manner, whipping, and even beheading some of the fiercest of the controversialists. Even in the time of the tolerant emperor Nobunanga, a terrible controversy was settled quite in the manner of our Henry VIII. in the last years of his reign. But this was not until the peace of the country had been seriously disturbed. " Never," says Mr. Meylan, " do we hear of any religious dispute among the Japanese, much less discover that they bear each other any hate on religious grounds. They esteem it, on the contrary, an act of courtesy to visit, from time to time, each other's gods, and do them reverence. While the Koboe sends an embassy to the Sintoo temple at Isye, to offer prayers in his name, he assigns, at the same time, a sum for the erection of temples to Confucius ; and the Mikado allows strange gods, imported from Siam or China, to be placed (for the convenience of those who may feel a call to worship them) in the same temples with the Japanese. If it be asked whence this tolerance originates, and by what it is maintained, I reply, from this, that worshippers of all persua-

* *Summary of the Journal of Don Rodrigo de Vivero y Velasco,* in *Asiatic Journal,* July, 1830,

sions in Japan acknowledge and obey one superior, namely, the Mikado, or "spiritual emperor," as we call him. As the representative and lineal descendant of God on earth, he is himself an object of worship, and as such he protects equally all whose object it is to venerate the Deity; the mode of their so doing being indifferent to him. Let it not be thought that I prize this tolerance too high, nor let the cruel persecutions of the Christians in Japan be objected to me : I ask whether this toleration was not one of the causes which so far facilitated the introduction of Christianity there? But that which with me is conclusive is, that could the preachers of the gospel in Japan have been tolerant as the Japanese—had they not mocked and despised the gods of the country—could it have been possible that the bishops chosen from the first missionaries should have receded from insisting on their right of total independence, and could they have been contented to place themselves under the protection of God's representative on earth, which the Japanese acknowledge in their Mikado—lastly, could they have forborne to meddle in affairs of politics and government, then would no persecution of Christianity, in all human probability, have taken place, and perhaps at this moment the doctrine of Jesus would have been triumphant over that of Confucius." Mr. MacFarlane continues :—

"Thunberg, Golownin, Fisscher, Siebold, and all the recent writers about the country, are agreed as to this easy toleration. Every Japanese citizen has a right to profess whatever faith he pleases—provided, only, it be not Christianity—and to change it as often as he may think fit. Nobody concerns himself whether he does so out of conviction or out of regard to his worldly interest. It is said to happen frequently that the members of one family follow different faiths or sects, and that the difference of belief does not disturb the family harmony.

"From all that we can collect on this subject," adds Mr. MacFarlane, "we are inclined to believe that if the government could only be relieved of its prejudices and implacable animosity against the Romanists, or thoroughly convinced of the difference between the Church of Rome and the Reformed Churches, that a troop of reformed missionaries might have a better chance of success than a powerful fleet and a great army of soldiers. But the missionary ought to be kept apart from every political scheme, and from every display of military force. Should the Japanese Government suspect the Americans [and the English] of any extensive design of occupation, conquest, or annexation, its hatred of the religion they profess will no doubt become quite as inveterate as that which has for more than two centuries been nourished against the Portuguese and the Church of Rome."

I confess, however, that I am by no means so sanguine as to the possibility of Protestant Christianity having any better chance of success with the Japanese *Government;* for that is the point to be considered, not the *people*, who certainly endured infinitely more for their faith during the persecution than the Catholics of England during theirs. The present treaty provides for a sort of toleration of Christianity. · " British subjects will be allowed the free exercise of their religion; and for this purpose will have the right to erect suitable places of worship." Our religion will be exercised; we shall erect places of worship, but if there be a word of truth in all that the Dutch have reported as to the determined political opposition of the Japanese Government to Christianity, will the Japanese be permitted to embrace it? This is not named in the bond. But there will certainly be *converts*. Will they not be *persecuted?* If so, we shall decidedly have *diplomatic complications*. The Japanese Government, so haughty, will probably resist; the Anglo-Saxon, so tenacious, will as probably insist: and the history of the past, in all our conquests, will be the history of the future with regard to Japan. But it may take some trouble to plant our standards on the rocks of hitherto unconquered Niphon.

If this most unexpected revolution in the politics of Japan has been brought about by the pressure of the recent events in China upon the Government—as is

DIVINITIES.

authoritatively averred*—possibly the same terror may
continue, and allow us to do as we please; but possibly it
may not, and the second state may not be a jot better
than the first.

Again, will the Protestant missionary be more protected

* Page 3 of this book.

than the Catholic by the majesty of England? Will not the Catholic missionary now strive again to plant his faith in the land consecrated to the memory of Xavier—perchance even fondly hoping that a remnant of the ancient flock may still be found, after the lapse of centuries, ready to relate the legends, the traditions of their providential preservation?

Here will be a battle of creeds. I dare not meditate the consequences of this religious antagonism; and here I leave the solemn question.

LADY PAINTING.

CHAPTER VI.

SOCIAL AND DOMESTIC LIFE.

THE Japanese are everywhere described as being essentially a sociable, pleasure-seeking people. They work hard the greater part of their time, but they must have their feasts and their frolics on the great holidays, which appear to occur rather frequently.

Music, dancing, and the theatre, are favourite amusements with all classes. Mummers and mountebanks parade the streets. Tumblers, conjurers, and all manner of jugglers exercise their callings to the great delight of the common people. We do not see any mention of Punch; but, as that mysterious personage—that great universality

—flourishes in China, and has been traced in Tartary and all through the Asiatic continent to the Bosphorus and Constantinople, there can be little doubt that he has some modified form of existence in the islands of Japan. Besides thronging the public theatres, the Japanese very frequently get up plays and farces among themselves in their own houses.   Private theatricals, indeed, seem to be even more fashionable with them than with us.

Fun and drollery appear to be very liberally diffused. Their beggars are merry rogues.

The mendicants exhibit touches of humour ; a troop, apparently of " halt, lame, and blind," will one moment solicit alms in doleful strains, and the next, throwing off disguise, leap about and chant merrily, in return for the guerdon that may have been bestowed on them ; or, calculating that they are more likely to gain their object by mirth than by persisting in the assumption of distress, the unreality of which can be easily detected.

Every writer who has treated of the subject, praises the great urbanity, mutual respect, and formal but real politeness of the people.

Their theatrical entertainments are said to be far superior to those of the Chinese in respect to scenery, costume, and decoration.   Their theatres have usually three tiers of boxes, in the front of which all the ladies who are young and pretty, or fancy themselves so, take care to show themselves.   The milliners of London might derive great benefit if our *beau monde* would only adopt a Japanese fashion during the Opera season.   " The ladies," says M. Fisscher, " who frequent the theatre make a point of changing their dress two or three times during the representation, in order to display the richness of their wardrobe ; and they are always attended by servants who carry the necessary articles of dress for the purpose."

With these frequent transmutations, the dear creatures must afford as much amusement as the actors on the stage.

Play-bills, or printed programmes of the piece about to be represented, are always in circulation, and, no doubt, the playgoer at Meako or Jeddo is invited to "buy a bill of the play" just as if he were going to a London theatre.

The Dutch writer from whom I last quoted throws an air of poetry as well as truth over some of his descriptions of social enjoyments. Secretary Fisscher had a lively eye for female beauty, and a susceptible heart. It will be as well to state that the passage of English verse in the following extract is of his own quoting.

" In the great world the young ladies find delight, at their social meetings, in every description of fine work, the fabrication of pretty boxes, artificial flowers, painting of fans, birds, and animals, pocket-books, purses, plaiting thread for the head-dress, all for the favourite use of giving as presents. Such employments serve to while away the long winter evenings. In the spring, on the other hand, they participate with eagerness in all kinds of outdoor and rural amusements. Of these the choicest are afforded by the pleasure-boats which, adorned with the utmost cost and beauty, cover their lakes and rivers. In the enjoyment of society and music, they glide in these vessels from noon till late in the night, realizing the rapturous strain of the author of Lalla Rookh :—

> ' O ! best of delights, as it everywhere is,
> To be near the loved one ! what rapture is his,
> Who, by moonlight and music, thus idly may glide,
> O'er the Lake of Cashmeer with that one by his side !'

" This is an enjoyment which can only be shared under the advantages of such a climate and scenery ; viz., the climate of Nice and the scenery of Lugano. Their lakes and rivers are, after sunset, one blaze or illumination, as it were, with the brightly-coloured paper lanterns displayed in their vessels. They play meanwhile that game with their fingers, which has been perpetuated from classic times in Italy. A floating figure is also placed in a vase of water ; as the water is stirred by the motion of the boat, the figure moves. The guests sing to the guitar the strain ' Anataya modomada,'—' He floats, he is not still,' till at last the puppet rests opposite some one of the party, whom it sentences to drain the saki-bowl, as the pleasing forfeit of the game. All this stands out in cheerful contrast to the dull debaucheries of the men, and the childish diversions of the women, among other oriental nations. The female sex, at least, have greatly the advantage over the scandal of the Turkish bath ; and the man has, equally with the Turk, the resource of his pipe, in the intervals of those better enjoyments which the admission of the female sex into society affords him, and which are prohibited to the Mussulman."*

Assuredly these are captivating, delicious pictures of life and manners.

Speaking of the Japanese ladies, the late James Drummond, Esq., Commissary-General, Commissioner of Accounts at Paris, &c., exclaimed :—" They have a natural grace which cannot be described. The Japanese are the most fascinating, elegant ladies that I ever saw in any country in the world. Take away a few peculiarities, to which one soon gets accustomed by living among them, and they would, at their first *debut*, be admired at St. James's, or in any other court of Europe."†

And he who bore this high testimony was a great traveller, who had been in nearly every country, and who had lived, in each of them, in the most refined, most accomplished circles of society.

In addition to this, I must state that the Japanese make no difference in the education of their children— boys and girls are educated according to the same system. Learned ladies are not rare in Japan, in spite of their fascinations. By all the accounts, the Japanese lady is as learned as she is pretty, and can thus attract by the resources of art as well as nature, which, it is said, is a praise that cannot be given to those ladies of Europe who drive the pen, or otherwise emulate the monster,

* Fisscher.

† MacFarlane, who adds :—" As these words were spoken many years ago, I need not now be much ashamed of confessing that it was they that first excited me to a deep and lively interest in the subject of Japan."

commonly called the lord of creation. It must be admitted that the Japanese ladies have plenty of time on their hands ; but this cannot detract from their merit in making the most of it. It seems that their teachers begin with forming their hearts, inspiring them with a high principle of honour and right reason. They are made to study their language with assiduity, so as to read, speak, and write it correctly. With them it is really a serious study. The doctrines of religion then follow, to be succeeded by logic, eloquence, morals, poetry, and painting. Amongst the most admired authors, historians, moralists, and poets of Japan, are found several female names. Like the men, they set no value on jewels and precious stones, which they do not wear.

Remembering Mr. Drummond's high testimony to the charms of woman in Japan,—inferring what a valuable, delightful, all-satisfying creature she must be from her education,—we naturally conclude that the position of " woman in Japan " must be exceptionable all the world over, in point of merited estimation and social standing ; but this is not the case it seems.

" The position of women in Japan seems to be unlike what it is in all other parts of the East, and to constitute a sort of intermediate link between their European and their Asiatic conditions. On the one hand, Japanese women are subjected to no seclusion ; they hold a fair station in society, and share in all the innocent recreations of their fathers and husbands. The fidelity of the wife and the purity of the maiden are committed wholly to their own sense of honour, somewhat quickened, perhaps, and invigorated, by the certainty that death would be the inevitable and immediate consequence of a detected lapse from chastity. And so well is this confidence repaid, that a faithless wife is, we are universally assured, a phenomenon unknown in Japan. But if thus permitted to enjoy and adorn society, they are, on the other hand, held during their whole lives in a state of tutelage, of complete dependence upon their husbands, sons, or other relations. They are without legal rights, and their evidence is inadmissible in a court of justice. Not only may the husband introduce as many subsidiary, unwedded helpmates as he pleases into the mansion over which his wife presides—and these women, though inferior to her in rank, dignity, and domestic authority, in proof of which, they are not permitted to shave their eyebrows, are not deemed criminal or dishonoured—but he has also a power of divorce, which may be called unlimited, since the only limitation proceeds from his sense of economy and expediency. A husband must support his repudiated wife according to his own station, unless he can allege grounds for the divorce satisfactory to a Japanese tribunal; among which grounds, barrenness is one that leaves the unfortunate, childless wife no claim to any kind of maintenance. Under no circumstance, upon no plea whatever, can a wife demand a separation from her husband. At home, the wife is mistress of the family; but, in other respects, she is treated rather as a toy for her husband's recreation, than as the rational, confidential partner of his life. She is to amuse him by her accomplishments, to cheer him with her lively conversation, not to relieve, by sharing, his anxieties and cares. So far from being admitted, like Portia, to 'partake the secrets of his heart,' she is kept in profound ignorance of his affairs, public or private; and a question relative to any such matters would be resented as an act of unpardonable presumption and audacity."*

Among the rich and great, the husband, in general, is thus very far from corresponding to the fidelity of the wife; and, among all classes, those pleasant vices that turn themselves into scourges to whip themselves, appear to be exceedingly prevalent. Incontinence is, in fact, the great national vice of the Japanese. Yet the purity of mothers and wives remains an indisputable and striking fact. Innumerable native stories bear testimony to it, and innumerable incidents, related by different travellers and their own writers, prove the respect in which a married woman is invariably held by the men.

* *Manners and Customs of the Japanese.*

The women of Japan strongly resent dishonour; and there is more than one instance recorded of death having been inflicted on her dishonourer by the injured woman. As an evidence of determination of character, the following anecdote is related:—"A man of rank went on a journey, and a noble in authority made overtures to his wife. They were rejected with scorn and indignation, but the libertine, by force or fraud, accomplished his object. The husband returned, and was received by his wife with affection, but with a dignified reserve that excited his surprise. He sought explanations, but could not obtain them at once. His wife prayed him to restrain himself till the morrow, and then, before her relations and the chief people of the city, whom she had invited to an entertainment, his desire should be satisfied. The morrow came, and with it the guests, including the noble who had done the wrong. The entertainment was given in a manner not unusual in the country, on the terraced roof of the house. The repast was concluded, when the lady rose and made known the outrage to which she had been subjected, and passionately demanded that her husband should slay her as an unworthy object, unfit to live. The guests, the husband foremost, besought her to be calm; they strove to impress her with the idea that she had done no wrong—that she was an innocent victim, though the author of the outrage merited no less punishment than death. She thanked them all kindly. She wept on her husband's shoulder. She kissed him affectionately, then suddenly escaping from his embraces, rushed precipitately to the edge of the terrace and cast herself over the parapet. In the confusion that ensued, the author of the mischief, still unsuspected, for the hapless creature had not indicated the offender, made his way down-stairs. When the rest of the party arrived, he was found weltering in his blood by the corpse of his victim. He had expiated his crime by committing suicide in the national manner —by slashing himself across the abdomen with two slashes, in the form of a cross."*

* Rundall, *Memorials*, from Ogilby.

Incidents like these furnish the groundwork of many of their dramas and popular novels.

Other tales are told in honour of female presence of mind, courage, and fortitude.

A great lord, named Tchouya, with his friend named Ziositz, entered into an extensive conspiracy against the emperor. Tchouya had a wife who had been greatly celebrated as well for her beauty as for her wit and heroic constancy.

An act of indiscretion on the part of Tchouya, after so many years (nearly fifty) of prudence, betrayed the conspiracy, and orders were issued for his arrest and that of Ziositz. It was deemed important to seize both, if possible, or at least Tchouya (who resided at Yeddo) alive, in the hope of extorting further disclosures. To effect this, it was indispensable to surprise him, and measures were taken accordingly. An alarm of fire was raised at Tchouya's door, and when he ran out to ascertain the degree of danger threatening his house, he was suddenly surrounded and attacked. He defended himself stoutly, cutting down two of his assailants, but, in the end, was overpowered by numbers and secured. His wife, meanwhile, had heard the sounds of conflict, and apprehending its cause, immediately caught up those of her husband's papers which would have revealed the names of his confederates (amongst whom were men of distinction and princes of the land), and burnt them. Her presence of mind remains even to this day a topic of admiration in Japan, where the highest panegyric for judgment and resolution that can be bestowed upon a woman is to compare her to the wife of Tchouya.*

Another historical anecdote elevates the character of woman in Japan to the heroic, if murder and subsequent suicide be raised to that dignity in the estimation of men, by the "circumstances" which so often alter "cases" in this incomprehensible state of existence.

"Early in the eighteenth century, the Siogoun, Tsouna-

* Rundall, &c., from Titsingh.

yosi, a profligate prince, who by his vices had destroyed
his constitution, accidentally lost his only son, and the
dignity of Siogoun having never been inherited by a
daughter, resolved to adopt an heir. This is a constant
practice in Japan with the childless, whether sovereign or
subject; but the established rule is, to select for adoption
the son of a brother, or other near relation ; in direct
contravention of which, Tsouna-yosi, disregarding the
claims of his nephew, fixed his choice upon an alien to his
blood, the son of a mere favourite of inferior birth.

" The prime minister, Ino-Kamon-no-Kami, remonstrated, alleging that a step so unprecedented would exasperate not only the princes of the blood, but all the
other princes of the empire. His representations proved
unavailing against the favourite's influence ; whereupon
he sought the empress, or *Midia*. To her the minister
revealed his master's illegal and dangerous design ; explained the probability, if not certainty, that a general
insurrection would be its immediate consequence ; and
declared that, unless she could avert it, the adoption and
its fearful results were inevitable. The *Midia*—a daughter
of the reigning *Mikado*, and high-minded, as became her
birth and station—meditated profoundly for some
minutes ; then, raising her head, she bade the alarmed
minister be of good cheer, for she had devised means of
prevention. But what these means might be she positively refused to tell him.

" Upon the day preceding that appointed for the adoption,
the daughter of the 'Son of Heaven,' who had long been
wholly neglected by her libertine husband, invited him to
take saki with her ; and, upon his assenting, prepared a
sumptuous entertainment. Whilst he was drinking, she
retired for a moment to her private apartment, wrote
and despatched a note of instructions to Ino-Kamon,
and then, placing in her girdle the ornamented dagger
worn by women of exalted rank, she returned to the
banqueting-room. Shortly afterwards, she announced her
wish for a private conversation with the Siogoun, and
dismissed her attendants.

" The Japanese annalist relates, that when they were alone, the princess earnestly implored her consort to grant the request she was about to prefer to him. He refused to pledge his word until he should know what she desired ; and she then said, ' I am assured that you purpose adopting the son of Dewano-Kami as your heir. Such a step, my most dear and honoured lord, must grievously offend all those princes whose claims would thus be superseded ; it would unavoidably provoke a general insurrection, and occasion the destruction of the empire. My prayer therefore is, that you will renounce so ruinous a design.'

" The Siogoun was incensed at such feminine interference with his projects, and indignantly replied, ' How darest thou, a mere woman, speak upon state affairs ? The empire is mine, to rule at my pleasure. I heed not female counsel, and never will I see or speak to thee more !" With these words he arose, and was leaving the apartment in a rage.

" The *Midia* followed, and detaining him by his sleeve, persisted with humble urgency, ' Yet bethink you, my sovereign lord. Reflect, I implore you, that should you execute this baneful resolution, the morrow's sun may see all Japan in rebellion.'

" The Siogoun was inflexibly obstinate ; her expostulations, gentle and submissive as they were, serving only to exasperate his resentment. The Heaven-descended lady, finding argument and solicitation fruitless, and hopeless of otherwise averting the impending disaster, suddenly plunged her dagger into his breast, and, withdrawing it, repeated the blow. Her aim was true ; the monarch fell, and his consort, dropping on her knees by his side, implored his pardon for having, in an emergency so critical, employed the only possible means left of securing the throne to the Gongen dynasty. She concluded with an assurance that she dreamed not of surviving him. The moment the Siogoun Tsouna-yosi had breathed his last, she stabbed herself with the same dagger, and sank lifeless upon his corpse. Her ladies, hearing the noise of her fall, ran in, and found both weltering in their blood.

"At this moment appeared Ino-Kamon, who, startled by the purport of the empress's billet, had flown to the palace. He was instantly admitted to the chamber of death, and stood confounded at the fearful spectacle it presented. After awhile, recovering himself, he exclaimed, "Lo! a woman has saved the empire! But for her bold deed, Japan would to-morrow have been convulsed, perhaps destroyed!"

"The self-slain princess had not, it seems, thought it sufficient thus effectually to prevent the Siogoun from executing his illegal design : she had further given Ino-Kamon, in her note, precise instructions as to the course he was to pursue. By obeying them, the minister secured the accession of the lawful heir, and alleviated the disappointment of the youth whom Tsouna-yosi had intended to adopt, by obtaining a principality for him from Yeye-nobou, the monarch he had been intended to supplant. Ino-Kamon's own services were recompensed by the new and grateful Siogoun, who rendered the office of governor of the empire hereditary in his family ; and this *Midia* is said to divide the admiration of Japan with the wife of Tchouya."*

All is wonderful, striking, singular, grand or horrible, pleasant or monstrous, in this matter of the Japanese. I know not what the ladies will think of the following account of the beginning and ending of that interesting event in their lives which is said to make their husbands "happy."

"Upon the first symptoms of pregnancy, a girdle of braided red crape is bound round the future mother's body, immediately below the bosom. This is performed in great ceremony, with religious rites appointed for the occasion ; and the selection of the person who presents the girdle is a point of extreme importance and dignity. This singular custom is, by learned Japanese, said to be

* *Ubi suprà.*

practised in honour of the widow of a *Mikado*, who, some sixteen centuries ago, upon her husband's death, being then in an advanced state of pregnancy, thus girding herself, took his vacant place at the head of the army, and completed the conquest of Corea. It is to be observed, however, that this lady was impelled to the girding in question by a motive peculiar to herself. She had prayed to the gods to postpone her confinement, lest it should impede her military operations; and her adoption of this tight filleting must be considered as in the nature either of a vow, to induce the gods to grant her petition, or of a means to facilitate the miracle she solicited. The name of this Amazon, herself of the *mikado* blood, was Sin-Gou-Kwo-Gou, and her exploits were rewarded with sovereignty. Whether she was actually acknowledged as a *mikado*, seems to be a disputed point amongst Japanese historians; but she certainly governed the empire during the remainder of her life, sixty-nine years, and, dying at the age of one hundred, was succeeded by the son she had borne to her husband after his death.[*] Both mother and son are deified. The more vulgar opinion represents the girding as a mere physical precaution, by which the unborn babe is prevented from stealing the food out of the mother's throat, and so starving her to death! But whichever be the cause, the red fillet must remain, as at first fastened, until the birth of the infant.

"Upon the occurrence of this happy event, the mother is relieved from her long-endured binding; but her sufferings from ceremonious or superstitious observances are not yet over. She is forthwith placed in an upright sitting posture upon the bed,[†] fixed in it by bags of rice under each arm, and at her back; and thus is she compelled to remain during nine whole days and nights, most sparingly fed, and actually kept wide awake, lest, by dropping asleep, she should in some way alter the prescribed position. Perhaps the most extraordinary

---

[*] Klaproth.   [†] Meylan and Fisscher.

part of the whole business is, that no ill effect is said to ensue to the patient. It is to be observed, however, that Japanese women recover more slowly than those of other countries from parturition ; probably in consequence of this severe treatment. For one hundred days after her delivery, the recent mother is considered as an invalid, and nursed as such; at the end of that period only, she resumes her household duties, visits the temple frequented by her family, and performs her pilgrimage, or any other act of devotion that she may have vowed in her hour of peril.

" The infant, immediately upon its birth, is bathed, and remains free from all swathing and clothing that could impede the growth and development of body or limb. Upon one occasion only is this early state of freedom interrupted, and that occasion is the bestowing a name upon the new member of society. This takes place on the thirty-first day of a boy's age, on the thirtieth of a girl's.* Upon the appointed day, the babe is carried in state to the family temple ; the servants follow, bearing a whole infantine wardrobe, by the abundance of which the father's wealth and dignity are estimated. Last in the procession walks a maid servant, with a box in her hand, containing money for the fee of the officiating priestess, and a slip of paper, on which are inscribed three names. These names the priestess submits, with prescribed rites, to the god to whom the temple is dedicated ; then announces which of the three is selected, and confers it on the child, whom she sprinkles with water. Sacred songs, chanted to an instrumental accompaniment, conclude the naming ceremony. The infant is then carried to several other temples, and, for its final visit, to the house of the father's nearest kinsman. He presents it with a bundle of hemp, destined symbolically to spin it a long life, talismans, relics, and other valua-

* Others say that children of persons of distinction receive a name on the seventh day after their birth : among the lower classes, boys being named at the expiration of thirty days, girls at that of thirty-one.

bles; to which he adds, if his new-born relation be a boy, two fans (as representatives of swords), implying courage; if a girl, a shell of paint, implying beauty.

"In the unconfined state above described the child continues for three years, at the expiration of which the clothes are bound at the waist with a girdle. Religious rites accompany this first girding, and the child is now taught to pray. At seven years old the boy receives the mantle of ceremony, and, what could hardly have been surmised, from the great importance apparently attached to the choice of the name given the baby, a new name. For this change, likewise, there is an appropriate religious ceremony; and, to avoid repetition, it may be said, once for all, that every change, every epoch in Japanese life, is consecrated by the rites of the national religion. After the reception of the mantle of ceremony, a boy is permitted to perform his devotions regularly at the temple.

"Children are trained in habits of implicit obedience, which, independently of any beneficial effects on the future character that may be expected, Japanese parents value as obviating the necessity of punishment. Children of both sexes, and of all ranks, are almost invariably sent to the inferior or primary schools, where they learn to read and write, and acquire some knowledge of the history of their own country. For the lower orders this is deemed sufficient education; but of thus much, it is positively asserted,* that not a day labourer in Japan is destitute. The children of the higher orders proceed from these schools to others of a superior description, where they are carefully instructed in morals and manners, including the whole science of good-breeding, the minutest laws of etiquette, the forms of behaviour, as graduated towards every individual of the whole human race, by relation, rank, and station; including also a thorough knowledge of the almanack, since it would be as vulgarly disgraceful as it could be disastrous, to marry, begin a journey, or take any other important step, upon

* Meylan.

an unlucky day.* Boys are further taught arithmetic, and the whole mystery of the *Hara-kiri*, literally meaning, 'happy dispatch'—but the proper appellation of the abdomen-ripping, by which a well-born man is often compelled to terminate his existence. They are taught not only the proper mode of performing the operation, and the several accompanying ceremonials, varying with the occasion, and with the consequent publicity or privacy, but also the nature of the occasions, that is, of the causes and situations, which render this form of suicide imperative upon a gentleman. Girls, in lieu of this fearful indoctrination, receive lessons in the craft of the needle, with every species of ornamental work, in the service and management of a house, and in whatever it is thought may be useful to them as mothers and mistresses of families.

"During this period of their lives, Japanese children are very ill-dressed. Even when accompanying their splendidly-attired mothers through the streets, their shabby appearance offers a disagreeable contrast to hers. The object of this is to prevent the noxious effects of the admiration which, if well-dressed, their beauty might excite; and it is not a little curious thus to find the same strange superstition of the *evil eye*, in the most remote and dissimilar countries, where intercommunication seems to be impossible.

"At fifteen education is deemed complete. The boy, as of man's estate, now takes his place in society; his head is shaved in Japanese fashion, and again he receives a new name. But even this third name is not destined to be permanent. Upon every advance in official rank—and half the Japanese above the working classes appear to hold office—the placeman takes a new name. Nor is it only upon an occasion thus agreeable, that he must change his designation; no official subaltern may bear the same name with his chief; so that whenever a new individual is appointed to a high post, every man under him who

* See p. 184 of this work.

chances to be his namesake must immediately assume a new denomination. The system of changing the name with the post, extends even to the throne, and occasions great perplexity to the student of Japanese history, whose undivided attention is requisite to trace, for instance, the progress of an usurper through all his varying appellations."

This strange custom produces still greater complications amongst the Chinese. In China the child first receives the name of the family; a month afterwards a diminutive is added to it, which is called the milk-name, and it is generally that of a flower, an animal, or anything according to fancy; at the commencement of his studies he receives another amongst his school-fellows; and when he becomes of age he takes another, with which he signs his letters; finally, should he obtain office, he takes a fifth name suited to his rank, and etiquette requires that he should be called by the last.*

"The Japanese marries early; but, as to marry beneath his rank is held to be utterly disgraceful, persons of the middle classes of society are commonly reduced to the necessity of espousing those whom they have never seen. The children of the governor of Nagasaki—who have no equals in the place—must get wives and husbands out of the families of men of the governor's rank in the distant cities and provinces. When no such obstacle prevents 'the course of true love' from running ' smooth,' and a youth has fixed his affections upon a maiden of suitable condition, he declares his passion by affixing a branch of a certain shrub (the *Celastrus alatus*) to the house of the damsel's parents. If the branch be neglected, the suit is rejected; if it be accepted, so is the lover; and if the young lady wishes to express reciprocal tenderness, she forthwith blackens her teeth; but she must not pluck out her eyebrows until the wedding shall have been actually celebrated.

"When the branch is accepted in the one case, or the

* Navaretto.

parents have agreed to unite their children in the other, a certain number of male friends of the bridegroom, and as many female friends of the bride, are appointed as marriage-brokers. These persons discuss and arrange the terms of the marriage contract; and when they have agreed upon these, they carefully select two auspicious days; the first for an interview between the affianced pair, the second for the wedding.

"At this stage of the proceedings the bridegroom sends presents, as costly as his means will allow, to the bride; which she immediately offers to her parents, in acknowledgment of their kindness in her infancy, and of the pains bestowed upon her education. Thus, although a Japanese lady is not subjected to the usual Oriental degradation of being actually purchased of her father by her husband, a handsome daughter is still considered as rather an addition than otherwise to the fortune of the family. The bride is not, however, transferred quite empty-handed to her future home. Besides sending a few trifles to the bridegroom, in return for his magnificent gifts, the parents of the bride, after ceremoniously burning their daughter's childish toys, in token of her change of condition, provide her a handsome *trousseau*, and bestow upon her many articles of household furniture—if the word 'many' can apply to articles of furniture, where the handsomely-matted floor answers the purpose of chairs, tables, sofas, and bedsteads. Those given on the occasion in question always include a spinning-wheel, a loom, and the culinary implements requisite in a Japanese kitchen. The whole of this bridal equipment is conveyed in great state to the bridegroom's house on the wedding-day, and there exhibited.

"With respect to the marriage-rites, some little difficulty is created by Titsingh's intimation that no religious solemnization takes place; but it is easy to conceive that, in such a country as Japan especially, a foreigner, even the head of the factory, should have been often invited to the formal ceremonies with which the bride is installed in her new home, without ever witnessing, or even hearing of the earlier religious celebration. In fact, Meylan distinctly states that marriage, although a mere civil contract, is consecrated by a priest. Fisscher adds, that it must be registered in the temple to which the young couple belong; and from the Swedish traveller of the last century, Thunberg, as also from old Montanus, we have a description of the religious solemnity. This appears to consist in the prayers and benedictions of the priests, accompanied by a formal kindling of bridal torches, the bride's from the altar, the bridegroom's from hers; after which the pair are pronounced man and wife.

"But the business of the day by no means terminates with this declaration. The bride is attired in white, to typify her purity, and covered from head to foot with a white veil. This veil is her destined shroud, which is assumed at the moment of exchanging a paternal for a conjugal home, in token that the bride is thenceforward dead to her own family, belonging wholly to the husband to whom she is about to be delivered up. In this garb she is seated in a palanquin of the higher class, and carried forth, escorted by the marriage-brokers, by her family, and by the friends bidden to the wedding-feast; the men all in their dress of ceremony, the women in their gayest, gold-bordered robes. The procession parades through the greater part of the town, affording an exceedingly pretty spectacle.

"Upon reaching the bridegroom's house, the bride, still in her future shroud, is accompanied by two playfellows of her girlhood into the state room, where, in the post of honour, sits the bridegroom, with his parents and nearest relations. In the centre of the apartment stands a beautifully-wrought table, with miniature representations of a fir-tree, a plum-tree in blossom, cranes and tortoises, the emblems, respectively, of man's strength, of woman's beauty, and of long and happy life. Upon another table stands all the apparatus for *saki* drinking. Beside this last table the bride takes her stand; and now begins a pouring out, presenting, and drinking of *saki*, amidst formalities, numerous and minute beyond description or conception, in which the bridemaids (as they may be called), under the titles, for the nonce, of male and female butterflies,* bear an important part, which it must require many a school-rehearsal to perfect. This drinking finished in due form, the ceremonial is completed. The wedding guests now appear, and the evening is spent in eating, and drinking *saki*.† The wedding feast is, however, said usually to consist of very simple fare,‡ in deference to the frugality and simplicity of the early Japanese, which many of the customs still prevalent are designed to commemorate. Three days afterwards the bride and bridegroom pay their respects to the lady's family, and the wedding forms are over.

" Whether the house in which the young wife' is thus domiciliated be her husband's or his father's, if yet living, depends upon whether that father has or has not been yet induced, by the vexations, burthens, and restrictions attached to the condition of head of a family, to resign that dignity to his son. These annoyances, increasing with the rank of the parties, are said to be such, that almost every father in Japan, of the higher orders, at least, looks impatiently for the day when he shall have a son of age to take his place, he himself, together with his wife and younger children, becoming thenceforward dependents upon that son. And among such a whole nation of Lears, we are assured that no Regans and Gonerils, of either sex, have ever been known to disgrace human nature."

In manners it is woman that makes the man. Where the gentler sex are graceful, elegant, and refined, the other sex are never found to be coarse, ungainly, and vulgar. The Japanese gentleman is invariably described as a person of pleasing address and most polished manners. Even among the commonest people, brawlers, braggarts, loud-tongued disputants, dirty slovens, or men

---

* Titsingh.　　　　　† Siebold.
‡ Fisscher.

with coarse, repulsive manners, are very seldom met with. The poorest labourer, toiling by the wayside for his daily bread, expects a civil question, and is always ready with a civil answer. In their most familiar intercourse with one another, they scrupulously observe the set forms of politeness. Unless it be some person in authority, they will not reply to the man that addresses them in an insolent or rough way. They will even refuse to work for a violent or coarse-tongued employer.

Thunberg says : " Although gravity forms the general character of the Japanese nation, this serious disposition does not prevent them from having their pleasures, their sports, and festivities. These are of two kinds—occasional or periodical—and constitute part of their worship. Their chief festivals of all are the ' *Feast of Lanterns*,' and what is called the *Matsuri*.

" The Lantern Festival, or Feast of Lamps, is celebrated towards the end of August, and is called by the natives *Bong*. It last three days ; but the second afternoon, with the following night, are kept with the greatest festivity. It was originally instituted in memory and honour of the dead, who, they believe, return annually to their kindred and friends on the first afternoon of these games, every one visiting his former house and family, where they remain till the second night, when they are to be sent away again. By way of welcoming them on their arrival, they plant stakes of bamboo near all the tombs, upon which they hang a great number of lanterns, with lights, and those so close to each other, that the whole mountain appears illuminated : these lanterns are kept alight till nine or ten o'clock at night. On the second evening, when the spirits of the defunct are, according to their tradition, to be sent away again, they fabricate a small vessel of straw, with lights and lanterns in it, which they carry at midnight in procession, with vocal and instrumental music, and loud cries, to the seashore, where it is launched into the water, and left to the wind and waves, till it either catches fire and is consumed or is swallowed up by the waves. Both of these illumi-

nations, consisting of several thousand fires, exhibit to
the eye an uncommonly grand and beautiful spectacle.*

"The feast of *Matsuri*," continues Thunberg, "is celebrated upon some certain festival-day, and in honour of
some particular god. Thus, for instance, in the town of
Nagasaki, where I was present at one of these festivals, it
is celebrated in memory of *Suwa*, the tutelar deity of the
town. It is celebrated on the ninth day of the ninth
month, which is the day of the idol's nativity, with games,
public dances, and dramatic representations. The festival
commences on the seventh day, when the temples are frequented, sermons preached, prayers offered up, and public
spectacles exhibited ; but the ninth day excels all in
pomp and expensive magnificence, which they vary every
time in such a manner, that the entertainments of the
present year bear no resemblance to those of the last ;
neither are the same arrangements made. The expenses
are defrayed by the inhabitants of the town, in such manner that certain streets exhibit and pay the expenses of certain pieces and parts of the entertainment. A capacious
house, resembling a large booth, raised upon posts, and
provided with a roof and benches, was erected on one
side, for the convenience of the spectators. These consisted not only of the magistrates and ecclesiastics, but
likewise of foreigners ; and a guard was placed to keep off
the crowd. First of all appeared the priests, carrying the
image of the idol *Suwa;* and took their places, habited in
black and white. A company of ten or twelve persons
played upon instruments of music, and sang the exploits of
their gods and heroes ; in the meantime that a party of
virgins dancing displayed the most enchanting elegance
in their gestures and deportment. The music consisted
of a mere rattling noise, which might, perhaps, sound
more grateful in the idol's than in human ears. A large
parasol was next introduced, inscribed with the name of
the street, and emblazoned with its coat-of-arms, followed
by a band of musicians, in masks, with drums, flutes,

* Thunberg, Kämpfer.

bells, and vocal music. These were succeeded by the device itself, which was different for every street; then followed a band of actors; and, lastly, the inhabitants of the street, in solemn procession, with an innumerable and promiscuous crowd at their heels. This progressive march lasted nearly a whole hour, after which they marched back again in the same order, and a second procession succeeded in its place: this was followed by a third; and so on, during the whole forenoon. The inhabitants of each street vied with each other in magnificence and invention, with respect to the celebration of this festival, and in displaying, for the most part, such things as were characteristic of the various produce of the mines, mountains, forests, navigation, manufactures, and the like, of the province from which the street derived its name, and whence it had its inhabitants."

Kämpfer enumerates three other great annual festivals. I cannot do better than give, at full length, his account of one of them, because it contains, in addition to some very agreeable pictures of festive life, a wild Japanese romance or legend. The passage may, therefore, be taken as a specimen of old native literature as well as an illustration of manners and customs :—

" The second *sekf*, or great yearly festival, is called *Sanguatz Sannitz,* because of its being celebrated on the third day of the third month. On this, also, after the usual compliments and visits, which friends and relations pay one to another, and inferiors to their superiors, every one diverts himself in the best manner he can. The season of the year—the beginning of the spring, the trees, chiefly plum, cherry, and apricot trees, which are then in full blossom, and loaded with numberless white and incarnate flowers, single and double, and no less remarkable for their largeness and plenty, than for their singular beauty, invite everybody to take the diversion of the country, and to behold nature in her new and inimitable dress. But this same festival is, besides, a day of pleasure and diversion for young girls, for whose sake a great entertainment is commonly prepared by their parents, whereto they invite their nearest relations and friends. A large and spacious apartment is curiously adorned with puppets to a considerable value, which are to represent the court of the Mikado, or ecclesiastical hereditary Emperor, with the person of *Finakuge*. A table, with Japanese victuals, is placed before each puppet, and among other things cakes made of rice and the leaves of young mugwort. These victuals and a dish of saki the guests are presented with by the girls, for whose diversion the entertainment is intended ; or if they be too young, by their parents.

"The following story gave birth to this custom :—A rich man, who lived near *Rinsagava*, which is as much as to say the Bird River, had a daughter called *Bundjo*, who was married to one *Symmias Dai Miosin*. Not having any children by her husband for many years, she very earnestly addressed herself in her prayers to the Kamis or gods of the country, and this with so much success, that soon after she found herself big, and was brought to bed with five hundred eggs. The poor woman, extremely surprised at this extraordinary accident, and full of fear that the eggs, if hatched, would produce monstrous animals, packed them all up in a box, and threw them into the river Rinsagava, with this precaution, however, that she wrote the word *fosjoroo* upon the box. Some time after, an old fisherman, who lived a good way down the river, found this box floating, took it up, and having found it full of eggs, he carried them home to present them to his wife, who was of opinion that there could not be anything extraordinary in them, and that certainly they had been thrown into the water for some good reason ; and therefore she advised him to carry them back where he found them. But the old man replied : 'We are both old, my dear, and just on the brink of the grave ; it will be a matter of very little consequence to us, whatever comes out of the eggs, and therefore I have a mind to hatch them, and see what they will produce.' Accordingly, he hatched them in an oven, in hot sand, and between cushions, as the way is in the Indies, and having afterwards opened them, they found in every one a child. To keep such a number of children proved a very heavy burden for this old couple. However, they made a shift, and bred them up with mugwort-leaves minced, and boiled rice. But in time they grew so big, that the old man and his wife could not maintain them any longer, so that they were necessitated to shift for themselves as well as they could, and took to robbing on the highway. Among other projects, it was proposed to them to go up the river to the house of a rich man, who was very famous for his great wealth in that part of the country. As good luck would have it, this house proved to be that of their mother.

" Upon application made at the door, one of the servants asked what their names were, to which they answered, that they had no names, that they were a brood of five hundred eggs, that mere want and necessity had obliged them to call, and that they would go about their business, if they would be so charitable as to give them some victuals. The servant having taken the message in to his lady, she sent him back to inquire whether there had not been something writ upon the box in which the eggs had been found, and having answered that the word *fosjoroo* was found writ upon it, she could then no longer doubt but that they were all her children, and, accordingly, acknowledged and received them as such, and made a great entertainment, whereat every one of the guests was presented with a dish of *sokana*, with cakes of mugwort and rice, and a branch of the apricot-tree. This is the reason they give, why, on this festival, branches of the apricot-tree are laid over the kettle, and cakes made of mugwort and rice, which they call *futsumotzi*, that is, *mugwort cakes*, and prepared after the following manner : —The mugwort-leaves are soaked in water over night, then pressed, dried, and reduced to powder, afterwards mixed with rice, which hath been boiled in water, then again reduced to powder, and mixed with boiled rice and *adsuki*, or red beans, coarsely powdered, and so baked into cakes. The mother of these children was afterwards

T

translated among the goddesses of the country, by the name of Bensaitree. They believe that she is waited upon, in the happy regions of the gods, by her five hundred sons, and they worship her as the goddess of riches."

At one of the five great annual festivals, in the midst of good eating and drinking, the school-boys erect poles or posts of bamboo, and tie to them verses of their own making. At another—"Joy, mirth, and hospitality are universal. Not even strangers are suffered to pass by without being invited to make merry with the company. In short, one would imagine that the Bacchanals of the Romans had been brought over into Japan and established there. All sorts of diversions and public shows, dancing, plays, processions and the like, so greatly divert and amuse the people, that many choose rather to lose their dinners, than to give over sauntering and staring about the streets till late at night."

In addition to these five great yearly festivals, there are many more holidays observed at different seasons of the year. Honest old Kämpfer found them so numerous, that " it would be almost endless to mention them all."

In a morning call, pipes and tea are as invariably brought in at Jeddo, as pipes and coffee at Constantinople. At the conclusion of such call, sweetmeats or other dainties, to be eaten with chopsticks, are served up on a sheet of paper, sometimes purely white, and sometimes ornamented with tinsel or bright colours. Pocketing is not a vulgarism, but a duty strictly imposed by etiquette. If the visitor cannot eat all the dainties, he must fold up the remainder in the sheet of paper, and deposit them in his wide sleeve, which serves as a pocket. At grand dinners, each guest is expected to take with him a servant or two, to carry off, in baskets, the remnants of the banquet. At these social meetings, the ladies smoke as well as the gentlemen.

A Japanese feast usually consists of seven or eight courses. During the several removes, the master of the house walks round and drinks a cup of saki with each

A JAPANESE LADY'S BOUDOIR.

guest. This is their way of hobnobbing, or "taking wine." The viands consist of game, venison, poultry, fish, and all kinds of vegetables, seaweeds not excepted. Fish is, however, the *pièce de résistance*, the standing dish, the roast beef of the Japanese. As has been already mentioned, they eat of all sorts, not excluding the whale, nor even the shark. Each guest is served with a portion of every dish in a small, light lacquered bowl. Another bowl of the same description is placed at his side, and kept constantly replenished with rice. As whets, servants of both sexes, from time to time, hand round soy, other sauces, pickled or salted ginger, and small, nicely-cut morsels of salted fish, which are all eaten with the Chinese chopsticks. It is expected that the guests should compliment the giver of the feast on the beauty of his lacquered ware, on the splendour of his bowls, and on the richness and beauty of his domestic utensils, and furnishing in general.

None but personages of high hereditary rank dare presume to give a feast of the first order. A wealthy merchant must on no account entertain his friends like a lord or prince. It is, however, believed, that when a wealthy trader can conciliate all the spies that are watching over him, by making them partakers of the banquet, he sometimes ventures to give, quietly, as grand a " spread " as any of his betters.*

It appears that the feasts are generally enlivened by music, and followed by music and dancing, and copious libations of saki and tea. Occasionally some new little play or interlude, analogous to the occasion, is introduced and performed by amateur actors. According to honest Captain Cock, all the Japanese in his time were much

---

* Titsingh, Kämpfer, Golownin, *Atlas Japon.* It appears that Meurs, who was an engraver as well as a bookseller, really compiled the last work and that the person designated on the title-page as Arnold Montanus, merely put in the learning, furnishing the classical allusions, Latin quotations, and the like. The engravings, which are very curious, and very full of character, appear all to have proceeded from the industrious hands of the engraver-bookseller Meurs.

addicted to the good old hospitable fashion of giving "house-warmings," and considered that no dwelling could be prosperous or stand long on its foundations that was not, on its being finished, opened with a banquet and a jovial carouse. But it was the custom, on every such occasion, for all the neighbours of the master of the new house to send him liberal presents of eatables and drinkables.*

Tobacco, that herb so pleasant, which has become so indispensably necessary to so many millions of men, is a mighty favourite with the Japanese. Given to them by the Portuguese, it is almost the only relic they have retained of that detested nation. They have no name for it in their language, but call it tobacco, and smoke it cut as fine as the hair of the head, in small metal pipes, with a stem about a foot long. The bowl does not hold more than a thimbleful, and they thus enjoy the fragrance without spoiling the tobacco by the moisture generated at the bottom of large bowls—what they lose in time and trouble by constant filling, they gain by enjoyment. All smoke, men and women, high and low, from the imperial palace of Jeddo to the humble cot of the peasant. They literally smoke and drink tea all day long.†

All classes of them make a very frequent use of the bath, and are scrupulous as to partial ablutions, at certain fixed periods of the day. This alone does not insure cleanliness. The Turks bathe, or rather stew themselves, as often as the Japanese ; but the Turk puts on foul, unchanging clothes over a clean skin, and has generally a house encumbered with filth, and swarming with bugs, fleas, and other intolerable vermin ; but the Japanese

---

* *Journal and Notes,* as given by Mr. Rundall, *Memorials of the Empire of Japan.* In Cock's time no English or Dutch vessel was ever allowed to leave port for Batavia, or for Europe, without receiving presents, and holding a good drinking bout. The people went off to the ship, carrying with them good store of foreign wines, and of native potables, to drink success to the voyage. The Japanese, like our English tars of the old school, had no notion of "parting dry."

† Tiedemann, Thunberg, &c.

contrives usually to put clean clothes over his clean skin, and to be neat and tidy at home.' Kämpfer observes :— " They are, indeed, very nice in keeping themselves, their clothes, and houses clean and neat." To every house of any pretension to respectability there is attached an apartment called a " *Fro*," which is fitted up with vapour-baths, and with warm and cold baths. One or the other of these the Japanese use every morning and every evening. The loose nature of their costume renders the operations of undressing and dressing very quick and easy. Unfasten the girdle that encircles the waist, and the whole of the simple habiliments drop at once to the ground, as before stated. It is mainly to this practice of constant bathing that our learned German doctor attributes the generally robust health and longevity of the people in this empire.

Both hunting and hawking are frequently mentioned by the early travellers, as common pastimes of "the nobility and gentry." Hawks of a wonderfully fine breed, and of admirable training, are also mentioned ; but, as I have previously stated, it seems that these sports are not now very common, and that the Japanese gentlemen have quite lost their taste for equitation, although, when rich, they always keep a numerous, if not a good stud in the stable, and are very rigorous with the grooms who neglect the feeding and proper cleaning of their horses. Some of these stables are said to be as neat as a drawing-room.

" Of music the Japanese are passionately fond, and their traditions give the art a divine origin. According to this account, the Sun Goddess, once upon a time, in resentment of the violence of an ill-disposed brother, retired into a cave, leaving the universe in anarchy and darkness. Music was devised by the gods to lure her forth. But, though the existence of daylight is evidence that the invention succeeded, Japanese music, as described to us, corresponds but ill with the high purpose of its birth. It has, indeed, produced many instruments— stringed, wind, and of the drum and cymbal kind—of which the favourite is the *syamsie*, or guitar, with three strings. two in the octave, the middle giving the fifth, touched with a flat piece of horn, held between the thumb and third finger. But with all this variety of instruments (twenty-one in number), the Japanese have no idea of harmony; and when several are played together, they are played in unison. Nor are they much greater proficients

MUSICAL INSTRUMENTS.

in melody; their airs, we are told, boasting neither 'wood notes wild,' nor any portion of science. Yet to this music they will listen delightedly for hours; and the girl must be low-born and low-bred indeed,* who cannot accompany her own singing upon the *syamsie.* And this singing is often extemporary, as it appears that there scarcely ever is a party of the kind mentioned in which some one of the

* Meylan.

ladies present is not capable of *improvising* a song, should opportunity offer.

"The dancing is of the Oriental style, and depending upon the arms and body rather than the feet, which remain nearly immovable and concealed, as usual, beneath the robes.   It is, in fact, pantomimic in character, and generally designed to represent some scene of passion, of absurdity, or of every-day life.   These domestic *ballets* are performed by the ladies, the men gazing in rapturous admiration; although the utmost praise their Dutch visitors can bestow upon the exhibition is, that it is perfectly free, as might be anticipated from the character of the dancers, from the indecent and licentious character of those of the Oriental dancing-girls.   The country does not appear, however, to be destitute of this class of performers.

"Cards and dice are prohibited; and although the law is said to be secretly transgressed in gaming-houses, at home the Japanese respect it, and resort to other kinds of games.   Chess and draughts are great favourites."

The Japanese game of Sho-ho-yé, analogous to our game of chess, is played by two persons, with forty pieces— twenty on each side—and upon a chequer board of eighty-one squares—nine upon each side.   The board is of one uniform colour; the pieces also are of one colour, as they are used at pleasure by either party, as his own, after being captured from the adversary.   They are of various sizes, long and wedge-shaped, and sharpened from side to side in front; and the name of each piece is inscribed upon it, both the original and the one assumed, upon being reversed or turned over.   Each player knows his men, or pieces, by their pointed and thin end being always forward or directed from him.   They are laid flat upon the board, front forward, and thus their names are plainly visible. They capture, as in chess, by occupying the places of the captured pieces.   The "King," *Oho-shio*, being the chief piece, cannot remain in check, and when checkmated, the game is lost.*

* *United States Expedition,* Tomes's Abridgment, p. 413.

"There is also a favourite game resembling the Italian *moro*. Upon occasions of their games of forfeits, the trammels of ceremony are completely broken, and the most extravagant merriment prevails, often ending in results very contrary to our English notions of the temperance of tropical and Oriental climates. *Saki* is drunk, as a penalty or voluntarily, to intoxication by the men, who then sober themselves with tea, and again inebriate themselves with *saki*, until, after several repetitions of the two processes, they are carried away insensible.

"In summer, their joyous meetings usually take the form of rustic, and especially water parties, formed expressly for the enjoyment of fine scenery. Large companies will spend the afternoon, evening, and part of the night, upon the lakes, rivers, or innumerable bays of the sea, in their highly ornamented boats, with music and banquets. During the heat of the day, they lie moored in some shady nook, protected from the sun's rays, but open to the sea-breeze, whence they command a pleasing view. In the evening the waters are all alive with music, and illuminated with the moving light from the coloured paper lanterns of the several boats.

"In order to divert the company, should conversation flag, and their own music pall on the ear, professional musicians, jugglers, posture-makers, and the like, are hired for the day. To these are added a variety of the story-telling genus, very different in character from the species ordinarily found in the East. These persons make it their especial business to learn, not romances, but all the gossip of a neighbourhood, which they retail for the entertainment of their employers. Some of these traders in scandal are frequently hired to relieve the tedium of a sick-room; but those engaged to divert a party of pleasure have a second and somewhat startling duty—it is to set an example of politeness and high breeding, to improve the tone of the society that requires their services. These several and not very homogeneous functions they are said to combine in a most extraordinary manner. We are assured that, although in their capacity of amusers they indulge in extravagant buffoonery, rudeness, and impudence, they remain perfectly self-possessed, and at the proper moment resuming their polished demeanour, recal the whole company to order and good breeding."*

Wrestlers appear to be much in vogue in Japan. The officers of the American Expedition had a sight of these artists—"monstrous fellows who came tramping down the beach like so many huge elephants. They were professional wrestlers, and formed part of the retinue of the Japanese princes, who keep them for their private amusement, and for public entertainment. They were twenty-five in all, and were men enormously tall in stature, and immense in weight of flesh. Their scant costume—which was merely a coloured cloth about the loins, adorned with fringes, and emblazoned with the armorial bearings of the prince to whose service each belonged—revealed their gigantic proportions, in all the bloated fulness of fat and breadth of muscle. Their proprietors, the princes, seemed proud of them, and were careful to show their points to the greatest advantage before the astonished spectators. Some two or three of the huge monsters were the most famous wrestlers in Japan, and ranked as the champion Tom Cribs and Hyers of the land. Koyanagi, the reputed bully of the capital, was one of these, and paraded himself with the conscious pride of superior immensity and strength. He was brought especially to the Commodore, that he might examine his massive form. The Commissioners insisted that the monstrous fellow should be minutely inspected, that the hardness of his well-rounded muscles should be felt, and that the fatness of his cushioned frame should be tested by the touch. The Commodore attempted to grasp his arm, which he found as solid as it was huge, and then passed his hand over the enormous neck, which fell, in folds of massive flesh, like the dew-lap of a prize ox. As some surprise was naturally expressed at this wondrous exhibition of animal development, the monster

* *Manners and Customs of the Japanese.*

himself gave a grunt, expressive of his flattered vanity.

" They were all so immense in flesh, that they appeared to have lost their distinctive features, and seemed only twenty-five masses of fat. Their eyes were barely visible through a long perspective of socket, the prominence of their noses was lost in the puffiness of their bloated cheeks, and their heads were almost directly set upon their bodies, with only folds of flesh where the neck and chin are usually found. Their great size, however, was more owing to the development of muscle than to the mere deposition of fat; for, although they were evidently well fed, they were not the less well exercised, and capable of great feats of strength. As a preliminary exhibition of the power of these men, the princes set them to removing the sacks of rice to a convenient place on the shore for shipping. All the sacks weighed one hundred and twenty-five pounds a-piece, and there were only two of the wrestlers who did not each carry two sacks at a time. They bore the sacks on the right shoulder, lifting the first from the ground themselves, and adjusting it, but obtaining aid for the raising of the second. One man carried a sack suspended by his teeth, and another, taking one in his arms, kept turning repeated somersaults as he held it, and apparently with as much ease as if his tons of flesh had been only so much gossamer, and his load a feather.

" After this preliminary display, the Commissioners proposed that the Commodore and his party should retire to Treaty House, where they would have an opportunity of seeing the wrestlers exhibit their professional feats. The wrestlers themselves were most carefully provided for, having constantly about them a number of attendants, who were always at hand to supply them with fans, which they often required, and to assist them in dressing and undressing. Whilst at rest, they were ordinarily clothed in richly-adorned robes of the usual Japanese fashion ; but when exercising, they were stripped naked, with the exception of the cloth about the loins. After the performance with the sacks of rice, their servitors spread upon the huge frames of the wrestlers their rich garments, and led them up to the Treaty House.

" A circular space of some twelve feet diameter had been inclosed within a ring, and the ground carefully broken up and smoothed in front of the building ; while in the portico, divans covered with red cloth were arranged for the Japanese Commissioners, the Commodore, his officers, and their various attendants. The bands of the ship were also present, and enlivened the intervals during the performance with occasional stirring tunes. As soon as the spectators had taken their seats, the naked wrestlers were brought out into the ring, and the whole number being divided into two opposing parties, tramped heavily backward and forward, looked defiance at each other, but not engaging in any contest, as their object was merely to parade their points, to give the beholders, as it were, an opportunity to form an estimate of their comparative powers, and to make up their betting-books. They soon retired behind some screens placed for the purpose, where all, with the exception of two, were again clothed in full dress, and took their position on seats in front of the spectators.

" The two who had been reserved out of the band, now, on the signal being given by the heralds, presented themselves. They came in, one after the other, from behind the screens, and walked with slow and deliberate steps, as became such huge animals, into the centre of the ring. Here they ranged themselves, one against the other, at a distance of a few yards. They stood for awhile eyeing each other with a wary look, as if both were watching a chance to catch their antagonist off his guard. As the spectator looked on and beheld these overfed monsters, whose animal natures had been so carefully and successfully developed, and as he watched them glaring with brutal ferocity at each other, ready to exhibit the cruel instincts of a savage nature, it was easy for him to lose all sense of their being human creatures, and to persuade himself that he was beholding a couple of brute-beasts thirsting for one another's blood.

"They were, in fact, like a pair of fierce bulls, whose nature they had not only acquired, but even their look and movements. As they continued to eye each other, they stamped the ground heavily, pawing, as it were, with impatience, and then stooping their huge bodies, they grasped handfuls of the earth, and flung it with an angry toss over their backs, or rubbed it impatiently

JAPANESE WRESTLERS.

between their massive palms, or under their stalwart shoulders. They now crouched down low, still keeping their eyes fixed upon one another and watching each movement, when, in a moment, they had both simultaneously heaved their massive frames in opposing force, body to body, with a shock that might have stunned an ox. The equilibrium of their monstrous persons was hardly disturbed by the encounter, the effect of which was but barely visible in the quiver of the hanging flesh of their bodies. As they came together, they had flung their brawny arms about each other, and were now entwined in a desperate struggle, with all their strength, to throw their antagonist. Their great muscle rose with the distinct outline of the sculptured form of a colossal Hercules, their bloated faces swelled up with gushes of red blood, which seemed almost to burst through the skin, and their huge bodies palpitated with savage emotion as the struggle continued. At last, one of the antagonists fell with his immense weight upon the ground, and being declared vanquished, he was assisted to his feet and conducted from the ring.

"The scene was now somewhat varied by a change in the kind of contest between the two succeeding wrestlers. The heralds, as before, summoned the antagonists, and one having taken his place in the ring, he assumed an attitude of defence, with one leg in advance as if to steady himself, and his body, with his head lowered, placed in position, as if to receive an attack. Immediately after, in rushed the other, bellowing loudly like a bull, and, making at once for the man in the ring, dashed, with his head lowered and thrust forward, against his opponent, who bore the shock with the steadiness of a rock, although the blood streamed down his face from his bruised forehead, which had been struck in the encounter. This manœuvre was repeated again and again, one acting always as the opposing and the other as the resisting force, and thus kept up this brutal contest until their foreheads were besmeared with blood, and the flesh of their breasts rose in great swollen tumours from the repeated blows. This disgusting exhibition did not terminate until the whole twenty-five had successively, in pairs, displayed their immense powers and savage qualities."

The American writer adds somewhat comically in national self-laudation :—"From the brutal performance of the wrestlers, the Americans turned with pride to the exhibition to which the Japanese Commissioners were in their turn invited, of those triumphs of civilization, the telegraph and the railroad." And he assures us that these Japanese, who had enjoyed this human bull-fight, far less revolting perhaps than any bull-fight, bowie-knife encounter, &c., turned with admiration and intense interest to the contemplation of these "triumphs of civilization." Most assuredly the men who generally enjoy, amongst us, such brutal displays, have no taste whatever for the "triumphs of civilization." That is the difference, then, between the Japanese and their Western critics.*

The love, obedience, and reverence manifested by children towards their parents are stated to be un-bounded. On the other hand, it is said that the con-fidence placed by parents in their children is equally without limit. Parents frequently select their elder sons to be arbitrators in their disputes with others, and submit implicitly to their decisions.

Next to the vices before alluded to, the great defect of the national character, though coupled with a keen sense of the point of honour, appears to be the thirst and madness of revenge. This passion, as we have intimated, also furnishes great staple materials for their dramatists and other writers; and it seems to be illustrated in numerous popular stories.

Some of these tales throw more light on the Japanese character than can be derived from any other source.

"Fakaki-fikoyemon, the governor of Nagasaki, having obtained permission of the Siogoun to wear two sabres, and to have a pike in his coat of arms, his people became in consequence so insolent that they treated every one with the utmost haughtiness and disdain.

"On the twentieth of the twelfth month of the four-teenth year Gen-rok (1701), they were carrying his daughter in a sedan-chair to the temple, to receive a name. Heavy rains had rendered the road very muddy. Fokka-fouri-kouanseïmon, that is, the governor of the

* In the *United States Expedition* will be found a wood-cut of these monstrous wrestlers, who must be a peculiar race in Japan, if the Japanese have not discovered a method for promoting the growth of men as well as vegetables.

village of Fokka-fouri, hastily passing by the chair, had the misfortune to splash it. Fikoyemon's people began to abuse him, and, regardless of his excuses, fell upon and beat him, and then ran to his house in the street called Ouya-goto-matche, where they destroyed all the furniture.

"The servants of Kouanseïmon took a boat, and lost no time in carrying to him intelligence of what had happened. After deliberating on the means of revenging this insult, which could not be washed away but with blood, they returned to Nagasaki, with several of the inhabitants of Fokka-fouri, assembled to the number of more than two hundred before the residence of Fikoyemon, and as soon as the door was opened, rushed in and attacked the master and his people. Fikoyemon valiantly defended himself; but his foot having unfortunately slipped, his adversaries fell upon him and cut off his head, which they carried in triumph to Fokka-fouri, as a trophy of their vengeance.*

"It was conveyed to Nagasaki, and interred with the body near the temple of Fon-ren-si, together with a white dog, which had rushed among the assailants to defend his master, and been killed after wounding several of them.

"Two of Kouanseïmon's people ripped themselves up on the bridge, near the residence of Fikoyemon, calling loudly upon the people to witness the courage with which the inhabitants of Fokka-fouri suffer death in order to revenge injuries."†

"M. Caron relates a remarkable instance, which occurred within his own knowledge. It appears that two high officers of the court met on the palace-stairs and jostled each other. One was an irascible man, and immediately demanded satisfaction. The other, of a placable disposition, represented that the circumstance was acci-

---

* "While I was in Japan, a woman was still living at Nagasaki, who recollected seeing the murderers pass by, holding by the hair his head dripping blood."—Titsingh.

† Titsingh, *Illustrations of Japan.*

dental, and tendered an ample apology : representing that satisfaction could not reasonably be demanded. The irascible man, however, would not be appeased, and finding he could not provoke the other to a conflict, suddenly drew up his robes, unsheathed his katana, and cut himself in the prescribed mode. As a point of honour, his adversary was under the necessity of following the example, and the irascible man, before he breathed his last, had the gratification of seeing the object of his passion dying by his side."

" Having a keen sense of the slightest insult, which cannot be washed away but with blood, they are the more disposed to treat one another in their mutual intercourse with the highest respect."

The Japanese must rank among the—

> "Souls made of fire and children of the sun,
> With whom revenge is virtue."

" Forgiveness of an injury Mr. Meylan asserts to be unknown, or only to be stigmatized as a weakness or a sin. Of their courage it would be hard to speak, the article not having been tested on a large scale for two centuries. Mr. Meylan states that in the armies of the infant Dutch East India Company were many Japanese soldiers, who did excellent service, as before stated, and he believes them to be far braver than the other nations of the East. Suicide is frequent ; and the duellist of Europe, however desperate, is far excelled, in our judgment, by the Japanese, who, in the presence of applauding, and frequently imitating relations and friends, rips his own abdomen to escape dishonour.

" This was the conduct and fate of the Governor of Nagasaki in 1808, when an English frigate found an entrance into that harbour, detained as prisoners the Dutch who boarded her, and demanded—in that ignorant and wanton violation of the religious law of the country, which we regret to say so often marks the conduct of British adventurers—fresh beef as their ransom. The beef was supplied, but the governor, as soon as the Dutch under his protection were released, anticipated disgrace and ruin by the suicidal process above mentioned, and, as we have heard, others of his house swelled the sacrifice. We cannot too seriously inculcate upon our countrymen the folly and injustice of which they are too often guilty, in endeavouring to subject the nations they happen to visit to their own very peculiar habits and practice.   Mr. Meylan concludes that in the case referred to the governor deemed himself too weak to attack the vessel.   It is certain that he was taken by surprise—for access to the harbour for a ship without a pilot is considered next to impossible, and the Dutch ânnual vessel is always towed in by native boats.   We have heard, however, that the English captain, warned of his danger by the Dutch whom he had thus unjustifiably detained, only escaped in time, for that within a few hours fourteen thousand armed men were mustered on the coast, and that more than a hundred junks had been collected for the purpose of being sunk in the only channel by which the frigate could regain the open sea." *

Whatever the people or the Government may be, both are certainly raised far above the contempt with which Europeans usually regard Asiatics.   We cannot find a single writer, whether of a remote or of a recent period, that gives other than a high, manly character to the Japanese.   The reader will remember the testimony delivered by Adams the mariner, and Xavier the sainted missionary.   Father Froes, after a residence of some years, eloquently defended the people against all detractors. "They are," said he, " as gifted a nation as any in Europe."

In another letter the same missionary says, " That which is proper to give great consolation and joy, and Christian hope for the future, is the good natural disposition of these people : the young men we have in our

* _Quarterly Review_, November, 1834. I shall have occasion to revert to this unfortunate affair in the sequel.

seminary at Arima are so well conducted. They are
nearly all of noble birth ; they live like so many devout
recluses ; they are modest, quiet, and studious, friends of
purity, most tractable and obedient, and quick at their
studies. They literally adhere to the rules set down for
them. Their hours are so distributed that they never
lose any valuable time. They learn our languages and
literature, as also music, both vocal and instrumental.
In sooth, they are by nature docile and of a lively
genius."*

Don Rodrigo, the noble viceroy, who suffered shipwreck
on the coast, gives the people a very high character ; but,
like a sober Spaniard, he blames the men for being too
fond of drink.

On the whole, it appears that there is no disputing the
short general estimate presented by a very recent English
writer, who had carefully collected and perused all ac-
cessible authorities.

"To sum up the character of the Japanese : They
carry notions of honour to the verge of fanaticism, and
they are haughty, vindictive, and licentious. On the
other hand, brawlers, braggarts, and backbiters, are held
in the most supreme contempt. The slightest infraction
of truth is punished with severity ; they are open-
hearted, hospitable, and, as friends, faithful to death. It
is represented that there is no peril a Japanese will not
encounter to serve a friend ; that no torture will compel
him to betray a trust ; and that even the stranger who
seeks aid will be protected to the last drop of blood. The
nation, with all their faults and vices, evinced qualities
that won the hearts and commanded the esteem of the
missionaries."†

"The studied politeness which marked their intercourse
with our officers was evidently not assumed for the occasion, for it is so habitual with them, that in their ordinary
relations with each other they preserve the same stately

---

* *Nuovi Avvisi del Giapone.* Venetia. 1586.
† Rundall, *Memorials.*

courtesy ; and it was observed that, no sooner had Yezai-
man and his interpreters entered their boat alongside the
Susquehanna than they commenced saluting each other
as formally as if they had met for the first time, and were
passing through the ceremonials of a personal introduction."*

" Though always preserving a certain gentlemanly
aplomb, and that self-cultivated manner which bespeaks
high breeding, these Japanese dignitaries were disposed
to be quite social, and shared freely and gaily in conversation. Nor did their knowledge and general information
fall short of their elegance of manners and amiability of
disposition. They were not only well-bred, but not ill-
educated, as they were proficients in the Dutch, Chinese,
and Japanese languages, and not unacquainted with the
general principles of science and of the facts of the geography
of the globe. When a terrestrial globe was placed before
them, and their attention was called to the delineation of
the United States, they immediately placed their fingers on
Washington and New York, as if perfectly familiar with
the fact that one was the capital, and the other the commercial metropolis of the country. They also, with equal
promptitude pointed out England, France, Denmark, and
other kingdoms of Europe."

From the pleasures and formalities that mainly occupy
the life of a Japanese, we must now turn to his closing
scene. When the father or mother of a family is attacked
with any serious malady, when all hope of recovery is
at an end, and the fatal hour seems to be approaching,
they change his or her garments, and put on clean ones.
Men are tended by men, women by women. They then
ask the last wishes of the dying sinner ; they write them
down : all is done in profound silence. When life de-
parts, his relatives bewail him with mournful demeanour.
They carry his body to another place, and cover it with
his robe—but they take care to place the skirt over his
head, and the sleeves over his feet. His head is turned

* *United States Expedition.*

towards the north ; his face, covered with a piece of gauze, towards the east. They use light gauze, in order not to hinder him from coming to life, should he be only in a swoon or trance. Round the body they place screens, to keep away the cats. They say, if a cat leaps upon the body, the dead will come to life ; that if you strike then the cat with a broomstick, the body dies again ; but if you strike the cat with anything else, the body will continue to live again—hence a severe law never to drive away cats with a broomstick. I suppose they think that by screening the body from the cats all accidents will be prevented.

The son and heir (*Sozu*) of the defunct must, together with his wife, his children, brothers and sisters, show by their white garments and demeanour their deep affliction. Sometimes they tie up their hair with a hempen cord. They must neither wash nor eat for three days. If they cannot fast so long, their friends or acquaintances must come to their aid by presenting them with *kan-si* or moist rice. Confucius says, in the *Li-ki*, that it is not allowed to make a fire in the house during the three days after a death.*

Sometimes death precedes interment during a long interval.

"Many Japanese of the higher order die *nayboen*, that is, 'in secret,' either in the course of nature or by their own hands. If a man holding office dies, his death is concealed—it is *nayboen*—and family life proceeds apparently as usual, till the reversion of his place has been obtained for his son. If such a person be deeply in debt, the same course is adopted for the benefit of his creditors, who receive his salary whilst he, though well known to be dead, is nominally alive. Again, if he has incurred any disfavour, or committed any offence, the conviction of which would be attended with disgraceful punishment, confiscation, and corruption of blood, he probably rips himself up, either in his family circle, if any good to his

* Titsingh.

family be contingent upon his death's remaining for a time *nayboen;* or publicly, in a solemn assembly of his friends, if the object be solely the satisfaction of justice, and the obviating of punishment. The *hara-kiri* operation is, upon some occasions, performed in a temple after a splendid entertainment, given to and shared with relations, friends, and the priests of the temple.

" When the necessity for the *nayboen* ceases, or when a Japanese openly dies, either naturally or by the national *hara-kiri,* the first symptom of mourning that appears[*] is the turning all the screens and sliding doors throughout the house topsy-turvy, and all garments inside out. A priest then takes his place by the corpse. The family is supposed to be too much absorbed in sorrow to admit of their attending to the minor cares and preparations requisite upon the melancholy occasion; wherefore, they are permitted to weep in unmolested solitude, whilst their most intimate friends supply their places in all matters of business or ceremony. One of these kind substitutes directs the laying out of the corpse, whilst another orders the funeral. One stations himself at the house-door, in his dress of ceremony, to receive the formal visits of condolence paid by all the friends and acquaintance of the deceased, but paid outside the door, to avoid the impurity incurred by entering the house of death. The digging of the grave is superintended by a fourth friend. This is situated in the grounds of a temple, is shaped like a well, and lined with strong cement, to prevent the infiltration of water. If the deceased be married, the grave is usually made sufficiently capacious to receive husband and wife. A monument is prepared, bearing the name of the deceased, and, if married, the name of the survivor is added in red letters, to be blackened, or sometimes gilt, when this surviving partner shall rejoin in the grave the partner who has gone before.

" When all preparations are completed, the corpse, washed, and clad in a white shroud, on which the priest

---

[*] Meylan.

has inscribed some sacred characters, as a sort of passport to heaven, is placed in the sitting posture of the country, in a tub-shaped coffin, which is enclosed in an earthenware vessel of corresponding figure; and the funeral-procession begins. This is opened by a number of torch-bearers, who are followed by a large company of priests, bearing their sacred books, incense, &c. Then comes a crowd of servants carrying bamboo poles, to which are attached lanterns, umbrellas, and strips of white paper inscribed with sacred sentences. These immediately precede the corpse in its round coffin, borne upon a bier, and covered with a sort of white paper chest, having a dome-fashioned roof, over which a garland is suspended from a bamboo carried by a servant. Immediately behind the body walk the friends and acquaintance of the deceased, in their dress of ceremony, accompanying, attending, and surrounding the masculine portion of the family and kindred, who are attired in mourning garments of pure white. White mourning is also worn by the bearers and household servants of the deceased. The procession is closed by the ladies of the family and their female friends, each in her own palanquin attended by her female servants. The palanquins (norimons) of relations are distinguished from those of friends by the white mourning dresses of the attendants. In families of lower rank, the female relations and their friends walk after the men.

"The sorrowful train is met at the temple by another detachment of priests, who perform a funeral service, and the corpse is interred to a peculiar sort of funeral music, produced by striking copper basins. During this ceremony, two persons, deputed from the house of death, sit in a side chamber of the temple, with writing materials, to note down the names of every friend and acquaintance who has attended.

"In former times, obsequies were, in many various ways, far more onerous; for it seems that, even in secluded and immutable Japan, lapse of years has wrought its ordinary softening effect, and lessened the propensity to make great sacrifices either of life or property. In the early times alluded to,* the dead man's house was burnt, except so much of it as was used in constructing his monument. Now it is merely purified by kindling before it a great fire, in which odoriferous oils and spices are burnt. At that period servants were buried with their masters, originally, alive; then, as gentler manners arose, they were permitted to kill themselves first; and that they should be thus buried was, in both cases, expressly stipulated when they were hired. Now, effigies are happily substituted for the living men.

"The mourning is said by some of our writers to last forty-nine days; but this must mean the general mourning of the whole family, inasmuch as Dr. Von Siebold expressly states that very near relations remain impure— which, in Japan, is the same thing—as much as thirteen months. It appears, also, that there are two periods of mourning in Japan as with us, a deeper and a subsequent lighter mourning, which may help to explain the discrepancy. During the specified forty-nine days, all the kindred of the deceased repair daily to the tomb, there to pray and offer cakes of a peculiar kind, as many in number as days have elapsed since the funeral; thus presenting forty-nine on the forty-ninth day. On the fiftieth day, the men shave their heads and beards, which had remained unshorn and untrimmed during the seven weeks. All signs of mourning are laid aside, and men and women resume the ordinary business of life, their first duty being to pay visits of thanks to all who attended the funeral. It should be added, however, that for half a century the children and grandchildren of the deceased continue to make offerings at the tomb."†

* Siebold.

† *Manners and Customs of the Japanese.* In Titsingh's *Cérémonies usitées au Japon*, there are well-executed engravings of all the marriage and funeral ceremonies,—the former being copied from a Japanese manual.

ENGRAVING BLOCKS FOR PRINTING.

CHAPTER VII.

LANGUAGE, LITERATURE, SCIENCE, MUSIC, PAINTING, SCULPTURE,
MANUFACTURES.

As the language of a nation is necessarily part and
parcel of its manners and customs, the reader will not
be surprised to find that the Japanese is as curious and
characteristic as anything belonging to this original

"type of mankind." One of the old Jesuits, Father Oyanguren, compiled a grammar of it, but utterly declined to explain its mode of writing, which, he said, had been invented by the devil to perplex poor missionaries, and impede the progress of the Gospel.

As yet very few Europeans have acquired anything like a perfect familiarity with Japanese, although it seems to be less difficult, and certainly more interesting, than many other Oriental languages. As friendly relations have been established with the government, and greater freedom of intercourse permitted, doubtless we shall soon have accomplished Japanese scholars amongst American citizens and British subjects. The study recommends itself by the fact that the native interpreters are not to be trusted in diplomacy; and without a knowledge of their language it will be found very difficult to make any progress with the people; although it is more than probable that they will "pick up" our language without delay, as they seem to be very ready linguists. One of Xavier's first Japanese Christians learnt to read, write, and speak Portuguese within eight months.*

The difficulties which beset us in considering the mental and bodily characteristics of the various races of men are vastly increased when we turn to their languages. The miraculous confusion of tongues at the Tower of Babel is satisfactory on religious grounds; and to support this explanation by the aid of science, we must infer that the same miracle completely altered the minds, the way of thinking, the manner of feeling of the men who then forgot their primitive language; since, if there be an incontestible fact in the experience of precise scientific research, it is that all languages, whether

* At the College of Goa, A.D. 1548. This is the same Paulus Samfidius before mentioned—one of three Japanese youths who seem to have found their way to Malacca, and become converts to the preaching of the Fathers. Paul must indeed have made great progress to have written the admirable letter to the Fathers at home, which stands second in the collection now before me. The document is invaluable as the account of the manners, customs, &c. of his countrymen by a Japanese.—*Epist. Japon.* Louanii. 1570.

original, derived, or corruptions, completely reflect the
mental organization, the habits of life, the manner of
feeling and way of thinking, of the people who speak
them.* All languages " hold as it were the mirror up to
the nature" of the men who use them ; the investigation
is as easy as it is interesting ; and I propose, in a page
or two, to glance at the topic in the case of the language
of Japan.

If there be amongst the numerous national characteristics of our own language, the English, one which stands
out most demonstratively, it is the well-poised, firmly-
gravitating, unmistakeable Anglo-Saxon pronoun " I."
What is the German *ich*, the Dutch *ik*, the French *je*,
the Spanish *yo*, to the race-dominant Anglo-Saxon "I"?
The gifted Hungarian, Kossuth, admirably said, lately :—
"With the English, the man, the individual, is everything. Society is to him but the frame in which he
expands his individual energies ; but it is not on society
he relies ; he relies on himself. We read of St. Olof,
that on asking one of his warriors, ' In whom dost thou
believe ?' the warrior answered, ' I believe in myself.'
That man must have been the progenitor of the Anglo-
Norman race."† We did not get this magnificent "I" from
the Britons, the Saxons, the Danes, the Normans, the
French, or any other race, with whom we are interminably in blood amalgamated—for we are, beyond a doubt, the
most mixed people on the face of the earth. Whence did

---

* It should be considered, however, that in chapter x. of Genesis,
it is distinctly stated that the isles of the Gentiles were " divided in
their lands,—every one *after his tongue*, after their families and
nations ;" and in the last verse we read :—" and by these were the
nations divided in the earth *after the flood*. The following chapter
immediately gives the incident of the Tower of Babel—"and from
thence did the Lord scatter them abroad upon the face of the earth."
—Gen. xi. 9. It seems to me that the whole difficulty or apparent
contradiction rests on the interpretation of the words "Lord" and
" the face of *all the earth*,"—a subject which it would be out of place
here to discuss.

† The whole lecture is well worth perusal.—*Times*, November
22nd. But read also the well-put, matter-of-fact remarks in the
Times' leader, in reply, November 23rd, 1858.

it come, this "I?" Heaven only knows. Here it is however, and hitherto it has stood up amongst the nations,
meaning "my house is my castle;" "the Bill of Rights;"
"free discussion;" "liberty of the press;" "every man
equal in the eye of the law;" and, lastly, "sympathy for
the down-trodden nationalities," for which it has sacrificed millions, and will be ground down by taxation for
ever. That's our "I." Now what's the Japanese? Why,
they haven't got one at all, properly speaking, since they
have no less than eighteen, all which have evidently
some distinct etymological meaning, and apparently were
originally pronouns of the third person subsequently applied to the first. In Japan all classes have an *I* peculiar
to themselves, which no other class may use; and
there is one exclusively appropriated by the Mikado or
"spiritual emperor," as we call him, and one confined to
women! When you speak in Japan you must of course
speak with deference, scrupulous politeness, and outward
humility at least, and your "I" becomes mystified into one
of the following Japanese representatives : *ware, warera,
watakousi, soregasi;* the two last never to be used in
writing.

If you are speaking to a superior,—and everybody has
a superior in Japan, beneath the emperor,—you may use
mi, miga, midomo, midomo-*raga, kotsi, kotsiga.* Observe,
that the *i*'s in these words are pronounced as soft as
double *e* in *feet.*

The Bonza or monk says *gousò.* Old men dwindle into
gourò. Women need not show their blackened teeth in
warbling such *I*'s as *midzoukara, varawa, wagami;* and
the common people must confine themselves, amongst
each other, to *wara* and wo-*rara.* Finally, *Tsinga* is the
Yo el Rey or *We* of Japan's mouth royal.

If it be probable that in many, if not all languages,
the pronouns of the first and second person were pronouns of the third, or rather nouns or adjectives designating in some way the person speaking, it would be highly
interesting to know the specific meaning of all these Japanese representatives of *I.* Humboldt suggests that

gousò of the Bonza or monk, which, we are told, is equivalent to *ego indignus,*—"I, the unworthy,"—may be the same word as *gou,* signifying "ignorant :" certain it is, that in the Malaya language all the pronouns of the first person—excepting one whose meaning seems to be lost—are nouns designating various degrees of humility.

Now, do we not detect in this wonderful distribution of personalities—or rather complete abnegation of personalities—the very mirror of the man of Japan so utterly cribbed, cabined, and confined in the meshes of a governmental system—such as it is described—which refuses him the right of free action, confines him to his street under lock and key, fashions his house and its mats, makes a spy of him, and sets a spy upon him—and yet, withal, unable to crush within him that high sense of honour and dignity which strengthens his arm—in the hour of disgrace, or when he cannot take revenge on some sneaking coward—to rip up his own abdomen ?

The same curious distribution is made with regard to the second and third persons. There are eight pronouns of the second person peculiar to servants, pupils, and children, to some of which the terminations *me* and *ga* are sometimes added to express contempt or the deepest humility, and nothing, in point of fact, can surpass the self-debasement of a Japanese in the presence of his superior.*

* Slavery in the Empire of Japan is different from that prevailing in the western hemisphere. The person of a party, male or female, may be sold under certain circumstances, or a party may sell his or her service for a stipulated period for a sum of money which may be agreed on, and which must be paid down at once in the gross. On the expiration of the stipulated period, the party is free to dispose of his or her person again. Masters have power over the lives of their slaves, if they commit offences which by the law are punishable with death ; but if a man should kill his slave for any cause that the law does not deem worthy of death, the offender is adjudged guilty of murder, and subjected to the penalty of the crime. Formerly servants agreed to die at his death—nay, it is said, would kill themselves in the usual way for the entertainment of himself and friends ! "The Japanese are never forgetful of the respect they think due to rank, and graduate their obeisance according to its degrees. From

I observe, however, that this termination *ga*, expressive
of the deepest humility, is in the personal pronoun of the
" spiritual emperor"—namely, *Tsinga :* it reminds us of
the Pope's *servus servorum Dei,* " the servant of the servants of God."*

But there is a very singular fact in relation to the pronoun : the same word may be *I* or *thou,* or *he,* according
to circumstances—which seems to prove that it is really
a significant *noun*—in fact, the so-called first personal
pronoun is not personal at all, as it may belong to *any*
person. One grammarian tells us that *Watakusi* is " I ;"
another, that it is "thou :" *waga* is " thou" according to
one, and " I" according to another : we are told by one
that *konata* is " thou" and " he ;" another says it is " I "
and " thou ;" and a third insists that it is *I, thou,* and

the Emperor to the lowest subject in the realm there is a constant
succession of prostrations. The former, in want of a human being
superior to himself in rank, bows humbly to some Pagan idol ; and
every one of his subjects, from prince to peasant, has some person
before whom he is bound to cringe and crouch in the dirt. One is
reminded, as he looks upon an universal nation on their knees, ' in
suppliance bent,' of the favourite amusement of childhood, where a
number of blocks are placed on end in a row, one shoves the other,
and the first being knocked down, topples over the second, and so on
in succession, until all are tumbled upon the ground. The crouching
position in which an inferior places himself, when in the presence of
his superior in rank, seems very easy to a Japanese, but would be
very difficult and painful for one not accustomed to it. The ordinary
mode pursued is to drop on the knees, cross the feet, and turn up the
heels, with the toes, instep, and calves of the legs brought together
into close contact. . . . They all showed a wonderful elasticity
of muscle and suppleness of joint, which could only have been
acquired by long practice, and reminded one of those skilful contor-
tionists or clowns, who exhibit their caoutchouc accomplishments to
the wonderment of the spectators. These worthies, humble as they
were in the august presence of the commissioners, had their worshippers in turn, who were more humble still, and who outdid them,
even in their bowings and prostrations. Every Japanese is thus by
turns master and slave, now submissively with his neck beneath the
foot of one, and again haughtily with his foot upon the neck of
another."—*United States Expedition,* 348.

* These observations are founded on the *Elémens de la Grammaire
Japonaise,* by Rodriguez, and Humboldt's *Notice sur la Gramm.
Japon. du P. Oyanguren.*

he ! This confusion, again, seems to prove that these words are merely nouns applied with a meaning : each grammarian wrote according to his experience.

Of course we say " you" in speaking to a single person ; the Italians say *ella* for " you" and " she ;" the Germans use *sie* for " they" and " you," and *er* for " he" and " you ;" and royalty, the journalists, and critics lord it over us with " we ;" but all these are merely conventional absurdities : they are not the analogues of the Japanese pronominal system, which, I suspect, holds in reserve for the future philologist a rich mine of curious investigation.

Space will not permit me further to pursue this reading of the Japanese nation in its language on the present occasion : I may be permitted to do so elsewhere, for this people, together with others, should health and strength permit.* I proceed to give some account of the language.

" The Japanese language has been usually said to be unlike all the languages of the globe, and, in one point of view, the statement is true ; but it is in its structure analogous to the languages of the Tartar or Scythic class ; and although in the lexicographic portion the language differs from all others of that class, so far as we know, this can hardly be a foundation for making a general distinction, because they differ very considerably from each other in this respect. It would seem as though languages less fully organized than those of the Indo-Germanic class, those which are merely pegged together, and not dovetailed like the work of a cabinet-maker—to use Dr. Johnson's metaphor—more readily change the form and meaning of their words ; and that while Sanskrit and English, for instance, after a separation of half the age of the world, still retain very many roots perfectly alike, two tongues like the Mordwin and Cheremiss, spoken by neighbouring tribes on the Volga, who were probably one not many centuries ago, have now distinct

* In *Man all the World over: the Comparative Manners and Customs of all Nations,* &c., on which I have been for some time diligently engaged.

words in most cases for their most ordinary ideas. This may be theorizing too far, perhaps ; much of the variation may have arisen from the fact that those languages have never been cultivated, and that the people who speak them are nomad.

" The features of the Japanese language which coincide with those of the Tartar tongues are these :—The substantives have no gender ; they form all their cases and other modifications by subsequent particles ; and these particles are too numerous to come under our strict ideas of grammatical declension. As an instance, we take the word *fito*, man : *fito-bito, fito-dono, fito-tato*, and some other expressions, signify men ; *fito-no,* or *fito-ga,* of a man ; *fito-ni,* or *fito-ye,* to a man ; there is also *fito-wa, fito-wo, fito-yori,* &c. ; and these are not indiscriminately used, but they answer to what the Finnish grammarians call the predicative, factive, adhesive, allative, and other cases, in addition to our well-known datives and accusatives."

They have no possessive pronouns : " mine" is literally " of me"—as *wate-ga,* " mine," *sanata-no,* " your."

The verbs have their tenses produced by additions to, and not changes of, the root ; the word *yo,* to read, may be an example. We have *yomi,* I read ; *yoda,* I did read ; *yoma, yomozu,* or *yomozuru,* I shall read ; *yomokasi,* might I read ; *yomeba,* when I read ; *yomaba,* if I read, &c. &c., to a considerable extent : there is also, as in Turkish, a negative incorporated with the verb, as *yomami,* I do not read ; *yomananda,* I did not read, &c., and through all the same variations as the affirmative verb. And not only so, but the word *yomi* means also *thou, he, she, we, you, they read.*

There are two sorts of adjectives, one of which is very peculiar ; it is, in point of fact, a conjugated verb : thus, the *high mountain* is *takai yama,* literally, " the mountain which is elevated ; *atorasy iye, new house,* that is, " house which is new ;" *yoy fito, good man,* that is, " man who is good." The other sort is formed from a verb—as from *foukai* " to be deep," we have *foukade* "deep wound ;" from *takai* " to be high," *takayama* " high mountain ;"

and from *akai* " to be red," they say *akago*, " red child," that is, a newly-born infant.

They have no relative corresponding to *who, which,* &c.; they supply its place by placing the antecedent immediately after the verb to which the relative refers :—*the man who sees*, is, literally, " he sees man," namely, *manita fito.* Can conventionality go much further ?

Perhaps these few instances will suffice to give some idea of the singular language spoken by this singular race ; but not content with their own they adopted the Chinese, and say they have two languages, the *Yomi* and the *Koye ;* but the fact is, that *Koye* is pure Chinese with a different pronunciation, though still monosyllabic. As the Japanese write the Chinese sounds with alphabetic symbols, these Japanese pronunciations may represent the sounds of the Chinese characters as they were fifteen or twenty centuries ago ; for an alphabet, however imperfect, must contribute to retain more of the sounds than any ideographic character ; and a study of these sounds might be useful in comparisons of tongues, and help to form a judgment upon the ethnographical position of the Chinese nation.

" Practically, the Japanese mix the Koye or Chinese with their own language to the best of their ability ; the most learned inflicting such a mass of Chinese upon their readers or hearers as to be unintelligible to all but those as learned as themselves.

" They speak of two kinds of style—the *mai-den,* or the most learned or religious style, and the *gheden,* the secular ; each of these has its subdivisions, but scarcely any is free from admixture with Chinese words. Japanese poetry is composed most commonly in Yomi only, in feet of five or seven syllables : it is now and then mingled with prose, as is done by Persians and Turks ; and even the prose has often a cadence of rhythm in imitation of poetry. The recitation is said to be very harmonious."

The language is usually written with a syllabarium of forty-seven characters, each character representing a syllable," as in Chinese ; in other words, each character is as significant as the figures 1, 2, 3, &c., to all European nations. They write, like the Chinese, in columns, proceeding from the right to the left, and descending from the top to the bottom of the page. St. Francis Xavier asked his interesting and intelligent convert before mentioned why the Japanese did not write according to our horizontal method ? The convert—Paul by name—answered after the manner of the Irish, by asking why the Europeans did not write after the manner of the Japanese ; which reminds me of the venerable Scotch lady who, dining with the *suite* of Charles X. at Holyrood House, asked one of the Frenchmen the French for *bread.* "*Du pain,*" said he. " Ah !" she exclaimed, striving in vain to imitate the Frenchman's intonation, " wha dinna ye ca' it *breed ?* " However, the intelligent convert Paul advanced, at last, a beautifully philosophical reason for this vertical mode of writing :—" As Nature," said he, " placed man's head above, and his feet below, in an humble position, why should we not, in writing, imitate the order of Nature ?" * It is a curious fact that their syllabarium is named after the three first syllables, *I-ro-fa,* just as our alphabet is so called from the two first letters.

" There are two systems in use, one very easy, and the other extraordinarily difficult ; and of course the latter is selected for general use, the easy one being employed only for notes, glosses, and interlineary versions. The latter, which is called *katagana,* is very simple, each sound having one invariable representative. The other style, called *hiragana,* employs at least six characters, radically different from each other, for each sound ; varying each of these characters at the pleasure of the writer, and, notwithstanding this barren redundancy, employing, in addition, any Chinese character which the writer may choose to adopt, twisted into any cursive form he pleases,

* *Epist. Japon.*

X

instead of using one of the characters more generally known.*

" The probability is, that it is this habit of adapting new Chinese characters which has caused the *hiragana* syllabarium to grow to its present incredible extent, and bids fair to render it at last utterly illegible. The extent of this system may be judged from the fact, that the Vienna printing-office, in order to produce a copy of a Japanese novel with moveable types, was obliged to cast a fount of four hundred and eighty-one Japanese types for the ordinary syllabarium, and two hundred and twenty-seven more for the additional Chinese types which the writer chose to adopt; and the learned scholar Pfitzmayer, who has, with much learning and incredible pains, edited the above novel with a translation, complains that the types are not nearly numerous enough to represent the variety of forms used. All this is for an ordinary tale, intended to be intelligible to the many.

" The translation of the Gospel of St. John, which was, I believe, made by Gutzlaff, with the aid of a native, is printed very judiciously in the easy, or katagana character.

" It must be admitted that a good proportion of this large number of types cast by the Vienna type-founders was unnecessary, many of them being required merely to imitate the irregular writing of the Japanese scribe."†

* " In the early part of the eighth century, the syllabic systems, denominated *katagana* and *hiragana*, were invented and found completely adapted to the idiom of the country. The use of this species of writing is now almost universal in Japan ; it is rare to find a person unable to read it."—*Chinese Repository*, vol. iii. p. 206. Canton. 1835. The authority quoted is that of the learned Orientalist, Klaproth.

† The preceding account of the Japanese is taken from Mac-Farlane, who states that it was written by a learned and most ingenious philologist. I have added to it, as the reader will have perceived ; and must now, in deference to Mr. MacFarlane, add in a note a compliment he pays to the imperial house of Austria ; which, however, will not permit any books to be printed without being examined by two or three censors :—" The liberal and extraordinary efforts made by the imperial government of Austria (with-

Paper came into use in Japan as early as the beginning of the seventh century; and printing, from engraved wooden blocks, in the Chinese manner, was introduced A.D., 1206, about two hundred and fifty years before that invaluable árt was invented in Europe.

From the moment the Japanese acquired a written language, their literature advanced rapidly, and it appears to have improved from age to age. Unfortunately, in Europe it is scarcely known; but from the few Japanese

out any immediate view to self-interest) to promote Oriental learning, and facilitate the means of studying the languages of the East, entitle that government to the gratitude of the whole civilized world, and are deserving of far more praise than they seem hitherto to have obtained. Certain deep-rooted, ill-considered prejudices, arising chiefly out of political feelings, cool or entirely suppress European gratitude. It has been a fashion to consider the ancient house of Austria as an enemy rather than friend to letters, science, and art. Yet that house is now, and has long been, spending annually vast sums of money upon these objects, while, from our own constitutional and *liberal* government it is always a most difficult task to procure a grant of a few hundred pounds for any such purpose. It will be found out some day,—perhaps when too late,—that all things cannot be conducted by private enterprise, and upon purely commercial principles, and that the application of those principles is, in certain cases, detrimental to the national spirit, to real intellectual progress, and to the honour and even safety of the country.

"Where is the enterprise among booksellers, where the commercial principle, by which so elaborate and costly a work as the immense Japanese dictionary of Professor Pfitzmayer, now in course of printing at Vienna, could have been produced? It is calculated that, if this dictionary be continued and concluded on its present ample scale, it will run to twenty volumes. We may safely venture to say that by such means the book could not have been brought out in any country in Europe. Yet no one will deny the value and importance of the work, or question the now increasing necessity of our possessing such a lexicon. Private speculation has its limits, and it is when it reaches them, and halts upon them, that the State ought to step in. Societies or learned associations may do a good deal, and some of them have done much, but it should seem that their resources are far too narrow, and the number of their subscribers too uncertain, to permit of their prosecuting any very extensive enterprises and labours. Where is now the Oriental Translation Fund attached to the Royal Asiatic Society of Great Britian? To retain its valuable vitality, it ought to have been nourished by an annual government grant."

x 2

books that have fallen into the hands of learned foreigners, and from the accounts left us by the missionaries and other travellers, it is evident that these people possess works of all kinds,—historical compositions, geographical and other scientific treatises, books on natural history, voyages, and travels, moral philosophy, cyclopædias, dramas, romances, poems, and every component part of a very polite literature.

The wide diffusion of education, which has been more than once mentioned, is of no recent date. The first of all the missionaries who visited the country found schools established wherever they went. St. Francis Xavier mentions the existence of four "Academies" in the vicinity of Meako, at each of which education was afforded to between three and four thousand pupils; adding, that considerable as these numbers were, they were quite insignificant in comparison with the numbers instructed at an institution near the city of Bandone; and that such institutions were universal throughout the empire.*

Nor does it appear that these institutions have decreased in modern days. Speaking of the early part of the present century, M. Meylan states that children of both sexes and of all ranks are invariably sent to rudimentary schools, where they learn to read and write, and are initiated into some knowledge of the history of their own country. To this extent, at least, it is considered necessary that the meanest peasant should be educated. Our officers who visited the country as late as the year 1845, ascertained that there existed at Nagasaki a college, in which, additionally to the routine of native acquirements, foreign languages were taught. Among the visitors on board our ship, many spoke Dutch. Some understood a little French. One young student understood English slightly, could pronounce a few English words, caught readily at every English expression that struck him, and wrote it down in his note-book. They all seemed to be tolerably well acquainted with geography, and some of

* Charlevoix.

them appeared to have some acquaintance with guns, and the science of gunnery. The eagerness of all of them to acquire information greatly delighted our officers.*

" The Japanese are extremely fond of reading ; even the common soldiers when on duty are continually engaged with books. This passion for literature, however, proved somewhat inconvenient to us, as they always read aloud, in a tone of voice resembling singing—much in the same style in which the psalms are read at funerals in Russia. Before we became accustomed to this, we were unable to enjoy a moment's rest during the night. The history of their native country, the contests which have arisen among themselves, and the wars in which they have been engaged with neighbouring nations, form the subjects of their favourite books, which are all printed in Japan. They do not use metal types, but print with plates cut out of pieces of hard wood." †

In the *United States Expedition*, or its abridgment, by Mr. Tomes,‡ will be found a very interesting narrative of an attempt to escape, by two Japanese students of the higher ranks, in order to visit " the five great continents" in pursuit of knowledge. They contrived to get on board the American ship—were of course refused admission without the consent of their government—and, on returning to the shore, they were caught and " caged ;" but, it seems, finally pardoned, as was intimated to the commodore. They wrote a preliminary letter to the Americans, which is very interesting and significant.

" The two scholars from Jeddo, in Japan, present this letter for the inspection of ' the high officers and those who manage affairs.' Our attainments are few and trifling, as we ourselves are small and unimportant, so that we are abashed in coming before you. We are neither skilled in the use of arms, nor are we able to discourse upon the rules of strategy and military discipline ; in trifling pursuits and idle pastimes our years and months have slipped

* *Voyage of H.M.S. Samarang*, ii.
† Golownin, *Memoirs of Captivity*, &c.
‡ Page 292, *et seq.*

away. We have, however, read in books, and learned a little by hearsay, what are the customs and education in Europe and America, and we have been for many years desirous of going over the ' five great continents,' but the laws of our country in all maritime points are very strict ; for foreigners to come into the country, and for natives to go abroad, are both immutably forbidden. Our wish to visit other regions has consequently only ' gone to and fro in our own breasts in continual agitation,' like one's breathing being impeded, or his walking cramped. Happily, the arrival of so many of your ships in these waters, and stay for so many days, which has given us opportunity to make a pleasing acquaintance and careful examination, so that we are fully assured of the kindness and liberality of your excellencies, and your regard for others, has also revived the thoughts of many years, and they are urgent for an exit.

"This, then, is the time to carry the plan into execution, and we now secretly send you this private request, that you will take us on board your ships as they go out to sea ; we can thus visit around the five great continents, even if we do, in this, slight the prohibitions of our own country. Lest those who have the management of affairs may feel some chagrin at this, in order to effect our desire, we are willing to serve in any way we can on board of the ships, and obey the orders given us. For doubtless it is, that when a lame man sees others walking, he wishes to walk too ; but how shall the pedestrian gratify his desires when he sees another *riding ?* We have all our lives been going hence to you, unable to get more than thirty degrees east and west, or twenty degrees north and south [the geographical extent of the empire] ; but now, when we see how you sail on the tempests and cleave the huge billows, going lightning-speed thousands and myriads of miles, skirting along the five great continents, can it not be likened to the lame finding a plan of walking, and the pedestrian seeing a mode by which he can ride ? If you who manage affairs will give our request your consideration, we will retain the sense of the favour ;

but the prohibitions of our country are still existent, and if this matter should become known, we should uselessly see ourselves pursued and brought back for immediate execution without fail, and such a result would greatly grieve the deep humanity and kindness you all bear towards others. If you are willing to accede to this request, keep ' wrapped in silence our error in making it' until you are about to leave, in order to avoid all risk of such serious danger to life ; for when, by-and-bye, we come back, our countrymen will never think it worth while to investigate bygone doings. Although our words have only loosely let our thoughts leak out, yet truly they are sincere ; and if your excellencies are pleased to regard them kindly, do not doubt them nor oppose our wishes. We together pay our respects in handing this in.— April 11."

In this disposition of the people of Japan, what a field of speculation, and, it may be added, what a prospect full of hope open for the future of that interesting country—if we do not abuse the providence !

The poor fellows seemed to bear their misfortune with great equanimity, and were greatly pleased, apparently, with the visit of the American officers. On one of the visitors approaching the cage in which they were con- fined, the Japanese wrote on a piece of board that was handed to them the following sentiments, which, as a remarkable specimen of philosophical resignation under circumstances that would have tried the stoicism of Cato, deserves a record :—

" When a hero fails in his purpose, his acts are then regarded as those of a villain and a robber. In public have we been seized and pinioned and caged for many days. The village elders and head men treat us disdain- fully, their oppressions being grievous indeed. Therefore, looking up while yet we have nothing wherewith to re- proach ourselves, it must now be seen whether a hero will prove himself to be one indeed. Regarding the liberty of going through the sixty states as not enough for our desires, we wished to make the circuit of the five great continents. This was our hearts' wish a long time. Suddenly our plans are defeated, and we find ourselves in a half-sized house, where eating, resting, sitting, and sleeping are difficult; how can we find our exit from this place? Weeping, we seem as fools; laughing, as rogues. Alas! for us; silent we can only be. (Signed) ISAGI KOODA, KWANSUCHI MANJI."

As a specimen of composition these documents—we are assured, literally translated—speak well for the intellect of " Young Japan," and prove that the educator there does his duty to a genial nature.

The Japanese printers keep the market well supplied with cheap, easy books, intended for the instruction of children, or people of the poorer classes. The editions or impressions of books of a higher order appear to be uncommonly numerous. Most of these books are illustrated and explained with frequent woodcuts, which are engraved on the same wood-blocks with the type. Like the Chinese, they only print on one side of their thin paper. An imperial cyclopædia, printed at Meako, in the Mikado's palace, is most copiously embellished with cuts.

According to Balbi, the libraries at Jeddo and Meako contain 150,000 volumes.

All are agreed that reading is a favourite resource and recreation with both sexes, and that the Daïri, or court of the Mikado, is eminently a learned, literary court.

It is said that few sights are more common in Japan, during the sunny seasons of the year, than that of a group of ladies and gentlemen seated by a cool running stream, or in a shady grove, each with a book in hand. Whatever their literature may be, it is evident that it delights them, and that it has polished their manners.

It is scarcely fair to judge of the literature of any country by mere translations. The difficulty of so judging is vastly increased when the language of the original writer and that of the translator differ so entirely as does the Japanese from Dutch, German, French, English, or any European dialect. Then again, we possess as yet but very few and fragmentary translations from the Japanese of any kind. In this our uninformed condition, it appears to have been rather premature in any English writer to sit in judgment on the literature of these people. The few specimens of their histories or annals have been called jejune, trivial, and monotonous; the specimens of their geographical works dry and dull. But in the multiplicity of native authors and books, the best may not have been chosen, or the very few Europeans who have tried their hands at the task may not have been the best of translators.

It is said that every Japanese is fond of quoting poetry, and enlivening his conversation with verse. So far he seems to be a perfect Doctor Pangloss. But of the metre, or rhyme, or construction of Japanese poetry we can scarcely be said to know anything. It appears pretty evident that their poets delight in point, anti-thesis, epigrammatic turns, and what we call *concetti*, or conceits.

They have many historical ballads, which are said to be not very unlike our *Chevy Chase*. In the preface of a work entitled the *Tale of the Six Folding Screens*, occurs the following quaint and characteristic passage :—

" The reader will find in this book nothing about fight-ing with enemies, or about conjurors or magical works, or fairy discourses, or jackals, or wolves, or toads : nothing about pedigrees, or jewels, or any other lost property. Here are no stories of confusion between the names of father and son, or elder and younger brother; no sealed-up boxes, or hair-pins, or mysterious revelations of the gods and Buddhas, by means of dreams; no mortal swords pointed against each other; nothing which makes the blood run cold can at all be found in it. Convinced of the incorrectness of the adage, that ' Men and folding screens cannot stand unless they be bent,' we have here hastily put together, upon this perishable paper, covered with figures, the brief notes of good counsel, as a border or frame, to the tale of six such folding screens under the new forms of this transitory world, who have wholly disdained to bend; and we publish the same to the world."

In their *Mirror of Female Education*, published at Jeddo, in 1534, we have pictures of female occupations and pastimes; pictures of ladies at their toilette, and others showing how they ought to behave themselves in company; in fact, a perfect Japanese "interior."

The Japanese have the counterpart of our very useful lines :—

> Thirty days hath September,
> April, June, and November;

but they do not make up the months of the year as we do. Here is the curiosity :—

> Si yo daï mi o
> Mou sio ni nikou mo ou,
> Nanats ou bo si
> I ma si kou si re ba
> Si mo no si ya wa si.

These lines contain the names of all the Japanese months of thirty days, as well as of those that have but twenty-nine days. Yet the same verses being read in their ballad sense, signify—

"All the grandees of the empire abhorred the bear (the arms of Yamassiro, which are seven stars); let it shine no more; it is a happy event even for the lowest servants."

They appear to have a great many of these aids to memory, some of their verses fixing the dates of historical events, like the late Dr. Valpy's chronology in rhyme, which we learned by heart in our schoolboy-days, and which still clings to our memory in spite of the mediocrity of its verse :—

> Through sixteen centuries the revolving sun,
> And summers fifty-six his course had run,
> When sinful man drew Heaven's just vengeance down,
> In one wide deluge the whole earth to drown, &c.

Some of their poems seem to consist of religious dogmas

or moral apothegms. The following might have been uttered by a pious Christian :—

> Kokoro da ni makoto,
> No mitri ni kana fi nabo
> I ! no ra tsoe to te mo kami,
> Jamo mo ramoe.

> Upright in heart be thou and pure,
> So shall the blessing of God
> Through eternity be upon thee ;
> Clamorous prayers shall not avail,
> But truly a clear conscience,
> That worships and fears in silence.*

---

* It is stated that the Japanese have a complete *corpus poetarum*, or collection of all their poets, with short memoirs to each. I have selected these few " specimens" from MacFarlane, and others will be found in the *Manners and Customs* before quoted; but truly the rest seem to have been injudiciously chosen or badly translated : they do not accord with the idea of Japanese intellect. If compilers must give " a brick of the building," care should be taken to give a " brick," and nothing less. We must wait for better things.

The best short account of the Japanese language, and the different modes in which it is written, is given by Professor H. Brockhaus, in a review of Hoffmann and Von Siebold's *Bibliotheca Japonica* (Gersdorff's Repertorium. Lipz. 1846, p. 372, ff.)

The first part of the great Japanese Dictionary by Dr. Pfitzmayer, lately published at Vienna, has been already noticed. Several papers on Japanese dialects, grammar, and poetry, by the same savant, have appeared in the report of the Transactions of the Imperial Académie des Sciences, Vienna, 1849 and 1850. A grammar was in course of preparation by the celebrated Chinese scholar, Professor Stephan Endlicher, of Vienna, but interrupted by his death.

Two recent works, by an Englishman, are said to be easy and useful. *An English and Japanese, and Japanese and English Vocabulary*, by W. H. Medhurst, Batavia, 1830 ; and *Translation of a Comparative Vocabulary of the Chinese, Corean, and Japanese Languages*, by the same author, Batavia, 1835.

Brief as they are, these last notes may possibly be found of some service to such as think of commencing the study of the Japanese language, a knowledge of which will certainly be in great demand.

Some valuable remarks on the affinities of language and the connexion between the Japanese, Tartars, and other eastern peoples, will be found in two articles, ''The Ethnology of Eastern Asia,'' and ''The Ethnology of South-Eastern Asia,'' in that valuable publication, the *Journal of the Indian Archipelago and Eastern Asia*, vol. iv. Singapore, 1850. Both these papers are written by the editor, J. R. Logan, Esq., member of the Asiatic Society, &c.

Many of their prose tales and romances appear to be exceedingly interesting, and far more imaginative, and at the same time more natural, than the general run of Oriental narrations.* I have given some short specimens, and more will be found in the works of Titsingh. Japanese gentlemen throw off, at their festive meetings, rhymed toasts, like Italian improvisatori.

The dramas, which so attract and fascinate the Japanese, are said to admit, in one and the same piece, a Shaksperian mixture of the tragic and comic, and to bid a bold defiance to what classicists and the French of the old school call the "Unities." They think nothing of passing, in the twinkling of an eye, from one island to another, or from Japan to China or Corea, or from earth to heaven, or to the regions under the earth. These plays are generally founded on national history or tradition, presenting the exploits, loves, and adventures of Japanese heroes and gods. Some of them may be called didactic, as they are designed to illustrate and enforce certain moral precepts. Their general tendency is said to be elevating, patriotic, and excellent; but they sometimes exhibit, in broad and revolting light, the unfavourable features of the national character; such as a demoniacal passion of revenge, and a fondness for witnessing punishments and tortures. M. Fisscher saw, on the stage, at Osacca, the representation of one of their punishments by torture, which he describes as astoundingly cruel.

It appears that more than two actors are seldom, if ever, upon the stage at the same time.† The theatres are very large, and, to fill them with their voices, the actors have a sad habit of roaring and ranting. As in the old times, in England and every other European country, the female parts are filled not by actresses but by smooth-chinned boys. This we believe to arise, in Japan,

---

* The monotony and want of imagination in *real* Eastern tales, almost force us to adopt the theory of the brilliant author of Eöthen —that the *Arabian Nights' Entertainments* had a Greek origin. Perhaps they were inspired by *opium!*

† Thunberg.

from the excessive fatigue attendant on the profession, to which no woman's strength would be equal. The players begin business soon after the hour of noon, and seldom leave off until late at night. The actor is most esteemed who can most frequently change parts in the same piece, in the manner of Charles Mathews, of facetious and yet of mournful memory. The "stars," or very great favourites, are said to be enormously paid. But the profession is held in great contempt, the Japanese maintaining that the man who will give up his own character to assume that of another, for pay and profit, can have no sense of honour. As a natural consequence of their ban and proscription, the Japanese actors are the most immoral, licentious, and depraved people in the empire.

But the most singular point of all that has been told us about the Japanese stage is the order of performance. Three long pieces are frequently represented on the same day ; not, as with us, one after the other, in wholes, but in portions ; namely, first, the first act of one, then the first act of a second, then the first act of a third ; then, returning to the first play, the second act of it, and, successively, the second acts of the second and third plays, and so on till all the three plays are played out. By this curious arrangement, any of the audience who wish only to see one of these pieces, or who have not patience to sit out the whole, may withdraw to attend to business or to other diversion, or to smoke their pipes and drink rice-beer, whilst the dramas they have no wish to see take their turn on the stage ; and they can then return, refreshed, to see and hear the next act of their favourite play. It is said, however, that the Japanese ladies seldom avail themselves of this facility, having no objection to sit out all the three intermingled pieces, and employing some of their time in changing their dresses in the manner already related. Little more is known of their theatres, except that, in general, the actors are magnificently attired, and change their dresses on the stage still more frequently than the ladies change theirs in the boxes.

The perfection of jugglery in Japan entitles it to be ranked amongst the fine arts. An eye-witness thus describes the performance of a Japanese juggler. " Here are some of his feats :—No. 1. He took an ordinary boy's top, spun it in the air, caught it on his hand, and then placed it (still spinning) upon the edge of a sword, near the hilt. Then he dropped the sword point a little, and the top moved slowly towards it. Arrived at the very end, the hilt was lowered in turn, and the top brought back. As usual, the sword was dangerously sharp. No. 2 was also performed with the top. He spun it in the air, and then threw the end of the string back towards it with such accuracy that it was caught up and wound itself all ready for a second cast. By the time it had done this it had reached his hand, and was ready for another spin. No. 3 was still performed with the top. There was an upright pole, upon the top of which was perched a little house, with a very large front door. The top was spun, made to climb the pole, knock open the said front door, and disappear. As well as I remember, the hand end of the string was fastened near the door, so that this was almost a repetition of the self-winding feat. But feat No. 4 was something even more astonishing than all this. He took two paper butterflies, armed himself with the usual paper fan, threw them into the air, and, fanning gently, kept them flying about him as if they had been alive. " He can make them alight wherever you wish ! Try him !" remarked the Kami (Prince), through the interpreter. Mr. H—— requested that one might alight upon each ear of the juggler. No sooner expressed than complied with. Gentle undulations of the fan waved them slowly to the required points, and there left them comfortably seated. Now, whether this command over pieces of paper was obtained simply by currents of air or by the power of a concealed magnet Mr. H—— could not tell or ascertain. One thing however was certain, the power was there."*

* *Philadelphia Ledger.* The suggestion about a " magnet " is simply absurd, and obviously so.

In science the Japanese have particularly cultivated medicine, astronomy, and mathematics.

The Japanese computation of time is, as may be expected, very singular, if not incomprehensible. For chronology they use three different and independent cycles, but all three together. One is called the *nengo*, used for historical dates, borrowed from the Chinese, of an arbitrary length, and consequently always variable; a sort of ending and beginning again, just as the Mikado thinks proper, from some remarkable event or accident which he thinks worthy of commemoration, such as the building of a temple, and, of course, an earthquake. He gives it a name simply indicative of the event, or indulges in metaphor, allegory, or enigma : thus a Mikado, at his abdication, inaugurated a new era with the title of *nengo genrohf*, that is, "the nengo of the bliss of nature and of art ;" intending therefore to insinuate that such would be his own enjoyment in his retirement, like Charles V. at the monastery of St. Just, where he took to watchmaking, and learnt, too late, that he could not make them "go together" any more than he could make men *think* together, "of one mind" in his scheme of government. They also date by the reign of the Mikado, and also by that of the Siogoun, and the latter is the date found in the title-page of Japanese books. They have, thirdly, a computation of six years' duration, somewhat incomprehensibly founded on their Signs of the Zodiac and their Five Elements. They call the Signs *ziguni no shi*, that is, "the twelve branches." They are the Rat, the Cow, the Tiger, the Hare, the Dragon, the Snake, the Monkey, the Cock, the Dog, the Boar ;* in Japanese *Ne, Oushi, Tora, Ou, Tats, Mi, 'Mma, Hitsouri, Sarou, Tori, Inou, I.*

The elements† of the Japanese are more original. They are held to be five in number, excluding air, and

---

* The Tartar names for these twelve signs are :—1. Mouse. 2. Ox. 3. Leopard. 4. Hare. 5. Crocodile. 6. Serpent. 7. Horse. 8. Sheep. 9. Ape. 10. Hen. 11. Dog. 12. Hog.
          † Meylan.

including wood and metal as elementary substances. But these five are whimsically doubled, by taking each in a twofold character, and separately, as one in its natural state, and another as adapted to the use of man, yet in each an element. This is so strange, as to be worth giving at length, and in the proper order.

1. *Kino-ye* is wood in its natural state, as a tree : this is the first element, and becomes,

2. *Kino-to,* when cut down, and converted into timber.

3. *Fino-ye* is the element of fire in its original state, as appearing in the sun's heat, lightning, volcanic eruptions, &c.

4. *Fino-to* is fire kindled by man, with wood, oil, &c.

5. *Tsoetsno-ye* is earth in its uncultivated state, on mountain-tops, at the bottom of the sea, &c.

6. *Tsoetsno-to* is earth as wrought by the hand of man into porcelain, earthenware, and the like. To which of these two elements tilled ground appertains, does not appear.

7. *Kanno-ye* is the metallic element in its native state of mineral ore.

8. *Kanno-to* is the metallic element smelted, &c.

9. *Mietsno-ye* is water as it flows from springs and in rivers ; and

10. *Mietno-to* is the other watery element, as stagnant in pools and morasses : a curious deviation from the principle laid down, that adaptation to human use constitutes every second element.

Now, these ten elements being five times combined with the twelve signs of the Zodiac, in some way more complicated than intelligible, sixty compound figures are said to be obtained, each of which stands for a year in this most scientific cycle.

The year, which begins in February, is divided into twelve lunar months, but contains more than the number of days naturally belonging to such a year, because the *mikado* and his astronomers add a couple of days to several of the months, announcing always in the almanack of the year how many and which of the months they have thus increased. The difference between the lunar year, even thus lengthened, and the sidereal year, is corrected by inserting every third year an intercalary month, of varying length, according to the number of days the *mikado* has been pleased to make requisite.

But perhaps the most whimsical, and certainly the most inconvenient, division of time in Japan, is that by hours. A natural day and night is there divided into twelve hours, of which six are always allotted to the day—that is to say, to the interval between the rising and the setting of the sun ; the other six to the night, or the period between sunset and sunrise. Thus, the hours of the day and of the night are never of equal duration in Japan, except at the equinoxes ; in summer, the hours of the day being long, those of night short, and in winter *vice versâ*. Strictly speaking, the length of the hours should vary from day to day ; but such extreme accuracy is dispensed with, and the variations are regulated only four times in the year, upon averages of three months.

Again, the numbering of these twelve hours, which seems so straightforward a matter for people who can count twelve, is in Japan so strangely complicated, that had not the expedient been adopted of bestowing upon each hour the name of a sign of the Zodiac, in addition to its number, it would have been no easy task to answer the seemingly plain question of " What's o'clock ?"* Unfortunately, their abhorrence of everything that is dead has prevented any proper study of anatomy by dissection. They cannot, therefore, be good surgeons. But as physicians, they very frequently give the best test of ability, for they cure their patients of alarming, and even dangerous diseases. Kämpfer, Thunberg, and nearly all the medical men who have ever travelled in the country, speak favourably both of their skill and of their ardent desire to acquire professional European knowledge.†

* *Manners and Customs of the Japanese*, or *Chinese Repository*, x., where an attempt is made to explain the system. See also Knight's *Companion to the Almanac* for 1830.
† See particularly Dr. Von Siebold's valuable work.

Y

Acupuncture and *moxa*-burning are both Japanese inventions. They were brought from Japan into Europe, and were, during a very long series of years, adopted in the practice of every European country.

Acupuncture — that is, sticking with a needle—is chiefly practised in a violent endemic colic of Japan. According to Japanese theory, this colic is caused by *wind*, and to let out this wind several small holes—nine being a favourite number—are made with needles, prepared for the purpose, generally in the muscles of the stomach or abdomen, though other fleshy parts of the body are, in some cases, chosen for the operation. These needles are nearly as fine as a hair, made of gold and silver generally, but sometimes of steel, by persons who profess a particular skill in tempering them. The bony parts, nerves and blood-vessels, are carefully avoided, and while they are passed through the skin and muscle, they are twirled about in a peculiar manner. There are many practitioners who confine themselves to this practice alone.*

The still more favourite and universal remedy, employed quite as much for prevention as cure, is burning with the moxa—the finer woolly part of the young leaves of the wormwood (*Artemesia*), of which the coarser kind is used for ordinary tinder. It is procured by rubbing and beating the leaves till the green part separates, and nothing remains but the wool, which is sorted into two kinds. When applied, it is made up in little cones, which, being placed on the part selected for the operation, are set fire to from the top. They burn very slowly, leaving a scar or blister on the skin, which, some time after, breaks and discharges. The operation is not very painful, except when repeated in the same place, as it sometimes is, or when applied to certain tender parts. It is thought very efficacious in pleurisies, toothache, gout

---

* See a sensible article on this subject by Remusat (*Nov. Melanges Asiat.* vol. i.), in which he gives an analysis of a Japanese treatise on acupuncture, which, with a translation of it, was brought home by Titsingh.—Hildreth.

and rheumatism—disorders which, like the colic above-mentioned, are rapid in their operation, and of which the paroxysms tend to a speedy termination under any medical treatment or none at all. The Japanese have very elaborate treatises as to the effects produced by the moxa, according to the part to which it is applied, and its application forms a science and profession by itself. The fleshy parts, especially of the back, are ordinarily selected. It is used still more by way of prevention than for cure, every person, young and old, male and female, even prisoners in the gaols, submitting to the operation, at least once in six months.* Another remedy is friction, applied by certain professors, and which proves of great use in pains of the limbs, arising from the prevailing changes of the weather. Wonderful virtues are ascribed to certain drugs ; and, on the whole, the Japanese appear, as in the use of unicorn's horn and ginseng, to have been not less deluded by quack medicines and medical theories than more enlightened nations.† Titsingh professes to speak from his own personal knowledge and experience, in the following astonishing statement :—

" Instead of inclosing the bodies of the dead in coffins of a length and breadth proportionate to the stature and bulk of the deceased, they place the body in a tub, three feet high, two feet and a half in diameter at the top, and two feet at the bottom. It is difficult to conceive how the body of a grown person can be compressed into so small a space, when the limbs, rendered rigid by death, cannot be bent in any way.

" The Japanese to whom I made this observation told me that they produced the result by means of a particular powder called *Dosia*, which they introduce into the ears, nostrils, and mouth of the deceased, after which the limbs, all at once, acquire astonishing flexibility. As they promised to perform the experiment in my presence, I

* Kämpfer treats at length on acupuncture and moxa, and gives in his appendix a translation of a Japanese treatise on the parts to be chosen for burning, according to the object in view.

† Hildreth.

could not do otherwise than suspend my judgment, lest I should condemn as an absurd fiction a fact which, indeed, surpasses our conceptions, but may yet be susceptible of a plausible explanation, especially by galvanism, the recently discovered effects of which also appeared, at first, to exceed the bounds of credibility.

"The experiment accordingly took place in the month of October, 1783, when the cold was pretty severe. A young Dutchman having died in our factory at Desima, I directed the physician to cause the body to be washed, and left all night exposed to the air, on a table placed near an open window, in order that it might become completely stiff. Next morning several Japanese, some of the officers of our factory, and myself, went to examine the corpse, which was as hard as a piece of wood. One of the interpreters, named Zenby, drew from his bosom a *santock*, or pocket-book, and took out of it an oblong paper, filled with a coarse powder resembling sand. This was the famous *Dosia* powder. He put a pinch into the ears, another pinch into the nostrils, and a third into the mouth ; and, presently, whether from the effect of this drug, or of some trick which I could not detect, the arms, which had before been crossed over the breast, dropped of themselves, and in less than twenty minutes, by the watch, the body recovered all its flexibility.

" I attributed this phenomenon to the action of some subtle poison ; but was assured that the *Dosia* powder, so far from being poisonous, was a most excellent medicine, in child-bearing, for diseases of the eyes, and for other maladies. An infusion of this powder, taken even in perfect health, is said to have virtues which cause it to be in great request among the Japanese of all classes. It cheers the spirits and refreshes the body. It is carefully tied up in a piece of white cloth and dried, after being used, as it will serve a great number of times before losing its virtues.

" The same infusion is given to people of quality when at the point of death ; if it does not prolong life, it prevents rigidity of the limbs; and the body is not exposed to the rude handling of professional persons—a circumstance of some consequence in a country where respect for the dead is carried to excess.

"I had the curiosity to procure some of this powder, for which I was obliged to send to Kidjo, or the Nine Provinces, to the temples of the Sintoos, which enjoy the exclusive sale of it, because they practise the doctrine of Kobou-Daysi, its inventor. It was after the death of Kobou-Daysi, in the second year of the *nengozio-wa* (A.D. 825), that this sand came into general use in Japan. The quantity obtained in consequence of my first application was very small, and even this was a special favour of the priests, who otherwise never part with more than a single pinch at a time.

"At my departure, in 1784, however, I carried with me a considerable quantity of the *Dosia* powder. Part was put up in lots of twenty small packets each, with the name written on the outside in red characters ; the rest was in small bags : this was only a coarse powder, in which were to be seen here and there particles of gold, and which probably was not yet possessed of the requisite virtues. One small packet only had undergone the chemical operation which insures its efficacy, and this was a powder as white as snow.

"The discovery of the *Dosia* powder is ascribed to a priest named Kobou-Daysi : he became acquainted with the properties of this wondrous mineral on the mountain of Kongosen or Kinbensen, in the province of Yametto, where there are many mines of gold and silver, and he carried a considerable quantity of it to the temple to which he belonged, on the mountain of Kojas-an.

"The priests of this temple continue to chant hymns of thanksgiving to the gods who led Kobou-Daysi to the important discovery. When their stock is exhausted, they fetch a fresh supply from the mountain of Kongosen, and carry it away in varnished bowls. In all ages the common people are apt to attribute phenomena surpassing human comprehension to the agency of celestial spirits ; and, accordingly, the priests do not fail to pretend that the

Dosia powder owes all its efficacy to the fervour of their prayers. As soon as the new supply arrives, it is put into a basin, varnished and gilt, and set before the image of the god Day-nitsi, or Biron-sanna. The priests, ranged in a circle before the altar, and turning between their fingers the beads of a kind of rosary, repeat, for seven times twenty-four hours, a hymn, called *Guomi-singo*, the words of which are :—

"Ou o bokja Biron saunanomaka-godora mani,
Fando ma, zimbara gara, garetaga won."

The priests assert that, after this long exercise, a kind of rustling is heard in the sand ; all the impure particles fly out of the vessel of themselves, and nothing is left but the purified *Dosia* powder, which is then divided among all the temples of the Sintoos."*

In 1799, Charpentier-Cossigny examined this wonderful powder, and subjected it to severe analysis. It turned out to be a compound apparently of ashes and earth, pyrites and mica. He tried it on dead bodies—at single, double, and triple doses—but they remained as stiff as ever, after waiting fifteen, thirty, and sixty minutes. "Besides," says he, " I declare that I took a whole dose of *Dosia* without feeling the slightest effect in any way whatever. It is scentless, and has no taste but that of sand in the mouth. * * * Its mysterious origin confirms me in the opinion that its use is connected with some religious belief."†

Chemistry appears to be very imperfectly studied. Botany, on the other hand, is said to be diligently and successfully cultivated, at least as far as it is connected with the knowledge of simples. Some of the vegetable

---

* Titsingh, *Illustrations of Japan*, &c.

† Note in Titsingh's *Ceremon. usit. au Japon*, p. 240. In not one of the books on Japan which allude to this wonderful powder is there mention of the fact that it was found to be "humbug" by Cossigny. Kobou, the inventor, a great sage and saint, discovered also, by profound meditation, that the great scourges of mankind are four :—1. Sigokf, *hell ;* 2. Goki, *woman ;* 3. Tükusio, *the man with a perverse heart ;* and 4. Sioura, *war.*

medicines are described as effective and excellent. The people, however, place their main dependence upon diet, and upon acupuncture, and the *moxa*, which are still universally practised among them.

In astronomy, their proficiency really appears to be very considerable. They pursue this study with great ardour. Their best astronomers are said to be well acquainted with Lalande's Treatises, and other profound works which have been translated into Dutch. This surely disproves the assertion that they have only "some little knowledge of mathematics." They have learned the use of most of our astronomical instruments. They have even taught Japanese artisans to imitate and reproduce them to perfection. They have excellent telescopes, chronometers, barometers, and thermometers of native workmanship; and they have learned to measure the height of mountains by the barometer. The courts of both the Emperors are centres of science as well as of literature. Good almanacs, including the calculation of eclipses, are annually published by the colleges of Jeddo and Meako. From the few observations made by the officers of the *Samarang*, we are disposed to believe that if we only knew more of them, the Japanese would be found to be in possession of far more scientific knowledge than the amount for which they have received credit.

It is quite clear that they are skilled in trigonometry, and in some of the best principles of civil engineering.

The mechanical arts, or all such portions of them as tend to abridge manual labour, and deprive people of the employments to which they have been bred, are discouraged, and in fact repressed by the Government. The Siogoun would not accept, as a present, a European oil-mill : he said that it was very ingenious, but that if such a machine were generally adopted in the country, it would throw all the old Japanese oil-pressers out of work and out of bread.

Although they are passionately fond of it, the national music—like that of all Oriental nations—appears to be utterly insupportable to European ears.   Perhaps. however, this condemnation is too sweeping and general.

"We have heard," adds Mr. MacFarlane, "some of the music of the Japanese ladies highly commended by one who possessed a good musical ear.   The *samsie*, or native guitar, is even more invariably a part of female education than is the pianoforte in England.   Its touch is the signal for laying aside ceremony and constraint.   The Japanese gentleman—truly a *gentleman* in this respect—has no notion of social enjoyment or conviviality without the company of the ladies.   Every fair one takes with her to their parties her *samsie*, and they sing and play by turns, while the gentlemen smoke their pipes and take the cheering glass.   At every feast it is the lady of the house that presides.

"In the arts of design and painting they certainly possess both skill and taste, although they are somewhat negligent in the study of 'the human form divine.'

"This art," says M. Fisscher, "appears to have developed itself to a considerable degree in very early times. Many screens and decorated walls in their temples have the stamp of a remote antiquity.   Yet I never heard of a good portrait-painter in Japan, and am of opinion that a reluctance exists among their artists to devote themselves to this branch of their profession, founded on superstitious feelings.   In all such works their attention is principally directed to accuracy in the details of costume and to the general air ; the face is never a likeness."

It has been appositely remarked that "their Tartar brethren of St. Petersburgh, whose criticism on the portrait of Alexander, by Lawrence, was first directed to the great painter's delineation of his Imperial Majesty's epaulettes, crosses, and ribbons, displayed similar feelings with respect to the fine arts."*

It is curious to trace over the broad earth these Mongol affinities—these long lingering proofs of a common type among so many and such distant nations.   Those other

* *Quarterly Review*, vol. lii.

brethren of the Japanese, the Osmanli Turks, would not, until quite a recent period, allow the human face or the human form to be depicted, or carved, or sculptured at all. It is true that the Koran prohibits all such representations; but we believe that the old Mongol antipathy had more to do with the interdict than any religious feeling or scruple; for we have seen Turks, who had no religious convictions whatever, express a strong dislike at the sight of a very agreeable English portrait.

The illustrations of M. Fisscher's own book, all copied from the productions of Nàgasaki artists, would in themselves be sufficient to prove that their painters have really very considerable skill, and can give to their works all that beauty of finish which we find in the illuminations of the best of our old missals. It is at least reasonable to suppose that the artists of Jeddo or Meako surpass those of the provinces, as our London painters and the other artists excel those of our provincial towns. Considering the interdict laid upon exportation, we may also suppose that the best specimens of Japanese art have not yet reached Europe, or been seen and examined by competent European judges.

The native delineations of flowers, fruits, and more especially of birds, are exquisitely beautiful. " We have frequently had in our hands," adds Mr. MacFarlane, " a small cup, or rather saucer, which is ornamented with the figures of two cranes. Nothing can be more perfect in drawing, more true in colouring, and more perfect in finish, than this admirable miniature. The object is preserved in the Museum of the Royal Asiatic Society, New Burlington-street, and may be seen by any one, upon application to the Secretary, or to a member of the said Society.

" Japanese artists produce beautiful maps of their own country, which, by law, are not allowed to be exported, or even to be seen by foreigners. In procuring copies of the best of these maps of the empire, Dr. Von Siebold became involved in very grievous troubles. An English officer—a very competent judge of such matters—to whom we have been indebted for some valuable assistance, saw these Japanese copies of the Imperial maps, three years ago, in Von Siebold's own house at Leyden, and he assures us that they are most admirably executed.*

"If we had more good specimens before us we might, no doubt, have much more to say on the subject of the fine arts in Japan; but we trust that enough has been said to impress the reader with the belief that these people—these super-refined Tartars, if you like—have, at least, artists of high taste and very extraordinary skill."

As previously observed, precious stones are not valued in Japan; they have, therefore, no lapidaries. Charlevoix says that the women fix a pearl to the end of the hair-pin over their left ear: but jewels seem to be either rejected by Japanese vanity, or forbidden by law; and yet they buy Dutch and French tinsel. They trade in pearls with the Dutch and the Chinese; a good one—about as large as a small pea—is worth two kobangs, or about fifty-two shillings.

Die-sinking cannot be deficient in Japan, to judge from the engravings of their coins, which are cast, not struck; but the finish of the work, and the sharpness of the im-pression, whether in silver, gold, or copper, would do honour to European artists.†

* The Japanese call Europe *Ziagatara*. The word was evidently adopted under the notion that the island of Java was the country of the Hollanders. Ziagatara is a corruption of *Jacatra*, a district in Java, of which Batavia (the Amsterdam of the east) is the capital. At all events, it was applied to "Asiatic" Europe, and "Holland" in Java.

† The comparative value of Japanese money is somewhat obscure in the books. The kobang seems to be worth about 26s., the *tael* (a Chinese adoption) about 7s., others say 4s. 7½d. The *oho-bang*, the largest gold coin, is worth 20 kobangs; but it is only used for gifts. These two beautiful coins are very flat, and oval in shape; they bear, as other coins, the arms of the Mikado,—a flower and three leaves of the tree *kiri* (*driandra*). There are also half, quarter, eighth kobangs of silver. The smallest copper coin, the *seni*, seems to be the eighth of a farthing. Siebold mentions perfectly round kobangs in the province of Kai. The Japanese have paper-money, called *fouda* or *sats*. These notes are issued for the smallest amounts—even the eighth of a kobang, little over three shillings.

In their "nursery-books" we are assured they "show a humorous conception and a style of treatment far in advance of the mechanical trash which sometimes composes the nursery-books found in our shops. A people have made some progress worth studying who have a sense of the humorous, can picture the ludicrous, and good-naturedly laugh at a clever caricature. The constant recurrence in the margin of the pages of these Japanese books of what is usually called by architects "the Greek fret or border," is certainly curious. We are surprised by a classic form that we would not have expected to find an established feature in Oriental art. Not less surprising also is it to find another architectural form belonging to what is usually termed the "Gothic" style. These are singular coincidences. There is great scope for sculpture in the image-worship of the Japanese religion; and, accordingly, statues of stone, metal, and wood abound in the temples, shrines, and by the waysides. The mechanical execution of these generally exhibit much manual skill, but none of them are to be named as works of art. The wood-carving is often exquisitely cut, and when representing natural objects, particularly the lower animals and familiar parts of vegetation, is often remarkably close to truth. The sculptured cranes, tortoises, and fish, which are amongst the most frequent subjects carved upon the entablatures and cornices of the houses and temples, were continually admired for their fidelity to nature."*

There is but one opinion as to the industry, ingenuity, and manual dexterity of the Japanese. These people, to use the words of an old Italian missionary, work admirably well in iron, silver, gold, and all metals; also in wood and bamboo, and in all such materials as they possess in that fair country. They also have the art of making

Various expedients are applied, as with us, to prevent forgery: the penalty is death. The bullion price of gold is only eight and a half times that of silver, instead of sixteen times, as with us.—Siebold, Jancigny, Hildreth, *United States Expedition.*

* *United States Expedition,* 463.

good use of many materials which by us are thrown away as of no value.

"Arts and manufactures," says Thunberg, "are carried on in every part of the country, and some of them are brought to such a degree of perfection, as even to surpass those of Europe ; whilst some, on the other hand, fall

ORNAMENTAL VASES.

short of European excellence. They work extremely well in iron and copper, and their silk and cotton manufactures equal, and sometimes even excel, the productions of other eastern countries. Their lacquering in wood, especially their ancient workmanship, surpasses every attempt which has been made in this department by other nations. They work likewise with great skill in *sowas*, which is a mixture of gold and copper, which they understand how to colour blue or black with their tousche, or ink, by a method hitherto unknown to us. They are likewise acquainted with the art of making glass, and can manufacture it for any purpose, both coloured and uncoloured. But window-glass, which is flat, they could not fabricate formerly. This art they have lately learned from the Europeans, as likewise to make watches, which they sometimes use in their houses. In like manner, they understand the art of glass-grinding, and to form telescopes with it, for which purpose they purchase mirror-glass of the Dutch. In the working of steel, they are perfect masters, of which their incomparable swords afford the most evident proof. Paper is likewise manufactured in great abundance in this country, as well for writing and printing as for tapestry, handkerchiefs, cloths for packing of goods, &c., and is of various sizes and qualities. They prepare it from the bark of a species of mulberry-tree.*

* *Morus papyrifera.* The method is as follows :— After the tree has shed its leaves, in the month of December, they cut off the branches about three feet in length, which they tie up in bundles, and boil in a ley of ashes, standing inverted in a covered kettle, till such time as the bark is so shrunk, that half an inch of the woody part is seen bare at the ends. They are then taken out and left in the open air to cool, cut up lengthwise, and the bark is stipped off. Upon this the bark is again soaked, three or four hours, in water, and when it is become soft, they scrape off the fine black skin with a knife. The next thing to be done is to separate the coarse bark from the fine, which produces the whitest paper. The older the branches are, the coarser is the paper. The bark is now boiled again in fresh ley, and the whole continually stirred with a stick, and fresh water added to it. A nice and delicate operation is then performed in a brook, by means of a sieve, by stirring the bark incessantly about till the whole is reduced to the consistence of a fine pap, and, thrown into water, separates in the form of meal. It is then further mixed in a small vessel with a decoction of rice and the *Hibiscus-manibot*, and stirred well about, till it has attained a tolerable consistence. After this it is poured into a wider vessel, from whence the sheets are taken and put into proper forms, made of grass-straw, and laid one upon another in heaps, with straw between, that they may be easily lifted up. They are further covered with a board, and pressed, at first lightly, but afterwards, and gradually, harder, till the water is separated. When this is done, they lay the sheets upon a board, dry them in the sun, and then gather them into bundles for sale and use. An inferior kind of paper is likewise manufactured from the *Morus Indica.*

" The *lacquered* woodwork which is executed in Japan
excels the Chinese, the Siamese, and indeed that of all
other nations in the world. For this purpose they make
choice of the finest sort of firs and cedars, and cover them
with the very best varnish, which they prepare from the
Rhus vernix, a tree that grows in great abundance in
many parts of the country. This varnish, which oozes
out of the tree on its being wounded, is procured from
stems that are three years old, and is received in some
proper vessel.   When first caught, it is of a lightish
colour, and of the consistence of cream ; but grows thicker
and black on being exposed to the air.   It is of so transparent a nature, that when it is laid, pure and unmixed,
upon boxes and other pieces of furniture, every vein of
the wood may be clearly seen.   For the most part a dark
ground is spread underneath it, which causes it to reflect
like a looking-glass ; and for this purpose recourse is frequently had to the fine sludge which is caught in the
trough under a grinding-stone.   At other times, ground
charcoal is used, and occasionally some blacker substance
is mixed with the varnish, and sometimes leaf-gold,
ground very fine, when it is called *Salplicat.*   This
lacquered work is afterwards, for the most part, embellished with gold and silver flowers and figures laid on
upon the varnish, which, however, are liable to wear off
in time."*

* "Fashion, that most absolute of all tyrants, has almost entirely
exiled these beautiful Japanned wares from our houses ; but we are
old enough to remember the time when nearly every respectable
drawing-room, dining-room, and boudoir, presented specimens of
them, in the shape of screens, desks, cabinets, caskets, or other
objects of ornament and utility.   They were rather more numerous
in Scotch than in English houses, and this from the very obvious
reason that, mainly in grace of the patronage of hearty Henry
Dundas, Lord Melville, so many Scotchmen sought and found
fortune in the East.   Many of these articles were most admirable
specimens of the arts of the cabinet-maker, japanner, and gold-
embosser.   It is said, however, that the finest specimens were never
allowed to be exported out of Japan.   The finest collections existing
in Europe are those of Von Siebold and his Majesty the King of the
Netherlands, at the Hague."—MacFarlane.

Generally, Japanese workmanship has more strength, solidity, and real finish than that of the Chinese. They seem to have a contempt for all that is flimsy. Their common packing-cases are nearly always strong and finished specimens of materials and workmanship. There may be said to be about the same difference between Chinese and Japanese work that there is between French and English; but, if the French, in most things, can claim over us a superiority in taste of design, no such superiority can be claimed by the Chinese over the workmen of Japan.

In the art of making and tempering steel, they must possess some valuable secret or most extraordinary skill. The finest blade we ever handled was an indisputable old blade of Japanese make.* It beat all the Damascus blades and Andrea-Ferraras we ever saw. It is mentioned, as a notorious fact, that a sword of this sort would, at a blow, cut a man's body in two.

"With respect to steel manufactures," says Golownin, "the Japanese sabres and daggers surpass all others in the world, those of Damascus perhaps excepted. They bear extraordinary trials. The edge of the sabre is kept as sharp as that of a razor. The Japanese are extremely skilful in polishing steel, and all other metals. They make metal mirrors, which, for their object, are scarcely inferior to our looking-glasses. We often saw carpenters' and cabinet-makers' tools made in Japan which might be compared with the English. Their saws are so good, that the thinnest boards may be sawed out of the hardest wood."†

In cotton fabrics they appear to have little skill. As before stated, they use a coarse, thick, spongy paper, made from a tree, for pocket-handkerchiefs, for napkins, and for other purposes in which we employ calico, silk, or muslin.

I have mentioned the inferiority of the native silk; but rich and beautiful articles are manufactured out of

* MacFarlane.   † *Recollections of Japan.*

silk imported from China. These valuable silk goods are
said to be produced only by unfortunate noblemen and
gentlemen, who are exiled to a lonely island, and compelled to work for their own livelihood.

Some of the trades are followed up in a grand, wholesale way. Among these are their iron works, tobacco
manufactories, breweries, and distilleries. Some of the
last are said to be very extensive. Many thousands
are constantly employed in the manufacture of straw
shoes, straw hats, and mats. The consumption of
this straw, made out of a native grass, must be truly
prodigious.*

As before observed, the Japanese have little furniture
in their houses beyond the apparatus for their kitchen,
and what they use at their meals. Of these, however,
as likewise of clothes and other necessaries, there is such
an incredible quantity exposed for sale in the shops of
their tradesmen, both in town and country, that the
wonder is, where they can find purchasers, and it might
be supposed that they kept magazines here to supply the
whole world. Here the native may select, according to

---

* "When on a journey," says Thunberg, "all the Japanese wear
a conical hat, made of a species of grass, platted, and tied with a
string." He also observed that all the fishermen wore hats of the
same material and shape. But, in addition to this extensive use, the
Japanese hardly ever wear any shoes or slippers but such as are made
of platted straw. This is the most shabby and indifferent part of
their dress, and yet in equal use with the high and the low, the rich
and the poor. They are made of rice-straw platted, and by no means
strong. They cost, however, a mere trifle ; they are found exposed
for sale in every town and in every village, and the pedestrian supplies
himself with new shoes as he goes along, while the more provident man
always carries two or three pair with him for use, throwing them
away as they wear out. "Old worn-out shoes of this description are
found lying everywhere by the sides of the roads, especially near
rivulets, where travellers, on changing their shoes have an opportunity at the same time of washing their feet." In very wet weather
they use wooden clogs, which are attached to their straw-platted
shoes by ties also made of straw-plat. People of very high rank
sometimes wear slippers made of fine slips of rattan neatly platted.
It is said that the common people count the length of a journey by
the number of these straw shoes they wear out in making it.

his varying taste and fancy, all his clothes ready made, and may be furnished with shoes, umbrellas, lacquered ware, porcelain, and a thousand other articles, without having occasion to bespeak anything beforehand.*

FLOWER-BASKETS AND VASES.

In their great fondness for dishes and vessels of light lacquered ware, they rather neglect the porcelain fabrics ; but they are said to produce, in this line, some articles that far exceed the finest Chinese.

Nothing can well be more light, neat, and graceful, than the superior kinds of their lacquered cups. They are generally painted in a very pretty style, and are so

* Thunberg. Kämpfer.

z

exceedingly light as scarcely to be felt in the hand through their weight.

Although these various manufactories are spread all over the empire, the principal ones are said to be confined to the cities of Meako, Jeddo, and Osacca.

" On the first arrival of the Dutch, the Japanese were allowed to visit foreign countries. Their ships, though built on the plan of the Chinese junks, boldly defied the fury of tempests. Their merchants were scattered over the principal countries of India ; they were not deficient either in expert mariners or adventurous traders. In a country where the lower classes cannot gain a subsistence but by assiduous labour, thousands of Japanese were disposed to seek their fortune abroad, not so much by the prospect of gain, as by the certainty of being enabled to gratify their curiosity with the sight of numberless objects that were wholly unknown to them.

" This state of things formed bold and experienced sailors, and at the same time soldiers, not surpassed in bravery by those of the most warlike nations of India.

" The Japanese, accustomed from their infancy to hear the accounts of the heroic achievements of their ancestors, to receive at that early age their first instruction in those books which record their exploits, and to imbibe, as it were with their mother's milk, the intoxicating love of glory, made the art of war their favourite study. Such an education has, in all ages, trained up heroes : it excited in the Japanese that pride which is noticed by all in the whole nation."

Here is a description of their junk :—

" In the afternoon, one of the Japanese junks left the harbour, laden with upwards of two hundred peculs of sugar, bound for Satzuma, a port in Japan, lying about four hundred miles N.N.E. from Loo-Choo. In coming out, she struck on a reef, but was soon got off without apparent damage, and as she passed the ship, we went in the gig to examine her. The hull was made of pine, and, in its general form, resembled a Chinese fast boat ; the bow was sharp, without bowsprit, but, instead, there was a high beak, like that of an ancient galley, with a fender, in case she should run stem on. The solitary mast was about forty feet high, and supported by a huge forestay, under which hung a yard, in form like two cones united at their bases ; this was raised by halliards passing over the top of the mast, aft, to the quarters, where they went over a sort of windlass, and then round a capstan below deck. The sail was made of very coarse heavy cotton, and the bolts were loosely laced together with cords, each being four or five inches apart, giving the sail a singular appearance ; at the bottom, several ropes secured it in its proper place. There was no sternpost, and the open work permitted us to look directly into the cabin, where, at this time, the crew were hoisting sails with loud cries. The rudder was about fifteen feet long and eight broad, with a tiller like a spanker-boom, reaching forward nearly to the mast. The long-boat was lashed athwart the vessel, near the bow, the ends projecting over each side about five feet, placed, one would suppose, in a very hazardous manner. Three or four grapplings lay on the bows, attached to large hausers ; and a double-headed anchor placed athwart the vessel near the mast, with the flukes outside, for the purpose of strengthening the sides. The stern was high out of the water, as in the junks of China, and upon it was her name, *Hozammah*, painted in large Chinese characters ; upon the bow was a bird rudely carved, and the character *pin*, 'ashore,' all neatly ornamented with copper, which here, as in other parts of the vessel, was laid on profusely. The capstan stood in the cabin, which, like every other part of the vessel, was kept very clean ; her sides fell in above the water-mark, and she was rudely, though strongly built. The crew numbered about fifteen, one or two of whom wore the singular leggings seen in Japanese pictures ; but most of them were scantily clad."*

In another place the same writer says :—" The boats

* *Narrative of a Voyage of the Ship Morrison,* &c. By S. Wells Williams.

in which the natives came off were rudely, though strongly, built of pine ; and most of them carried a sail of coarse cotton canvas, suspended from a single moveable mast. Their progress was accelerated by three or four large sculls attached to each side, near the stern, on pivots, and formed of two pieces lashed together like the Chinese ; with this difference, that the loom was very broad at its lower end, in its general shape resembling a paddle ; the upper surface was convex, and the rounded edges made the under somewhat concave : this form appeared to be for convenience in sculling. Some of the largest of the boats were thirty feet long and six wide, having the two ends open like a scow, and carrying between twenty and thirty men. In two or three were a few women, of whom we did not see much, for they were fully occupied in protecting themselves from the rain, piling bamboo cloaks and hats upon their persons, in a very singular manner, while they lay in the bottom of the boats."

The number of these boats and junks was such as to denote a most active coasting trade ; and it seems that we might exclaim now as honest old Kämpfer did more than a century and a half ago—" How much commerce is carried on between the several provinces and parts of the empire ! How busy and industrious the merchants everywhere are ! How full their harbours of ships ! How many rich and mercantile towns up and down the country ! There are such multitudes of people along the coasts and near the seaports, such a noise of oars and sails, such numbers of ships and boats, both for use and pleasure, that one would be apt to imagine that the whole nation had settled there, and that all the inland parts of the country were left quite empty and deserted."

" The brisk trade of the bay was carried on as usual, and Japanese boats, both large and small, were moving up and down in constant circulation. The various towns and villages grouped about the bay were thus interchanging their elements of life, and stimulated into commercial activity by the throb from the busy heart of the great city, poured into Jeddo their overflowing abundance. There were no less than sixty-seven junks counted as passing up the bay during the single day."

Yet, according to all accounts, trade is as active in the interior of Niphon and the other great islands, as it is

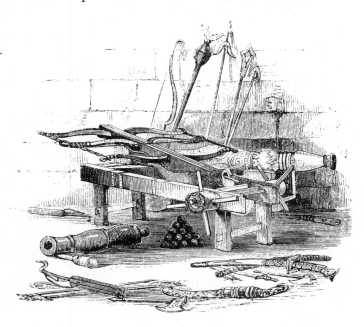

JAPANESE INSTRUMENTS OF WAR.

along the coasts. All the chief towns of the interior are " remarkable" for some distinct produce or manufacture, the interchange of which keeps the whole empire in ceaseless activity. In one it is saki, silk manufactures, fish, wild geese, cast-iron kettles; in another, cotton fabrics, rock-crystal, sulphur; in a third, saltpetre, tin, lead, bamboos, hawks, and dogs for hunting, bricks and frying-pans; in a fourth, whales, edible roots, earthenware, mats, porcelain, sugar, and brass guns; in a fifth salted fish, oranges, leather trunks, flints,* grindstones, and tobacco pipes ; in a sixth, camphor, cinnamon, trained horses, and tobacco ; and so on throughout a long catalogue of wares "too numerous to mention."†

As has been already mentioned, any theft or robbery is a most difficult matter in Japan. The roads are perfectly safe. The merchant loads his bullocks with the richest goods, or with gold and silver, and travels cheerily along without any fear of robbers. This result is not all produced by legislation, severe laws, and municipal and police regulations ; the Japanese, as a proud people, have a contempt or abhorrence of cheating, pilfering, stealing, or robbing. In this respect they are most advantageously contrasted with the Chinese.

Finally, we are assured that the Japanese are eager for knowledge. "Never was there a people more ready to adapt themselves to the changes and progress of the world than they are. It is curious that while some of their customs are what we would deem rather barbarous, and while they are ignorant of many common things—while they still rip themselves up, and shoe their horses with straw, because ignorant of any other method, they have jumped to a knowledge of certain branches of science which it has taken nations in Europe hundreds of years to attain. At Nagasaki they can turn out of their yard an engine for a railway or steamer ; Japanese captains and engineers command their men of war, of which three are steamers ; they understand the electric telegraph ; they make thermometers and barometers, theodolites,

---

* Yet it has been supposed that the *absence of flints* in Japan was the cause why the Japanese have clung so long to the old matchlock. Doubtless they will now see the necessity for adopting all our warlike appliances, arms, and discipline, to provide against the future.

† See *Asiatic Journal*, vi. 196, *et seq.* The empire is distributed into eight grand divisions or countries, denominated *Do*, or " ways," namely, Gokynay, Tokaydo, Tosando, Foo-koo-ro-koodo, San-in-do, San-yo-do, Nan-kay-do, and Say-kay-do. These are subdivided into sixty-eight kokofs or provinces, which again contain 622 koris or districts.

and, I believe, aneroids. Their spy-glasses and micro-scopes are good, and very cheap. They have a large glass manufactory which turns out glass little inferior to our own. They have a short line of railway somewhere in the interior, given by the Americans. Many of them speak Dutch, some English, all anxious to learn ; every-thing is done by themselves, and when it is considered that it is not much more than ten years ago since they made this start, the advance they have made in that short time is perfectly wonderful." *

* *Times* Correspondent.

PART II.

———

CHAPTER I.

IF you ask a Japanese of what race he is, whence he came, he will tell you with great pride that the Japanese are lineally descended from the gods, and had their origin in the islands where we found them. Everything relating to them seems to uphold their belief in this respect; we may designate the ethnological branch to which they may be referred, but we can form no notion whatever as to whence the primitive inhabitants of Japan could have migrated. The night of obscurity overhangs the origin of all nations that form types of mankind; and it is as difficult to imagine any other than an indigenous source for the Japanese as for the quadruman or monkey of Japan. For a certainty the monkey did not migrate into Japan; no animal dreads water or the sea more intensely; hence the rarity of his remains in the fossil-state, for he clings to his primeval woods and forests, dies on the surface, and his bones decompose in the face of heaven. No floods can cover him with alluvium where he pitches his tent; hence has he rarely, in the fossil-state, testified with other animals to the age of the earth and her revolutions.

The Japanese are insulted by those who attempt to draw their descent from the Chinese. Because a good many Chinese usages prevail amongst them, this belief in their descent was entertained in Europe. Ethnologically they are referred to the great Mongol type, which has peopled so vast a portion of the Eastern world, and which now fills the undefined country of Tartary, a great part of the Russian empire and central Asia, and is found in other offshoots, in the Turkomans, Calmuks, Turks, Tongus, and the like ; that is to say, certain well-defined characteristics seem to point to a common mould in their creation, with reference to the regions which they were to inhabit ; and, for a certainty, the functions which they were to perform in the grand economy of Providence. There may thus be numerous races formed on a common type, yet diverging immensely according to the circumstances in which they were to live and fight the battle of life ; but, nevertheless, to fight it after the fashion resulting from the common mould, or in accordance with the common type.

The Japanese seem decidedly to be an original race, however nearly or remotely they may touch other races fashioned in the same mould, or organized according to the same type.

Although, in their writing and printing, they frequently drop in a Chinese character, to express a Chinese thing or idea, the two characters, however identical in their origin, are now totally distinct. Nor is there any affinity between the two languages, although the Japanese frequently borrow Chinese terms, rather to parade their learning than from any deficiency of equivalent expressions in their own tongue.

There can scarcely be a greater difference than in the pronunciation of the two peoples : it should seem, as Kämpfer remarks, that the very instruments of voice are different in the Japanese to what they are in the Chinese. The pronunciation of the Japanese language in general is sharp, articulate, and distinct, there being seldom, according to our alphabet, more than two or three letters combined together in one syllable ; the pronunciation of the Chinese, on the contrary, is nothing but a confused noise of many consonants, pronounced with a sort of sing-song accent, very disagreeable to the unaccustomed ear. The same strong difference appears with regard to particular letters. Thus the Chinese pronounce our letter *h* very distinctly, but the Japanese can give it no other sound but that of an *f.* Again, the Japanese pronounce the letters *r* and *d* very distinctly, while the Chinese always make an *l* of them, even such as are well skilled in the European languages. There are other instances equally striking. I allude to the language merely as connected with the question of race ;—no two languages can differ more, in essential characteristics, than those of China and Japan.

Another argument against the descent of the Japanese from the Chinese, is drawn from the difference between the ancient religions of the two nations. If the Japanese were a colony of the Chinese, they would have brought with them into these islands the faith and worship of their mother country. But the original religion of the Japanese, by them called *Sintoo*, is peculiar to their own country, and has not the slightest resemblance to the ancient belief of the Chinese. Buddhism exists in both countries, but is to both of exotic growth, and was not introduced into either until a comparatively recent period. Besides, the Japanese say that they received Buddhism not from China but from Corea.

There are also differences in physical conformation. Although strongly marked with the Mongol type, the Japanese bear a stronger resemblance to the European family, and their eyes are not so deeply sunk in their heads as those of the Chinese. Generally, it may be said that the Japanese are not so strong as Europeans, but they are well made and have stout limbs. Their eyes show their Mongol origin, not being round, but oblong and small. Their hair is black, thick, and shining, and their noses, although not flat, are rather thick and short. Their complexion is yellowish. They seem to resemble most the inhabitants of Corea and the Ainos, on the island of Tarakai. In a country so vast and so various in climate as China, there are great differences between the inhabitants of the several provinces; but, in general terms, it may be admitted that the Japanese are a stronger, hardier, and a braver race than the Chinese.

(FEMALE.) JAPANESE. (MALE.)

In some parts of the islands, even the common people, if dressed in our costume, might pass for Portuguese, or southern Italians, or Sicilians. Many of the upper classes, or members of the old families, are tall, exceedingly handsome in figure and countenance, and are far more like Europeans than Asiatics.

Then again the Japanese greatly differ from the Chinese in many of their customs and ways of life, as in eating, drinking, sleeping, dressing, shaving of the head, saluting, sitting, and many others. There is also a remarkable difference in the national characters of the two. The Chinese are peaceable, timid, much given to a sedate, ruminating way of life ; cunning, suspicious, greedy, and much addicted to fraud and usury; the Japanese are quick and volatile, daring, fond of an active, exciting life, frank, liberal, and open-handed, having many of the virtues of the nomadic tribes. Of course I speak of the people, and not of the Government.

In their governmental and municipal institutions, in their law of primogeniture, in their hereditary nobility, and in many other institutions, they widely differ from the people of the Celestial Kingdom.

Although this singular people seem always to have been somewhat jealous of intermixture, or even of intercourse with foreigners, they appear to have admitted from time to time small colonies from China, Corea, and perhaps from some other neighbouring countries.* The Japanese themselves make frequent mention in their histories of learned Chinese, who brought over into Japan their books, and the knowledge of useful arts and sciences, though not until the latter ages, when their own original stock had vastly increased and multiplied, and Japan had

* Nothing was done by war, or invasion and conquest. The Chinese never made good an invasion of Japan. But the Japanese invaded, and for a time occupied, Corea, or, at least, the maritime parts of that peninsula, and made frequent inroads on China. As we speak of virgin fortresses, so we may call Japan a virgin empire, for it has never been conquered by any foreign foe. This, in spite of the oppressiveness of their internal government, no doubt contributes materially to the independent bearing of the people.

already become a powerful empire. " And, indeed," says old Kämpfer, "since so few foreign words have been brought into the Japanese language, that it is hardly visible that there hath been any alteration at all made in it, and since the religion and old customs subsist till now, it appears plainly that whatever foreign colonies did from time to time voluntarily or by chance come over into Japan, their number must have been very inconsiderable with regard to the bulk of the Japanese nation."

I have before mentioned that old Kämpfer traced the Japanese from the Tower of Babel; his hypothesis is very pleasant and amusing, much more so, I fear, than must have been the journey of the emigrants seeking a settlement. At the confusion of languages, or dispersion of peoples, he brings the Japanese family by slow marches from Mesopotamia to the shores of the Caspian Sea, where they would find a large and fertile country extending itself far eastward, offering abundance of pasture to their cattle and their flocks, and the means of easily and leisurely pursuing their journey. He supposes that they then proceeded through the valleys of the Yenisi, Silinga, and parallel rivers until they came to the Lake of Argueen, where the cold northern climate would not invite a long stay. From that lake arises a large river of the same name, the valley of which would bring them to the still more considerable river, the Amoor, which runs E.S.E., and the long valley of which would bring them to the eastern coasts of Asia, into the then uninhabited peninsula of Corea, where the Amoor loses itself in the Eastern Ocean. Once at Corea, the passage over to Japan was neither long nor (in the summer weather) dangerous, especially as there are many little islands at almost regular distances between the main and the large islands which constitute the Japanese empire. In fact they might have crossed over in common fishing-boats. In the many broad rivers and vast lakes they had crossed, or on whose banks they had sojourned during their long migration, they must have made themselves familiar with the use of boats, and a short residence in Corea, on the coast of a sea abounding with fish, must soon have made fishermen and expert boatmen of these pastoral tribes.

It is not supposed that this immense march was made in one, in fifty, or in a hundred years. The ancestors of the Japanese would probably remain in any favourable region until they felt their rear pressed upon, or their flank annoyed, by other nomadic tribes. Then they would collect their flocks and herds, and move forward in quest of other regions and "pastures new." They could make a home wherever they could find streams of pure water and pasture for their flocks and herds. Something of the same sort may still be seen in many parts of the East. Even so near as Asiatic Turkey, when certain pastoral tribes are oppressed in one pashalic, they move on with all that they possess to another; and should the same inconvenience follow them, they go on to a still greater distance; and were the countries in their front not occupied (however thinly), it would be difficult to put an imaginable limit to their migrations. What Kämpfer fancies is, that from the purity or freedom from admixture of the Japanese language, that people could not have made any very considerable stay in any one country, or with any one people then existing. Had they made such stay, they must have adopted some words of the language of that nation into their own. Having brought them across the seas to Niphon, the most considerable of their islands, he carries them from the western coast to the southern extremity of the land, where the soil is most fruitful, the air most mild and salubrious, and where every advantage was offered in the way of security, tranquillity, and pleasant abode. To this day the Japanese look upon this part of their country as the place where their ancestors first dwelt, and as such they honour it with frequent pilgrimages and other acts of devotion.*

---

* This hypothesis is about as probable as the others by which men strive to make the action of the Creator,—so all-providing, so full of purpose, so definite—a mere thing of chance or accident in the distribution of Earth and her inhabitants. Thus, we read, in 1845,

Another essential characteristic of the Japanese race is its decided tendency to advance in the march of civilization. It is a fact, now universally acknowledged, that every nation that does not advance in civilization must inevitably retrocede. No people can be stationary. There is abundant evidence to prove this retrocession in the Chinese, who are very far from being so civilized now as they were in the thirteenth century, and the days

three Japanese were carried to Ningpo, in China, by the American frigate, *St. Louis.* These three men had been blown or drifted right across the Atlantic in a little junk, from the coast of Japan, all the way to Mexico, where they had remained two years. "After this," says Sir John F. Davis, "there can be little difficulty in accounting for the original peopling of America from Asia." (!)—*China during the War and since the Peace*, &c.

It really appears that some Chinese junk was drifted to the coast of Mexico, and that America was known to that singular people many centuries before its discovery by Christopher Columbus. In the year 499 a Bonze wrote an account of a country in the far west, which he called Fou-Sang, and the description of which closely agrees with what we know of Mexico in its flourishing and most civilized time. The only thing that startles belief is this : the Bonze speaks of horses, and it has always been assumed that there were no horses on any part of the American continent, until they were carried thither by the Spaniards. The Bonze mentions a sort of deer which the natives of the country employed as beasts of burden. This was clearly the Alpaca. The Bonze, though a great traveller, was evidently no great naturalist, and may have described some other animal as a horse. On this curious subject the reader may be referred to *Recherches sur les Navigations des Chinois du Côté de l'Amérique*, &c. Par M. de Guignes. *Mémoires de l'Académie des Inscriptions*, &c. vol. xxviii. p. 503. Paris : 1761 ; and to *L'Amérique sous le Nom de Pays de Fou-Sang*, &c. Par M. de Paravey. Paris : 1844 ; and to *Nouvelles Preuves que le Pays du Fou-Sang, mentionné dans les livres Chinois, est l'Amérique*, by the same author.

An interesting account of these poor Japanese mariners is given by the American medical officer, Dr. Pickering, in his *Races of Man, and their Geographical Distribution.* According to Dr. Judd, an American missionary, who had previously had some communication with educated Japanese, these poor fellows were fishermen of the lowest class. Their boats resembled the flat-bottomed skiffs of New England. Dr. Pickering shows how naturally and almost inevitably a bark, carried away from Japan in a storm, would drift to the coast of Mexico or California.

of Marco Polo. Some writers have supposed that the Japanese also must have declined; but the hypothesis does not appear to be made out by the books and the other authorities which I have consulted.* The numerous facts which have been presented to the reader must have convinced him that the Oriental stagnation of Japan is of a different sort to that of any other Eastern nation; it seems rather to consist in advancing according to its own method or organization—the method alone being stagnant—for that was fashioned for them from the beginning.

It would but fatigue the reader to enter into any lengthy detail of Japanese history; a few points, however, may prove interesting to him, after having been made perfectly acquainted with the nature of the people, their manners and customs; for surely to give the history of nations before telling us what sort of people they are, how they live, and think, and feel, is little to the purpose of forming a right understanding of the subject.

Though pretending to a descent from the gods, and of course to a remote antiquity—like all the superior races of men—their writers are not so extravagant as are those of the Celestial Empire. Passing over the obscure times when the country was divided into clan or tribe governments, they fix the foundation of their monarchy, under Syn Mu, about the year before Christ 660. The Government was strictly hereditary and theocratical: Syn Mu was at once the high priest, or representative of the divinities, and King or Emperor of the people. He civilized the inhabitants of Japan, introduced chronology among them, dividing the time into years and months, and reformed the laws and government of the country. Having fully secured the throne to his posterity, and attained to the fabulous age of 156 years, he died full of

* A gentleman who is well acquainted with Von Siebold assures us that the impression on that able writer's mind is, that there has been rather progress than decline in the arts and civilization of Japan.—*MacFarlane.*

honour and sanctity. If there were troubles in the islands, they appear not to have been recorded; one theocrat quietly succeeding to another in their annals. But when the Empire was about two hundred years old, a civil war is first mentioned by their historians. For a long succession of years, nothing is chronicled but an occasional earthquake, volcanic eruption, meteoric phenomenon, comet, or fiery dragon, always excepting, however, great efforts made by Emperors and sages to discover the philosopher's stone, or the elixir vitæ, or some compound which should make the life of man immortal. In the same ages, and long after, the same fancies haunted the imaginations of the Emperors and philosophers of the Celestial Empire. From the East, the whim flew to Europe; and, as an old writer slily observes, the Europeans were not more unsuccessful than the Japanese in their pursuit of the means of transmuting metals and prolonging life.

In the nineteenth year of the reign of the Emperor Siunsin (B.C. 78) merchant ships and ships of war were first built in Japan; and under Siunsin's son and successor "it rained stars from heaven in Japan." It is also noted that in this same reign of Synin, the Japanese first began to make fishponds in their islands, and to cultivate rice-fields, and to inclose the same with ditches. This Emperor was on the throne at the time of our Saviour's birth, and also at the time of the Crucifixion.

These Emperor-theocrats, called in the language of the country Mikados, claimed to rule by divine right and inheritance. They were high priests as well as kings; they were held as representatives of the gods upon earth, and like gods they were worshipped. No subject ever addressed them except on his knees. They were thoroughly despotic; and even after they had ceased to head their own armies, and intrusted the military command to sons and kinsmen, their power long remained undisputed and uncontrolled. "Even to this day," says Kämpfer, "the princes descended from the family, more particularly those who sit on the throne, are looked upon as persons most holy in themselves, and as Popes by birth."

Passing over much that is uninteresting, we come to points which are curious as national coincidences, or otherwise noteworthy.

Singukogu was an Empress of great renown, who began her reign with the third century of the Christian era. She was the widow of the Emperor Sin Ai, and his blood relation in the fifth degree. She is described as an Amazon. She carried on war against the Coreans, and at the very beginning of her reign went over to that country with a numerous army, which she commanded in person. But, finding herself in an interesting situation, she hastened back to Japan, and was delivered of a son, who, in due course of time, succeeded her, and was so renowned a monarch that at his death he was honoured with the divine title of the "God of War." This Empress, according to the ancient annals, consulted by Kämpfer, reigned gloriously for the space of seventy years, and dying, in the hundredth year of her age, was placed by her grateful people among the gods and goddesses of the country.

It may be here noted that the Japanese bestow a marvellous longevity on all their good and great sovereigns. An age equal to that of Methusalem is by no means a rarity in their earlier mortal reigns. Their celestial kings reigned their millions of years.

Frequently allusions are made to the contemporary history of China, and there appears to have been, through a long series of years, a free and active intercourse between the two nations. Under the Emperor Kin Mei—a very religious prince, who reigned about the middle of the sixth century—there was a great importation of priests and idols from China, and the Buddhist worship was spread with great success in Japan. Abundance of idols, idol-carvers, and priests also came over from several other countries beyond sea. At the end of the sixth, and beginning of the seventh century, there was another female reign. In the sixth year of this Empress, some

A A

crows and peacocks were brought over from beyond sea
as presents to her.   " Both kinds of birds are still sub-
sisting, and the crows particularly multiplied to such a
degree that at present they do a great deal of mischief."
During her reign all Japan was shaken by earthquakes
in a dreadful manner, and vast numbers of buildings
were overthrown and swallowed up.   The next year after
these calamities, fire fell from heaven, and after that there
fell such a quantity of rain, that many towns were laid
under water.

About the end of the eighth century, a foreign people,
"who were not Chinese, but natives of some more distant
country," came over to invade Japan in a hostile manner.
The Japanese did what they could to get rid of them,
but as their losses in battle were constantly made up by
fresh recruits who arrived from beyond sea, this work was
very difficult, and the strangers were not entirely defeated
and dispersed till eighteen years after their first arrival.
Some have thought that these strangers proceeded from
the Malayan Peninsula, others that they came from the
Peninsula of Kamtschatka, or from Siberia and the
regions round the Baikal Lake.   Between the ninth and
twelfth centuries several new religions or idolatries are
mentioned as being introduced by foreign priests, or by
Japanese returning from foreign countries.   About the
year 987, the Emperor Quassan, a very young man, was
suddenly seized with such a desire of retirement and a
religious life, that he left his palace privately in the
night time, and retired into the lone monastery of Quansi,
where he changed his name, and caused his head to be
shaved like the rest of those monks or bonzes.   He
lived twenty-two years in this manner, and was only
forty years old when he died.   From various causes,
abdications of the throne were very frequent.   The historical reader will not fail to remember that it was just
about this period, during our " Middle Ages," that precisely the same sort of things came to pass in Europe.
And in other respects the curious coincidence holds good,
even if the precise year mentioned, A.D., 987 (the year

of *Hugh Capet's accession* to the throne of France) be
uncertain. For, we are told by the Japanese historians
that civil wars arose very prejudicial to the empire—
that the princes of the empire espoused different interests,
and these quarrels, or " wars of the Roses," seldom ended
but with the entire destruction of one of the contending
parties, followed by a cruel extermination of whole
families. It would appear, however, that these civil wars
in Japan were of rarer occurrence, and were waged with
far less ferocity than similar contests in the Celestial
Empire. We nowhere read of such wholesale massacres,
such suicides by thousands and tens of thousands at a
time, as cast so deep a shade of horror over Chinese
history.

In another respect, however, the historic parallel is
entirely at fault, but decidedly in favour of the Japanese
blood royal.

Horace Walpole might have swelled his catalogue of
royal authors from the annals of Japan. Several of the
emperors, while sitting on the prison-throne, or after
their abdication, wrote books. Nearly all of them en-
couraged letters, and such sciences as the country possessed. The reign of the Emperor Itsi Sio (987-1012)
was famed for a great epidemic and mortality all over
Japan, and for many eminent and learned men who then
flourished at court.

The Japanese have their legend of St. George and the
Dragon. Thus, under the Emperor Kon Jei (1142-56),
there lived Jorimassa, a prince of the blood, and another
Japanese Hercules. By the assistance of the God of
War, Jorimassa killed with his arrows the infernal
dragon *Nuge*, who had the head of a monkey, the tail of
a serpent, and the body and claws of a tiger. This
monstrous beast inhabited the emperor's own palace, and
was exceedingly troublesome, both to his sacred person
and to all his court, particularly in the night-time, making
very improper noises, and frightening them, and disturbing the poor courtiers out of their sleep. This is, of
course, a myth, upon the interpretation of which we

need hardly venture. The Japanese take the story in its natural, or rather, non-natural sense ; and they have many such. The same dragon-slayer, Jorimassa, bore an heroical part in the civil wars carried on between the four most powerful families of the empire, and was slain in battle, after which his whole family was extirpated. But these sharp executions did not put an end to the dissensions of the country. In fact, Japan seemed on the point of resolving herself into her primeval chaos—or that of a congeries of small independent states, with about as many princes and governors as there were provinces in the islands. The early Portuguese and Spanish writers, speaking of the state of the country in the old times, enumerate as many as sixty-six or sixty-eight principalities, or rather kingdoms, which all managed separately their own affairs, and did little more than acknowledge the nominal suzerainty of the *one* emperor. About the middle of the twelfth century, during the reign of the above-named emperor, Kon Jei, these provincial potentates formed confederacies hostile to the central government.

In this situation of affairs, the court thought it expedient to entrust the command of its entire army to the celebrated Yoritomo, a young soldier of high birth (he was a scion of the ancient imperial stock), very valorous, successful, and ambitious. He was the first that received the office and title of Siogoun, or generalissimo of the crown, as before related.* His widow was the valiant lady, honourably mentioned in a previous page, who had renounced the world, and became a Buddhist nun, but, after our own mediæval fashion, returned from her convent when required, and governed the empire for her son —Ama Siogoun, the Nun-General, as she is styled in the annals of Japan.

The conquest of China by the Mongol Tartars (A.D. 1260-81) carried alarm to Japan, and induced that cautious government to break off all intercourse with the Chinese. In the year 1268, the great Mongol conqueror,

---

* Page 70.

Kublai Khan, sent a letter and envoys to Niphon to call upon the Japanese emperor for his alliance, offensive and defensive, and to apprise him of the far-spreading power and the irresistibility of the Mongols. "I apprehend," said Kublai, "that the true state of things is not, as yet, well known and understood in your land, and therefore I send envoys with a letter, to acquaint you with my views. I hope we may understand each other. Already philosophers desire to see all mankind form one family. But how may this one-family principle be carried into effect if friendly intercourse subsist not between parties ? I am determined to call this principle into existence, even though I should be obliged to do so by force of arms. It is now the business of the *wang* (king) of Niphon to decide what course is most agreeable to him."

How much this missive of the Tartar reminds us of that other Tartar, Nicholas of Russia, in the matter of the Turks ! The Mikado and Siogoun refused to admit the envoys to an audience at court, and dismissed them without any answer to their great monarch's epistle. Two other missions dispatched by Kublai, one in the year 1271, and the other in 1273, were treated in precisely the same manner. The haughty conqueror then resorted to arms. In 1274* a Mongol-Chinese fleet and army, with a contingent drawn from a part of Corea which had been conquered by Kublai, appeared off the coast of Japan. But the Japanese had taken warning, and were well prepared. The Siogoun came down to the coast with an immense army, and the ecclesiastical emperor, in the quiet recesses of his palace, put up prayers to the gods, and appointed general prayer days to be observed throughout the empire. Some of the old Japanese annalists assert that the enemy merely ravaged a small part of the island of Kewsew, and then retreated in dismay and confusion ; but others affirm that the Mongols were defeated, with great loss, in a general action. According to Marco Polo, it was a terrible and pro-

---

* Marco Polo dates this expedition a few years earlier.

vidential storm that scattered this Tartar armada ; and, to keep up the parallel, it seems, according to Marco Polo, that the Effinghams and Drakes of Japan followed up the victory of the elements " in numerous boats" to make prisoners of the shipwrecked Tartars.*

Kublai Khan, however, would not forego his " one-family" principle. In the very next year he sent fresh envoys to Japan. This time the Tartars were admitted to the presence of the Siogoun, or crown general ; but the answer they got from him was not very satisfactory : " Henceforward no Mongol subject shall set foot upon this soil under pain of death." In spite of this warning, Kublai sent over some other ambassadors ; and the Japanese, firm in their resolution, cut off the head of every man of them !

Kublai Khan, who would not forego his " one-family" principle, sent another armada against Japan, in 1281, but with precisely the same result. The storm arose, and the sea swallowed up the invaders. God grant that every armada against Japan, as against England, may meet with the same disaster !

For the space of nearly a hundred years, during which the Mongols held dominion in China and the adjacent states, the Japanese would have no intercourse with any of them, enforcing the law of proscription and death which they had pronounced to the envoys of Kublai ; but when, in 1366, the Chinese dynasty of Ming expelled the Mongols, and re-established the ancient government, communications were re-opened both with China and Corea, and a commercial intercourse was renewed upon the old cautious conditions. It appears, however, that the number of annual junks from those countries was strictly limited ; that every vessel on her arrival in a Japanese port was subjected to a most rigid search, and that the foreigners were placed under strict surveillance during all the time that they remained in the country.

We trace in another succession of voluntary or forced

---

* *Travels of Marco Polo,* edited by William Marsden, p. 569 to p. 571.

abdications of the spiritual imperial crown, the growing
prepotency of the Siogouns who were then very efficient
and active rulers, and not the secluded, inactive princes
they now appear to be. Ever since the time of Yoritomo,
these high functionaries had, as we have noted, virtually
held the sovereign power. At last they possessed themselves of the name as well as the substance. The disturbed state of the country again called for a man of
action—a man of the sword. This was found in the
celebrated Taiko Sama, a soldier of fortune, who is said to
have raised himself merely by his courage and merit. The
spiritual emperor invented new titles for him, and entrusted
him not only with the supreme command of all the troops,
but also with the management of all the secular affairs of
the empire. About the year 1585, this Taiko Sama took
to himself the title of *Kubo*, or lord-general. He is considered as the first absolute secular monarch of Japan ;
that is, the first who assumed to himself the absolute
government of the empire, whereof the ecclesiastical
hereditary emperors had, till then, preserved some share.
Ever since that time, the Kubo, or secular monarch, has
continued almost entirely independent of the ecclesiastical
emperor, except in matters spiritual. The evils which
might have been expected from such a state of things do
not appear to have arisen. "From the close of the
sixteenth century, when the Japanese *Maire du Palais*,
Taiko Sama, separated the empire into its two lay and
spiritual divisions, civil war has ceased, the pageant of
government has been played on, without interruption, by
the two principal actors and their subordinates, and the
operations of the real executive have been continued with
all the regularity and precision of machinery. The
founder of these institutions must, surely, have been no
ordinary legislator. The sceptre which he wielded has,
indeed, become a bauble in the hands of his descendants,
for the Kubo, or lay emperor, equally with his spiritual
counterpart, wears out his life in one long dream of ideal
sovereignty ; and so profound and subtle is the spell of
habit, custom, and etiquette, which wraps them in that

charmed sleep, that it is impossible to anticipate the period of its dissolution, or the process by which it can be broken."*

Taiko Sama,† the most celebrated character in the annals of Japan, is represented to have been ill-favoured, if not absolutely ugly and repulsive in person. He was below the average height, and corpulent to excess ; but, withal, endowed with immense strength, extraordinary activity, and a spirit of daring beyond conception. On one hand he had six fingers ; his eyes were so prominent that they seemed ready to start from their sockets ; his chin was destitute of the appendage of a beard ; and his features altogether were of so singular a mould, that he obtained the unenviable cognomen of "The Ape." ‡ Yet these disadvantages were overcome by the high qualities of his mind. He commenced his career as a hewer and carrier of wood. From this menial occupation he was taken into the service of an officer attached to the court of Nobounanga, the Siogoun. In the capacity of a private soldier, he attracted the attention of the Siogoun, who had the reputation of being a shrewd judge of men. His advancement was rapid. At length he obtained a separate command, and in a short space of time was recognised as one of the most skilful generals of the empire. His patron, the Siogoun, now reaped the fruits of his discernment, and Taiko zealously strove to repay to his sovereign the favours he had received from him. It

---

* *Quarterly Review,* vol. lii. 1834.

† *Taiko Sama* was known by various names, viz :—1. *Toyotomo:* 2. *Toquixero;* 3. *Cicuquidono;* 4. *Faxiba;* " dont la signification," Charlevoix observes, "faisoit allusion aux armes ou quelque devise du Roi de Nanguto," who had been in rebellion, and was reduced to submission by Faxiba, on whom the Siogoun, Nobounanga, conferred the title. 5. *Quabaucondono,* which, by some writers, is said to mean " *The Lord of the Treasure.*" Captain Cook states (East India House MSS.), it is equivalent to the " *Cæsar*" of the Romans. 6. *Taiko Sama,* which signifies " *The Most High and Sovereign Lord.*"—Rundall's *Memorials.*

‡ According to Charlevoix. Titsingh says *Sarout Soma,* or " *Monkey Face.*"

was owing to his skill and valour that the cause of Nobounanga was maintained against a host of powerful opponents.
But, though powerful against hosts, Taiko was unable to
restrain private malice. Nobounanga fell beneath the
sabre or dagger of an assassin, leaving, as his successor,
a grandson, a youth possessed of little influence or talent.

Presently, on the death of Nobounanga, the most
disaffected, turbulent, and ambitious of the princes and
nobles of the land flew to arms, contending among themselves for the seat of power. For a time, anarchy
reigned; but at length, Taiko, who had been fighting
the battles of his late sovereign in a distant part of the
land, arrived, by a succession of rapid marches, at the
scene of action; and, falling suddenly on the contending
parties, put their forces to the rout. The leader of a
numerous and well-disciplined army, Taiko felt his power,
and installed himself the successor of Nobounanga.

The superiority of the Mikado was at first acknowledged
by the new Siogoun. After a few months he declared
himself independent and absolute. Irresistible in might
and skill, he crushed every attempt at opposition; and,
ruling the princes and nobles with a rod of iron, he reduced them to a state of abject submission. Adding
policy to force, he declared war against Corea, which, in
the lapse of ages, had regained its independence, and
despatched a force of 200,000 men for the conquest of
that country.

In this army the most dangerous characters in the empire
were absorbed. Few of the leaders returned to their native
land, and the few who did return were not in a condition
to excite any apprehension for the peace of the country.
So far successful, he proceeded to devise means by which
the restless spirits in the realm might be permanently
kept in subjection. The measures he adopted remain
part of the policy of Japan to the present day, and have
proved efficient.

As a legislator, as well as warrior and politician, Taiko
distinguished himself. He introduced laws which bear
the impress of great severity, but they were necessary to

meet the exigencies of the times, and were adapted to the temper of the people, which, at that period, whatever it may be now, is represented to have been "no less fiery and changeable, than the neighbouring sea is stormy and tempestuous."

Magnificence and profusion were two of the leading habits of this Siogoun ; but, as he taxed the aristocracy, and left the people unburthened with imposts, the plebeian part of his subjects were well content.

The renown of Taiko was not confined within the limits of the empire. It extended to China, and was acknowledged in Europe. His alliance was courted both by the Emperor of the Celestials and by the King of Spain.

In reply to the overtures of an ambassador despatched by the Viceroy of the Spanish Indies, the Siogoun gave the following brief account of his career :— "The kingdom of Japan," he said, "containeth above sixty states, or jurisdictions, which, from long time, had been sorely afflicted with internal broils and civil wars ; by reason that wicked men, traitors to their country, did conspire to deny obedience to their sovereign lord. Even in my youth did this matter grieve my spirit, and from early days I took counsel with myself how this people might best be made subject to order, and how peace might be restored to the kingdom. That so mighty a work might be brought about, I especially essayed to practise these three virtues which follow :—Therefore, I strove to render myself affable to all men, thereby to gain their good-will. I spared no pains to judge all things with prudence, and to comport myself with discretion ; nothing did I omit to do that might make men esteem me for valour of heart and fortitude of mind. Now, by these means have I gained the end I sought. All the kingdom is become as one, and is subject to my sole rule. I govern with mildness, that yields only to my energy as a conqueror. Most especially do I view with favour the tillers of the ground ; they it is by whom my kingdom is filled with abundance.

"Severe as I may be deemed, my severity is visited alone on those who stray into the ways of wickedness.

Thus hath it come to pass, that at this present time. peace universal reigns in the empire ; and in this tranquillity consisteth the strength of the realm. Like to a rock, which may not be shaken by any power of the adversary, is the condition of this vast monarchy under my rule."

Testimony to the merits of Taiko Sama is borne by Charlevoix ; and he derived his information entirely from Roman Catholic sources. In a style of admirable candour, the learned Jesuit gives the following review of this Siogoun's reign :—" Never," he says, " was Japan better ruled than under Taiko, and the condition of the country at that period affords a proof that the Japanese, as well as most other nations, only require to be subject to a man who knows how to govern, to conduct themselves peaceably and obediently. Vice was punished, virtue was rewarded, merit was acknowledged, and occupation was found for the restless, or they were coerced into quietness. Excepting the persecution of the Christians, in which, however, the emperor exhibited a degree of moderation hardly to be expected from a man of his character, no just complaint can be urged against his government. It is true, he was not an object of affection ; but he was feared and admired. Moreover, the traditions of the country seldom fail to do justice to the memory of a sovereign, whether meriting applause or reprobation. To the present day, the name of Taiko Sama is revered throughout Japan, and his actions continue to be the theme of admiration."[*]

The Lutheran Kämpfer is equally warm in his praise of this rare man—a warrior and a statesman suited to his country and to the times in which he lived.[†]

There have been some civil wars since this division of authority ; but, on the whole, Japan has enjoyed more tranquillity than ever it did before, and certainly more

---

[*] Charlevoix. *Nipon o Daï,* by Titsingh and Klaproth.
[†] *Memorials of the Empire of Japan in the Sixteenth and Seventeenth Centuries,* published by the Hakluyt Society. London: 1850.

internal peace and more uniformity of government than has been known by any European nation during the nearly three hundred years which have elapsed since 1585. One of the very latest of the Dutch writers conjectures that by a quarrel between the Siogoun and the Mikado, and by such an event alone, can any innovation or revolution ever take place in the existing political institutions of Japan.[*] He does not indicate the nature of the contingency which could produce the collision between the two rulers; but it is not difficult to conjecture various means by which such a collision might be brought about. The very peculiar system is indeed fenced in with innumerable laws, regulations, and precautions; but these may all be taken as indications of doubt and apprehension, if not as something very like proofs, that the Japanese grandees, governing under the emperors, are oppressed with the conviction of the frailty of the institutions. Suspicion and distrust must prevail through every link of the social chain, and the precautions against foreigners are said to be equalled by those adopted against innovation or disturbance within. Japan is a country filled with spies. A system of espionage extends itself throughout the empire, embracing not only every public functionary—including the Mikado and the Siogoun themselves—but every component part of society.[†]

Taiko Sama, who is still considered by the Japanese as one of their greatest heroes, is said to have contemplated

---

[*] J. F. Fisscher.

[†] There is, opposite the imperial palace at Jeddo, a square box, called *meyas fako*, or *zosio fako*, that is, "a box to receive complaints." Any one who thinks he has been deprived of his rights may put in his petition. It is opened once a year. There are similar boxes in all the principal cities: two officers constantly guard them. The governor opens these six times a year, and they serve to check the magistrates. Rarely more than two or three petitions are inserted during the year; which may arise from the fact that if the case be not proved, the petitioner or plaintiff has his head cut off after subjecting him to great indignities. Titsingh saw one of these executions at Jeddo.

the conquest of China, when his brilliant career, in 1598, was arrested by death. His son and successor highly favoured the Japanese Christians and their teachers, and was strenuously supported by the Jesuits in his contentions and wars with some refractory native princes and provincial chiefs. It was fully expected that the young man would openly profess Christianity ; but he was supplanted in the Siogounship by a near relative, from whom is lineally descended the emperor who now occupies the lay throne.

CHAPTER II.

THREE hundred years ! 'Tis a long time ago. But what a doleful meditation it must be for a nation which can look back through this vista of years and see herself at that epoch one of the greatest on earth—rolling in wealth, irresistible in power, spreading her conquests illimitably over the fairest provinces of the golden East— filling that terrestrial paradise with devastation and blood, utterly sacrificed to the unbridled lust and insatiate avarice of the adventurers led on by Vasco de Gama and the intrepid Albuquerque. It was the epoch when an Indian of Malabar exclaimed :—" Oh, divine Providence ! how well Thou hast done in merely sprinkling the earth with Portuguese as Thou hast with lions and tigers !"

About a month or two ago this nation, once so mighty, so omnipotent, was cruelly insulted—and with impunity —by an emperor, a man who, some ten years ago, was an adventurer in London !*

Three hundred years ago, then—it was in 1542—a Portuguese ship, bound for Macao, in China, was driven from her course, and dashed by a storm on one of the islands of Japan. That was the discovery of Japan by the Portuguese.

After great danger and much suffering, the ship came

* The Portuguese cruisers seized a French ship manifestly engaged in the slave trade, under the pretence of engaging free emigrants. The Emperor of the French ordered the King of Portugal to give up the ship and pay down an indemnity ; and the King of Portugal gave up the ship, and told the Emperor to name the sum, and he would pay it down, and so the matter ended. But *whose* turn will come next ?

safely to anchor in the harbour of Bungo, on the island of Kewsew. The Portuguese were received with courtesy and kindness, and freely allowed to traffic with the inhabitants. They were much, struck with the beauty, fertility, and high state of cultivation and populousness of the empire, and by the evident abundance of gold, silver, and copper. The honour of the first discovery of Japan, by the way of the Indies, is thus unquestionably due to the Portuguese, though it happened accidentally.

The first two of them who set foot on shore on this "unknown land" were named Antonio Mota and Francesco Zeimoto. The Japanese have preserved portraits of them, which are said to be very curious and characteristic specimens of native art. It is quite evident that their memory must have been cherished with affection, and that the first impression they made on the Japanese must have been highly favourable to their own nation.

From this time, by an arrangement with the prince or viceroy of Bungo, a Portuguese ship, laden with woollen cloths, furs, manufactured silks, taffetas, and other commodities in request, was sent once a year to the same island.

In 1548, only seven years after the discovery, a young Japanese fled to the Portuguese settlement of Goa, on the Malabar coast, and there meeting with some missionaries of the Church of Rome, he was converted to the Christian faith, and baptized. Like many of the Japanese, he was shrewd, intelligent, and enterprising. This is the same Paul honourably mentioned in a previous page. He showed the Portuguese merchants the great gains they might make by extending their commerce in Japan, and by supplying other provinces with their manufactures; and he discoursed with the Jesuits_ as to the facility or possibility of Christianizing his countrymen.[*]

At that time a Jesuit, subsequently canonized by his Church, St. Francis Xavier was filling the east and the

---

[*] There were two others with him. *Hi magna de Japaniâ promittunt*, says Xavier.—*Epist. Japan.*

west with the renown of his victories over Paganism—
his conversions to Christianity. Together with Paul, the
Japanese, he embarked on board a Chinese junk, and
after some accidents and perils of the deep, he reached
Japan, as he says, " in spite of the devil and his minis-
ters, in the month of August, on the Festival of the
Blessed Virgin, in the year 1549," and at the port of
Congazima.

This high-born Spaniard had all the accomplishments
and qualities most calculated to command success as a
missionary among a people like the Japanese ; and his
zeal and courage were never surpassed by mortal man.
Some of his friends at Goa endeavoured to turn him from
his project, by representing the great length of the
voyage—good thirteen hundred leagues—the great risk
of falling among Malay pirates, who pitilessly massacred
all the prisoners they took ; the dangers of the rocky
coasts of Japan, which had not been surveyed by any
mariner ; the dangers of whirlpools which were known
to exist there ; and the perils of those tremendous hurricanes called typhons, which prevail at certain seasons on
the ocean between Japan and China. But the ardent
propagandist said it were a shame that he should be
afraid to venture for the sake of religion where sailors
and merchants went for the mere love of worldly gain ;
that missionaries ought to have as much courage as they;
and he felt that it was the will of God that he should
go.* He went, and truly wondrous was the success
which attended him.

Xavier assures us that he was received with the greatest kindness by the governor of the city, that the people

* Père Bouhours, *Vie de Saint François Xavier, Apôtre des
Indes et du Japon.* Other interesting notices of the first proceedings
of the Christian missionaries in Japan will be found in the following
works:—Padre G. Marini, *Delle Missioni del Giapone,* &c. 4to. Roma,
1663; F. Luigi Frois, *Avvisi Nuovi del Giapone,* &c. Venezia, 1586 ;
and C. W. King, *Claims of Japan and Malaysia upon Christendom,
exhibited in Notes of Voyages made in* 1837, 2 vols. 8vo. New York,
1839. But nothing can equal Xavier's own account in the *Epistolæ
Japanicæ.*

wondered how a priest should come from so remote a
country to visit Japan ; but that they did not wonder at
the fact that Paul had changed his religion and embraced
Christianity, indeed they were very far from being
offended thereat ; they rather congratulated him on his
fortunate peregrinations in foreign lands, the sights he
must have seen ; and eagerly questioned him concerning
the usages, power, and possessions of the Portuguese in
India, all to the evident delight of the governor of
Congasima. "Paul had an image of the Blessed Virgin.
As soon as the governor saw it, he not only was much
pleased with it, but fell upon his knees and worshipped
it, and required the by-standers to do the same, and
showed it to his mother ; and as soon as she saw it she
was not less struck with it, and ordered one like it to
be made for her ; but as there was no artist there equal
to the work, it could not be done."*

Xavier congratulated himself that there were neither
scoffing Mahomedans nor sordid Jews in Japan, *non
Mauri nec Judœi incolunt ;* and he declared that he had
found no nation amongst the infidels which had pleased
him so much ; "men endowed with the best of dispositions, of excellent conduct, free from malice and gall."†

And the convert Paul, writing to the Fathers, informed
them that the Japanese believed in one God and a
Trinity ; that they had five commandments ; 1. Not to
kill ; 2. Not to steal ; 3. Not to commit fornication ;
4. Not to lie ; 5. To abstain from wine ; that they practised a baptism, which could not be omitted without
grievous sin ;‡ that the priests visited the sick and prepared them for death ; that they practised dreadful
macerations of the flesh, and mortifications or penance ;
that they practised public confession of sins, used "beads"
or a "rosary," and prayed in a foreign tongue, "as

* *Epist. Japan.*

† Optimis moribus conversationeque præditi sunt, expertes
malitiæ et fellis.—*Epist. Japan.*

‡ Si quis non lotus . . . . gravissimè peccatum esse credunt.—
Ibid.

B B

Catholics pray in Latin ;"* that they used the sign of the cross in the shape of the letter X ; that their monks took vows of chastity, poverty, and obedience, and had to undergo a probation before they were admitted into the order.†

It appears also to comprise the existence, death, and resurrection of a Saviour born of a virgin, with almost every other essential dogma of Christianity.‡ The fact is inexplicable, excepting on the supposition sometimes emitted by the Fathers, that such coincidences were the pre-contrivances of the devil to mock the true faith.

This religion bore so near a resemblance to the doctrines introduced by the Portuguese, that it must have greatly favoured their reception. Besides, there was no *one* established, dominant religion in the country ; the most ancient faith was split into sects ; and there were at least three other religions imported from foreign countries, and tolerated in the most perfect manner.

Then the pomp and impressive ceremonials of the Roman Church, and the frequency of its services, delighted the impressionable Japanese, who in all probability would have paid far less attention to a simpler form of worship.

* Quòd peregrinâ linguâ scripta sit, recitant, ut nos latinè. —*Epist. Japan.*

† *Epist. Japan.* p. 10 *et seq.* ed. 1570. I may remind the reader that all these practices are essential to Buddhism, one of the ancient religions of India—a religion which took its rise long before Christianity—and not derived, as the Jesuits pretended, from the Nestorians, a Christian sect said to have penetrated into the centre of Asia. See an excellent article on the subject by Alfred Maury in the *Encyclopédie Moderne,* " Bouddhisme."

‡ " If this be a true statement and correct description," adds a writer in the *Quarterly Review,* " and if we add to it the tradition that this form of religion was introduced under the reign of the Chinese emperor Mimti, who ascended the throne in about the fiftieth year of the Christian era, can we avoid admitting the conclusion that some early apostle reached the eastern extremity of Asia, if not the islands themselves of Japan."—Vol. xlii. 299. (November, 1834.) " We believe that there is other evidence to show that the doctrines of Christianity were conveyed to India in the first century after the death of our Saviour."—MacFarlane, *Japan.*

The first missionaries, moreover, were men of exemplary lives—modest, virtuous, disinterested, and most tender and charitable to the poor and afflicted. They sought out cases of distress ; they attended the sick ; and some knowledge they possessed of the superior science of medicine, as practised by the most advanced nations of Europe, was frequently of great benefit to the natives, and another means of facilitating their conversion.

The Portuguese—mariners, merchants, padres, and all— were received with open arms, not only at Bungo, but at whatsoever other part of the empire they chose to visit or live in. The local governments and the minor princes, who then enjoyed a considerable degree of independence, vied with each other in inviting them to their ports and towns. They went wherever they pleased, from one extremity of the empire to the other, and by land as well as by sea. The merchants found a ready and a most profitable market for their goods ; the missionaries an intellectual, tolerant people, very willing to listen to the lessons which they had to teach them.

Xavier quitted Japan for China in 1551, and died on the 2nd of December of the following year, at Shan-Shan, on the Canton river, not far from Macao ;* but he left able and enthusiastic missionaries behind him, and others soon repaired to the country.

It is said that the immediate successor of Xavier (he died in 1570) founded fifty churches, and baptized, with his own hands, more than 30,000 converts. These early

* " It is worthy of notice that poor Fernam Mendez Pinto, who by no means merits the very hard names bestowed upon him by a Spanish writer of romances, and an English writer of plays, performed several voyages with the fearless missionary Xavier. He records with great reverence many of the learned father's deeds and disputations with the Bonzes, or native priests. It was not his fortune to be present at Xavier's death.

" Not for the sake of my own humble performance, but for the sake of rescuing the fame of a brave, adventurous, and much-traduced sailor, I would recommend the reader to a short account of his life and adventures contained in my little book called the *Romance of Travel*, vol. ii. p. 104 to p. 192. "—MacFarlane, *Japan*.

missionaries are unanimous in their praise of the good, docile, kindly disposition of the natives ; and speak of them as eminently a grateful people. In one of his letters, the sainted Xavier says, " I know not when to have done when I speak of the Japanese. They are truly the delight of my heart."

The current of conversion, however, was not always smooth and unimpeded ; for, at this period of greatest success, we hear occasionally of a persecution, and, though less frequently, of an apostasy.

It was so much the more easy to the Portuguese to bring their trade into a flourishing condition, and at the same time to advance and support the conversion of the Japanese to the faith of our Saviour, as the neighbouring city of Macao, in China, which they were then already possessed of, could furnish them at command with a sufficient stock of European and Indian commodities, and a competent number of priests. Their co-religionists, the Spaniards, established at the city of Manilla, in the Philippine Islands, not very remote from Japan, were likewise at hand to assist them in case of need ; and the city of Goa itself, as the Rome of India, and the metropolis of all the Portuguese dominions in the East, though at a greater distance, yet could easily, and without prejudice to its own inhabitants, send over fresh recruits of ecclesiastics. Hence it is not matter of wonder that the Portuguese should, in a short time, attain to a high pitch of fortune in this insular empire.*

These local advantages and facilities of the Portuguese for any enterprise on the country were in themselves enough to awaken the jealousy of that Asiatic government ; but many years passed ere any such feeling disturbed the intercourse. Perhaps, however, the comparative weakness of the central government, and insubordination and almost independence of many of the provinces, promoted the interests of the strangers as much as any other circumstance or cause then in operation. It is evident, from some of the early missionaries,

* Kämpfer.

that several of the princes or viceroys paid no attention to the edicts of the emperor.*

About the year 1566, the Portuguese first pointed out to the prince of Omura the great advantages of the harbour of Nagasaki over the ports they had been accustomed to frequent. Their suggestions led to the formation of a settlement, which, ere long, became an important city, and which retains a somewhat unhappy celebrity down to our own day.†

The traders brought their cloths, silks, European stuffs, wines, drugs, medicines, and a great variety of other goods, and in return became possessed of "the golden marrow of the country." The missionaries had to struggle for some time with the difficulties of the language.

"At first, the fathers, being unacquainted with the policy, customs, manners, and language of the Japanese, were obliged to get their sermons and lessons to the people translated into Japanese by not over-skilful interpreters, and the Japanese words written in Latin characters, which being done, they read out of these papers what they did not understand themselves, and in a manner, as may be easily imagined, which could not but expose them to the laughter of the less serious part of their audience. But in process of time, when they came to familiarize themselves with the natives, learning their language, studying their religion, their customs, and inclinations, they then met with a success infinitely beyond their expectations. The number of converts, particularly upon the island of Kiusjú (Kewsew), where they first settled, was almost inconceivable, and this the rather, as the princes of Bungo, Arima, and Omura, did not only openly espouse the interest of the Christian religion, but were converted themselves, and baptized." ‡

* Fernam Mendez Pinto says that the emperor was recently dead, and that the Japanese were for some time engaged in a civil war.

† C. W. King, *Notes of the Voyage of the "Morrison" from Canton to Japan.* New York, 1839.

‡ Kämpfer. See also Arnold Montanus and the other early Dutch writers ; also Thunberg's travels.

The Jesuits, after giving them a careful education, admitted a good number of young natives into their Society.

The Japanese Christians even went so far as to send an embassy, consisting of seven persons, well furnished with letters and presents, to the city of Rome, there to do homage to Pope Gregory XIII., and to assure his holiness of their entire submission to his church. Being very long on their voyages and journeys, they did not reach the Eternal City until the year 1585, when they were present at the enthronization of Gregory's successor, Pope Sixtus V. Returning homewards, they did not reach Japan again until 1590, thus having been absent eight years from their country.* In the course of the two years which followed on their return (1591-2), no fewer than 12,000 Japanese are said to have been converted and baptized. It is even stated that the Emperor then reigning, with many of his courtiers and of the chiefs of his army, professed a strong inclination to the Jesuits, and the doctrines which they had taught with such signal success. Yet the heathen priests, who found that they were losing both their revenues and their influence with the people, had influence enough at court to procure a proclamation, forbidding, under pain of death, the practice or profession of the Christian religion; and there were occasional and fierce outbreaks of fanaticism and persecution. It should appear, however, that these were directed solely against the native converts, and that the Portuguese remained exempt from any serious molestation. Many of them married native ladies of the best families—of course baptized. The merchants in their trade, and the priests in the propagation of their gospel, prospered equally well. The three ports that were most used were Bungo, Firando, and Nagasaki. The gain upon the goods imported was at least cent. per cent., and their profits on the goods they exported were very high. It is

* An account of this remarkable embassy to Rome is given by Thuanus in his history.

confidently asserted that upwards of three hundred tons of gold, silver, and copper were exported every year; for at that period the Portuguese had full liberty to import and export whatsoever they pleased, without limitation as to quantity. They traded in fine large ships, the arrival of which was always held as a holiday by the natives. "It is believed," says the valuable old German writer, so frequently quoted, "that had the Portuguese enjoyed the trade to Japan but twenty years longer, upon the same footing as they did for some time, such riches would have been transported out of this Ophir to Macao, and there would have been such a plenty and flow of gold and silver in that town, as sacred writ mentions there was at Jerusalem in the time of Solomon."*

The Portuguese were at this period, with the exception of the Italians, as civilized a nation as any in Christendom; elegant in their attire and manners, fond of the arts and of music and poetry. Traces of their civilization are yet distinguishable among the upper classes of Japanese, curiously blended with the Chinese and Indian elements of civilization. Old Kämpfer, who loves to trace resemblances and affinities of races, says that there was a certain natural resemblance between the minds, dispositions, and inclinations of the Japanese and Portuguese, "both being born nearly under the same clime."

It is worthy of remark, that to English skill and courage, the Dutch owe *their* first access to Japan. The *Erasmus*, the first Dutch ship which ever reached that coast, in 1599, was piloted by William Adams, "a Kentish man, born in a town called Gillingham, two English miles from Rochester, and one mile from Chatham, where the Queen's ships do lie"—to use his own quaint and simple language. His skill in mathematics and the art of shipbuilding which he contrived to practise without ever having learnt it, procured him a long but honourable detention in Japan—a favourite of the Emperor—but in the midst of his honours and wealth yearning in vain to return home to his wife and dear children. "Thus," says

* Kämpfer.

this excellent man, concluding a letter, " I am constrained to write, hoping that, by one means or another, in process of time I shall hear of my wife and dear children : and so with patience I wait the good will and pleasure of God Almighty, desiring all those, to whom this my letter may come, to use the means to acquaint my good friends with it, that so my wife and children may hear of me ; by which means there may be hope that I may see my wife and children before my death : the which the Lord grant, to his glory and my comfort. *Amen.*"

He never had that comfort. Detained by the Emperor, he lived many years on the island, and there he died, at Firando, in 1619 or 1620. He deserves a high place in the list of the heroes of naval discovery and enterprise, and equally so among the diplomatists of commerce and civilization.*

The first Dutch factory, on a very humble scale, was established at Firando, where Adams breathed his last. Having in vain attempted to prevent its establishment, the Portuguese intrigued and laboured hard to bring about its destruction. The hatred between the two European nations was as irreconcileable as it was violent —no gust of passion, but a deep-welling perpetual hatred. If the Portuguese called the Dutch vile Lutherans, schismatics, accursed heretics ; the Dutch were always ready to retort by calling the Portuguese worshippers of wood and rotten bones, lying papists, foul idolaters. The religious animosities certainly led to many melancholy occurrences, and rendered it impossible that the two nations should live peaceably together in the same country ; but the Catholic writers are incorrect in asserting that it was owing to the malice of the Dutch that the missionaries of their church and their native converts were first subjected to Japanese persecution. That persecution had commenced before William Adams reached the country, and before the name of the Dutch was known

* Mr. MacFarlane (*Japan*, p. 13, *et seq.*) gives a long account of Adams. See also Harris's *Collection of Voyages*, i. 856, and Purchas, 688.

to the natives ; and it appears to have originated, in good part, from the enmities and dissensions which broke out among the different monastic orders in the East. If the work of Japanese conversion had been left wholly in the hands of those who began it and made so rapid and wonderful a progress in it, perhaps it is at least probable that there would have been no persecution at all, and that the great bulk of the population would have been brought within the pale of the Church of Rome. But the politic, wary, and accomplished Jesuits were soon far outnumbered by a host of Franciscan, Dominican, Augustine, and other friars, of more zeal than discretion, who flocked in from Goa, Malacca, Macao, and other Portuguese settlements, and who, instead of conciliating the Government and people, set their laws and usages at defiance. The Franciscans quarrelled with the Dominicans, and all the orders together quarrelled with the disciples of Loyola. There was then frequently exhibited the unseemly spectacle of one body of Christians intriguing with heathens against another, and what was scarcely more decorous, a Japanese convert labouring to reconcile these foreign Christian rivals.

The greatest vice of the Japanese is incontinence. It is hinted that the struggles of the missionaries to subdue this vice contributed very materially to the overthrow of their church. The princes and great men would not put away their numerous concubines—for them, the harem must go with the church. According to one account, it was the passion of love that led to the religious catastrophe. A prince (some say the emperor himself) became enamoured of a Christian lady, and was transported into fury at finding that the fair one would not conform to the old, easy customs of the country.

Orders were issued by the imperial court that no more friars or missionaries of any kind should be admitted into the country; and the Portuguese captains and traders were strictly commanded not to bring any more in their ships ; nevertheless, they continued to smuggle in fresh recruits of ecclesiastics. Certain Franciscan friars, who

came from the Spanish settlements in the Philippines,
formed processions, preached in the public streets of
Meako, and built a new church there, contrary to the
imperial edict, and contrary to the advice and earnest
entreaties of the Jesuit fathers. They had nothing to
plead in justification of their rashness but an ardent, impatient longing after the crown of martyrdom. In vain
the Jesuits urged that such conduct would prove in the
end not only fatal to their own persons, but highly prejudicial to the advancement of Christianity and the good
of the church. It was this indiscreet zeal that brought
on the first serious persecution in the year 1597, or three
years before Adams and the Dutch reached the country.
Japanese tradition concurs with the early Dutch writers
in representing the crisis as having been precipitated by
the pride, rapacity, and sensuality of the religious orders.
It is said that even the native converts were astonished,
and grew impatient, when they saw that their spiritual
fathers aimed not only at the salvation of their souls, but
had an eye also to their money and lands, and that their
pride was so great that they refused the prescribed marks
of respect to men of the highest hereditary rank. In the
same view, it is said that their growing riches and unexpected success in the propagation of the gospel wonderfully
inflated them ; that those who were at the head of the
clergy thought it beneath their dignity to walk on foot
any longer, in imitation of the apostles ; that nothing
would serve them but they must be carried about in
stately chairs, mimicking the pomp of the Pope and his
cardinals at Rome; that they not only put themselves
upon a footing of equality with the greatest men of the
empire, but, swelled with ecclesiastical pride, fancied that
even a superior rank was nothing but their due. As an
example, the following story is told, as a thing that happened in 1596, and led immediately to the great persecution. It chanced one day that a Portuguese bishop met
upon the high road one of the greatest officers of state,
who was on his way to court. The haughty prelate would
not allow his chair or sedan to be stopped, in order to

alight and pay his respects to the great man, according to the usages of the country, but, without showing him the common marks of civility, or taking the least notice of him, he turned his head aside in contempt, and ordered his bearers to carry him on. It is added, that so imprudent a step, at a time when the Portuguese had already lost the best part of that esteem and favour in which they had formerly been held, could not but be attended with fatal consequences, highly prejudicial to the interest of the whole nation; that the grandee, exasperated at the affront, conceived a mortal hatred to the Portuguese, and forthwith drew to the emperor an odious picture of their vanity, pride, and insolency.*

Such an incident may really have happened, and there may have been individual cases of rapacity and sensuality. We may doubt, however, that these vices were at all common or prevalent among the missionaries.

"These vices are usually the attendants of long and undisputed possession rather than of the circumstances in which these missionaries of a religion struggling into life were placed. It is likely that the hostility of the Dutch rivals may have magnified individual instances of such errors, and that the zeal of triumphant persecution may have perpetuated the imputation."†

Father Trigaut, the Jesuit, makes a striking remark with reference to the causes of the persecution. He says:—"It is a strange thing to see how much the life of the Christians offend the Japanese, even the idolaters, if it does not correspond with the sanctity of their law, although they do not appear to see their own abominable sins."‡

The whole of the preceding account of causes which led to the persecution is what appears in all the Protestant versions of the matter. One of them appears in the Catholic version, but it is really very difficult to see the

---

* Kämpfer. He here follows Arnold Montanus and other early Dutch writers and compilers.

† *Quarterly Review,* vol. lii.

‡ *De Christ. apud Jap. Triump.*

cogency of the causes as detailed in the Jesuit narratives excepting some acts of violence perpetrated by the Spaniards.

But the oddest fact recorded, as a cause, is nothing less than that it was an *Englishman* who, possessed of the devil, and being asked whence and why he came, declared that he came from England, where he had remained for many years teaching the heretics to persecute the Catholics; and that he had come for the purpose of inducing the pagan Japanese to persecute the Christians of Japan: it was by the suggestions of this " doctor"—of divinity, I suppose—that the tyrant was led to persecute the Christians.*

For my own part, I believe that governmental suspicion, a policy suggested by the growing influence of foreigners in Japan, was the true cause of the persecution; subsequently aggravated, as usual, by resistance on the part of the converts.

In 1597, twenty-six professing Christians were executed on the cross, there being in the number one or two Jesuits and several Franciscan friars. But most of them appear to have been native converts. The friars flew out too violently against idol-worship. Their neophytes, with all the zeal of a recent conversion, not only told their countrymen that so long as they continued their heathen worship they had nothing to expect but eternal damnation; but they even proceeded to insult the bonzes or priests, to overthrow their idols, and to pull down their temples. This provoked further persecution. The emperor, and his hitherto tolerant government, could see in these demonstrations nothing but an intention to revolutionize the whole state.

In the year 1612, when Adams was living tranquilly at Firando, and when the Dutch were as yet only beginning to establish their influence, a dreadful persecution commenced. It raged with still greater fury in 1614, when many of the Japanese converts, who would on no account recant, suffered cruel deaths. The monks and

---

* *De Christ. apud Jap. Triump.*

friars were scattered; many left the country; but, apparently, as many more either concealed themselves, or returned stealthily.

The crosses they had erected were cast down and trampled under foot; their schools were closed; their churches razed to the ground; their faith was declared infamous, subversive of all ancient institutions, and of all authority and government.

For a long time the persecution did not reach the Portuguese merchants and traders. The Japanese could not dispense with the foreign commodities they brought them, and the Dutch trade was not sufficiently developed to promise a regular supply. But as they continued to smuggle in missionaries, the Portuguese were no longer allowed the free use of the ports, but were strictly limited to, and confined in, the little islet of Desima, in the harbour of Nagasaki. In the year 1622 a frightful massacre of native Christians and some of their foreign teachers was perpetrated on a rock in the immediate neighbourhood of that place. The Jesuit father Spinola, a Dominican friar, and a Franciscan, were in the number of those who suffered, having been convicted of returning to the country after the emperor had decreed their perpetual expulsion. Horrible tortures were employed, of which harrowing and revolting representations are given in the illustrations of the books of several of the old Dutch and Jesuit writers. Decapitation was the most merciful. The Christians were burnt to death; immersed in boiling-water from the hot-springs; beaten to death with clubs; suspended from the branch of a tree head downwards; crucified and speared; swung under a beam, feet and hands tied together over the back; their legs compressed between two blocks of wood, on which men trampled; hacked to pieces by bits at a blow; and finding that the means as yet employed had little effect upon the missionaries and their native assistants, a new and more effectual, because more protracted, torture was invented—the *Torment of the Fosse*.

A hole was dug in the ground, over which a gallows

was erected. From this gallows the sufferer, swathed in bandages, was suspended by his feet, being lowered for half his length, head downward, into the hole, which was then closed by two boards, which fitted together around the victim so as to exclude the light and air. One hand was bound behind the back, the other was left loose, with which to make the prescribed signal of recantation and renunciation of the foreign creed; in which case, the sufferer was at once released.

This was a most terrible trial indeed. The victim suffered under a continual sense of suffocation; the blood burst from the mouth, nose, and ears, with a twitching of the nerves and muscles, attended by the most intolerable pains. Yet the sufferer, it was said, lived sometimes for nine or ten days. It was by this dreadful tortue that the Jesuit, Ferreyra, before mentioned, was forced to yield and betray his companions.[*] There were other expedients resorted to; the modesty of women was brutally outraged. But enough as to the means employed by the Japanese government to root out Christianity—means so hideous, that we almost conclude that the rulers of Japan are a different race to the people.[†] The heroic constancy of the poor Japanese to the faith which they had embraced is an indubitable historical fact, attested as well by the Lutheran or Calvinist Dutch as by the Portuguese and other Catholics.

Considering the immense spread of Christianity in Japan—and the fact seems scarcely to admit of a doubt—coupled with the evident tenacity of the people, their fortitude, which equalled that of the earliest martyrs of the Christian faith—a surmise lurks in the mind that their

---

[*] In the *De Christianis apud Japonios Triumphis*, by Trigaut, the reader will find engravings of these horrible tortures.

[†] It was in this year, 1622, that the Dutch disgraced themselves in the Molucca islands, by that dark deed, which is known in our history under the name of "The Massacre of Amboyna." They put eighteen Englishmen to the rack, and afterwards cut off the heads of nine of them. One Portuguese and nine Japanese were put to death at the same time, as accomplices with the English.—MacFarlane.

religion could not have been utterly exterminated—
unless, indeed, we infer that this inconceivable endurance
under the most atrocious torments was but part and
parcel of the national character, and by no means indicative of the faith or the hope that was in them.   In
truth, judging merely on natural grounds, we feel disposed to believe that Japanese Christianity could scarcely
have been much more than Buddhism under a different
name.   Experience proves that where two sects
amongst us are similar in form or formalities, their
members mix and blend without scruple, in habitual
communion.   We shall probably now be in a position to
discover whether any permanent effect was produced
by the Christianity of the Japanese before it was proscribed two hundred years ago.   We do not read of any
affectionate or grateful remembrance of the missionaries.
Not a single writer speaks of anything of the sort ; on
the contrary, it would seem that the mass of the people
has entirely forgotten the event, or look upon the introduction of Christianity as a national calamity.   According to the Russian Golownin, it should seem that
the thinking portion of the people lament two evils,
brought upon them by the missionaries, their faith and
the use of tobacco !   I know not what reliance is to be
placed on this Russian's statement—I hope he speaks
falsely.   Here are his words :—

" Tobacco is an article which is equally indispensable to
the Japanese.   The Catholic missionaries were the first
who introduced this plant, and taught them its use.
From them, too, the Japanese received its name, and
still call it tobacco, or tabago.   It is astonishing how the
use of this *worthless herb* should have spread, in so short
a time, over the whole earth ; as it is entirely without
taste, without any agreeable smell, without use to the
health, and a mere amusement for idle people !   Our
interpreter, Teske, one of the most sensible of our Japanese
acquaintances, was himself a great smoker, but often said,
that the Christian priests had not done the Japanese
so much injury by the introduction of their faith, which

only produced among them internal commotions and civil wars, as by the introduction of tobacco; for the former was a transitory, long-forgotten evil, but the latter diverted, and probably would divert for centuries to come, large tracts of land and a number of hands from the production of useful and necessary articles, which are now dear, but might otherwise be cheaper. Besides, the workmen could not then so often interrupt their labour, but now they were continually resting themselves in order to smoke their pipes."*

At this time the power and consideration of the Por-

---

* *Recollections of Japan.* He adds, " I do not know how many species of this plant there are in nature, nor how many of them the Japanese have ; but I saw various kinds of prepared tobacco among them—from the most pleasant to the most disgusting. They cut both the good and the bad tobacco very small, as the Chinese do. In the manufacture of the better sort they use saki to moisten it, and sell it in papers which weigh about a Russian pound. The Japanese consider the tobacco from Sasuma as the best, then that from Nagasaki, Sinday, &c. The worst comes from the province of Tgyngaru ; it is strong, of a black colour, and has a disgusting taste and smell. The tobacco from Sasuma is, indeed, also strong, but it has an agreeable taste and smell, and is of a bright yellow colour. The tobacco from Nagasaki is very weak in taste and smell, perhaps the best, and of a bright brown colour. The tobacco from Sinday is very good, and was always given us to smoke. The Japanese manufacture tobacco so well, that though I was before no friend to smoking, and even when I was at Jamaica, could but seldom persuade myself to smoke an Havannah cigar, yet I smoked the Japanese tobacco very frequently, and with great pleasure. Snuff is not used in Japan. But enough of this plant. I could, indeed, for the pleasure of gentlemen who love smoking, write some sheets more on the article tobacco, for there was nothing concerning which we had such frequent opportunities to converse with the Japanese. The literati, the interpreters, and guards, all smoked ; and used, too, different kinds of tobacco, according to their respective taste or ability. Out of politeness, they frequently offered us their tobacco, and mentioned its name. In this manner a conversation usually began upon tobacco, which often lasted for hours together. We often had an opportunity to speak of other more important things, but the Japanese did not all like to converse upon them." But there is much worse smoking than tobacco-smoking. There is reason to fear that the Japanese are as much addicted to the opium-pipe as either the Chinese or the Malays, the Siamese or the people of An-

tuguese in the East was rapidly declining in all directions ; the splendid Indian empire, which the great Albuquerque had created for them, was falling to pieces ; the Dutch were dispossessing them of Ceylon and other rich settlements, and gradually obtaining nearly all the profitable trade which they had monopolized for nearly a hundred years. To blacken the Dutch in Japan, and drive them from that trade, they now represented them to the Emperor and Government as rebels to their former sovereigns, the kings of Spain—always a weighty argument in a despotic country—they renewed the accusations of robbery and piracy, which they had made on Adams's first arrival, and they resorted to every calumny that commercial and national jealousy and sectarian and personal hatred could suggest.* We have cleared the Dutch from unfounded aspersions ; but we now reach a point where their conduct is proved to have been of a nature to excite feelings very unfavourable to them. Few will agree with Kämpfer, who says that, " surely the Dutch were not much to be blamed for whatever attempts they made to keep up their own credit, to clear themselves of the calumnies of the Portuguese, and, withal, to take

nam. This vile habit is destructive of health, both mental and bodily."—MacFarlane.

I do not believe that the *use* of tobacco is injurious to man,—the damage of this use to his pocket is a different question, with which " the weed" has nothing to do ; but when a nation takes to opium-smoking or opium-consumption in any way as a "luxury," it is the beginning of downfall, or rather it is already indicative of an ending. We are assured that there exists in Paris a society called *Opiophiles*, who keep a journal in which the members must record the feelings and fancies they experience during the operation of the fumes of opium habitually smoked. We are also assured that opium-smoking has begun in Great Britain—in London to wit—and that the consumption of the drug is on the increase. In 1850 the importation was 103,718lbs. ; in 1851, 118,915lbs. ; in 1852, 250,790lbs.— Tiedemann, *Geschichte des Tabaks*, 418.

* Every old writer, being a member of the Roman Church, seems to have considered himself in duty bound to keep up the charge of *piracy*. The Père Bouhours, in his life of St. Francis Xavier, and Père d'Orléans, in his life of the missionary and martyr Spinola, never mention either English or Dutch except as *pirates*.

C C

what revenge they could upon their enemies." Even Kämpfer himself, like an honest man, afterwards condemns what he here excuses or extenuates.

The Dutch captured a Portuguese ship, and alleged that certain treasonable letters, which they produced to the Japanese authorities, were found on board ; these implicated a native and the Jesuits in a conspiracy to overturn the government by aid of ships and soldiers promised from Portugal. The Jesuits utterly denied the fact, declared that the letters were forgeries, as did the native concerned, but all in vain. Poor Moro, the native Christian, was burned alive, and in the course of the year 1637 an imperial proclamation was issued, decreeing that "the whole race of the Portuguese, with their mothers, nurses, and whatever belongs to them, shall be banished for ever," and definitively laid down those stringent laws against all intercourse with foreigners, as against the Christian religion, which have endured to the present time.

Some of the Portuguese were scared away at once ; but others lingered in their narrow factory or prison at Desima, hoping that the wrath would blow over, and that they might yet be allowed at least a little traffic. But the emperor was resolved to get rid of them entirely ; and on the assurance of the Dutch that they would regularly supply the country with the goods and commodities required, he again declared the Portuguese enemies of the empire and forbade them for ever to import even the goods of their own country.*

Thus the Portuguese lost their profitable trade with Japan, and they were totally expelled the country before the close of the year 1639. They accused the Dutch as the chief cause of their expulsion, and it is not easy to see how the charge can be either denied or doubted.

But worse followed. The Portuguese were rivals in commerce, and in every way implacable enemies ; they would fain have done to the Dutch that which the

---

* The imperial palate must have acquired a taste for port and sherry (no bad drinks in a cold Japanese winter), for the wines of Portugal and Spain were excepted in the prohibition.

Dutch succeeded in doing to them; but the poor Christian natives stood in no such position of rivalry, hatred, and unappeasable hostility.

Though deprived of their padres, or European teachers, and though menaced, not only with imprisonment, but also with torture and death, the converts persevered in their faith. Oppression drove them into open rebellion, and they took refuge, and made an heroical stand against the troops of the emperor, in the province of Simabara. The imperial government called upon the Dutch to assist them in their war against these Christians, and the Dutch promptly gave the aid required of them. The fact is admitted by all their own countrymen who have written about Japan, from their first writers in the middle of the seventeenth century, down to the year 1833. M. Fisscher, the very last on the list, says that the Dutch were *compelled* to join in the persecution against the stubborn remnant of that Christian host. Others would soften the matter by saying that the Dutch *only* supplied the heathen Japanese with gunpowder and guns, taught them a little artillery practice, and sent ammunition, arms, and troops in their ships to the scene of action. But Kämpfer, who was only a German in the Dutch service, most distinctly and positively assures us that the Christian traders acted as auxiliaries and belligerents. The stronghold of the native Christians was an old fortified place, which the emperor's troops could not take.

A recent writer, a right-hearted and right-minded American, says—" The walls of Simabara were unquestionably battered by the Dutch cannon, and its brave defenders were slaughtered. Some apology might be made for this co-operation at the siege of Simabara, had the defenders been the countrymen of Alva, or Requesens, or John of Austria, or Alexander Farnese. But truth requires that the measures of Kockebecker should be regarded as the alternative, which he deliberately preferred to the interruption of the Dutch trade."*

* C. W. King, *Notes of the Voyage of the " Morrison,"* &c.

It appears that the siege was converted into a long and close blockade, and that when the indomitable converts of Xavier were reduced and in good part exterminated by famine, a storm and an atrocious massacre ensued, none being spared, because none would recant and beg quarter; but men, women, and children being all butchered in heaps. In this war of religion, according to the most moderate estimate, there fell on both sides 40,000 men. According to the Catholics, the number of native Christians alone was far greater than this, and all the atrocities and horrors of the Diocletian persecution were repeated, exaggerated, and prolonged. The magnitude of the holocaust does indeed afford some measure of the depth and tenacity with which Christianity, in its Roman form, had struck its roots into the soil.

Over the vast common grave of the martyrs the Japanese Government set up this impious inscription :—" So long as the sun shall warm the earth, let no Christian be so bold as to come to Japan ; and let all know, that the King of Spain himself, or the Christians' God, or the great God of all, if he violate this command, shall pay for it with his head."

The Dutch were very far from deriving all the benefits they expected from their intrigues and mean compliances ; they never attained to the consideration and liberty in the islands which had been enjoyed by the Portuguese ; and they may be said to be, even at this moment, a despised set of traffickers.

Listen to the terrible words of honest old Kämpfer, the historian of Japan :—

" By this submissive readiness to assist the emperor in the execution of his designs, with regard to the final destruction of Christianity in his dominions, it is true, indeed, that we stood our ground so far as to maintain ourselves in the country, and to be permitted to carry on our trade, although the court had then some thoughts of a total exclusion of all foreigners whatsoever. But many generous and noble persons, at court and in the country, judged unfavourably of our conduct. It seemed to them inconsistent with reason that the Dutch should ever be expected to be faithful to a foreign monarch, and one, too, whom they look upon as a heathen, whilst they showed so much forwardness to assist him in the destruction of a people with whom they agreed in the most essential parts of their faith (as the Japanese had been well informed by the Portuguese monks), and to sacrifice to their own worldly interest those who followed Christ in the very same way, and hoped to enter the kingdom of heaven through the same gate. These are expressions which I have often heard from the natives, when the conversation happened to turn upon this mournful subject. In short, by our humble complaisance and connivance, we were so far from bringing this proud and jealous nation to any greater confidence, or more intimate friendship, that, on the contrary, their jealousy and mistrust seemed to increase from that time. They both hated and despised us for what we had done. In the year 1641, soon after the total expulsion of the Portuguese, and the suppression of Christianity among the natives, we were ordered to quit our comfortable factory at Firando, and to confine ourselves, under a very rigid inspection, to the small islet of Desima, which is more like a prison than a factory. So great was the covetousness of the Dutch, and so strong the alluring power of the Japanese gold, that rather than quit the prospect of a trade (indeed most advantageous) they willingly underwent an almost perpetual imprisonment—for such in fact is our residence at Desima—and chose to suffer many hardships in a foreign and heathen country, to be remiss in performing divine service on Sundays and solemn festivals, to leave off praying and singing of psalms, entirely to avoid the sign of the cross, the calling upon the name of Christ in presence of the natives, and all the outer signs of Christianity; and, lastly, patiently and submissively to bear the abusive and injurious behaviour of these proud infidels towards us, than which nothing can be offered more shocking to a generous and noble mind.

" The poor Japanese people, sociable in their dispositions,

and with no antipathy to foreigners, visibly regret all these harsh regulations, but dare not transgress the letter of the law, or give offence to their Government."

The ill-meant, mocking, impious jests of Voltaire, as to the Dutch going through the ceremony of trampling on crosses and crucifixes, may not have been, at every period, quite destitute of truth. As Lutherans or Presbyterians, they may have entertained no more reverence for crosses and crucifixes, and images of saints, than was felt by our English Puritans, who, in the days of their prepotency, found a rude delight in destroying such articles, and treating them with every imaginable disrespect.* The Portuguese, when driven to despair through their hated rivals, nearly involved the Dutch in their own ruin by announcing to the Imperial Government that they were Christians like themselves. It behoved the Dutch to convince the Japanese that there was the widest difference between them ; that they belonged to a sect quite hostile to that of the Portuguese ; that they hated Pope, Jesuits, Franciscans, Dominicans, and all manner of monks and priests. We can, therefore, easily credit that, if put by the Japanese Government to that test, the Dutchman would not much scruple to trample upon the cross in the manner described by Voltaire. A bigoted Presbyterian would even find a pleasure in so doing.† Indeed, after any lengthened residence in the country, such religion as these Dutchmen carried with them must have almost wholly evaporated. The life led in their prison at Nagasaki was little calculated to foster devotional feelings. Kämpfer says that in

---

* We ourselves once met in the island of Sicily a fanatical Presbyterian skipper, who wanted to pull down and burn all the crosses in the country, and who could never pass a wooden cross by the roadside without committing some assault upon it. He was a disagreeable and dangerous travelling companion, for his conduct greatly enraged the country people, and might have led to very serious consequences.—MacFarlane.

† The Russian officer Golownin and the companions of his Japanese captivity found it expedient to deny, over and over again, that they followed the same religion, and exercised the same rites, as the Portuguese and Spaniards.

his time they lived like a set of heathens,—that the principles of Christianity were so little conspicuous in their
lives and actions, that the Japanese were absurd in fearing
that they would attempt the conversion of the heathens.
But good and religious men have gone through this ordeal
without any detriment to their faith or to their morals;
so let not these remarks be taken as uncharitable, or as
disrespectful to the Dutch.

The precautions to which the Dutch have to conform
are not the least curious features of the Japanese character and Dutch endurance for the sake of commerce.
We have no reason to doubt that they have been altered
since the time of Thunberg's visit, who thus describes
them ;—some may concern us in our coming intercourse
with Japan :—

" Custom-houses are not known, either in the interior
of the country or on its coasts, and no customs are demanded on imports or exports of goods, either from
strangers or natives. But, that no prohibited goods may
be smuggled into the country, so close a watch is kept,
and all persons that arrive, as well as merchandize, are
so strictly searched, that the hundred eyes of Argus might
be said to be employed on this occasion. When any
European goes ashore, he is first searched on board, and
afterwards as soon as he comes on shore. Both these
searches are very strict ; so that not only travellers'
pockets are turned inside out, but the officers' hands pass
along their bodies and thighs. All the Japanese that go
on board of ship, are in like manner searched, excepting
only the superior orders of banjoses. All articles exported or imported undergo a similar search, first on
board the ship, and afterwards in the factory, except
large chests, which are emptied in the factory, and are so
narrowly examined, that they even sound the boards,
suspecting them to be hollow. The beds are frequently
ripped open, and the feathers turned over. Iron spikes
are thrust into the butter-tubs and jars of sweetmeats.
In the cheese a square hole is cut, in which part a thick-
pointed wire is thrust into it towards every side. Nay,

their suspicion went even so far as to induce them to take an egg or two from among those we had brought from Batavia, and break them. The same severe conduct is observed when any one goes from the factory to the ship, or into the town of Nagasaki, and from thence to the island of Desima. Every one that passes must take his watch out of his pocket, and show it to the officers, who always mark it down whenever it is carried in or out. Sometimes, too, strangers are searched. Neither money nor coin must, by any means, be brought in by private persons; but they are laid by, and taken care of till the owner's departure. No letters to be sent to or from the ship sealed; and if they are, they are opened, and sometimes, as well as other manuscripts, must be read by the interpreters. Religious books, especially if they are adorned with cuts, are very dangerous to import; but the Europeans are otherwise suffered to carry in a great number of books for their own use; and the search was less strict in this respect, as they looked into a few of them only. Latin, French, Swedish, and German books and manuscripts pass the more easily, as the interpreters do not understand them. Arms, it is true, are not allowed to be carried into the country; nevertheless, we are as yet suffered to take our swords with us.

" The Dutch themselves are the occasion of these over-rigorous searches, the strictness of which has been augmented on several different occasions, till it has arrived at its present height. Numerous artifices have been applied to the purpose of bringing goods into the factory by stealth; and the interpreters, who heretofore had never been searched, used to carry contraband goods by degrees, and in small parcels, to the town, where they sold for ready money. To this may be added, the pride which some of the weaker-minded officers in the Dutch service very imprudently exhibited to the Japanese, by ill-timed contradictions, contemptuous behaviour, scornful looks and laughter, which is greatly increased upon observing in how unfriendly and unmannerly a style they usually behave to each other, and the brutal treatment which the sailors under their command frequently experienced from them, together with the oaths, curses, and blows with which the poor fellows are assailed by them. All these circumstances have induced the Japanese, from year to year, to curtail more and more the liberties of the Dutch merchants, and to search them more strictly than ever ; so that now, with all their finesse and artifice, they are hardly able to throw dust in the eyes of so vigilant a nation as this.

"Within the water-gate of Desima, when anything is to be exported or imported, are seated the head and under banjoses, and interpreters, before whose eyes the whole undergoes a strict search. And that the Europeans may not scrape an acquaintance with the searchers, they are changed so often that no opportunity is given them.

"This puts a stop to illicit commerce only, but not to private trade, as everybody is at liberty to carry in whatever he can dispose of, or there is a demand for, and even such articles as are not allowed to be uttered for sale, so that it be not done secretly. The camphire of Sumatra, and tortoiseshell, private persons are not permitted to deal in, because the Company reserve that traffic to themselves. The reason why private persons prefer the smuggling of such articles as are forbidden to be disposed of by auction, is, that they do not receive ready money for them, but are obliged to take other articles in payment; but when the commodities can be disposed of underhand, they get gold coin, and are often paid twice as much as they would have had otherwise.

"Some years ago, when smuggling was still in a flourishing state, the greater part of the contraband wares was carried by the interpreters from the factory into the town ; but sometimes they were thrown over the wall of Desima, and received by boats ordered out for that purpose. Several of the interpreters, and other Japanese, have been caught at various times in the fact, and punished with death.

"Smuggling has always been attended with severe punishments ; and even the Dutch have been very largely fined, which fine has of late been augmented ; so that if any European is taken in the fact, he is obliged to pay 200 catties of copper, and is banished the country for ever.   Besides this, a deduction of 10,000 catties of copper is made from the Company's account ; and if the fraud is discovered after the ship has left the harbour, the chief and the captain are fined 200 catties each.

"The Company's wares do not undergo any search at all, but are directly carried to the storehouse, on which the Japanese fix their seal, where they are kept till they are sold and fetched away.

"The interpreters are natives of Japan, and speak with more or less accuracy the Dutch language.   The Government permits no foreigners to learn their language, in order that, by means of it, they may pick up any knowledge of the country ; but allow from forty to fifty interpreters, who are to serve the Dutch in their factory with respect to their commerce, and on other occasions. These interpreters are divided into three classes.   The oldest, who speak the Dutch language best, are called head-interpreters ; those who are less perfect, under-interpreters ; and those who stand more in need of instruction, bear the denomination of apprentices or learners. Formerly the Japanese apprentices were instructed by the Dutch themselves in their language, but now they are taught by the elder interpreters.   The apprentices had also, before this, liberty to come to the factory whenever they chose ; but now they are only suffered to come when they are on actual service.   The interpreters rise gradually and in rotation to preferments and emoluments, without being employed in any other department. Their duty and employment consist in being present— generally one, or sometimes two of each class—when any affairs are transacted between the Japanese and Dutch, whether commercial or otherwise.   They interpret either *vivâ voce,* or in writing whenever any matter is to be laid before the governor, the officers, or others, whether it be a complaint or request.   They are obliged to be present at all searches, as well at those that are made on board ship as at those which take place at the factory, and likewise to attend in the journey to court. They were formerly allowed to go whenever they chose to the Dutchmen's apartments ; but now this is prohibited, in order to prevent smuggling, excepting on certain occasions. They are always accompanied, as well to the ships as to their college in the island of Desima, by several clerks, who take an account of everything that is shipped or unloaded, write permits, and perform other offices of a similar nature.

" Kambang money, or the sums due for goods that are sold, is never paid in hard cash, as the carrying it out of the country is prohibited ; but there is an assignment made on it, and bills are drawn for such a sum as will be requisite for the whole year's supply, as also for as much as will be wanted at the island fair. This kambang money is, in the common phrase of the country, very light, and less in value than specie, so that, with the money which is thus assigned over, one is obliged to pay nearly double for everything. All these kambang bills are paid at the Japanese new-year only. Every man's account is made out before the ship sails, and is presented and accepted at the college of the interpreters, after which the books are closed. All that is wanted after the new-year is taken up upon credit for the whole year ensuing.

" The 18th of February is, with the Japanese, the last day of the year. On this day all accounts between private persons are to be closed, and these, as well as all other debts, to be paid. Fresh credit is afterwards given till the month of June, when there must be a settlement again. Among the Japanese, as well as in China, in case of loans, very high interest is frequently paid—from eighteen to twenty per cent. I was informed that if a man did not take care to be paid before new-year's day, he had afterwards no right to demand payment on the new year.

" When the Dutch do not deal for ready money, their commerce can hardly be considered in any other light than that of barter. With this view, a fair is kept on the island, about a fortnight before the mustering of the ship, and its departure for Papenberg, a small island near the entrance of the harbour, when certain merchants, with the consent of the governor, and on paying a small duty, are allowed to carry their merchandize thither and expose it to sale in booths erected for that purpose.

"The copper, the principal article of export, was brought from the interior and distant parts of the country, and kept in a storehouse ; and as soon as the ship was in part discharged, the loading it with the copper commenced. This latter was weighed, and put into long wooden boxes, a pecul in each, in presence of the Japanese officers and interpreters, and of the Dutch supercargoes and writers, and afterwards conveyed by the Japanese to the bridge, in order to be put on board. On such occasions a few sailors always attend, to watch that the labourers do not steal it ; which they will do if possible, as they can sell it to the Chinese, who pay them well for it.

"When the ship is nearly laden, she is conducted to Papenberg, there to remain at anchor, and take in the residue of her cargo, and all the merchandize and other things belonging to the officers, the ship's provisions, &c. A few days after, when the ship has anchored in the harbour, the governor points out the day when she is to sail ; and this command must be obeyed so implicitly, that, were the wind ever so contrary, or even if it blew a hard gale, the ship must depart without any excuse, or the least shadow of opposition. Before the ship leaves the harbour, the powder, arms, and the chest of books that were taken out, are returned ; the sick from the hospital are put on board ; and whilst she is sailing out, the guns are fired to salute the town and the factory, and afterwards the two principal guards at the entrance of the harbour."

It appears that the Government allow the free importation of foreign books, provided only they have nothing to do with the Christian religion, and that scientific books from Europe are eagerly sought after by many.

The Dutch commerce is distinguished into that which is confined to Government and public trade, or *kambang*, as

it is called. Of late years the public trade has not ex-
ceeded the value of £2,500 per annum. It is fraught
with stock-jobbing, intrigue, and usury, fraud and disreputable transactions of every kind. During the last
few years this impure traffic has caused dismal events at
the factory : one interpreter, convicted of smuggling, was
decapitated, another committed suicide.*

The profits of the kambang are considerable. Siebold
estimates them at cent. per cent., and even higher. The
Government importations are woollen goods, silks, velvet,
printed calico, cotton stuffs, and a variety of articles in
gold and silver, and a small quantity of tin, lead, and
quicksilver. The export, always on the Government
account, consists of only two articles, copper in bars, and
camphor. The kambang imports consist of numberless
articles of grocery and chemicals, and an immense assort-
ment of manufactured wares, which are usually denominated " French goods," or *articles Paris*, as the French
call them. From the detailed list given by Siebold, it is
evident that the taste for the frivolous trifles of European
industry is on the increase amongst the Japanese. Contrary to what we have been told as to the rejection of
jewellery by Japanese vanity, this list includes counter-
feit stones, jewellery of base metal, false pearls, agates,
and the like. The kambang exports are tree-wax,
prepared from the fruit of the *rhus succedaneum*, in
Japanese, *faze-no-ki*, which is considered almost equal to
bees-wax, and is used for making their candles ;† bam-

---

* See on this subject, and Japanese commerce in general, *Essai
Historique, Statisque, &c. du Japon*, by Siebold, in the *Moniteur des
Indes.*

† See *antè*, p. 183, where Kämpfer describes Japanese candles ;
but Siebold says that now instead of cotton wick or a rush they
make a cylinder, of paper, coated with the marrow of a rush called
wi, and secured by a red silk thread, which sticks to it. The smoke
is concentrated in this cylinder and is consumed with it,—a very
clever invention decidedly, and worthy of the attention of Messrs.
Palmer and Co. The tree grows in the southern provinces, and is
planted in the midst of corn-fields, or cultivated like the fruit-trees
of the country.

boos, saki, soy, mustard, silk stuffs, straw boxes, bamboo
baskets, Japanned ware, parasols, fans, porcelain, common
crockery, water vases, and the like.

It appears that the average imports of Japan, from 1825
to 1833 inclusive, amounted at most to about £24,280,
or 289,050 florins ; the exports for the same period are
estimated at 702,685 florins, or about £48,673, just
double the imports.   Since 1833 these figures have
diminished, but still we are struck with precisely the
same proportion between imports and exports, whilst in
1846 the balance was still more in favour of Japan.   As
compared with the value of the trade in the seventeenth
century (1685), the result is a diminution by one-half,
the imports for Government and the kambang being then
about £48,000.

If the Japanese have hitherto prospered with these
small figures of imports, it is clear that our merchants
must tempt them into extravagance to make trade answer.
For many years only one Dutch ship has sufficed for the
trade, and it seems certain, that in maintaining this
abnormal commerce, the Japanese Government has rather
flattered its own vanity than acted in accordance with
what it considers its own interests, for the imperial
treasury is a loser by the wretched commercial transactions, of which the factory of Desima is the theatre.

The Government monopolists of Jeddo, Meako, Osacca,
Sakaï, and Nagasaki, which dispose of the government
imports, are losers by the transaction, for they must
supply the Dutch with camphor and copper at half the
price that they would fetch in the country !*   It seems
evident that both the Dutch and the Chinese have merely
been tolerated, permitted to import such articles as are
absolutely necessary, and no more ; the kambang is a
different matter, of course, and time will show whether
this exponent of the popular will, wants, and desires, is
capable of further development under the fostering hand
of Anglo-Saxon and American speculation.

* Siebold, *ubi suprà ;* Jancigny, *Japon.*

The subjects of the Celestial Empire live in as prisoned a state as the Dutch. " The Chinese," says Thunberg, "have almost from time immemorial traded to Japan, and are the only people in Asia who have engaged in the trade, or are allowed to visit the empire. Formerly, they proceeded to Osacca harbour, although it is very dangerous, on account of rocks and shoals. The Portuguese showed them the way to Nagasaki. At first the annual number of their vessels amounted to upwards of one hundred. The liberty which they then enjoyed is at present greatly contracted, since they have been suspected by the Japanese of favouring the Catholic missionaries in China, and have made attempts to introduce into Japan Catholic books printed in China. They are therefore as much suspected and as hardly used as the Dutch. They are also shut up in a small island, and strictly searched whenever they go in or come out.

" When a vessel arrives from China, all the crew are brought on shore, and all charge of the vessel is taken from them till such time as everything is ready for their departure ; consequently, the Japanese unload it entirely, and afterwards bring the vessel on shore, where, at low water, it is quite dry. The next year it is loaded with other goods.

" The Chinese are not suffered to go to the Imperial Court, which saves them considerable sums in presents and expenses. They are allowed to trade for twice as large a sum as that granted to the Dutch ; but as their voyages are neither so long nor so dangerous, they are obliged to contribute more largely to the town of Nagasaki, and therefore pay more, as far even as sixty per cent. *fanndgin*, or flower-money.

" Their merchandize is sold at three different times in the year, and is brought in seventy junks. The first fair takes place in the spring, for the cargoes of twenty vessels ; the second in the summer, for the cargoes of thirty vessels ; and the third in autumn, for the cargoes of the remaining twenty. Should any more vessels arrive within the year, they are obliged to return without being

allowed to unload the least article. Although their
voyages are less expensive than the Dutch, and they are
not under the necessity of sending an ambassador to the
emperor, nor is any director put over their commerce,
but interpreters, a guard, and supervisors are appointed
to them, the same as the Dutch ; yet, on account of the
greater value per cent. deducted from their merchandize,
their profits are less than those of the Dutch ; and as
they are no longer allowed to carry away any specie,
they are obliged to purchase Japanese commodities for
exportation ; such as copper, lackered ware, &c., many of
which are produced in their own country.

"When their vessels are loaded, and ready for sailing,
they are conducted by a number of Japanese guard-ships,
not only out of the harbour, but likewise a great way out
to sea, in order to prevent their disposing to the smug-
glers any of the unsold wares they may have been obliged
to carry back."

Dr. Ainslie, who visited the port of Nagasaki in 1814,
states that the Chinese trade is limited to ten junks
annually, which are fitted out from the province of
Nankin, bringing principally sugar, with other trifling
articles, and a large quantity of English woollens. In
return, 1000 peculs* of bar copper are allotted to each
junk ; the remainder of the cargo consists of lackered
ware, dried fish, whale oil, &c. He adds, that the Chinese
are treated in Japan with great indignity ; and that their
intercourse is tolerated chiefly on account of certain drugs
which are produced in China, and to which the Japanese
are attached.

* The pecul is about 133 lbs. avoirdupois. For further information on these matters the commercial reader may consult Siebold's
article before mentioned in the *Moniteur des Indes,* tome ii.

CHAPTER III.

IT is something wonderful to think that a nation which
was at an early period so devoted to commerce, that they
trafficked with sixteen different countries, could thus be
shut up by the will of a government which otherwise
holds them in such inconceivable bondage. Such, however, was not the case before the unhappy religious feuds
and complications. Before these deplorable events, the
kindness of the Japanese to strangers who had been
wrecked upon their coasts, and the accounts given by
them of their wealth and commercial character, soon
brought many other traders and adventurers to the
islands besides the Dutch and Portuguese.

At the beginning of the seventeeth century, when the
English were beginning to make considerable commercial
progress in India, our East India Company obtained what
appeared to be a good footing in Japan. This was years
before the great massacre of the Christians, and the total
expulsion of the Portuguese. That truly remarkable
man, William Adams, who led the Dutch to the country,
and procured for them all their privileges, was also the
real founder of the English settlement. The two letters
which he sent to Batavia were conveyed to London, and
submitted to the "Worshipful Fellowship of the Merchants of London trading into the East Indies," the title
then borne by the lately defunct Honourable East India
Company. They attracted immediate attention, and
Captain Saris, in command of the good ship *Clove*, was
despatched on a mission to the Emperor of Japan, being
accredited with a letter, and charged with presents from
our immortal King James the First, who was then,

according to his own account, screwing £36,000 per annum out of the recusant Catholics, by way of fines for clinging to his own mother's religion.* No doubt he fancied Japan would put money in his pocket for his favourites to squander.

The *Clove* came to anchor in the vicinity of Firando, on the 11th of June, 1613, not two years after the date of Adams's letters. The king of the island and his grandson went on board the ship and welcomed the captain, who "had prepared a banquet for them, and a good concert of music, which much delighted them."

The old king received with much joy the letter from the King of England, but put off reading it till *Auge* (as Adams was called) should come into his presence.† After the king retired, multitudes of the chief men and soldiers entered the ship, bringing presents of venison, fowl, fruit, fish, &c. On the following day the ship was surrounded with boats full of people, and the decks soon became crowded with men, women, and children. The captain took several of the better sort of women into his cabin, where a picture of Venus and Cupid "did hang somewhat wantonly, set out in a large frame, which, mistaking it for the Virgin and her Son, some of those women kneeled to and worshipped with great devotion," at the same time whispering in a low tone, that they might not be overheard by their companions, that they were *Christianos;* by which it was understood that they were converts of the Portuguese Jesuits.

Soon after, King Foyne came again on board, and brought with him four women of his family. They were bare-legged, except that a pair of half-buskins were bound by a silk ribbon about their insteps, and were clad in a number of silk gowns, one skirt over another, bound about their waists by a girdle, their hair very black and long, and

---

* Hardwick Papers, i. 446.

† Adams writes it *Angiu.* " I am called in the Japanese tongue Angiu Sama. By that name am I known all the coast long." It means "pilot;" therefore *Angiu Sama* is "Lord Pilot," though perhaps not more than our Mr.

tied in a comely knot on the crown of the head, no part of which was shaven, like the men's. They had good faces, hands, and feet, clear-skinned and white, but wanting colour; which, however, they supplied by art. They were low in stature and very fat, courteous in behaviour, of which they well understood the ceremonials according to the Japanese fashion. At first they seemed a little bashful; but the king " willing them to be frolic," and all other company being excluded except Captain Saris and the interpreter, they sang several songs, playing on an instrument much like a guitar, but with four strings only, which they fingered very nimbly with the left hand, holding in the other a piece of ivory, with which they touched the strings, playing and singing by book, the tunes being noted on lines and spaces, much the same as European music.

Not long after, desirous to be " frolic," the king brought on board a company of female actors—such as were common in Japan, little better, it would seem, than slaves and courtesans, being under the control of a master, who carried them from place to place, selling their favours, and " exhibiting comedies of war, love, and such like, with several shifts of apparel for the better grace of the matter acted."[*]

Early in July, the king or viceroy of another island came to visit " the excellent English ship." " So he was well entertained aboard, banqueted, and had divers pieces shot off at his departure, which he very kindly accepted, and told me that he should be right glad to see some of our nation come to his island, whither they should be heartily welcomed." Such was the freedom of intercourse only a few years before the political hurricane brought on by the Portuguese and the Dutch.

Saris then visited the imperial court at Jeddo, accompanied by our old mariner Adams and ten other Englishmen. They went from island to island in a royal galley, and performed nearly all the journey by water, stopping

* Hildreth.

D D 2

at several cities which they describe as being densely peopled, and quite as large as the London of their day. " Everybody very civil and courteous; only at our landing, and so through the country, the boys, children, and worser sort of idle people, would gather about and follow after us, crying, ' *Coré, Coré, Co-coré waré,*' that is to say, 'You Coréans with false hearts' [on account of their enmity with that nation]: wondering, whooping, hallooing, and making such a noise about us, that we could scarcely hear one another speak, sometimes throwing stones at us (but that not in many towns); yet the clamour and crying after us was everywhere alike, none reproving them for it. The best advice that I can give those who shall hereafter arrive is, that they pass on without regarding those idle rabblements; and in so doing they shall find their ears only troubled with the noise."

In most of the towns the general and his goodly company were most hospitably entertained; and they appear to have been freely admitted to the society of the Japanese ladies. In the latter stages of the journey, Saris was carried in a norimon on six men's shoulders, and had a spare horse, very handsomely caparisoned, whereon to ride when it so pleased him. The general, when in presence of the emperor, well maintained the honour of his country and his own personal dignity. There was no crawling like a crab, no humiliation, no ceremony unbecoming the representative of a powerful sovereign. Through the help and admirable diplomacy of Adams, a commercial treaty, or a series of privileges, more favourable than any ever enjoyed by Portuguese or by Dutch, was granted to the English, and apparently without any demur or delay on the part of the Imperial Court.

The first article in these original privileges of 1613, runs thus:—"We give free license to the King of England's subjects, Sir Thomas Smith, Governor, and Company of the East India Merchants, for ever, safely to come *into any our ports* or empire of Japan, with their ships and merchandise, without hindrance to them or their goods; and to abide, buy, sell, and barter, according to their own manner with all nations; and to tarry so long as they will, and depart at their pleasure."

The second article exempted English goods from all manner of customs or duties; the third granted to the English full freedom of building houses in any part of the empire, which houses, at their departure, they might freely sell; the fourth article placed the property of any English subject that might die in the empire under the sole control of the captain, merchant, or English resident, and exempted entirely all English subjects, whatever their offences, from the somewhat summary process of Japanese law; and the three remaining articles were all in the same liberal and most friendly spirit.*

These privileges were, however, somewhat modified in 1616, when the English, wherever they might arrive on the coast, were ordered to repair immediately to the port and town of Firando, there to sell their merchandise, and not to stay at or trade in any other port whatsoever. But it was ordered, at the same time, that, in case of contrary winds or bad weather, the English ships might abide in any other port without paying anchorage duties; and the people were enjoined to treat such ships in a friendly manner, and to sell them whatsoever they might require. At the same time, all the other valuable privileges of 1613 were confirmed. Captain Cock, who established himself at Firando, and remained in the country long after the departure of Saris, paid more than one visit to the Imperial Court at Jeddo.†

* See *Minutes of Evidence*, appended to the *Report of the Select Committee of the House of Commons on Commercial Relations with China*. 1847. Purchas, *His Pilgrimage*, and the Notes to Mr. Rundall's valuable Memorials.

† MSS. in the East India House (Japan Series), as quoted by Thomas Rundall, Esq. in *Memorials of the Empire of Japan in the Sixteenth and Seventeenth Centuries*. Printed for the Hakluyt Society. London : 1850. Captain Cock was at Firando in 1620, when William Adams closed his adventurous life. The captain took charge of the old pilot's will and property, and remitted the money to Adams's family in England. The original will is preserved in

Our factory at Firando, or rather, perhaps, those who managed their shipments in England, made an injudicious selection of merchandise, sending out commodities which were not in request in that country. In this manner the trade was conducted rather at a loss than profit, and this, with some other circumstances of discouragement, induced the East India Company prematurely to abandon the experiment.

"Of the English," says a recent English writer, "it is simply to be observed that in their commercial project they failed, and that they retired with honour, and regretted, from the scene of their misadventure."* In the year 1623, after upwards of £40,000 had been uselessly expended, they entirely withdrew from that country and trade. But though commercially unsuccessful, the Engglish left an unimpeached character behind them, and worthy Captain Cock and his associates, honoured by the esteem of the higher classes, were blessed and regretted by the humble in condition.† It was, perhaps, fortunate in more ways than one, that our countrymen were far from the empire long before the days of the terrible persecution, civil war, and slaughter. We should grieve to see our national fame blotted by conduct at all resembling that pursued by the Dutch at that dreadful crisis.

In 1673, when an English ship was sent to attempt a revival of intercourse, the first question asked by the Japanese authority was, whether it was long since the English king had married a daughter of the King of Portugal? Our Charles II. had married the Portuguese Infanta, Catherine of Braganza, twelve years before. The Dutch had made the Japanese acquainted with the fact; and this alliance with a hated nation led to a total refusal of the Japanese to permit any renewal of English intercourse, it being declared that "no trade could be

the East India House, as is also the inventory of the estate of the deceased. Too much praise can hardly be given to Mr. Rundall for his industrious researches into these matters.

* Thomas Rundall, Esq., *Memorials of the Empire of Japan*, &c.
† Ibid.

permitted with the subjects of a king who had married
the daughter of the greatest enemy of Japan, and the
English ship must, therefore, sail with the first fair wind."
The English captain was even denied permission to sell
his cargo, which he had brought from so great a distance.*
Yet, in other matters, our people were courteously received
and hospitably entertained.

This base trick of the Dutch, and their grasping commercial tactics, rendered them hateful to the people of
England, and at the commencement of the seventeenth
century, Salmon gave vent to the national indignation as follows : — " Had we our share of the spice
trade, we should have occasion to send very little
treasure to India ; whereas now we send hardly anything
else : spices are as much valued in Asia as in Europe, and
perhaps the Dutch sell more on the other side of the
Cape of Good Hope than on this side. With these it is
they purchase the merchandize of one kingdom to transport to another. Bullion itself is not as valuable as the
spices they have taken from us. And of these precious
commodities do they root up and destroy vast quantities
every year, to enhance the prices ; so that in this respect
they may be looked upon as the common enemies of mankind. God has bountifully furnished the world with
spices as well as oil and wine, to render his creatures
happy ; and these monopolizers would deprive mankind
of them, and defeat the design of the Creator. Two-
thirds of the world at least never taste or smell those
fragrant fruits ; our Dutch neighbours choosing rather
to destroy them than they should become common. And

---

* The name of this ship was the *Return*. She had been despatched
by the English East India Company, with the sanction of Charles II.
All on board of her appear to have been convinced that they were
thwarted more by Dutch jealousy than by anything else. In the
United States Expedition, i. 38, will be found the long interrogatory
to which the English captain was subjected on this occasion, —
referring to religious matters, to " God," and " Christ," the " St.
George's Cross" in the flag, &c.—all which seem to have been cunning suggestions of the Hollanders. It is much too long for quota-
tion, but is really worth reading in this curious matter of Japan.

could they engross all corn and wine into their hands, no
doubt but they would destroy those too, if they had the
like prospect of gain. 'Tis happy for the world, in some
respects, it must be acknowledged, that so sordid a spirit
possesses that people :—had their ambition been equal to
their covetousness, and private merchants did not openly
cheat the public, and connive at each other's frauds to
advance their private interests, they would by this time
have been masters of the world."*

After this unsuccessful experiment there is no record
of another English visit to Japan for considerably more
than a century. Captain Cook, in his last voyage, merely
coasted the western side of the empire.

But, in 1791, the *Argonaut*, an English vessel employed
in the fur trade with the north-west coast of America,
made an attempt to trade and barter with the Japanese.
She made for the western side of the islands, but met
with no welcome. At the only port in which she anchored, she was immediately surrounded by lines of boats,
and her people were cut off from all intercourse with the
shore ; and after getting a gratuitous supply of wood and
water, she was obliged to sail away. In 1803, an
English merchantman, the *Frederick*, was sent from Calcutta with a rich cargo of goods ; but her captain was
refused admittance to the harbour, and enjoined to leave
the neighbourhood within the space of twenty-four hours.

The progress of our vast conquests and annexations on
the Indian continent were of a nature to excite the jealous
fears and increase the estrangement of people like the
Japanese. They were uncommonly well informed of the
particulars of that history, from the time of the great Lord
Clive downwards. This complete information could be
obtained only by means of the Dutch. To the people of
that nation India was a sore subject. They had at one
time aimed at supremacy in Hindostan, but Clive had
shattered their hopes by the blow he struck at their settlement of Chinsura, above Calcutta, and under Warren

* *Modern History,* i.

Hastings their Indian continental power had dwindled to a mere shadow. They could not recover that power by criticising and condemning English ambition to the Japanese ; but by this process it was certainly easy to excite the alarm of that people, to induce them vigilantly to bar their ports and harbours to the English, and thus leave such trade as yet survived in Japan solely in the hands of the Dutch.

The French, though long powerful in India, and at one time all-powerful in Siam, made no effort in this direction. It appears, however, that when the celebrated Colbert took charge of the deranged finances of France, he projected an expedition to Japan, upon which he counted for a good supply of gold and silver, and for other advantages. But, from causes which are not explained, his project was never carried into execution.

Towards the close of the last century, Russia made more than one attempt to open an intercourse. Possessing one-half of the Kurile Islands, while the Japanese possessed the other half, these two powers were, in a manner, next-door neighbours.

With the shipwrecked Japanese before mentioned,* Catherine II. sent, indirectly, Lieutenant Laxman to attempt a commercial and diplomatic intercourse with the nation. Laxman was treated with great courtesy, though kept in a sort of confinement, but was dismissed on condition of never approaching, under any pretence, any part of the coast but Nagasaki. Catherine was forced to content herself with establishing a professorship of the Japanese language in a school for navigation at Irkutsk, —selecting the professors from the Japanese shipwrecked from time to time on the coast of Siberia.

In 1804, the Russian Czar sent Count Resanoff with imperial credentials and valuable presents to Japan ; but after a detention of nearly six months, he received a flat refusal of all his imperial requests, and even the presents from his emperor were declined ; but in the midst of all

* Page 142.

his annoyances—and they were many—everything was done with the greatest show of politeness by the Japanese officials.

Nothing daunted by these repulses, the Russians made another attempt in 1811, and this time sent the unfortunate Golownin — whose "Recollections" have been quoted in the previous pages—in the sloop of war, *Diana*. Entering the harbour of Kunaschier, two guns were fired at the *Diana* from a fort, hung round, in the fashion of the country, with blue and red striped cloth; and troops were seen in the town and on the seashore. Golownin endeavoured by signals and ingenious symbols to intimate that he only wanted provisions and water. After various misunderstandings and adventures on the part of the Russians, and very great cunning on that of the Japanese, Golownin was tempted to land, with a weak party consisting only of a midshipman, a pilot, four Russian seamen, and a Kurile interpreter. He was received with great courtesy, and entertained at dinner, and treated with tea and saki—the native drink brewed from rice ;— but when he and his party would have returned to their ship, they were all made prisoners, and bound with thick cords, and swung up by arms and legs to a beam, their pockets having been first searched and emptied. The Japanese then sat down on their heels and coolly smoked their pipes for an hour. At the end of that period the party were loosened from the beam, the cords were removed from their legs, in order that they might be able to march, and they were led out of the castle and through a wood, each of them having a conductor holding the end of the main one of the ropes with which he still remained bound, and a grim-looking Japanese soldier by his side.

On ascending a hill, they heard a cannonade, and saw their ships standing away under sail. "There goes our *Diana*! Take a last look of her!" said the pilot. As they hurried him along, the rope round Golownin's neck became so tightened that he was all but strangled. In the evening they arrived at a small village, and being carried into an empty apartment, were offered boiled rice and fish, the staple food of these people : they were then stretched on the floor, and the ropes by which they had been led were made fast to strong iron hooks driven into the wall. Their conductors then sat down to smoke pipes and drink tea. Such is Japanese custom. At daylight the following morning, Golownin was tied down to a plank or flat tray, like a sheep or dead pig, and carried away on the shoulders of two strong men, he knew not whither. He took a last farewell, as he fancied, of his companions in misfortune. In brief time, however, he found himself in a boat, into which all the rest of the Russians were brought, one by one, in the same manner, with an armed soldier between each of them. The boat shot across the narrow strait to the island of Matsmai, where they were placed in other boats. They proceeded along the shore, which appeared to be very populous, the whole of that day and the following night.

Though the Japanese would not relax the tight ropes with which they were bound, they were most attentive to their wants in all other respects, feeding them with rice and broiled fish, and constantly flapping away the gnats and flies which annoyed them. In a village a venerable old man brought them some saki, and stood by while they were drinking it, with marks of pity in his face. But everywhere they experienced humane and kindly attentions from private persons, and Golownin, who, from his book, appears to have been rather a weakheaded, but a very right-hearted man, left Japan, after all his sufferings, with the most favourable impressions of the benevolence and generosity of the people. His testimony in this respect may be considered as conclusive and important.

Some of his "recollections" of his intercourse with the Japanese in his captivity are worth attention. One question seems rather to have puzzled the Russians. They were asked why they had carried off wood and rice from a village where they had landed, without the consent of the owners ; and whether, under the circumstances of leaving other articles in lieu, as they had done, any law existed in Russia to justify the deed ? Golownin acknowledged that there was no such law ; but added, that if a man took only what was necessary to support his existence, and left an equivalent, he would not be considered guilty. " With us," replied the Japanese, " it is very different ; our laws ordain that a man must sooner die of hunger than touch, without the consent of the owner, a single grain of rice which does not belong to him."

The Russians were astonished to find how many trifling circumstances, unconnected either with themselves or with Resanoff, or Chwostoff, were brought to bear on the suspected views of the Russian Government against Japan. The visit of Captain Broughton to one of the Kurile islands, and the visit of an English frigate to the Bay of Nagasaki, with some insinuations of the Dutch of that place, had confirmed the Japanese in their belief that the Russians and the English intended to divide China and Japan between them.

His detention was in retaliation for some violence perpetrated by the Russians at one of the Kurile islands. On the return of the *Diana*, a Japanese junk was captured, whose captain, upon being required by the Russians to act in a manner which they thought proper to open communications, threatened to kill the chief officer of the *Diana*, and then to kill himself. But when the Russian officer left this resolute and clever man to act in his own way, all went well on shore, and Golownin and his comrades were soon liberated. Being landed, on his promise to do his best, he exhibited a declaration, which had been procured, by his advice, from the Russian governor of Irkutsk, that the violent proceedings at the Kurile islands had been wholly unauthorised ; and of his own knowledge and experience he bore testimony to the good feelings of the Russians toward Japan. No doubt he was aided by his affluence and his connexions ; but it would appear that, but for his extraordinary address and abilities, even he would have failed.

Golownin and those with him were set at liberty.

They soon reached the *Diana,* which had been allowed to come round to the port of Chakodade. It must have been long ere they forgot their caging.*

In 1808, the British frigate *Phaeton* appeared off Nagasaki. She was commanded by Captain Pellew—subsequently the second Lord Exmouth—who had been ordered by Admiral Drury, the head of our fleet in the Eastern seas, to cruise off the Japanese islands, for the purpose of intercepting the Dutch traders to Nagasaki. We were at war with Holland, which for some years had been a mere dependency of France. Her troops were fighting in the armies of Bonaparte, her ships were conveying his troops and stores, and her war-ships and privateers were doing us all the mischief they could. After cruising in vain for a month in those stormy seas, Captain Pellew, thinking that the Dutch traders had reached the harbour of Nagasaki, had determined to look for them there ; and being there, and finding no Dutchmen, he endeavoured to have some little communication with the shore, and asked for provisions and fresh water. The result of this visit has been given in a previous page,† to illustrate Japanese manners and customs, and the reader probably remembers the severe remarks of the writer there quoted, on the suicide of the governor of Nagasaki in particular, and the conduct of the British navy in general. Assuredly, Captain Pellew would never have willingly caused such a disaster. If ordered to cruise off Nagasaki, he was bound to obey ; and we have no right to assume that his conduct was dictated by insolent aggression, since it is obviously explained by a simple error in judgment.‡

* *Narrative of my Captivity in Japan during the years* 1812 *and* 1813 ; *with Observations on the Country and People.* By Captain Golownin, R.N. ; to which is added, *An Account of the Voyages to the Coasts of Japan, and of the Negotiations with the Japanese for the release of the Author and his Companions.* By Captain Rikord. London : 1818.

† Page 289.

‡ The Dutchman, M. Doeff's account of these occurrences is marked with considerable prejudice, animosity, and unfairness to the

As if the Japanese themselves did not furnish us with oddities enough, an incident occurred in 1813, under British contrivance, as amusing as anything in Japan. In the summer of 1813 two vessels bearing the Dutch flag, and showing a private Dutch signal, approached the coast. A letter was sent on shore, announcing the arrival of M. W. Waardenaar, formerly president of the factory, and M. Cassa, appointed to replace M. Doeff, with three assistants. No suspicion crossed the mind of M. Doeff, who sent an officer and clerk of the factory on board. The officer soon returned, saying that he had recognised M. Waardenaar and the Dutch Captain Voorman, but that things looked very strange on board the ship, and that Waardenaar had told him he could deliver the papers with which he was charged to none but M. Doeff in person. It was observed that nearly all the

English. But something must be pardoned in the poor Dutchman, who found himself, for a number of years, completely cut off from all communication with Europe and with his countrymen in the east, by the conquering, ubiquitous fleets of Great Britain. He and his companions at Nagasaki wore out their last coats, their last pantaloons, and their last shoes, and were obliged to go half-naked, or to dress themselves like natives. They drank out all their schiedam, and (woe for jovial Dutchmen!) they could get no more gin.

A moderate and excellent article on this subject will be found in the *Quarterly Review,* vol. lvi. p. 415.

On the 7th of September, 1854, just before the last visit of the *Mississippi* and *Susquehanna* to Simoda, a British squadron of three steamers and a frigate arrived at Nagasaki, under Admiral Sterling. These British vessels, which found the annual Dutch trading ship, two large Chinese junks, also a Dutch steamer, lying in the harbour, encountered the usual reception, being served with notices, surrounded with boats, and denied liberty to land. At length, however, after a deal of negotiation and threats to proceed to Jeddo, it was agreed to furnish supplies, tea, rice, pigs, &c., and to receive payment through the Dutch. On the 15th the admiral landed, and was conducted in state to the governor's house. The guard-boats were withdrawn, and the men were allowed to land on an island to recreate themselves. Other interviews followed, presents were interchanged, and on the 19th, the squadron left. These particulars are drawn from the published letter of a medical officer on board, who describes the supplies furnished as very good, and the Japanese soy as cheap and nice, but who does not seem to have relished the saki, which he likens in taste to acetate of ammonia water. —Hildreth.

people on board spoke English, but thence it was only concluded that the vessels were Americans hired by the Dutch, who, during the war, had very frequently sought security for person and property under the flag of the United States. To ascertain the truth, M. Doeff boldly went on board. There M. Waardenaar, with evident embarrassment, handed him a letter. Doeff declined to open the letter till he should return to his residence, whither he was presently accompanied by Waardenaar and his clerk. Being opened at the factory, the letter presented matter that astounded and bewildered the poor Dutch president, who, for nearly four years, had been cut off from the world by the successful operations of our fleets, and kept in total ignorance not only of the occurrences in Holland and the rest of Europe, but also of what was passing in the Indian seas. The letter, which announced that M. Waardenaar was appointed Commissary in Japan, with supreme power over the factory, was signed, " Raffles, Lieutenant-Governor of Java and its dependencies." "Who is Raffles ?" said the puzzled president, who had never heard the name, and who believed Java to be still in the hands of the Dutch, as the rich and magnificent island had been for ages. In reply, M. Doeff was informed that Java had been captured by the English ; that Holland had lost her nationality, and had been incorporated with the French Empire, and that Waardenaar, together with an Englishman, Dr. Ainslie, had been appointed by the British Government as Commissioners in Japan. Doeff instantly refused any compliance with the order set forth in the letter, maintaining that they came from the government of a colony in possession of the enemy, and that Japan was not to be considered as a dependency of Java, or affected by any capitulation into which the Dutch in Java might have entered with the English.*

* *Herinneringen uit Japan,—Recollections of Japan.* By Hendrick Doeff, formerly President of the Dutch factory at Desima. 4to. Haarlem, 1835. This curious Dutch work has not been translated into English, but numerous passages from it have been given in the *Quarterly Review*, vol. lvi. 1836.

" This ingenious and bold attempt to get a footing in the Dutch factory, and to smooth the way for future intercourse with the exclusive Japanese, proceeded from the spirit of enterprise which distinguished Sir Stamford Raffles, one of the many very remarkable men sent out to the East by the Hon. East India Company. His views extended all over this vast Archipelago; his darling object was to establish an insular empire, as magnificent, and even more extensive, than our continental empire in India. Sir Stamford was a great man, yet we cannot but agree with those (persons friendly to him) who think that his zeal in this instance overstepped his discretion, and that he arranged his scheme without a sufficient knowledge of the country and of the character of the Government and people of Japan.* Success could be gained only by entire acquiescence and collusion on the part of M. Doeff; and the lives of the crews and of all on board the two ships (which were only weak trading vessels), were placed in the hands of that Dutch functionary, who, by a word, could have given them over as Englishmen and enemies to the vengeance of a nation revengeful beyond measure, and still furious with the recollections of the visit paid to them by the *Phaeton* frigate. It appears to us that Doeff, whose hatred to the English was intense, and had been increased by years of segregation, suffering, and absolute privation, would really have taken this course, but for the happy circumstance that M. Waardenaar was not only his countryman, but his very old friend and patron. Fortunately, too, Waardenaar was known and respected in Japan, having formerly been president of the factory; the ships bore the Dutch flag, and no suspicion that the English had a Dutch agent in their service had as yet reached the Japanese authorities. This rendered it comparatively easy to keep the secret if M. Doeff would only connive ; and this, upon certain conditions of commercial profit to his country, he consented to do. The cargoes of the two

* See his *Life* and *Asiat. Journ.*, i. 295 (1830).

ships were delivered to him in the usual manner, and copper was obtained in return, and these transactions being completed, the *Charlotte* and *Mary* sailed away with all speed. Those on board were certainly not out of danger until they were well out at sea, for they were too weak to defend themselves against an attack which would certainly have taken place if the Japanese Government had made any discovery. At the court of Jeddo was established, at this very moment, in great power and favour, the son of that governor of Nagasaki who had committed suicide in consequence of the visit of the English in 1808. At Nagasaki itself, the garrison consisted of the troops of the Prince of Fizen, who had suffered one hundred days' arrest for his imputed negligence in the same affair ; and doubtless the friends and relations of the other victims of the transaction were living there and panting for vengeance on any Englishman that might fall into their hands.

" But what would have happened if M. Doeff had obeyed the orders of Sir Stamford Raffles, and had left his appointed successor and the English surgeon Ainslie to explain to the Japanese the British authority under which they were appointed ? Nothing less, in all probability, than the destruction of the factory, the execution of its officers, and the final cessation of all intercourse with Europe.

" In the following year (1814) Sir Stamford Raffles renewed his attempt by sending the Dutch agent Cassa, in the *Charlotte*, to Nagasaki ; but although the enterprise was conducted with rare skill and circumspection, it failed most completely."＊

In 1818, Captain Gordon, of the British navy, entered the Bay of Jeddo, in a little brig of sixty-five tons, begging permission to return with a cargo of goods for

---

＊ " In relating these English attempts we have followed M. Doeff's own account, in his *Recollections of Japan,* and the remarks thereon by the able writer in the *Quarterly Review,* vol. lvi."— MacFarlane.

sale ! He was visited immediately by two Japanese officers, whom he supposed to be of high rank. They said he must unship his rudder and allow it, with all his arms and ammunition, to be taken on shore. The vessel was then surrounded by a circle of about twenty small boats, and beyond them, by another circle, of about sixty larger guard and gun-boats, besides two or three junks, which mounted a number of guns. Two interpreters then came on board, one speaking Dutch, the other knowing something of Russian, and both a little English. They inquired if the vessel belonged to the East India Company, if the English were now friends with the Dutch. They knew the names and uses of our various nautical instruments, and said that the best of these, and other articles of manufacture, were made in London. At a subsequent visit, they firmly, but politely, told Captain Gordon that he could not be permitted to trade to Japan, as by their unalterable laws, all foreign intercourse was interdicted, except at Nagasaki, and even there allowed only with the Dutch and Chinese, and that the governor of the province desired they would take their departure the moment the wind should be fair. They declined some trifling presents which the captain offered, saying that they were prohibited from accepting them. The rudder, with everything else that had been taken on shore, was carefully returned, and about thirty boats were sent to tow the vessel out of the bay. Ten years had now passed since the visit of the *Phaeton* frigate, and, very fortunately, Gordon had put into a very different port, on a different island. He speaks in high terms of the polite and affable conduct of the Japanese towards him and his people, and towards one another. He also speaks of the great mineral riches of Japan, and thinks that, if their Government would only consent, a profitable trade might be carried on with them in our woollen cloths and other manufactures. The worthy officer is praised by those who have seen the details of his expedition, for admirable prudence and conduct. Perhaps, under less judicious guidance, the expedition of the little brig would have ended in some other tragical catastrophe.*

At last the Americans made an attempt, and, after the fashion of the Russians, charitably covered the enterprise with "shipwrecked Japanese." In the course of the year 1831, a Japanese junk was blown off the coast into the Pacific Ocean, and, after drifting for a long time, was cast ashore in America, near the mouth of the Columbia river. The poor castaways were kindly treated, and after four years of varied adventures, they were conducted to Macao, where they were taken care of by the English and Americans. It was reasonably supposed, by those who did not know the imperial decree of 1637, or who could not conceive that that decree would still influence the conduct of the Japanese authorities,† that, to carry the poor people back to their own country would be a good and sufficient reason for appearing at Japan. An American merchantman, called the *Morrison*, was excellently equipped for the purpose; but, unfortunately, her guns and armament were taken out of her, as a recommendation to the confidence of the Japanese. This very circumstance became the cause of her unceremonious expulsion and bad treament. The defenceless ship, with a medical missionary on board, to administer to the sick, reached the Bay of Jeddo. The first care of the officers who visited her from shore was to inspect her keenly, and ascertain her strength, by rowing round and peering in at the sides. When it was discovered that she was wholly unarmed, the greatest contempt and insolence were betrayed by these official visitors, and early the next morning the *Morrison* was saluted by a discharge of shotted guns from the shore, at very short distance. Badly as the guns were directed, their point-blank range, and the unarmed condition of the ship, made it necessary to weigh anchor with all speed. The Americans then

* MSS. Journal of Captain Gordon, as cited in the *Quarterly Review*, vol. xx. p. 119.
† The second clause of that decree is simply to this effect:—" All Japanese, who return from abroad, shall be put to death.

ran westward to the neighbourhood of Kagosima, the principal town of the island of Kewsew, where they anchored in a deep and spacious bay.

Mr. C. W. King, a highly respectable merchant of New York, conducted the negotiations with tact, good humour, and ability. On his arrival in the port, he prepared a paper to be laid before the Emperor. "The American vessels," said he, "sail faster than those of other nations. If permitted to have intercourse with Japan, they will communicate always the latest intelligence. . . . . . Our countrymen have not yet visited your honourable country, but only know that, in old times, the merchants of all nations were admitted to your harbours. Afterwards, having transgressed the law, they were restricted or expelled. Now we, coming for the first time, and not having done wrong, request permission to carry on a friendly intercourse on the ancient footing."

The natives seemed very friendly, and it was thought at first that the negotiations for landing the shipwrecked Japanese was in a fair train; but, after a period of uncertainty, striped canvas cloths were seen stretched along the shore.* Their Japanese passengers, in great dismay, told the Americans that these were warlike preparations; lines of this cloth repeated, one in the rear of the other, being used to deaden the effect of shot, and to conceal the gunners. The anchor was again weighed, when a battery on shore opened savagely on the defenceless ship. Nothing was left for it but to return to Macao with the shipwrecked people.†

In 1846, seeing the absolute necessity of protecting their own subjects frequenting those seas, the United States made an attempt to open negotiations with the

* The English sailors laugh at the Japanese warlike demonstrations, and say that the Japanese put their batteries in petticoats. Nothing, in a warlike sense, is more contemptible than these batteries! The guns (of brass) are laid on level platforms, without parapet or protection of any kind, unless we accept as such the petticoats, or striped cloth.

† C. W. King, *Notes of the Voyage of the "Morrison" from Canton to Japan.* New York. 1839.

obstinate court of Japan. The *Columbus,* of ninety guns, Commodore Biddle, attended by the United States frigate, *Vincennes* arrived at the entrance of the Bay of Jeddo on the 20th of July. The ships were immediately surrounded by about four hundred guard-boats, each containing from five to twenty men, who were generally without arms. Going on board the *Vincennes,* the smaller of the ships, a man placed a stick with some symbol on it at the head, and another stick of the same sort at the stern. As the Americans thought that this looked rather like taking possession, they ordered the sticks to be removed ; and this was instantly done, without any objection on the part of the Japanese. Sir J. F. Davis thinks, that in this respect, the Japanese resemble their Chinese neighbours :—"They go as far as they dare, until a check occurs. Thus they tried at first to prevent communication between the *Columbus* and *Vincennes,* and a triple line of boats made no attempt to move ; but, on the seamen being ordered to cut the connecting ropes, no opposition was made." The interpreter was a Japanese, who, like many of his countrymen at Nagasaki, understood Dutch perfectly. The superior officers were very civil, well-conducted, sociably, and even jovially inclined. The Americans thought them generally a much better-looking people than the Chinese. Although the two ships remained ten days at anchor, not a soul went on shore. A reference being in the meanwhile made to the Emperor, the written reply arrived in about seven days. It was sufficiently curt :—"No trade can be allowed with any foreign nation, except Holland." On their departure, the *Columbus* and *Vincennes* were towed out by the whole fleet of boats.

It was the opinion of the illustrious Humboldt, that an opportunity for opening a liberal and honourable communication between Europe and Japan would not occur until the two great oceans (the Atlantic and the Pacific) should be united by a canal cut across the Isthmus of Panama, when the productions of the west and north-west coasts of America, China, and Japan would be brought more than 6000 miles nearer Europe and the United States, and when alone any great change could be effected in the political and commercial policy of eastern Asia. "For this neck of land," said Humboldt, "has been for ages the bulwark of the independence of China and Japan."

A very recent English writer said, "Since, however, this opinion was expressed, the bulwark has been breached, and various circumstances have transpired to alter the features of the case, and to bring about a rapid change in the tide of commerce, and the progress of trade. The British have established themselves on •the frontiers of China, and in the heart of the Eastern Archipelago, and have compelled respect to their flag and freedom to their trade. Energy and enterprise have constructed a railroad across the Isthmus of Panama, and the gold discoveries of California, and the colonization of Vancouver's Island, have settled a vast and industrious population on the western seaboard of the American continent, and led to the establishment of new lines of steam navigation, and an immense tide of commerce and emigration. The opening of the Nicaragua, Tehuantepee, and other practicable routes of intercommunication between different points on the Atlantic and Pacific, has been undertaken by various companies. Steam communication has been extended from India to China, and recently to our Australasian settlements, by the way of Singapore and Java. There has also been a great increase in the European and American shipping employed in the India and China trade in general, commerce, and the whale-fishery in the Pacific. The Americans, particularly, have largely extended their whaling fleet, and prosecuted the fishery very successfully to the seas and coasts of Japan and her northern dependencies, to the gulfs of Tartary and Okotsk, the Sea of Kamtschatka, Behring's Straits, and the Arctic Ocean.

"The Port of San Francisco, California, is destined to become the great mart and entrepôt for American commerce in the Pacific, with China, Japan, and all the maritime countries of Asia, Polynesia, Oceanica, and Australasia, which embrace an aggregate population of upwards of six hundred millions. Our own excellent port and harbour of Sidney, from proximity and central situation, having now the advantages of regular steam communication, possesses even superior advantages for carrying on a most extensive and lucrative trade with the coasts and islands of Asia and the Eastern Archipelago.

"Japan is directly opposite the American possessions on the Pacific coast, and the two great islands of Niphon and Jesso form the Strait of Sangar, through which hundreds of its whale fleet are compelled annually to pass. To land, however, on any of the shores of this empire for supplies of wood, water, or the necessaries of life, or to be forced upon them by stress of weather, subjects the unfortunate whaler to robbery and death.

"Japan not only refuses to hold commercial intercourse with the rest of the world—a very questionable right— but she goes further; and, occupying as she does an enormous extent of sea-coast, not only refuses to open her ports to foreign vessels in distress, but actually opens her batteries upon them when they approach within gun-shot of her shores. And when driven upon them by stress of weather, she seizes upon, imprisons, exhibits in cages, and actually murders the crews of such ill-fated vessels.

"The world, however, is one of progress, and in the march of human events it is highly probable that the Japanese will be persuaded of the error of their present policy, and induced to pursue a more liberal course.

"The insular geographical position of Japan, her excellent ports and harbours, dense and industrious population, her boundless productive resources and vast capabilities for commerce, the superior intelligence and refinement of her princes and nobles, together with the skill, energy, and enterprise of the Japanese people, justly entitle her to rank above every other Asiatic nation. By a judicious relaxation of her restrictive policy, all these unrivalled, natural, and political advantages could be made available for conducting a very extensive and profitable trade with various countries both on the Atlantic and Pacific, without compromising either her sovereignty, national religion, or peculiar institutions.

" This isolated and mysterious empire, which has been since 1637 hermetically sealed to all foreign intercourse and trade, except with the Chinese and Dutch, will now be compelled by force of circumstances to succumb to the progressive commercial spirit of the age, and the Japanese islands will eventually become in the East what the British islands are in the West."*

Nothing can be more reasonable than these observations. Accordingly, in 1852, the American President sent an expedition to Japan, whose object was :—1. To effect some permanent arrangement for the protection of American seamen and property wrecked on these islands, or driven into their ports by stress of weather. 2. Permission to enter one or more of their ports to obtain provisions, to refit in case of disasters, a depôt for coal, it mattered not where. 3. Permission to American vessels to enter one or more of their ports for the purpose of trade. A long letter, well written, but much too long to quote, very plainly developed the President's views and the advantages that would accrue to all parties concerned by an amicable arrangement.

This mission failed ; the Japanese Government evaded the application, and the Americans departed, but to return in 1854, when Commodore Perry re-appeared in the Bay of Jeddo with three steam-frigates, four sloops-of-war, and two store ships. After vainly endeavouring to induce the Americans to retire to another station, a place was fixed upon for the negotiation.

" On the 8th of March," says a letter dated on board the *Vandalia,* and published in the New York *Journal*

---

* *Lawson's Merchant's Magazine, Statist, and Commercial Review,* vol. i.   No. 1.

of Commerce, " the day appointed for the first meeting, about nine hundred officers, seamen, and marines, armed to the teeth, landed, and, with drums beating and colours flying, were drawn up on the beach, ready to receive the commodore. As soon as he stepped on shore the band struck up, salutes were fired, the marines presented arms, and, followed by a long escort of officers, he marched up between the lines and entered the house erected by the Japanese expressly for the occasion. Thousands of Japanese soldiers crowded the shore and the neighbouring elevations, looking on with a good deal of curiosity and interest. The house was nothing but a plain frame building, hastily put up, containing one large room—the audience hall—and several smaller, for the convenience of attendants, &c. The floor was covered with mats, and very pretty painted screens adorned the sides. Long tables and benches, covered with red woollen stuff, placed parallel to each other, three handsome braziers, filled with burning charcoal, on the floor between them, and a few violet-coloured crape hangings suspended from the ceiling, completed the furniture of the room. As we entered we took our seats at one of the tables. The Japanese commissioners soon came in, and placed themselves opposite to us, at the other table; while behind us both, seated on the floor on their knees [rather on their heels] (their usual position, for they do not use chairs), was a crowd of Japanese officers, forming the train of the commissioners.

" The business was carried on in the Dutch language, through interpreters, of whom they have several who speak very well, and two or three who speak a little English. They were on their knees between the commissioners and the commodore. Our interpreter was seated by the side of the latter. It was curious to see the intolerable ceremony observed by them, quite humiliating to a democratic republican. A question proposed had to pass first through the interpreters, and then through several officers ascending in rank, before it could reach the commissioners, every one bowing his forehead to the floor before he addressed his superior."

The commissioners were exceedingly tenacious, even upon points of phraseology, but gave evidence of acting in entire good faith; and the commodore conceded everything which did not seem absolutely essential. The extent of the liberty to be allowed to American visitors was one of the greatest difficulties. Two ports, Simoda and Hakodade, were granted for the reception of American ships; protection for shipwrecked Americans; permission to "exchange gold and silver coin and articles of goods for other articles of goods, under such regulations as shall be temporarily established by the Japanese Government for that purpose"—but all through the agency of Japanese officers appointed for that purpose, and in no other manner. By the ninth article of the Treaty, Japan agrees to grant to the United States and their citizens, such privileges and advantages as she may concede to any other nation, "without any consultation or delay."[*]

The events of this very remarkable American success are admirably set forth in a work which I have frequently quoted. *Narrative of the Expedition of an American Squadron to the China Seas and Japan, under the command of Commodore M. C. Perry, United States Navy.* This book is a credit to the nation. It is well written, beautifully and profusely illustrated, and everywhere gives evidence of that intellectual as well as material advance which constantly commends the republic to our delighted contemplation.

The American war-steamer *Powhatan* visited Simoda in 1855, to complete the exchange of ratification. Sad to tell, the town of Simoda, one of the ceded ports, was found in a state of desolation and ruin, from the effects of a disastrous earthquake, on the previous 23rd of December —the same earthquake in which the Russian frigate *Diana*, then lying in the harbour, was so damaged as to sink in attempting to make a neighbouring port for repairs.

This dismemberment of the Japanese seclusion and exclusion—like the dismemberment of the Roman Empire

---

[*] *United States Expedition,* Hildreth.

—invited all the " barbarians" to take a share; and the recent war with China compressed into the space of a week or two events that all the begging and praying in the world, with charitable return of castaways, would not have brought about this side of the Day of Judgment.

On the 3rd of August, her Majesty's ships *Furious*, *Retribution*, and others, appeared at Nagasaki. A correspondent thus describes the incident :—

" There was soon a general flurry, for the Japanese appeared to have been waiting for their Dutch friends to awake, to inquire if we might be visited. Japanese officials, with pockets full of paper, pens, and ink, hurried off—jolly goodnatured-looking fellows, always ready to laugh, and in appearance resembling more the Kanaka races of the South Sea Islands than the Chinese we had left behind us. Their dress in some respects was Chinese, and their language sounding very like a composition of the discordancy of that most discordant of languages, and the soft liquid sounds of the Kanaka tongue. But how they interrogated us !—what was the ship's name, our name, the ambassador's titles—everybody's name and age—everybody's rank and business—what did we want —whither were we going—whence did we come—how many ships were coming—where was our Admiral ? Indeed, a Russian custom-house agent, or a British census paper, could not have put more astounding questions, whether in number or nature, than did these Nagasaki reporters. We were as patient as naval officers, or angels, may usually be supposed to be under such circumstances ; answered all their questions—allowed them to see, touch, smell, and hear everything, except our ambassador, who was in his cabin, and then dismissed them with a glass of sherry and a biscuit. The captain and first-lieutenant had hardly congratulated themselves that, at any rate, that portion of the pleasure of visiting Japan was over, when another boatful of reporters arrived, tumbled up the ladder, were very well behaved, but asked exactly the same questions, and went exactly through the same farce as the first party had done. They were, we learnt, duplicate reporters, whose statements served to check and correct those of the first set of inquirers. Directly they left us, a two-sworded official arrived—two swords in Japan, like two epaulettes in Europe, indicate an officer of some standing. He introduced himself through a Japanese interpreter, who spoke English remarkably well, as 'a chief officer,' who had an official communication to make. Would he sit down—would he be pleased to unbosom himself—could he not see the ambassador? Impossible! What! 'a chief officer' communicate with an ambassador? We were truly horrified. The chief officer must be simply insane ; did he couple the representative of the Majesty of Great Britain with some superintendent of trade? The chief officer apologized ; he was very properly shocked at the proposition that he had made ; he saw his error, and what was more to our purpose, the ambassador assumed a size and importance in his eyes which it would have been difficult to have realized. The 'chief officer' then put his quetion—Did Lord Elgin intend to call upon the Governor of Nagasaki? No ; he had no time to do so. Did he expect the Governor to wait upon him? The Governor could please himself—the ambassador would receive him if he came. If the Lieutenant-Governor called on Lord Elgin, would his Excellency receive him? Yes. This was all the chief officer had to say. His mission was a special one. He begged to wish us good morning, merely adding that the Governor of Nagasaki hoped the ambassador would kindly accept a small present which would shortly be sent. The present arrived shortly afterwards—a stout cob-built pig of three hundredweight, and a quantity of pumpkins."*

If this statement be correct, it seems that the day of Japan's humiliation has come. How strangely in contrast with all that we have read as to the deportment of Japanese officials on the intrusion of strangers within their sacred waters. How can we account for this wonderful

* *Blackwood's Magazine* for December.

NAGASAKI.

change in the minds and manners of those officials once
so proud, so haughty, so uncompromising ? It may be
only a flippant exaggeration ; but even then, it is painful
to contemplate the slightest foundation for so degrading a
change in officials, who, whether right or wrong, have
hitherto maintained so dignified a bearing. The *Times'*
Correspondent mentions nothing of the sort. He says :—

"Lord Elgin has returned to Shanghai after an absence
of exactly one month. This short interval, however, has
sufficed to enable him to conclude a treaty with Japan,
which, if it does not equal in commercial importance the
one recently signed at Tien-tsin, is invested with even a
higher character of historical interest and political significance.

"Having thus briefly adverted to the peculiar conditions
under which the treaty of Jeddo was negotiated, I shall
proceed to a general narrative of the principal events
which marked this most interesting episode in the diplomacy of Great Britain in the far East.

"On the 3rd of August, her Majesty's ships *Furious*,
Retribution, *Lee* (gunboat), and steam-yacht, *Emperor*,
destined as a present for his Majesty the Tycoon of Japan,
entered the port of Nagasaki, and steaming past the point
at which a line of junks have heretofore been moored to
bar the ingress of foreign ships, cast anchor immediately
off the city and Dutch factory of Desima. On the following day the *Calcutta*, having on board the Admiral, accompanied by the *Inflexible*, joined the squadron. Nothing can exceed in picturesque beauty the bay of Nagasaki and the situation of the city at its extremity ; swell-
ing hills covered with the most luxuriant verdure rise
from the water's edge. The steep thatched roofs of snug
cottages peep from out the dense foliage amid which they
are nestled ; white temples perched upon overhanging
points contrast brilliantly with the dark-green setting.
In some places precipitous walls of rock are mirrored in
the azure blue of the water at their base ; in others,
drooping branches kiss its calm surface. Green batteries
guard projecting points, and rock-cut steps ascend the

steep hill-sides, clothed with heavy forests or terraced
with rice-fields. Boats of quaint construction, with sharp-
pointed prows and broad sterns, above which flutter two
black and white flags—the Imperial colours — glance
across the harbour, propelled by stalwart naked figures,
who scull to the tune of a measured chant. The fore-
part of the boat is covered by a roof, and contains a posse
of two-sworded officials, who incontinently board each
ship as it anchors, speak very fair Dutch, are extremely
inquisitive, but very gentlemanlike and goodnatured, and
who, after official curiosity has been satisfied, proceed to
make their reports, and return, in all probability, to cir-
cumnavigate the ship as a guardboat during the rest of
its stay in the harbour. A Dutch merchant-ship and a
Japanese man-of-war screw-steamer were the only vessels
in harbour when we arrived and anchored about half a
mile from the shore. The city of Nagasaki covers a plain
at the end of the harbour, but it has outgrown its area,
and the houses cluster up the spurs of the hills that sink
into it, and the streets are in places so steep as to render
steps necessary. Formerly foreigners were not allowed to
enter the town, and the Dutch were only permitted to
leave their prison of Desima under a strong escort of
officials, and when permission had been formally asked
and obtained. Now the barriers had been so far broken
down that we explored at pleasure the shops and streets
of the town—not, as in China, an offensive and disgusting
operation, but a charming and agreeable amusement. The
streets are broad, clean, and free from foul odours ; the
people civil and courteous, and if the shops in the town
do not afford many interesting objects of speculation, the
bazaars, which are stocked with lacquer, china, &c., for
the express benefit of foreigners, are so tempting that few
can leave them without experiencing a considerable drain
upon their resources. Fortunately, this was a temptation
to which we were not exposed for any great length of
time. Immediately on the Admiral's arrival, it became
necessary to decide upon the steps which should be taken
for the presentation of the yacht. The distance of Na-

gasaki from the capital of the empire, and the comparative insignificance of the principal authority, rendered it
very undesirable that so important an act should be performed there. As Mr. Ward, who commanded the yacht,
had been instructed to deliver it over, if possible, at
Jeddo, it was therefore determined that he should proceed
at once to that place. Lord Elgin determined, by accompanying the yacht, to avail himself of the opportunity
which would thus be presented of gaining access to the
capital, as by these means additional facilities would doubtless be afforded for carrying out the object he had in view.

No sooner was it decided that the presentation of the
yacht should take place at Jeddo, than the *Furious*,
Retribution, *Lee*, and *Emperor* started for Simoda. Heavy
gales obliged all four ships to run in for shelter at the
bay of Nagasaki, and it was not until the morning of the
10th that they sighted the lofty volcanic mountain of
Fousi Yamma. Towering like Etna, to a perfect cone, with
an elevation of about 11,000 feet above the level of the
sea, it was first visible at a distance of upwards of one
hundred miles, its beautiful outline defined sharp and
clear with the first gray tints of morning. This celebrated
mountain, so dear to the Japanese, has been created by
him into a household god. Fousi Yamma is painted at the
bottom of the delicate china cup from which he sips his tea ;
it is represented on the lacquer bowl from which he eats
his rice. He fans himself with Fousi Yamma—he hands
things to you on Fousi Yamma. It is on the back of his
looking-glass, it is embroidered on the skirts of his garments, and is the background of every Japanese work of
art or imagination. Simoda is a lovely but dangerous
harbour. Its apparently sheltered nooks and secluded
coves woo you into their embraces, and when the south
wind blows fiercely, you are dashed to atoms upon their
ribs of iron. The earthquake, which wrecked the Russian frigate *Diana*, changed the surface of the bottom,
and there is now no good holding ground ; but it is a
fairy land to look upon, and in calm weather the picture
of repose and security. Here, too, there is a Goyoshi, or

Bazaar, and a better display of lacquer and china than at Nagasaki ; but it is a town of no local importance, containing some 3,000 or 4,000 inhabitants, and when, under the new treaty, the port is shut up, will sink into its normal condition of a fishing village. At the head of the bay, the American flag flaunts proudly ; for two years it has waved in solitary magnificence over the exiles who, during that period, have represented American interests in this remote corner of the globe. Cut off from all communion with their fellow-men, and sacrificing in the interests of civilization and commerce the blessings of all social intercourse, their efforts had at last been crowned with success, and the ambassador heard from Mr. Harris that he had only returned a few days from Jeddo, where he had concluded his treaty, and where Count Putiatine, who had proceeded to Japan direct from the Gulf of Pecheli, was at that moment negotiating. The Dutch resident at Nagasaki, Mr. Donker Curtius, had also been for some time engaged in negotiating at Jeddo, but had left before the intelligence had arrived there of the treaty of Tien-tsin, and had consequently failed altogether in signing any treaty at all. He was at that time on his return journey overland to Nagasaki. Had any doubts existed as to the propriety of proceeding without delay to negotiate at Jeddo, they were at once solved by this intelligence, for it became incumbent on the ambassador to lose no time in securing for Great Britain those advantages and privileges which other nations either had acquired or were acquiring, and in placing her, without delay, in the position of the other European powers, at that time represented in Japan. As, unfortunately, all the efforts made at Nagasaki to procure a Dutch interpreter had proved unavailing, an insuperable difficulty seemed to present itself, on learning that the only language in which the Japanese could communicate at Jeddo was Dutch. This obstacle was, however, removed by the friendly act of Mr. Harris, who, with great liberality and courtesy, placed his own interpreter, Mr. Huesken, at Lord Elgin's disposal. During the fortnight's stay of the squadron at Jeddo, the services of this gentleman were in constant request, and his readiness to oblige rendered him universally popular, while, in his official capacity, his knowledge of the people and familiarity with their habits, acquired during a residence among them of two years, must have rendered him invaluable. Simoda is about eighty miles from the city of Jeddo, situate at the extreme point of the promontory which forms one side of the capacious bay, or rather gulf, at the head of which the capital is placed. Up this bay the squadron proceeded, with a fair wind, on the morning of the 12th, and passing through the Straits of Uraga, the left shore of which is feathered with rich verdure, and indented with little bays, reached a point opposite the Port of Kanagawa, beyond which no foreign ships had ever ventured, and where the Russian squadron could then be discerned at anchor. Captain Osborn, however, professing his readiness to explore the unknown waters at the head of the bay, and to approach as near the city as possible, Lord Elgin seemed determined not to lose an opportunity of establishing a precedent likely to be so important in our future intercourse with Japan, and, to the astonishment of both Russians and Japanese, the British ships deliberately passed the sacred limit, without communicating with the shore, and a few minutes after were cautiously feeling their way round a long spit of land, which runs far out into the bay, and offers some danger to the navigator. An instinct for deep water must have guided the ships along the channel, which was afterwards found to be sufficiently narrow and tortuous ; but at last all doubts as to the feasibility of the enterprise were removed by the appearance of several large, square-rigged Japanese vessels at anchor, the draught of water of which was a guarantee for our own. Behind these rose gradually out of the waters of the bay a line of insulated forts, which marked the defences of Jeddo, while an extensive suburb running along the western shore formed a continuous street, as far as the eye could reach. The ships ultimately anchored in three fathoms of water, about a mile and a-half from this suburb, and the same distance from the fine island forts above mentioned, which are situated on a sandbank, the intervening channels being always covered with water. About a mile beyond these forts, and parallel to them, lay the main body of the city—the wooded height, on which is situated the Castle of the Tycoon, forming a conspicuous object. The arrival of the British squadron in waters which the Japanese had sedulously represented as being too shallow to admit of the approach of large ships, filled them with dismay and astonishment ; boats followed each other, with officials of ascending degrees of rank, to beg them to return to Kanagawa ; and finally, urgent representations were made to the ambassador on the subject. The pleas generally put forward were amusing and characteristic ; first, it was said the anchorage was dangerous, but the presence of their own squadron was referred to as an evidence to the contrary. Then, that it would be impossible to procure and send off supplies ; but it was protested that, if necessary, we could do without these. The merits and comforts of Kanagawa were expatiated on in vain ; the paramount duty was the delivery of the yacht at Jeddo, and to deliver the yacht there, it was necessary to remain at the present anchorage. No sooner was this settled, than the Japanese, in their usual way, became perfectly reconciled to the arrangement, sent off supplies with great willingness, and began to prepare a residence on shore for Lord Elgin and his staff. It appeared that Count Putiatine had been delayed for ten days negotiating on this subject at Kanagawa, and only succeeded in taking up his residence at Jeddo on the same day that we cast anchor before the town. He had made the journey overland from Kanagawa, a distance of eighteen miles.

The landing of a British ambassador in state at the capital of the Empire of Japan was only in keeping with the act of unparalleled audacity which had already been committed in anchoring British ships within the sacred limits of its harbour. Japanese officials were sent off to superintend the operation, but they little expected to make the return voyage in one of her Majesty's gun-boats, with thirteen ships' boats in tow, amid the thunder of salutes, the inspiriting strains of a naval band, and the flutter of hundreds of flags with which the ships were dressed. Close under the green batteries, threading its way amid hosts of huge-masted broad-sterned junks, the *Little Lee*, surrounded by her gay flotilla, steamed steadily, and not until the water had shoaled to seven feet, and the Japanese had ceased to remonstrate, or even to wonder, from sheer despair, did she drop anchor, and the procession of boats was formed ; the four paddle-box boats, each with a twenty-four pound howitzer in her bows, enclosing between them the ambassador's barge, the remainder of the ships' boats, with captains and officers all in full dress, leading the way. The band struck up " God save the Queen" as Lord Elgin ascended the steps of the official landing-place near the centre of the city, and was received and put into his chair by sundry two-sworded personages ; the rest of the mission, together with some officers of the squadron, following on horseback. The crowd, which for upwards of a mile lined the streets leading to the building fixed on as the residence of the Embassy was dense in the extreme ; the procession was preceded by policemen in harlequin cos-tume, jingling huge iron rods of office, hung with heavy clanging rings, to warn the crowd away. Ropes were stretched across the cross streets, down which masses of the people rushed, attracted by the novel sight ; while every few hundred yards were gates partitioning off the different wards, which were severally closed immediately on the passing of the procession ; thus hopelessly barring the further progress of the old crowd, who strained anxiously through the bars, and envied the persons com-posing the rapidly forming nucleus. During Lord Elgin's stay of eight days on shore, nearly all the officers of the squadron had an opportunity of paying him a visit. His residence was a portion of a temple situated upon the outskirts of what was known as the Prince's Quarter—in other words, it was the Knightsbridge of Jeddo. In front of it was a street which continued for ten miles, as closely packed with houses, and as densely crowded with people as it is from Hyde Park-corner to Mile-end. At the back of it stretched a wide and somewhat dreary aristocratic quarter, containing the residences of three hundred and sixty hereditary princes, each a petty sovereign in his own right, many of them with half-a-dozen town-houses, and some of them able to accommodate in these same mansions ten thousand retainers. Passing through the spacious and silent (except where a party of English were traversing them) streets, we arrive at the outer moat of the castle; crossing it we are still in the Prince's Quarter, but are astounded as we reach its further limit at the scene which now bursts upon us—a magnificent moat, seventy or eighty yards broad, faced with a smooth green escarpment as many feet in height, above which runs a massive wall, composed of stones Cyclopean in their dimensions. This is crowned, in its turn, by a lofty palisade. Towering above all, the spreading arms of giant cedars proudly display themselves, and denote that within the Imperial precincts the picturesque is not forgotten. From the highest point of the fortifications in rear of the castle a panoramic view is obtained of the vast city, with its two million and a-half inhabitants and an area equal to, if not greater than, that of London. The castle alone is computed to be capable of containing forty thousand souls.*

The interesting particulars of this rapid negotiation we expect with avidity: meanwhile we have an abstract of the most important stipulations of the treaty, as the text of the treaty itself cannot be published before it is laid before Parliament in February. It was signed at Jeddo on the 26th of last August.

This treaty, in the first place, engages that there shall be perpetual peace and friendship between her Britannic Majesty and the Tycoon of Japan; secondly, that her Majesty may appoint a diplomatic agent to reside at

---

* *Times,* November 2nd, 1858.

THE SIOGOUN, OR TEMPORAL EMPEROR AND HIS WIFE.

Jeddo, and the Tycoon a diplomatic agent to reside in London, both of them respectively to have the right of travelling freely to any part of the Empire of Japan, and to any part of Great Britain; also either Power may appoint consuls or consular agents at any or all the ports of the other. The ports of Hakodadi, Kanagawa, and Nagasaki, in Japan, are to be opened to British subjects on the 1st of July, 1859. Nee-e-gata, or if Nee-e-gata be unsuitable, another convenient port on the west coast of Nipon, is to be opened on the 1st of January, 1860; Hiogo on the 1st of January, 1863; and British subjects may permanently reside in all the foregoing ports, may lease ground, purchase or erect dwellings and warehouses, but may not erect fortifications. Within a certain distance of the specified ports they shall be free to go where they please, or, speaking generally, they have a tether of some twenty to thirty miles around either of them. From the 1st of January, 1862, they will be allowed to reside at Jeddo, and from the 1st of January, 1863, at Osacca for the purposes of trade. All questions of rights, whether of property or person, arising between themselves shall be subject to the jurisdiction of the British authorities; if they commit any crime against the Japanese, they will be tried and punished by their own authorities, and *vice versâ* Japanese subjects in the same predicament will be tried and punished by theirs; but in either case the British consuls are to act in the first instance as amicable arbitrators. In respect of debts contracted on either side, the respective authorities will do their utmost to enforce recovery, but neither Government will be held responsible for the debts of its subjects. The Japanese Government will place no restrictions whatever upon the employment by British subjects of Japanese in any lawful capacity. British subjects will be allowed the free exercise of their religion, and for this purpose will have the right to erect suitable places of worship. Foreign and Japanese coin may be used indifferently for commercial purposes. Supplies for the British navy may be stored at certain specified ports free of duty. If British vessels are wrecked or stranded, the Japanese authorities will render every assist-ance in their power. British merchants will be at liberty to hire Japanese pilots. Munitions of war are to be the only exceptions to articles of import and export, which last, on the payment of an *ad valorem* duty at the place of import, are to be subject to no further tax, excise, or transit duty. Such articles may be re-exported without the payment of any additional duty. The Japanese are to prevent fraud or smuggling, and to receive the benefit of all penalties or confiscations. The treaty is written in English, Japanese, and Dutch; the Dutch version to be considered the original. All official communications on the part of the British to the Japanese authorities shall, however, henceforward be written in English; though for five years from the signature of the treaty, to facilitate the transaction of business, they are to be accompanied by a Dutch or Japanese version. The treaty may be revised on the application of either of the contracting parties, on giving one year's notice after the 1st of July, 1872. All the privileges, immunities, and advantages granted, or to be granted hereafter, by Japan to any other nation, are to be freely and equally participated by the British Government and its subjects. The treaty is to be ratified within a year from the day of its signature.

For the regulation of trade the articles which are appended to the treaty are to be considered as forming a part of it, and as equally binding. The majority of these relate to the arrangements of the Japanese Custom-house, but the more important contain the tariff of duties to be levied. In the *first* class, as free of duty, are specified gold and silver, coined or uncoined, wearing apparel in actual use, and household furniture and printed books not intended for sale, but the property of persons who come to reside in Japan. On the *second* class a duty of *five per cent. only* will be levied, and this class comprises all articles used for the purpose of building, rigging, repair-ing, or fitting out ships, whaling gear of all kinds, salted provisions, bread and breadstuffs, living animals, coals, timber for building houses, rice, paddy, *steam machinery,* zinc, lead, tin, raw silk, *cotton and woollen manufactured goods.* A duty of thirty-five per cent. will, however, be levied on all intoxicating liquors; and goods not included in any of the preceding classes will pay a duty of twenty per cent. Japanese products which are exported as cargo will pay an export duty of *five per cent.* The above are substantially all the material stipulations of this important document.

It is impossible for me to conclude with more appropriate reflections than those put forth in the *Times'* leader of November 1st, 1858, excepting only the sentiment with regard to the " Portuguese missionary priests," whose " conspiracy" is said to have caused the extirpation of Christianity :—

" We do not entertain the hopes which have been expressed in some quarters as to the great commercial value of a trade with Japan, and we are sorry for the anguish of mind which must fall upon Mr. Bright when he comes to contemplate a set of estimates swollen by a salary for a resident minister at Jeddo. But we must, nevertheless, congratulate the country upon this accession of the Japanese empire to the comity of nations. They are a people who differ altogether from the Chinese. They are not only industrious and ingenious, but they are also inquiring and most desirous of civilization. Two hundred years ago they were upon the point of becoming a Christian people. They have what the Chinese have not—the capacity of a fervent faith, and it was a political necessity, and not a barbarous intolerance, that suggested the prohibitive and exclusive character of their modern policy. The conspiracy of the Portuguese missionary priests occasioned and almost justified the cruelties that are recorded in the Romish Martyrology ; but if our dealings towards them are conducted with as much good faith as is almost certain to appear in their dealings towards us, we may hope to base upon this treaty new friendships and new connexions in the East, of a different character, but scarcely less important in their results than those which Europe expects from the treaty of Tien-sin.

"We made no menaces and used no threats, but we fear there was something like the pressure of a force which was not altogether moral put upon these gentle Japanese. Our excuse must be that, if the Americans had obtained concessions upon the strength of the terror created by the roar of the lion, it would have been hard that the lion should get nothing on his own account. We need not tell how Lord Elgin went on shore in due state and lived in a gaudy temple, and negotiated for fourteen days, and visited many parts of the mighty city of Jeddo, with its two millions of inhabitants, and its hundred square miles of habitations; the result has been a treaty which gives us all we can require for the present. It gives us free commercial access to an interesting and amiable people, to a charming region in a beautiful climate, and to a country rich in coals and minerals. As we improve or abuse these opportunities so will the event be to our profit or our shame."

THE END.

GRAMMARS AND DICTIONARIES.

We are very much in the dark as to Japanese grammar and lexicography : it is certain that we have no authoritative work whatever on either subject. The *Elémens de la Grammaire Japonaise*, by Rodriguez, with *Supplément*, and a *Notice* by Humboldt, has been mentioned. I may add Siebold's *Epitome Linguæ Japonicæ*—a very slight affair indeed—and the *Introduction à l'Etude de la Langue Japonaise*, by Leon de Rosny, Paris, 1857 ; a compilation by a very young, but erudite Orientalist, who, however, has studied the language in Europe only. With regard to dictionaries or vocabularies, we have the Dominican Collado's *Dictionarium* . . *Linguæ Japonicæ*, Romæ, 1632 ; which is said to be "nearly obsolete," on what authority, I know not. Comparing it in many instances with the latest vocabularies, I have not found it wanting. It contains, besides, a most curious document—a *modus confitendi*, or method of confessing and examining a Japanese penitent in Japanese and Latin. This singular document throws some light on Japanese society, and certainly proves that human sins and vices of all kinds are pretty nearly the same all the world over. Compare the examination on the *Sextum Præceptum*, p. 37 *et seq.*, with the same subject, handled by Father F. M. Baccari, in his *Practica del Confessionale*, Napoli, 1841, *Parte terza, sezione quarta*, p. 217. On the authority of these two masters of the secrets of the confessional, it seems that vice in Italy assumes more hideous shapes than in Japan.

About two years ago, there were on sale at the shop of the universal bibliopole, Bernard Quaritch, two very rare lexicographical works—the *Sin Soou*, a Chinese-Japanese dictionary, and the *Ye ki ken*, or Dutch-Japanese dictionary—both of them strongly praised by Klaproth. Unfortunately, they did not find a purchaser in England, and went to France. I have alluded to Medhurst's English and Japanese vocabulary. I have since been lucky enough to procure a copy. It is a very curious specimen of *lithographic* printing, executed at Batavia, by a self-taught Chinese artist, who neither understood English nor Japanese ; Medhurst himself had never been in Japan, nor had an opportunity of conversing with the natives. There is a copy in the library of the British Museum.

Siebold's vocabulary, which is given in the *Voyage au Japon*, does not differ materially from Thunberg's (*Travels*, v. iii.), but the latter is much more extensive.

At the Museum there is an elegantly-written MS. Japanese vocabulary, by Klaproth.* The name of Klaproth goes a great way, of course ; but he states that it was compiled on the authority of one of those poor shipwrecked Japanese, before mentioned, whom Catherine of Russia converted into " Professors of Japanese" at the School of Irkoutsk.† It would be an odd thing for a Frenchman to compile an English vocabulary on the authority of a shipwrecked English sailor—curious and interesting, of

---

* Add. MSS. 21,437. *Japanisches Lexicon*, von Jul. Klaproth.
† *Antè* p. 409.

course—but clearly of no authority as to the language of England.* I should also mention the *Thesaurus Linguæ Japonicæ*, by Siebold and Hoffman.

Leon de Rosny is now publishing, in parts, a *Dictionnaire de la Langue Japonaise;* but how can he pretend to give us the true sounds of Japanese, never having been in Japan? For instance, Thunberg writes for *stomach*, *fii* (*i.e.*, feeye)—Rosny writes *wéy*—clearly the same sound rendered by different *organs,* but becoming very different sounds to a *Japanese ear.* It is the same throughout; we must therefore **wait for** better things from two or more competent authorities who shall have qualified themselves by residence and hard study to teach us how to warble Japanese. See *note*, p. 315.

* I observe that Klaproth gives the word *kamban*—that is, *kambang*—"affiche" (*i. e.*, *advertisement* of public sale), and as Japanese; but it is *Malaya,* not Japanese. See Doeff, *Herinner. uit. Japan*, 71.

SELECT JAPANESE VOCABULARY.*

⁎ *i* is pronounced as *e* in *me* or *i* in *fill;* *a* as *ah!* *e* as *a.*

A.

Agreeable, *Yurosikku.*
Agree (to agree for, to bargain), *makaru.*
Air, *sora.*
All, *mei.*
Alms, *fodokussu, segio.*
Allow, *yerusi.*
Ambergris, *kusera no fung.*†
Anchor, *ikari.*
Anchor (to), *ikakarú.*
Animal, *kedamono.*
Angry (to be), *ikaru, fandatsuru.*
Angry (to make), *sasura, faratate.*
Attend (wait upon), *neirurú.*
Ax, *warà, stono.*

B.

Back, *senaka.*
Bad, *faradate, farakaki, isnowari,* &c.
Barber, *kami, yui.*
Bath (warm), *isumi.*
Bath (in a tub), *furú.*
Bed, *nedokuri.*

Belly, *stabira, hara.*
Bird, *tori.*
Blood, *tyi kyets.*
Boat (**Dutch**), *obatera.*
Boat (Japanese), *temma.*
Book, *somots.*
Box (a), *iremono.*
Brandy (all spirits), *sotyu.*
Breast (of a woman), *tyityi.*
Breast (any other), *mone.*
Breeches, *fakama, hakama.*
Bug, *abramussi.*
Buy (to buy and sell), *baibai (!)*
Buy (to), *kawu, kao, kota.*

C.

Cable, *tyansuma.*
Camphor, *sono.*
Candle, *rosoku,* from *ro* "wax" and *soku* "wick."
Candlestick, *rosoks tatti.*
Cash, *sodan.*
Cheat, *damassu.*
Cloak, *hawori.*
Cloak (for rain), *toi.*
Clothes (suit of), *kimono.*
Coal, *isusumi.*

* From Thunberg and Rodriguez.
† Literally "whale's excrements." It is curious that the Persian for "amber" is *gau anberi,* "the excrements of the sea-cow," as the Persians supposed it to be. See an article of mine, "Amber in the Bible," &c., in *Notes and Queries,* Aug. 7, 1858.

Coffin, *kwanoki.*
Commerce, *akirawu, sobai.*
Court, *meako.*
Cup, *wang.*
Cut, *kiru, kar.**

D.

Debt, *sukugin.*
Door, *to*
Drink, *nomimono.*
Drink (to), *nomu.*

E.

Earth (the), *Tyi dsi.*
Earthquake, *dyisin.*
Ear, *mimi.*
Exchange (to), *kayurú.*

F.

Fan, *oge.*
Father, *tete, toto.*
Fire, *fi, finoko.*
Fire (a), *kwassi.*
Fish, *iwo, sakkana.*
Fisherman, *riosi.*
Friend, *ftoobai.*
Foreigner, *Yama midoss* (!)

G.

Garden, *hannabbataki.*
Give (to), *furerú, yarú.*
God, *Sin, Kami.*

Gold (or coin), *kin, kinsing.*
Good, *yukka.*
Goods, *mouo.*
Gun, *teppo, tippo.*

H.

Hair, *kami.*†
Hand, *koaka kowai.*
Handkerchief, *te-no-goi.*
Head, *kubi;* hence *kubo-sama,*
i. e. head-lord.
Hog, *sis* (*!*) Latin, *sus.*
Horse, *aki uma.*
Hysterics (in women), *skai.*
Hysterics (in men), *sakki.*

I.

Interpreter, *tsusi.*
Island, *dsima.*

K.

Kill, *korossú.*
Kiss, *umakutyi.*
Knife, *haka.*

L.

Lacquered work, *makie mono,*
nasis.
Letter (epistle), *syo, tegami.*
Loss, *song.*
Lie (to tell a) *suragoto.*

---

* It has been observed that the sound of *k* or the radical *kat* or *kas,* with the meaning *to cut* or *break,* is found in most languages of the world. The Japanese long sword or sabre is *kátana.* Thus: in Greek, κόπτω ; Latin, *cassus, cœdere;* Syriac, *kataf;* French, *casser, couper;* English, *cut;* Sanskrit, *kad* and *kout't', kas;* Turkish, *kes;* New Zealandish, *kotia;* Coptic, *kach;* Peruvian, *koutchoum, coutouni,* &c. &c. *Hari-kari* is *belly-cut.*

† *Kami* evidently does much service, since it means *God, hair,* paper, razor, and also *rich, great, powerful;* but this is a feature of all languages, especially the Oriental, and amongst these the *Arabic,* in which it is sometimes almost impossible to say what a word does not mean. The Christians were taught to say *Deus* for *God.*

M.

Man (mankind), *momo(!) nin-gen.*
Man (individual), *otoko.*
Mat, *tattami.*
Medicine, *kwassuri, gosuri.*
Merchant, *akibito, sonin.*
Milk, *tyi.*
Mistress (concubine), *sotekaki.*
Moon, *tsuki.*
Mouth, *kuts.*

N.

Name, *na.*
Neck, *nodor.*
Nose, *fanna.*

P.

Paper (writing), *kami.*
Paper (window), *minoganni.*
Paper (imperial), *otaka daisi.*
Paper (for hangings) *karakanni.*
Paper (gilt), *kinkarakami.*
Paper (nose paper, common), *fanaganni.*
Paper (nose paper, large), *sitkusumi.*
Parasol, *fisasi.*
Physician, *isa.*
Pillow (wooden), *makura.*
Pretty, *migotto.*

Q.

Question, *tsuru.*
Quick, *faiyo, faiyaki.*

R.

Razor, *sorri, yori, kami.*
Rice, *kome.*
Rice (early), *wase.*
Rice (threshed), *skigome.*
Rice (boiled), *mes.*
Rice (red), *tobose.*
Rice (white), *matyigome.*

Rice (fine), *domense.*
River, *kawa.*

S.

Sabre, *kátana.*
Sabre (short), *wagissassin.*
Saddle, *kwura.*
Shave (to), *soru.*
Ship, *fune.*
Shoe, *kwutsu.*
Sir, *sama, muss.*
Smith, *kasia.*
Smoke (to, tobacco), *tabaco nomú.*
Soldier, *bannin.*
Spy, *ying.*
Sun, *fi, nityi.*
Sword, *ken.*

T.

Tar, *tyan.*
Tea, *tsyaa.*
Tin, *susú.*
Tooth, *fagis, ha.*
Top (of anything), *toge.*

U.

Umbrella, *fisasi.*
Understand (to), *konogotukú.*

V.

Virgin, *imada.*
Velvet, *birodo.*
Vinegar, *su.*

W.

Wash (one's-self), *yosi.*
Water-tub (large), *furo.*
Water-tub (small), *yosi.*
Whale, *kusira.*
Wife, *niobo, yomego.*
Wind, *kase.*
Wood, *tagi.*
Write (to), *kakv, fisa.*

Y.

Year, *fosi,* i.e. " star."